With JESUS EVERY DAY

Daily Devotions through the Year

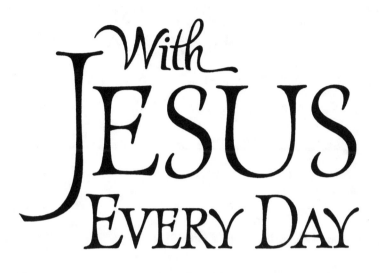

With Jesus Every Day

Daily Devotions through the Year

Rudolph F. Norden

SAINT LOUIS

Copyright © 1997 Concordia Publishing House
3558 S. Jefferson Avenue, St. Louis, MO 63118-3968
Manufactured in the United States of America

Library of Congress Cataloging-in-Publication Data

Norden, Rudolph F.
  With Jesus every day: daily devotions through the year / Rudolph F. Norden.
     p.   cm.
  ISBN 0-570-04987-3
  1. Devotional calendars—Lutheran Church. I. Title.
BV4811.N65 1997
242'.2—dc21   97-7999

1 2 3 4 5 6 7 8 9 10   06 05 04 03 02 01 00 99 98 97

To our grandchildren,

David, Elizabeth, Toby, and Erika

PREFACE

This is the third volume of daily devotions built around the theme of fellowship with Jesus on a day-by-day basis. It takes the author back to—even as it largely springs from—experiences in his childhood home in rural Nebraska. There both morning and evening devotions were held every day. In the years prior to World War I, they were conducted in German. America's entry into the war against Germany gave impetus to a gradual changeover to the English language. During the war the head of our house began to read devotions also in English, or as Dad Norden preferred to say, in the *American* language.

But what was available for reading? Books of devotions in German were used, as well as the religious "staples" of every Christian home: Bibles, hymnbooks, and catechisms. At the family altar, the family not only prayed together but also learned the Word of God. This called for a lot of grist for the mill—mostly for material in the increasingly used language of the land—English.

At about the same time two sources helped to supply the need. The first resource, and one on which God has heaped His blessing, was a dated devotional periodical, first issued in 1937, eventually named *Portals of Prayer*. The second resource was the prayer calendar, *Day by Day with Jesus*. This was written by Dr. Walter A. Maier, the Lutheran Hour founder, and continued by the late Dr. Eugene R. Bertermann. It was distributed largely through the International Lutheran Laymen's League. *With Jesus Every Day*, and its two similarly named predecessors, continues the prayer calendar.

This writer is most thankful to the Lord of the church for having had a part in both devotional publications. He served for 25 years as editor of *Portals of Prayer* (and of *Taegliche Andachten*, its German counterpart) and as author of the two predecessors of this present volume. This book, like the many other edifying materials issued by Concordia, is meant to strengthen the most basic institution, the family altar. It's purpose is to bring God's Word into the household, which, in the words of St. Paul to Philemon, is "the church that meets in your house." The home is the nursery of "family values" in a Christian sense.

Rudolph F. Norden

MAKING THE MOST OF LIFE IN THE NEW YEAR

Lord, You have been our dwelling place throughout all generations. Psalm 90:1

In their works of art, the native Maori people of New Zealand show the human hand with three fingers. These represent the three main human events: birth, life, and death.

Human life, for the New Zealand aborigines as well as for people in sophisticated cultures, consists of a beginning, a middle, and an end. The middle part varies greatly with individuals. For some, life is short; for others it is long, as Moses states in Psalm 90: "The length of our days is seventy years—or eighty, if we have the strength."

Birth, life, and death: What is important is that we make the most of the middle part—life. We have no control over our birth and, as far as death is concerned, it is in God's hands. But we do have much to say about life. We have a great responsibility toward our own life— how we spend it, what we do or leave undone, what we eat and drink, what time we allot to work and to rest, how we develop our talents. God has made us stewards, or caretakers, over our own lives.

Much is being said these days about improving the quality of life for ourselves and for others. It is important for Christians to make the most of life and to keep it on a high level. God the Father gave us life. Through Jesus Christ, His Son, He redeemed our life from sin and the fear of death, and through the work of the Holy Spirit in our hearts He gives a redeemed, sanctified, and fruitful life back to us. He wants us to make the most of it by serving Him with all our powers of body, mind, and spirit.

When you think of the three events—your birth, the living of your life, and death—you need not fear whatever may occur in the new year. When your life, whether short or long, glorifies God and benefits fellow human beings, it is eminently worthwhile.

Prayer Suggestion

Ask for Christ's help so that you may live more and more for Him who loved you and gave His life for you.

THE RIGHT COURSE FOR THE NEW YEAR

Jesus answered, "I am the Way and the Truth and the Life." John 14:6

Celebrated in story and song, and featured in a television series, was old U.S. Highway 66, which has since been absorbed into the interstate system. The highway led across the country to the west coast. Many people traveled on it, including the duststorm victims from Oklahoma of whom John Steinbeck wrote in *The Grapes of Wrath.*

Highways are not always happy ways. Some people must take the road to find new homes after losing their former ones. Others travel for the sake of their health or to attend the funeral of a loved one. Then again, highway travel can be a happy experience, like going on a honeymoon, taking a vacation, or coming home for the holidays.

We travel highways in a spiritual sense—roads people take in their search for something, such as finding peace with God. All roads lead to Rome, people said in ancient times. By the same token, say some, all roads—all religions—lead to heaven. Changing the comparison a bit, they claim: The spiritual vehicles taking us to heaven are many, just as one can go to Chicago, for example, by plane, train, bus, or private automobile.

Jesus teaches otherwise. In a very clear utterance He declared, "I am the Way and the Truth and the Life. No one comes to the Father except through Me" (John 14:6). That is also what the apostles taught. When the jailer of Philippi asked what he must do to be saved, or what road leads to heaven, St. Paul replied, "Believe in the Lord Jesus, and you will be saved" (Acts 16:31). Jesus died and rose again to gain eternal life for us all.

Old Highway 66 is gone, but the way of salvation in Christ is still there. It is the road we want to follow every day in the new year.

Prayer Suggestion

Ask the Holy Spirit for the wisdom and strength to follow Jesus Christ, who is the safe and sure Way to heaven.

OUR HAND IN HIS

Immediately Jesus reached out His hand and caught him.
Matthew 14:31

"Put your hand in the hand of the Man who stilled the water," states Gene MacLellan in a well-known song.

Peter was walking on the water to Jesus when suddenly the disciple began to sink. Jesus said, "You of little faith ... why did you doubt?" (Matthew 14:31) Then our Lord reached out His hand and drew Peter out of the water. And all this was followed by the Master performing the miracle of calming the sea.

What difference did it make in Peter's life—not only now but also at other occasions—that he trustingly put his hand "in the hand of the Man from Galilee"? Did he, as a result of this experience, look differently at himself and at others?

It certainly made a difference. In his later life Peter put his trust in Christ, confessing Him to be "the Son of the living God." He could assume his tremendous assignment to feed the flock of God which Christ had purchased with His own blood. He could proclaim, as he did at the beginning of his first epistle, "In His great mercy He has given us new birth into a living hope through the resurrection of Jesus Christ from the dead, and into an inheritance that can never perish, spoil or fade—kept in heaven for you" (1 Peter 1:3–4).

What is more, Peter could look at himself as the "rock man," as the name Peter indicates, only insofar as he relied on Jesus Christ, the true Rock. And he could look at other Christians differently because their trust was in Christ, who made them "a chosen people, a royal priesthood, a holy nation, a people belonging to God" (1 Peter 2:9). Himself steadied by Christ's hand, he could assure his readers at the end of the epistle: "The God of all grace, who called you to His eternal glory in Christ, ... will Himself restore you and make you strong, firm and steadfast" (1 Peter 5:10).

This will also be our experience when we confidently put our hand in Christ's hand during this new year.

Prayer Suggestion

Tell your Lord that you trustingly are putting your faith in Him, your dear Savior.

CHRIST'S PROMISE OF "TODAY"

Jesus Christ is the same yesterday and today and forever.
Hebrews 13:8

What is meant by "paradise"? First, it refers to the Garden of Eden, where our first parents lived. In the New Testament it stands for heaven, the place of bliss. In a vision, St. Paul "was caught up to paradise" (2 Corinthians 12:4), which earlier in the chapter he calls "the third heaven."

Jesus on the cross assured the believing thief, "I tell you the truth, today you will be with Me in paradise" (Luke 23:43). This promise was kept. Before the sun set on that first Good Friday, Jesus and this convert were reunited in the heavenly Father's presence. Heaven is open—fully and immediately open—to all who trust in the nail-pierced hands of the Savior.

Christ's everlasting, unchanging "today" stands as a landmark over against the swift passage of time. The beginning of a new year reminds us that time is fleeting. It will not be long before time advances to and through the many vicissitudes of the unfolding year. It is true: "As long as the earth endures, seedtime and harvest, cold and heat, summer and winter, day and night will never cease." All the while we, too, are passing through all the time cycles and are experiencing their effects. We speak the words of Henry F. Lyte after him:

> Swift to its close ebbs out life's little day,
> Earth's joys grow dim, its glories pass away.

But we are not discouraged or distressed. The empty cross and the vacated tomb are our pledge that Jesus Christ has completed our redemption and now sits at God's right hand to bless and guide our lives. In Him all commitments, including the promise of fellowship with Him in paradise, are "Yes" and "Amen," as St. Paul declares. What assurance this is to take with us into the new year!

Prayer Suggestion

The new year reminds us that time, and our lives with it, passes quickly. Ask Jesus, who is the same all the while, to guide and provide for you this year.

FOLLOWING THE RIGHT ROAD

Whoever follows Me will never walk in darkness, but will have the light of life. John 8:12

The poet Robert Frost found himself "invited" to enter the woods, which he describes as "lovely, dark, and deep." But he cannot accept their invitation to leisure and pleasure, for he has "promises to keep."

The forest, with its evergreen trees and stately oaks, can be inviting even in winter. Its mystery is intriguing. A song writer states that he wishes to know "What the tree tops say, Whispering secrets night and day."

One can get lost in the woods. This is also true spiritually speaking. Our world is like a forest in which many trees grow—the trees of pride, of self-proclaimed perfection, of immorality made attractive, of false religious beliefs. This has always been true. Jesus told His contemporaries that He was the Light of the world, that He had come to lead people out of the darkness of sin into the light of full salvation in Him. To this end He proclaimed the opening of the kingdom of heaven, the kingdom of repentance and faith. He accepted tax collectors, even former prostitutes, when they repented of their sins and believed in Him as their Savior. But many others, notably the Pharisees, persisted in following the path of self-righteousness. They became lost in the woods of unbelief. They could not see the forest of God's abundant grace because of the trees—the trees of their own would-be virtues.

Today people also get lost in the woods of unbelief, doubt, and self-glorification which they find "lovely, dark, and deep." The only way not to get lost is to follow Jesus Christ, who is the Way, the Truth, and the Life. John the Baptist pointed to Him as "the Lamb of God, who takes away the sin of the world!" (John 1:29) St. Peter, preaching in the home of the centurion Cornelius, declared, "All the prophets testify about Him that everyone who believes in Him receives forgiveness of sins through His name" (Acts 10:43).

As we follow Jesus in this new year and remain loyal to His Word, we will not get lost in the woods of a spiritually confused world.

Prayer Suggestion

Pray that the Holy Spirit may be your Guide, leading you closer to Jesus, your Savior.

EPIPHANY, AT HOME AND ABROAD

We saw His star in the east and have come to worship Him.
Matthew 2:2

Two important events reported in the Bible and observed by the Christian church this month are the coming of the Wise Men, January 6, and the conversion of St. Paul, January 25. Both have a strong mission emphasis. The first event, celebrated as the Epiphany festival, is important because Christ, the Light of the world, had begun to shine on the Gentile world. As for the second, St. Paul, more than any other apostle, proclaimed the Gospel in a pagan world. Isaiah had prophesied, "Arise, shine, for your light has come, and the glory of the LORD rises upon you. See, darkness covers the earth and thick darkness is over the peoples, but the LORD rises upon you and His glory appears over you. Nations will come to your light, and kings to the brightness of your dawn" (Isaiah 60:1–3).

This prophecy was fulfilled when the Wise Men, referred to in a song as "We three kings of Orient," came to Jerusalem, then to Bethlehem, to worship the newborn King. These representatives of Gentile nations (we don't know for sure whether they were kings and whether their number was three) did come to Christ, worshiped Him, presented Him with gifts, and returned to their homeland as converts and as witnesses of the world's Savior. We follow in their footsteps— and in those of the apostle Paul—when we proclaim the Gospel, teaching all nations and baptizing them. The church celebrates Epiphany the year around when it engages in Christian missions.

To be able to share the faith abroad, we need to preserve it at home. Christian missions abroad need to be supported by Christian education at home. Both activities are the alternate beats of the same heart, the diastole and systole, to say it in medical terms. Both are aspects of the one great effort that we, as Christ's church of today, put forth in behalf of the saving faith. The two themes go together: "Preach the good news to all creation" (Mark 16:15), and "Contend for the faith that was once for all entrusted to the saints" (Jude 1:3). This is putting meaning into the Epiphany festival, both abroad and at home.

Prayer Suggestion

Ask the Lord of the church, Jesus Christ, to bless Christian missions and Christian education.

THE SUN IS SHINING

I am the Light of the world. Whoever follows Me … will have the Light of life. John 8:12

During the summer, in the Arctic and Antarctic regions known as the lands of the midnight sun, the sun never sets. People grow accustomed to going to bed with the sun still shining. Then come the long, dark winters.

In the Epiphany hymn "As with Gladness Men of Old" William C. Dix invites us to rejoice with the Wise Men who followed a star leading them to the Christ Child. He envisions the time when, ransomed in heaven, we will need no star to guide us, for "Thou, its Sun [the heavenly country's], goes not down."

Jesus Christ is the Light of the world. He promises that His followers "will never walk in darkness, but will have the Light of life" (John 8:12). Also in this life Jesus is the Sun that doesn't go down. Not to follow Jesus leads to spiritual darkness, to dire consequences, as Jesus testifies, "If you do not believe that I am the one I claim to be, you will indeed die in your sins" (John 8:24). Not to believe in Jesus as the one whom the Father sent to effect our eternal salvation is to live in a world without sunshine. Without the warmth of His redeeming, life-sustaining love, we would live in a land of perpetual ice and snow. Without the Gospel working and sustaining faith in our hearts, there would be no fruits of faith worked by the Holy Spirit. In other words, there would be no true "love, joy, peace, patience, kindness, goodness, faithfulness, gentleness and self-control" (Galatians 5:22). Who wants to live in such a world?

But, thanks to Jesus Christ, we have a Sun that does not set; we have the Son who shines. We are protected and well provided for. Let come what may: the blizzards and blasts of evil temptations, the winds of war, the siege of sickness and suffering, and in the end trepidation in the moment of mortality, we know that Jesus Christ is the Sun of Righteousness that will never set.

Prayer Suggestion

Ask the Lord Jesus to keep you in the light of His love and to help you to be His messenger of light in an unbelieving world.

THE FATHER'S TESTIMONY

You are My Son, whom I love; with You I am well pleased.
Mark 1:11

The baptism of Jesus was a decisive event in His life, for it marked the beginning of His public ministry. "Here and now He really begins to be the Christ," observes Martin Luther. Of course, He was the Christ when He was born, but now He began His office as Christ. Jesus' baptism opened the door to His work as the Messiah, the world's Redeemer, the sinner's Substitute.

Sinners need baptism as the washing of regeneration, as the sacrament that works forgiveness of sins, delivers from death and the devil, and gives eternal salvation to all who believe the promises of God. Jesus, the sinless One made sin for us, was already at this stage the vicarious Savior. He submitted to a sinner's baptism that He might fulfill for them all righteousness by which they are saved. By being baptized Jesus did more than set an example; He did His work as our Redeemer.

It was for this that the Father sent His Son into the world. We recall the heavenly dialog as Paul Gerhardt reconstructs it in a hymn: " 'Go forth, My Son,' the Father saith, 'And free men from the fear of death, From fear and condemnation.' " And the Son replies, " 'Yea, Father, yea, most willingly I'll do what Thou commandest. My will conforms to Thy decree, I do what Thou demandest.' " From Jordan's waters to Calvary's cross Jesus is obedient.

The Father was pleased with His Son in His newly assumed role as the Redeemer. He declared for all the world to hear: "You are My Son, whom I love; with you I am well pleased" (Mark 1:11). Jesus is God's Son and our Savior. For this we have the Father's testimony.

Like Jesus' baptism, so also our own baptism elicits the testimony of God—of the triune God: Father, Son, and Holy Spirit. His testimony is: "You are My child; you are dear to Me."

Prayer Suggestion

Ask for the help of the triune God to fulfill your vow to be faithful to Him to the end.

THE HUMAN HARVEST

Ask the Lord of the harvest ... to send out workers into His harvest field. Luke 10:2

As Jesus sent out the seventy disciples to proclaim God's kingdom and to heal, He said, "The harvest is plentiful, but the workers are few" (Luke 10:2). Many are the people who are in spiritual and physical distress. They are in need of help. Jesus likens them to a grainfield ripe for the harvest. But there are never enough of the Lord's workers and witnesses to bring in the sheaves.

What can we do about this imbalance? For one thing, we can volunteer as harvesters; we can say yes when the Lord calls us. In Jesus' time not all His followers could be chosen for His twelve apostles. But they could be members of the larger group—the seventy disciples. Beyond that, they could be Christ's followers as they continued in their vocation.

Today not all Christians can become ordained missionaries, pastors, or teachers, but there is room for them, and a need for them, in the larger group of disciples who work and witness where they are: at home, in school, in office and shop, in the community. These are harvesters reaping the souls whom Christ redeemed with His blood.

We participate in the harvest of souls when we contribute to Christian ministry and mission at home and abroad. And, said Jesus, we should pray—"ask the Lord of the harvest, therefore, to send out workers into His harvest field" (Luke 10:2).

Fellow Christians, the harvest time is now! During the Epiphany season this hymn stanza is especially close to our hearts:

> Lord of the living harvest
> That whitens on the plain,
> Where angels soon shall gather
> Their sheaves of golden grain,
> Accept these hands in labor,
> These hearts to trust and love,
> And with them ever hasten
> Your kingdom from above.

Lutheran Worship 260, v.1

Prayer Suggestion

Pray not only for missionaries in general but especially for certain ones personally known to you.

REDEEMED THAT HE MIGHT REDEEM US

Joseph and Mary took Him to Jerusalem to present Him to the Lord. Luke 2:22

The presentation of Jesus in the temple 40 days after His birth was meaningful. It showed, for one thing, how completely He was "born under Law, to redeem those under Law" (Galatians 4:4).

Jesus' presentation has yet another dimension. Among the Israelites every firstborn son belonged to God to minister to Him as a priest. By giving their number 1 sons to God, parents were showing gratitude for the deliverance of their sons when the angel slew all the firstborn among the Egyptians.

Later the tribe of Levi took over the priestly functions. Then the parents in the other tribes could "redeem" their firstborn sons from obligatory temple service by bringing an offering, as Mary and Joseph did.

It was not God's intention that Jesus should be a regular, full-time temple priest or Levite, for He had other work in mind for His Son. Through the offering brought by His parents, Jesus was "redeemed" from the earthly priesthood to assume a heavenly one—to be our High Priest to redeem us by offering Himself.

Jesus redeemed us by His obedience to the Law and by the shedding of His blood on the cross. To be able to be our self-giving High Priest, He had to be "redeemed" from an earthly priesthood. Because He was now redeemed, He could pursue His work to redeem us.

Prayer Suggestion

Thank the Lord Jesus for being your Substitute in fulfilling the Law of God to its fullest extent.

WHAT REPENTANCE MEANS

Jesus said to him, "Today salvation has come to this house."
Luke 19:9

An American spy, who had turned over defense secrets to an enemy country, told a panel of congressmen, "I regret that I was caught." He added, almost as an afterthought, "I regret what I did to my country."

A thief, or any other kind of wrongdoer, whose only regret is that he was caught, shows no repentance, no sorrow for his sins. In the Greek language the word for repentance is *metanoia*, which means a change of mind, genuine grief, a turning away from sin, the willingness to make restitution for wrongs committed. We find these qualities in Zacchaeus, the once-crooked publican who had a change of heart. Likewise King David in Psalm 51 voiced true repentance.

Repentance is by no means a minor emotion. Salvation hinges on it. Jesus said He had come to call sinners to repentance. He wanted hearts truly changed. His message was, "The kingdom of God is near. Repent and believe the good news" (Mark 1:15). Only those who truly repent will find the Gospel of the forgiveness of sins "the good news." And that is what the Christian Gospel is: glad tidings. It proclaims and applies the grace of God to repenting and believing sinners. It declares: You are free to go. Your debt is paid. Jesus Christ settled your account with the price of His own blood.

The publican Zacchaeus made restitution for his thievery. He made a fourfold repayment to everyone he had cheated. He did it, not to earn God's favor and forgiveness—he already had that—but to fulfill love to the neighbor.

We also find peace with God when on a daily basis we repent, believe in Christ Jesus as Savior, and set things in order in our lives.

Prayer Suggestion

Confess all your sins, known and unknown, to your heavenly Father and trust assuredly that He will forgive you for Jesus' sake.

ADDING INSULT TO INJURY

Sin entered the world through one man, and death through sin. Romans 5:12

In a communist country a spy was executed by a firing squad. The victim's family not only lost a member but also—so it was reported—it received a bill for the ammunition used. This was a clear case of adding insult to injury.

Ever since sin came into the world, such things happen. Evil is interlinked with evil. Misdeeds draw penalties, and these are sometimes accompanied or followed by other aftereffects. Misery begets more misery. Sin demands payments. It wants not only the principal back but also interest—compounded interest.

The Bible tells us how sin and its penalties multiply. St. James tells us about evil desires in a person that entice the individual. But that is not all. He goes on: "Then, after desire has conceived, it gives birth to sin; and sin, when it is full-grown, gives birth to death" (James 1:15).

There is a way to prevent the chain reaction of sin and the price it demands. Better still, there is a way to turn the whole thing around so that there is faith instead of evil desire—faith which is the victory over sin and is followed by a succession of good things: the fruits of faith and love. St. Paul points to this when he completes the couplet: "The wages of sin is death, but the gift of God is eternal life in Christ Jesus our Lord" (Romans 6:23).

God's grace is truly amazing. It provides for us the Peacemaker, God's own Son, Jesus Christ, to be the sacrifice for our sins. With sins forgiven, the debt is paid; we are free to serve the living God. Declared just by faith, "we have peace with God through our Lord Jesus Christ" (Romans 5:1).

God does not add insult to injury—punish the penitent, believing sinner and send him a bill for administering the punishment. Instead He blesses the Christian with grace and healing of the soul.

Prayer Suggestion

Ask God to forgive you for Jesus' sake and to strengthen you for living a life of righteousness as a fruit of faith.

DEEDS THAT COME BACK TO BLESS

Give, and it will be given to you. Luke 6:38

In his short story *No Comeback* Frederick Forsyth tells about a self-willed rich man who, like King David in the Bible, wanted a husband removed so that he could marry the widow. The hired hit man promised that there would be no comeback. No one had seen him do it, he said, except the man's wife. So he killed her, too.

People sometimes become victims of their own designs, as Job declares in the Bible, God "catches the wise in their craftiness" (Job 5:13). There is a saying: He who digs a ditch for someone else will himself fall into it. How often doesn't this happen in life! Those who hate others will themselves become the objects of hate. Evil has a way of returning. During World War I an army released poisonous mustard gas, only to have the wind shift and blow the gas on the sender. Whatever we release against others—slander, gossip, lies, hateful words, harmful deeds—it often comes back with a vengeance.

How different when thoughts of love and kindness are put into words and translated into deeds! They, too, come back but to bless the giver. The writer of Ecclesiastes writes, "Cast your bread upon the waters, for after many days you will find it again" (Ecclesiastes 11:1). Many times it comes back to us not only as plain bread, but with butter on it, even marmalade.

In His grace God causes comebacks or rewards to crown our lives dedicated to serving Him and the neighbor. These return gifts are not merited. In love God sent His own Son, Jesus Christ, to save us from ourselves—from our selfishness and all other sins. In the same way He sends many other blessings to enrich our lives in this world. They are rewards of grace.

Prayer Suggestion

Thank God for all good things He has poured into your life and ask His help to enable you to share them with the needy.

NIGHT PEOPLE, DAY PEOPLE

Whoever lives by the truth comes into the light, so that it may be seen plainly that what he has done has been done through God. John 3:21

While most flowers respond to the sunlight and bloom during the day, the evening primrose, in yellow, white, or pink colors, opens only at night. It likes the dark.

Likewise we have night people and day people. We must have night people who wake and work while others sleep: police officers, firefighters, factory workers on graveyard shifts, staff members who put newspapers to bed. Day people, on the other hand, observe mostly nine-to-five hours and sleep at night.

There are other kinds of night and day people. Thieves and burglars like to do their nefarious work at night, under the cover of darkness. The darkness they prefer is not only physical but also spiritual. Sin bespeaks spiritual darkness, with sinners shunning the light of God's Word. Jesus tells us why they prefer darkness; it is a cover-up: "Men loved darkness instead of light because their deeds are evil. Everyone who does evil hates the light, and will not come into the light for fear that his deeds will be exposed" (John 3:19–20).

St. Paul urges us to be daylight people, "Let us behave decently, as in the daytime, not in orgies and drunkenness, not in sexual immorality and debauchery, not in dissension and jealousy" (Romans 13:13). "Rather," he goes on, "clothe yourselves with the Lord Jesus Christ" (Romans 13:14). Jesus is the light, and to believe in Him as the Savior from sin and death is to be clad with the robe of His righteousness. Jesus said: "Whoever lives by the truth [the truth He personified, procured, and proclaimed] comes into the light, so that it may be seen plainly that what he has done has been done through God" (John 3:21).

What kind of person are you? An evening primrose or, worse, a poisonous nightshade? Or are you a flower or plant that blooms and bears fruit in daylight? Christians have nothing to hide. They come out of dark closets and live in the open, where they let their light shine.

Prayer Suggestion

Give thanks to God for the bright light of the Gospel of Christ's redeeming love, for it enables you to shine as a light in the world.

HOW OLD ARE YOU?

Solid food is for the mature, who by constant use have
trained themselves to distinguish good from evil.
Hebrews 5:14

The Irish dramatist George Bernard Shaw once expressed the opinion that people could get to be 300 years old if they could avoid accidents. Ironically, he died at age 92 when he fell from a ladder while trimming a tree.

Age is not entirely a matter of calendar years. Much depends on how we guard our health. A dissolute actor who died at age 50 was said to have had the worn-out body of a 90-year-old man. Conversely, some people at age 80 are in better shape than those half their age. When Moses died at the age of 120, "his eyes were not weak nor his strength gone" (Deuteronomy 34:7).

How old are you? It could well be that you are younger than you think. You are young in *body* if you keep fit through daily exercise. You are young in *mind* if you keep on learning, maintain an interest in life around you, can adjust to changing conditions, and stay hopeful about the future.

Above all, we need to measure our age in the *spiritual* dimension of life—in our Christian faith. Here the emphasis is on growth. We don't want to remain what St. Paul calls "mere infants in Christ" (1 Corinthians 3:1) when we have the opportunity to be mature men and women. God has given us the means for spiritual development: His Word and the sacraments. He desires that we, in the words of St. Peter, may "grow up" in our salvation. To discover every day how wonderful is the love of God, who sent His Son to give us life and peace and pardon, is to stay spiritually young—in the psalmist's words, to renew our youth "like the eagle's" (Psalm 103:5). At the close of his Second Epistle St. Peter urges us: "Grow in the grace and knowledge of our Lord and Savior Jesus Christ" (2 Peter 3:18).

The post-Epiphany season offers many opportunities and incentives to let Christ's light of the Gospel shine in and through our lives.

Prayer Suggestion

Pray that through the Gospel the Holy Spirit may keep your faith fresh by drawing you closer to Jesus Christ.

USING OUR TALENTS

I remind you to fan into flame the gift of God.
2 Timothy 1:6

Edison, the inventor, had more than 1,000 patents. Picasso averaged more than 200 paintings a year. Mozart wrote more than 600 musical compositions, and all this before he died at age 35. "Great talents, these, but I don't have any," you say.

Not true! In most of us there is not this great capacity. Perhaps, too, most of us don't have the concentration of these persons. Edison said that genius was two percent inspiration and 98 percent perspiration.

However true that may be, we know that all people have some talents, endowments, and abilities—some more than others. You, too, have a talent. It may be a diamond in the rough, but it's there. Let's mention a few, and you can perhaps identify with one or more: a cheerful disposition, the ability to make friends, a readiness to listen when people present personal problems, skills in homemaking, a patience that goes with trying to help one who struggles, the giving of advice based on knowledge and experience, a good memory, a receptive mind, a compassionate heart. Little talents? No. They become big ones when rightly used.

When enhanced by the Christian faith, our gifts are profitably used in the service of Christ. And that is what makes our personal endowments so precious—with them we can glorify God and bring help into the lives of troubled and deprived people.

What a joy it is to our Savior Jesus Christ when He sees that He redeemed us not only *from* something—from the guilt of sin and the fear of death—but also *for* something—for serving Him and His brothers and sisters with our talents!

A deed of love done in His name can mean more than an invention by Edison, a painting by Picasso, a motet by Mozart. This is not to minimize great talent; it is to maximize what Christian love can do with even so small a personal talent.

Prayer Suggestion

Ask the Holy Spirit to stir up the gift that is in you and to help you use it in the service of Christ, our Savior.

Peace in the Home

May you live to see your children's children. Psalm 128:6

"He is happiest, be he king or peasant, who finds peace in his home." So declared the poet Goethe.

Peace in the home cannot be bought. We can purchase comfortable furniture, wall-to-wall carpeting, and television sets, but peace is not obtainable in the marketplace at any price. There are no substitutes for the happiness that peace brings. Lustful pleasure is no replacement. Alcohol and drugs may be relaxing for awhile—they may take the users into a world of fantasy and dreams, but that is not peace.

Many who in anger, frustration, or false expectations leave home to look for peace elsewhere usually don't find it. How many times has the sad experience of the Prodigal Son been repeated by young people today! The bright lights of the city, especially of its amusement area, spell out many words, but peace of mind and soul is not one of them.

Peace in the home—between husbands and wives, parents and children—is no accident. It is God's gift to us, in keeping with the directives and promises of His Word. Those who do the will of God, honoring father and mother and loving one another, have found the road to peace. The willingness and ability to let God's will prevail in all domestic relationships is not the result of some human philosophy but is a fruit of faith. Faith is the foundation of peace—faith in the Lord Jesus Christ, who walked the way of the cross to effect reconciliation and peace with God for all humanity. Peace in the home is a piece of the peace we have with God.

Prayer Suggestion

Ask God to grant peace in your home as you, for Jesus' sake, love and forgive one another.

Names That Honor Christians

You are a chosen people, a royal priesthood, a holy nation, a people belonging to God. 1 Peter 2:9

Sometimes people seek to enhance their position and the kind of work they do by inventing high-sounding titles. A barber becomes a tonsorial artist; an elevator operator, an engineer in charge of vertical transportation; and a bit on the humorous side, a soda jerk, a fizzicist.

People outside Christendom may wonder about the names and titles by which God honors His people. Christ's enemies may have wondered about His title: the Son of God. When Pontius Pilate had the lowly, beaten Jesus before him, he may have smiled when he heard Him affirm His divine kingship. But our Lord was indeed the King of heaven and earth, for He was the Son of the Highest.

Christians are called kings and priests in the Bible. These are not empty, pretentious titles. The exalted, enthroned Christ has truly made them rulers with Him in heavenly places. St. Peter tells all Christians: "You are a chosen people, a royal priesthood, a holy nation, a people belonging to God" (1 Peter 1:9). They came to be God's people because Jesus Christ purchased them with His blood and set them free so that they might declare God's praises, who called them out of darkness into His marvelous light. These God-given titles deal with reality.

So it is with every other name by which God honors Christians. They are truly His children—by adoption, yes, but truly His sons and daughters and the heirs of eternal life. The very name "Christian," although originally given them by the enemies of the Gospel, is an honorable designation, for it connects them with Christ.

Kings, priests, God's offspring, children of light, Christians—these are faith-implying, faith-strengthening titles. We are honored to bear them. What remains is that we live up to them by glorifying God.

Prayer Suggestion

Ask for God's help in your desire to honor Him by believing firmly in Jesus Christ as Savior and by living according to His Word.

Searching for the Treasure

Everything that was written in the past was written to teach us, so that through endurance and the encouragement of the Scriptures we might have hope. Romans 15:4

A treasure hunter in Florida searched for 16 years for the Nuestra Senora de Atocha, a Spanish galleon that sank in 1622 with a cargo of precious metals. In 1985 the ship was located, and 40 million dollars worth of gold and silver was salvaged. The approximate location of the ship was determined by searching ancient records.

The Word of God contains great spiritual treasures. These, declares the psalmist, "are more precious than gold, than much pure gold" (Psalm 19:10). The wisdom of the Holy Scriptures, which make us wise unto salvation through faith in Christ Jesus, "cannot be bought with the finest gold" (Job 28:15) says Job. The Word of God exceeds every earthly treasure, for only it can comfort people when they, like Job, have experienced afflictions and heavy losses. Only it enables a person to say with Job: "I know that my Redeemer lives" (Job 19:25).

Granted that the Holy Scriptures hold treasures to enrich and strengthen us spiritually, but how do we come into their possession? Jesus has the answer: Search the Scriptures! When we read, study, discuss, and apply the truths of God's Word, we, "through endurance and the encouragement of the Scriptures ... have hope," writes St. Paul (Romans 15:4).

Our growth in the grace and knowledge of our Lord Jesus Christ comes through the medium of God's written Word, but it does so only if we do persistent digging, exploring, and searching. Then, like the man in Florida who discovered the treasures of the Spanish galleon, we too will find a treasure, our Highest Good, and that is Jesus Christ, our Savior.

Have you been treasure hunting in the Bible?

Prayer Suggestion

Pray that the Holy Spirit may lead you deeper into the Holy Scriptures so that you may draw closer to Jesus, your Savior.

The Higher Loyalty

Peace I leave with you; My peace I give you. John 14:27

Jesus said, "Do not suppose that I have come to bring peace to the earth. I did not come to bring peace, but a sword" (Matthew 10:34). Yet He also said to His disciples: "Peace I leave with you; My peace I give you" (John 14:27). Some consider these statements contradictory.

We have to bear in mind: The peace of Christ—the peace we have with God through His reconciling death—is one thing; the peace of the world is another.

At the same time, as people who live both in Christ's kingdom and in the world, we often find ourselves in strange situations—in situations in which the greater loyalty to Christ supersedes personal relationships and friendships.

In our secular lives as well there may be conflicts. In the 1840s two young men were cadets at West Point Military Academy: Ulysses S. Grant and Simon B. Buckner. They were friends. In 1854, when Grant found himself without funds in New York City, Buckner made him a loan. Later the Civil War broke out, dividing not only states but also family members and friends. In the battle of Fort Donelson, Grant and Buckner were officers on opposite sides. Officially they were enemies, for their greater loyalty lay with their respective governments. When Buckner surrendered, Grant offered him financial assistance. In such situations we, too, may find ourselves.

What it boils down to is this: Christians and non-Christians must live together and share this one world. We deal with one another. We have many likes and dislikes in common. We are good neighbors. We work for the good of the community and country. However, in the final analysis—when it gets down to a spiritual crisis—our higher loyalty and love go to Jesus Christ. Not only our eternal well-being but also our peace of conscience lies with Him.

Prayer Suggestion

Ask God to give you love for all people, but fill you with the highest love for Jesus Christ, your Reconciler.

SPEAKING AND DOING THE TRUTH

Each of you must put off falsehood and speak truthfully to his neighbor, for we are all members of one body.
Ephesians 4:25

A national liar's organization is located in Burlington, Wisconsin. Obviously it is a tongue-in-cheek group, featuring fishing stories and other tall tales. People know what is involved: a form of entertainment.

All people, also Christians, lack perfect truthfulness. That comes out not only in what they say and do, but also in what they don't say and do. Take, for example, Ananias and Sapphira, members of the first Christian church in Jerusalem. They were liars, not only because of their lies but also their pretense, namely, that they had given all their money to the poor when they had kept some of it for themselves. Hypocrites are liars and dishonest persons.

Sometimes traces of untruthfulness are found among church people today, with some members trying to outdo one another by practicing a false liberality or a pretended holiness. St. Paul was aware of this tendency, writing to the Ephesians: "Each of you must put off falsehood and speak truthfully to his neighbor, for we are all members of one body" (Ephesians 4:25).

Jesus gives us the perfect example of truthfulness. St. Peter writes of Him, quoting the words of Isaiah: "He committed no sin, and no deceit was found in His mouth" (1 Peter 2:22).

It is one thing to admire an example, and another to follow it. A man in a wheelchair may admire one who can walk, but that doesn't mean that he can get up and do likewise. Jesus not only gives us the example of perfect truthfulness, but He also enables us to follow it. In giving His life for us, in rising from the dead, and in sending His Holy Spirit into our hearts, He made us His own—made us to be like Him. We have no reason to lie about ourselves. We are acceptable in the sight of God.

Prayer Suggestion

Pray for a truthful heart, fashioned after the truthful heart of Jesus, your Savior.

FIRST DOWN, THEN UP

Carry each other's burdens, and in this way you will fulfill the law of Christ. Galatians 6:2

Our Lord used a correct expression in saying at the beginning of His parable of the Good Samaritan: "A man was going *down* from Jerusalem to Jericho" (Luke 10:30). Jerusalem is 2,400 feet above sea level, while Jericho is 825 feet below sea level—a descent of nearly two thirds of a mile.

The man of Jesus' parable went down in another sense: "He fell into the hands of robbers. They stripped him of his clothes, beat him and went away, leaving him half dead" (Luke 10:30). The priest and the Levite who passed that way let him stay down.

But the Good Samaritan raised him up and ministered to him. He took the victim to the inn, cared for him for a day, and then engaged the innkeeper to attend him during the rest of his convalescence.

The man who was down came up again because somebody cared, somebody had compassion, somebody considered even a hostile racist to be his neighbor. And that is the point in the parable. "Who is my neighbor?" the scribe had asked. The reply of Jesus showed that it is anyone who is in need of our help.

Thank God, Jesus Christ was no respecter of persons. He disregarded race, color, social status, even moral self-achievement. While we were yet sinners—all of us—He died for us. We were all down, but now we are up. We are all one in Christ Jesus.

Let us then be up and doing. The mother of James and John asked Jesus whether her sons could *sit* on seats of honor in His kingdom. Yes, there is a time to sit and listen to Jesus' words, as did Mary of Bethany. All the while, whether we sit or stand, we remain *up* in our Christian living so that we may walk in God's ways and render service where it is needed.

Prayer Suggestion

Thank God for having granted you the upward look of faith in Christ Jesus, asking Him for help and willingness to reach out to the fallen.

KEEPING THE GOSPEL PURE

I do not set aside the grace of God, for if righteousness
could be gained through the law, Christ died for nothing!
Galatians 2:21

On the rock-bound coast north of Boston one can see the beautiful
home once belonging to Lydia Pinkham. Her company made a popular
remedy that many regarded as patent medicine. Perhaps some found
"relief" from it because it was 20 percent alcohol.

Jesus is our good Physician, and what He and His apostles dispensed was the pure Gospel, the only cure for sinful man. Our Lord
spoke the words of life, warning His hearers about false prophets, that
is, quacks, peddlers of useless spiritual medicines. Sometimes these
false teachers offered remedies that were a mixture of truths and
untruths. But true doctrine, when mixed with error, is no longer the
truth.

This fact becomes especially evident when the way of salvation by
faith is watered down, even poisoned, by claims of salvation by good
works or human merit. If, even to the smallest degree, we are made to
believe that we become right with God by our own goodness or good
deeds, the principle of divine grace is set aside.

St. Paul encountered this attempted mixture of God's mercy with
human merit among the Galatian Christians, many of whom were led
to believe that the deeds of the Law must still be done to gain God's
favor. The apostle calls this a gospel different from the one he had
preached. It was in fact no longer the Gospel. The Gospel that he
preached was that Christians lived by faith in the Son of God, Jesus
Christ, who loved them and gave Himself on the cross for them. The
idea of salvation by works, he says, sets aside the grace of God, "for if
righteousness could be gained through the Law, Christ died for nothing" (Galatians 2:21).

The "alcohol" of human merit can make people feel good, but only
the Gospel brings them peace with God.

Prayer Suggestion

Thank you for the gift of the Gospel and for the salvation it brings
through faith in Jesus Christ.

COMMUNICATING THE WORD

We write this to make our joy complete. 1 John 1:4

It is estimated that 26 million English-speaking people in the United States are illiterate, that is, they can't read the newspaper, address an envelope, write a check, or read a public notice.

When people are unable to read and write, it is much harder to get word to them—to communicate the Word of God. Of course, there is still the avenue of hearing and the use of visual material. But reading the Word—and writing it, as Christian authors do—is essential to the fulfillment of our Christian mission to share the Gospel of our Lord Jesus Christ.

Today, as in the past, missionaries have opened schools to teach the native tribes how to read and write. These skills open a new world to these people: They give them access to God's message in the Holy Scriptures. Of course, one can say, we can by word of mouth and over the radio tell the Gospel to the illiterate, and this is being done. But it is important, too, that the hearers of the Word become readers of it, so that they can learn firsthand what God has to say to them. Of the early Christians in Berea it is said: "They received the message with great eagerness and examined the Scriptures every day to see if what Paul said was true" (Acts 17:11).

While the ability to read and write is of great help to people in everyday life, it is especially important in one's relationship to Jesus Christ. He is the essence of the Holy Scriptures. They testify of Him as the Word through whom God made known His saving love. Jesus the Word not only *spoke* of and for the Father, He also *did* what the Father wanted Him to do: to give His life as a ransom for the redemption of all people.

Prayer Suggestion

Can you read and write? Thank God for this and see what you can do to help other people read and write, and to know about Jesus.

TRANSLATING THE WORD OF GOD

Do not merely listen to the Word, and so deceive yourselves.
Do what it says. James 1:22

More than 600 years ago John Wycliffe issued the first English Bible. Since then many translations have been published, not only in English but in more than 1,000 languages. Thanks to these translations, people everywhere in the world can read the Word of God in their own tongues and come to know Jesus Christ as their Savior.

There is another kind of translation of God's Word, that is, the translating of it into everyday Christian life. Several steps precede this. The first is *hearing* the Word, or reading it—making ear and eye contact with it. Then comes *believing* it. St. Paul, whose conversion the Christian church observes today, tells us that faith comes from hearing the message that comes from the Word of God.

From hearing the Word we go on to the doing of it, as St. James tells us. Only a believer can be a doer of works that God desires. The Bible states: "Without faith it is impossible to please God" (Hebrews 11:6). Faith in what? It is better to ask, Faith in whom? St. Paul gave a clear answer to the converted jailer of Philippi: "Believe in the Lord Jesus, and you will be saved" (Acts 16:31). Believe in Him as the one who gave His life to redeem you from sin and to enable you to be His follower.

Given hearing and believing, the translating of the Word into Christian action can begin. It began immediately for the jailer when he washed the wounds he himself had inflicted on Paul and Silas. Early Christians translated the Word of God when, to the astonishment of their heathen neighbors, they practiced love, also in their relation with enemies. Those who reveal the fruit of the Spirit in their lives are translators of the Word in terms of Christian virtues, and these are love, joy, peace, patience, kindness, goodness, faithfulness, gentleness, and self-control.

Practice this in the home, in the community, in school, and at work, and you are translating the Word of God.

Prayer Suggestion

Ask the Holy Spirit to strengthen your faith in Jesus so that you can bring the Gospel to life where you live and work.

THE WEALTH WE HAVE IN CHRIST

In [Christ] are hidden all the treasures of wisdom and knowledge. Colossians 2:3

Chapter 13 in St. Matthew's gospel contains nuggets of truth in its seven parables, and one of them does deal with a treasure: "The kingdom of heaven is like treasure hidden in a field. When a man found it, he hid it again, and then in his joy went and sold all that he had and bought that field" (Matthew 13:44).

The noun in the Greek text for "treasure" is *thesaurus,* a term commonly applied to a book containing a wealth of information on words, as in the case of *Roget's Thesaurus of English Words and Phrases.* In Greek a *thesaurus* meant, first, the place where valuables were kept: a treasure box or chest. Second, it meant the treasure itself.

According to Jesus' parable a man, quite by accident, found a cache in a plot of ground. He didn't abscond with the treasure. That would have been theft, and besides, it may have been too heavy to carry. So he hid it again, then went to great effort to obtain it legally by scraping together all his money and buying the field.

The purpose of the parable is not to instruct us on procedure when we find an earthly treasure. Nor is it an investor's guide on how to reconvert one's assets. The lesson is spiritual. The heavenly treasure some people find—unexpectedly, as it seems to them, but surely by God's guidance—is salvation in Jesus Christ. It is the forgiveness of sins, peace with God, the inheritance of eternal life. This treasure is so great that we gladly surrender everything else so that we might have and keep it. Christ is that valuable to us. We gladly sing, "Jesus, priceless treasure, Source of purest pleasure, Truest friend to me" (*Lutheran Worship,* 270).

Prayer Suggestion

Thank God for treasures He imparts to you in the Gospel of Jesus Christ, your Savior and Lord.

FORGIVING ANOTHER: IT LIFTS A BURDEN

Be kind and compassionate to one another, forgiving each other, just as in Christ God forgave you. Ephesians 4:32

In Jesus' parable of the prodigal son the father forgives his son. In Harold Bell Wright's *The Shepherd of the Hills,* which is the fourth most-read book in our country, it is a father who forgives his son-in-law. The father was long bitter because his daughter had died in child-birth. In the end, however, as the young man lay dying, old Matt found it in his heart to forgive.

Forgiveness is often a long time coming. Before it comes, hatred or a grievance corrodes the heart like an acid. Think of the feud between Isaac's twin sons, Esau and Jacob. After a 20-year absence because of Esau's jealousy, Jacob dared to come home with his family. The reunion was cordial. The brothers embraced.

Many people take their grudges with them through life, all the way to the grave. They refuse to forgive another for wrongdoing, even when forgiveness is asked for. Or they will say reluctantly: "Okay, I'll forgive, but I'll never forget," which comes close to being a contradiction in terms. An anger daily nursed and rehearsed can become a cancer of the soul. That's why St. Paul tells us to treat it early: "Do not let the sun go down while you are still angry" (Ephesians 4:26).

Forgiveness, though often hard, is possible because God in Christ forgave us. Again, the apostle: "Be kind and compassionate to one another, forgiving each other, just as in Christ God forgave you" (Ephesians 4:32). We came to God, confessing: "Great is our debt, and many are our trespasses of Your holy will." And He said to us: "Because My Son, Jesus Christ, whom you accept in faith as your Lord and Savior, died for your wrong-doing and set things straight, I forgive you—I forgive you the entire burden of your debt."

Shouldn't we then also forgive our neighbor the paltry debt he owes us?

Prayer Suggestion

Give thanks to God for His forgiveness to you in Christ and ask His help to forgive those who trespass against you.

AMAZING GRACE

It is by grace you have been saved, through faith.
Ephesians 2:8

"The last will be first, and the first will be last" (Matthew 20:16), said Jesus at the close of His parable of laborers in a vineyard. He said this to correct a misconception about the kingdom of heaven. Many Israelites expected God to reward them for their good deeds according to divine and human laws. Even the disciples were merit-conscious. Peter asked Jesus what their reward would be for having sacrificed more than others—for having "left everything to follow You!" (Matthew 19:27)

In the parable of vineyard workers, two things stand out: (1) The men hired last were paid first, and (2) all workers, even those who had labored for only one hour, received the same pay: a denarius, the usual day's wages. This is not the usual way of doing things in employer-employee relations.

Jesus did not intend to prescribe work schedules and wage scales for everyday life. He Himself subscribed to the principle that "the worker deserves his wages" (Luke 10:7). What He had in mind here was to underscore the terms God has ordained in the kingdom of grace. God is gracious, and when Jesus has the vineyard owner say "Don't I have the right to do what I want with my own money?" (Matthew 20:15), He is asserting God's right to be gracious.

Long-term Christians and veterans of the cross—those who have labored long for their Lord—and latecomers like the penitent thief on the cross are saved by grace alone. The former do not begrudge God's generosity to last-minute converts, for they too are saved by grace. And the latecomers? They join the hymn writer in saying: "Alas! that I so late have known Thee."

Prayer Suggestion

Build your prayer around God's saying to St. Paul, "My grace is sufficient for you, for My power is made perfect in weakness."

WHO IS YOUR MODEL?

Join with others in following my example, brothers.
Philippians 3:17

The 18th century English author, Oliver Goldsmith, wrote, "People seldom improve when they have no other model than themselves to copy after."

This is true for spiritual growth as well. St. Paul writes to the Philippians: "Join with others in following my example" (Philippians 3:17). It was hard for people who recently had come out of paganism to lead Christian lives. So let them copy the example of the apostle. He showed the converts how to exercise love, patience, and courage under difficult conditions. And St. Paul adds, "Take note of those who live according to the pattern we gave you" (Philippians 3:17). Members of the group can encourage one another as they walk together in the footsteps of their spiritual leader.

If early Christians followed the example of the apostles, who was the model for the apostles? It was Jesus Christ, their teacher and exemplar. After our Lord had washed the disciples' feet as an object lesson in humble service, He said: "I have set you an example that you should do as I have done for you" (John 13:15).

What the disciples learned from their Master, they passed on to others, especially how Christians should conduct themselves when they must suffer for the faith. St. Peter writes: "Christ suffered for you, leaving you an example, that you should follow in His steps" (1 Peter 2:21). With great forbearance He bore our sins in His body on the cross. He replied to curses and abuses with blessings and intercessions.

Early Christians had the apostles as models, and they in turn followed the example of Jesus Christ. We can go back one more step: The example for the Son of God was the heavenly Father, whose will Jesus followed and whose will He wants us to obey. He says: "Be perfect, therefore, as your heavenly Father is perfect" (Matthew 5:48). Again, be loving to all, for that is how God is, who lets His sun shine on the evil and the good, and sends rain on the just and unjust. How blessed we are to have all this guidance!

Prayer Suggestion:

Thank God for giving us His Son as the exemplar and enabler of Christian conduct.

FELLOWSHIP WITH CHRIST

Is not the cup of thanksgiving for which we give thanks a participation in the blood of Christ? And is not the bread that we break a participation in the body of Christ?
1 Corinthians 10:16

Hymn writers speak for Christians when they say, "Savior, I long to walk closer with Thee," or "Draw us to Thee," or "Nearer, my God, to Thee." Is this just a pious wish? Do we pray this in vain?

Our Lord has indeed made provision for us to enter into closer fellowship with Him. Besides Holy Baptism and the written Word, Christ has instituted the Sacrament of Holy Communion. This is a means of grace, a bridge or way by which He approaches us to strengthen us in faith and to enable us to live a Christian life in Him.

The faith we hold is this: Christ's body was given and His blood shed on the cross for the forgiveness of our sins. In receiving the consecrated bread and wine in Holy Communion, we are receiving, according to Christ's own words, His body and blood as pledges of His forgiveness and as spiritual food and drink to strengthen our fellowship in Him.

In writing to the Corinthians St. Paul speaks of this fellowship with Christ. He asks, "Is not the cup of thanksgiving for which we give thanks a participation in the blood of Christ? And is not the bread that we break a participation in the body of Christ?" (1 Corinthians 10:16) For "participation" he uses the Greek word *koinonia*, which means communion. Holy Communion—this is the closest fellowship we can have with Christ.

The apostle points to a wider outreach of this fellowship when he goes on to say, "Because there is one loaf, we, who are many, are one body, for we all partake of the one loaf" (1 Corinthians 10:17). This is a fruit of the sacrament; it both expresses and furthers the union among Christians, the communion of saints.

We see then that in this sacrament, which is the Gospel made visible, our Savior has made provision for us to walk closer with Him, to be near and dear to Him, to be drawn into closer fellowship with Him and with our brothers and sisters in the faith.

Prayer Suggestion

Give thanks to Christ for ordaining a sacrament which means Thanksgiving, the Holy Eucharist.

RICH IN GOD

In Him [Christ] we have redemption through His blood, the forgiveness of sins, in accordance with the riches of God's grace. Ephesians 1:7

Many people believe that *poverty causes crime*, that stealing and robbing would cease—at least be greatly reduced—if wealth were more evenly distributed. However, a recent spokesperson musters a great deal of evidence to show that the terms should be reversed: *Crime causes poverty*. The community deteriorates, and everything in it loses value, when crime infests it.

Part of the solution to poverty is not stealing and robbing but getting a job. St. Paul tells the Ephesians: "He who has been stealing must steal no longer, but must work, doing something useful with his own hands" (Ephesians 4:28). In doing this, he will not only overcome poverty by having a steady income but will "have something to share with those in need," the apostle declares.

Whatever a person's economic circumstances may be, the main concern of a Christian is to be "rich toward God," as our Lord said. God has provided spiritual riches. St. Paul writes: "to the praise of His glorious grace, which He has freely given us in the One He loves. In Him we have redemption through His blood, the forgiveness of sins, in accordance with the riches of God's grace that He lavished on us with all wisdom and understanding" (Ephesians 1:6–8).

By nature every person is—to borrow the words from the book of Revelation—"wretched, pitiful, poor, blind and naked" (Revelation 3:17). From Christ, as Charlotte Elliott says in her hymn "Just as I Am," come "sight, riches, healing of the mind." This is the grace of our Lord Jesus Christ: He became poor, He deprived Himself of every convenience, that we "through His poverty might become rich" (2 Corinthians 8:9).

We may lack riches. It doesn't bother us. It doesn't tempt us to commit the crimes of stealing and robbing. Our riches are in God, our heavenly Father.

Prayer Suggestion

Express your gratitude to God for all His blessings to you in Christ.

UNDERGIRDING MARITAL LOVE

*These three remain: faith, hope and love. But the greatest
of these is love. 1 Corinthians 13:13*

In Irving Stone's historical novel about Mary Todd, *Love Is Eternal,*
the future Mrs. Lincoln confides to her cousin Ann that she might
marry a Springfield, Illinois, lawyer because he has a promising political future and might someday be president. Her cousin replied, "Surely
you wouldn't marry a man for just that!" The cousin explained that she
would marry her beau only for love, adding, "What else is marriage?"
Mary's brief comment to that was that marriage is "a way of life."

Love is the essential ingredient. A popular song has it that love and
marriage go together like a horse and carriage. Much depends on what
is meant by love. It has to be more than infatuation. Mutual caring and
concern are part of it. It has to manifest itself in all good virtues:
patience, compassion, ability to forgive, thoughtfulness, a sharing of
joys and sorrows. Self-fulfillment? Yes, but not at the cost of sacrificial
love.

The strongest anchor for the ship of marriage on a stormy sea is
faith in Jesus Christ. You can compare faith and the love flowing from
it to anything else that gives stability: ballast in a ship, the rock foundation of a house, the girders of a bridge. The Bible has a great deal to
say about the love of Christ as sustaining our love to Him and to one
another. St. Paul bids husbands to love their wives as Christ loved His
bride, the church, and gave Himself up for her. Of course, the same
goes for wives in relation to Christ and their husbands.

Each of the young women quoted above spoke a part of the truth.
To marry a man primarily because of his position, present or future,
puts personal ambition ahead of love. To speak of love as the only pre-
requisite for marrying someone is likewise insufficient. Marriage does
have its practical side; it becomes a way of life for those who enter it.

St. Paul says of Christian love: "Love is patient, love is kind. It
does not envy, it does not boast, it is not proud. It is not rude, it is not
self-seeking" (1 Corinthians 13:4–5). That kind of love is needed to
undergird marriage.

Prayer Suggestion

Ask the Lord Jesus to strengthen your love toward one another,
that it may become more and more like His love.

OBEYING THE HIGHER LAW

Submit yourselves for the Lord's sake to every authority instituted among men. 1 Peter 2:13

In 18th-century Austria a special award, the *Pour Le Merite* (For Merit), was given to soldiers who had won signal victories by disobeying military orders that were obviously wrong. It was recognized that there were situations in which soldiers, in order to be *good* soldiers, had to fall back on their own intelligence and sense of personal responsibility.

In the lives of people today instances can occur when laws and rules have to be disobeyed to be obedient to the higher law, the law of God. More than a generation ago, in a European country, a government came to power that followed the "might makes right" principle, wantonly imprisoning and executing citizens who opposed its edicts. The victims, some of them Christians, accepted the consequences of their conscientious objections; they refused to act contrary to the moral laws of God. They followed the example of Christians in the Roman Empire who would not worship Caesar as God, even if the demanded act of loyalty was only taking a pinch of incense and offering it to Caesar.

"We must obey God rather than men" (Acts 5:29), said the apostle Peter when the religious authorities in Jerusalem demanded that the apostle no longer teach and preach in Jesus' name.

Christians stand by that principle today. They refuse to be disloyal to Him who died for them and rose again, Jesus Christ, whose name is above every name and who is to be confessed as Lord and Savior.

Jesus was not a revolutionary. He doesn't want His followers today to be disobedient for the sake of disobedience, or to be objectors when there is no proper ground for it. His position is clear, and workable: "Give to Caesar what is Caesar's, and to God what is God's" (Matthew 22:21).

Prayer Suggestion

Pray that God may guide all who are in authority in home, school, community, and at work to order what is right, but if they fail, to give you the courage to dissent.

A Prayer That Prevailed

Jesus answered, "Woman, you have great faith! Your request is granted." Matthew 15:28

Jesus had seemingly rebuffed the Canaanite mother who had asked for His help in behalf of her demon-possessed daughter. He had said, "It is not right to take the children's bread and toss it to their dogs" (Matthew 15:26). He meant to say that His time and effort belonged primarily to the Israelites; mostly with them must He share the bread of life.

The implied reference to the heathen as "dogs" is, according to the Greek text, softened by the use of a word meaning indoor dogs—little dogs, house pets—in distinction from outdoor dogs roaming the countrysides and city streets. Gross unbelievers are called dogs, as in the passage: "Outside are the dogs, those who practice magic arts, the sexually immoral, the murderers, the idolaters and everyone who loves and practices falsehood" (Revelation 22:15).

What Jesus said seems negative, but a yes is implied. In His comments He left Himself open to a rejoinder. His words gave the woman a handle and she was quick to grab it: "Yes, Lord, … but even the dogs [puppies] eat the crumbs that fall from their masters' table" (Matthew 15:27). The interceding mother is not asking for a great effort on Jesus' part—not asking the Good Shepherd to withdraw His love from "the lost sheep of Israel." She will be satisfied with leftovers to which, according to Jesus' own words, she is entitled.

A prayer of such urgency Jesus could not deny. The Good Shepherd laid down His life also for those "other sheep," for the Gentiles. He sent His apostles to teach the Gospel to all nations. His heart and ears are open to their prayers, and to ours also.

Prayer Suggestion

Meditate in prayer on the manifold blessings God has given you, especially on His greatest gift: His own Son, Jesus Christ, as your Savior.

The Marks of Life

Let no one cause me trouble, for I bear on my body the marks of Jesus. Galatians 6:17

When walking through city parks in St. Louis, one can see how dead trees, especially in spring and summer, distinguish themselves from living ones: They have no leaves and no fruit. By and by the park employees take an ax or hatchet to slash away a part of the bark and paint the spot with bright-red paint. They are marked for destruction and will soon be removed from the park.

People, too, bear marks of life or of death. Some are, as it were, a reverse plate of believers described in Psalm 1: Their leaves have withered; they bear no fruit. They are spiritually dead. Sooner or later the Lord will say with the owner in Jesus' parable of an unfruitful fig tree: "Cut it down! Why should it use up the soil?" (Luke 13:7). One could well imagine that they bear a red mark designating them for destruction.

Altogether different are people who have a living faith. Isaiah (61:3) calls them "oaks of righteousness." An outstanding example of such Christians was the apostle Paul. He was filled with spiritual energy and life—and he bore much fruit—because he had a living faith. He confessed, "I have been crucified with Christ and I no longer live, but Christ lives in me. The life I live in the body, I live by faith in the Son of God, who loved me and gave Himself for me" (Galatians 2:20).

Because St. Paul was such a devoted spokesman for Christ, he did not escape the attention of the enemies of the cross. The apostle, persecuted by them, could say, "I bear on my body the marks of Jesus" (Galatians 6:17). His enemies wanted these scars of whippings and stonings to be the marks of death. But in the sight of God they were the marks of life. We, too, like trees adding fruit to their foliage, bear the marks of Jesus as we confess our faith in Him and do His works.

Prayer Suggestion

Let your prayer be that Jesus may so live in you that His saving love may leave its marks on you.

PRAYER FOR THE LIVING

Pray for each other so that you may be healed. James 5:16

In his book *Roughing It* Mark Twain relates his observations during a trip to the Hawaiian Islands. The then-pagan natives, he says, believed they could pray their enemies to death. One needed to kneel down and pray before an article or item belonging to the intended victim, and this would kill him.

In the Bible we find the reverse, namely, people prayed back to life. The prophet Elijah prayed over the widow's dead son: "O LORD my God, let this boy's life return to him!" (1 Kings 17:21) God heard this prayer, and the son lived. In the book of Acts we read that the apostle Peter, taken to the upper room where the deceased Dorcas (or Tabitha) lay, "got down on his knees and prayed. Turning toward the dead woman, he said, 'Tabitha, get up' " (Acts 9:40). And she did. In answer to prayer, God brought this person, who had been a friend to the poor, back to life.

God has not promised that we can raise the dead with our prayers. But He has assured us that our prayers for the living will receive His attention, especially when people are sick or in any kind of need. St. James writes, "Is any one of you in trouble? He should pray. … Is any one of you sick? He should call the elders of the church to pray over him." He goes on: "The prayer offered in faith will make the sick person well" (5:13–15). God can effect healing as He desires—miraculously or through the means and ministrations of the medical profession.

There was a time when Philip Melanchthon, a Reformation scholar at the Wittenberg University, was deathly sick. Martin Luther prayed for him earnestly, telling God that the church needed this co-worker. A biographer of Melanchthon comes right out and says: "Luther prayed him well."

We note from the letters of St. Paul how he prayed frequently and fervently for his readers. Nowhere does it say that he prayed for the dead—always for the living in every circumstance of life. What he urges Timothy to do is what we should do also: "That requests, prayers, intercession and thanksgiving be made for everyone" (1 Timothy 2:1).

Jesus prayed for His enemies, His disciples, and for those who through the ages would believe in Him through their testimony—believe in Him as having died for them and risen again. We follow in His footsteps when we intercede for others—for the living.

Prayer Suggestion

Speak to God in behalf of someone in need of His help.

AN ACT OF MULTIPLICATION

Jesus then took the loaves, gave thanks, and distributed to those who were seated as much as they wanted. John 6:11

To feed the thousands who had come to Him in an uninhabited place, Jesus took the available food supplies—five loaves and two fish—blessed them, and so multiplied them that "all ate and were satisfied" (Matthew 14:20).

In another wilderness God nourished His people by providing manna from heaven, truly a miracle bread. On the occasion mentioned in today's reading the Son of God took earthly means and by His miraculous power multiplied them into rations sufficient for a multitude. In both wildernesses, divine love brought divine power into play for the nurture of needful people.

God is a true mathematician. He *adds*, as He lays blessings to blessings; He *subtracts*, as He removes what is harmful to us; He *divides*, as He makes parts of His bountiful supplies and "He gives … to each one, just as He determines" (1 Corinthians 12:11). He also *multiplies*, as He takes what little is at hand and increases it for the benefit of all. He routinely multiplies the seeds we sow into a harvest of many seeds. As a matter of course He uses earthly means, however, meager, to provide, to heal, to make us whole in our physical lives. These acts although commonly and frequently performed, involve miracles nonetheless.

The greatest miracle of divine love occurs when our Lord through ordinary food and drink—the consecrated bread and wine of Holy Communion—conveys to us His true body and blood once given and once shed for the remission of our sins. Thanks to His generosity, these gifts for our spiritual nurture are never exhausted. With each use they are multiplied.

Prayer Suggestion

Speak a word of praise to Jesus, your Lord and Savior, for all His benefits to you.

WE CAN LEARN TO LOVE

The grace of our Lord was poured out on me abundantly.
1 Timothy 1:14

A property owner who took pride in his lawn asked a plant expert what to do to get rid of dandelions. The reply was "Learn to love them."

Dr. Alvaro A. Carino, a prominent churchman in the Philippines, records this brief exchange in his autobiography *Saved to Serve.* He applies it to people of other cultures and races with whom we live: "Learn to love them."

This is good advice with regard to the whole human race, sinful as it is. As Christians we don't admire, imitate, or love peoples' sin, but we love the sinners.

This is what God Himself did. He loved all sinners despite their wrongdoing. We know He hates sin, for He is a zealously holy God. Yet He loves sinners—loves them enough to desire and devise their salvation. St. Paul tells Timothy: "Here is a trustworthy saying that deserves full acceptance: Christ Jesus came into the world to save sinners" (1 Timothy 1:15). Bringing this truth closer to home, the same apostle writes: "God demonstrates His own love for us in this: While we were still sinners, Christ died for us" (Romans 5:8).

While dandelions fall more into the class of weeds than flowers, their yellow rosettes are not without beauty and use. Wine can be made from the flowers, while the roots have medicinal value for liver disease. This being so, we need not fret when we see some dandelions in fields and meadows, even in our lawns and gardens.

People who seem useless, even obnoxious, often have redeeming qualities. Certainly we don't want to eradicate them. Many unborn infants are already being slaughtered. Do we want to extend this policy to other unwanted persons—the aged, the incurable sick, the imprisoned? God is pleased if, instead, we learn to love them and give them an opportunity to serve with the gifts God has given them.

It is easy to love roses—our friends who can return favors. It is harder to aid human dandelions, especially if they are our enemies. But that is the test of Christian love.

Prayer Suggestion

Ask the Holy Spirit to lead you closer to Jesus and to increase your love for Him and for fellow human beings.

GOD'S EYE IS ON THE SPARROW

Are not two sparrows sold for a penny? Yet not one of them will fall to the ground apart from the will of your Father. Matthew 10:29

In his highly regarded book *The Tin Drum* Günter Grass speaks of a man who could not make up his mind about sparrows. As he hunted them for pastime, he carried ammunition in one pocket of his jacket and bird food in the other.

Lowly creatures that they are, sparrows, in the comedian's words, "get no respect." Many people dislike seeing them at the bird feeders, preferring the more exciting and more colorful birds. Yet sparrows, despite their drab feathers, are cheerful, chatty, and sociable birds, so unlike the quarrelsome bluejays or the greedy starlings.

Visitors of old said that sparrows gathered in great numbers in the temple area in Jerusalem and on the Mount of Olives. That may have been the reason why Jesus spoke of them. He asked: "Are not two sparrows sold for a penny? Yet not one of them will fall to the ground apart from the will of your Father. ... So don't be afraid; you are worth more than many sparrows" (Matthew 10:29, 31).

Jesus is speaking about the providence of our heavenly Father. He encourages this logic of faith—a reasoning from the lesser to the greater: If God cares about the sparrows, He surely will do the same—and more—for us. The song writer stresses:

His eye is on the sparrow
And I know He's watching me.

The apostle Paul appeals to God's great love in a similar way when he writes: "If God is for us, who can be against us? He who did not spare His own Son, but gave Him up for us all—how will He not also, along with Him, graciously give us all things?" (Romans 8:31–32) Here the apostle reasons from the greater to the lesser: God had given us the great gift, His own Son, as the bread of life from heaven for our souls. From that we can draw the conclusion: The heavenly Father will provide also the lesser gifts of life. He conveys this truth to us through His messengers, even the lowly sparrows.

Prayer Suggestion

Ask God to strengthen your faith in His divine providence, especially in His promise to fill all your needs in Christ.

YOUR LIFE AS A NEWS STORY

*When David had served God's purpose in his own genera-
tion, he fell asleep. Acts 13:36*

This brief summary of a believer's life is like a news story that
answers the what, where, when, and why questions of an event.

We are told *what* King David did: He served God's purpose and did
His will. He was God's instrument when writing his psalms, ruling
God's people wisely and well, and lending support to the worship life
of priests and people.

The *where* of David's service was his generation, the people of
God in his kingdom, with Jerusalem its chief city. He served wherever
God placed him—out in the open where he tended sheep, in the army
where he overcame the giant Goliath, in the palace as king.

David rendered service to God and people in his lifetime. This was
the *when* of his activity. When his time was fulfilled, he fell asleep.

That leaves the *why* of David's service. Why did he serve? He was
prompted to do this by God's gracious purpose for him and his people.
He declares in Psalm 18, "I love You, O LORD, my strength." In Psalm 31
he urges us all, "Love the LORD, all His saints!" It is evident that David
loved his Lord, and for that reason served Him.

For all of us, life is measured out, for shorter or longer durations.
In our lives, too, are the what, where, when, and why questions to be
answered. The *what* is the rendition of service in fulfillment of God's
purpose—His purpose that all people should be saved and come to the
knowledge of the truth. The *where* is the place where we live and
work. The *when* is our lifetime, the time we share with our generation,
our contemporaries. And the *why* is our love to God, who first loved
us and gave His Son, Jesus Christ, to be our Savior. With these points
fulfilled, your life is a wonderful news story.

Prayer Suggestion

Turn to the Lord Jesus in prayer, asking Him to guide and strength-
en you in living a life of service.

ON BEING RESOURCEFUL

I have become all things to all men so that by all possible means I might save some. 1 Corinthians 9:22

"Ingenuity" is a word that may not occur in Bible translations. But often stressed is the need to use our minds, to apply our hearts to wisdom, to do original and creative thinking toward fulfilling God-pleasing purposes, to be opportunists in a good sense.

Jesus said that His followers should be wise in their generation, to be "as shrewd as snakes" (Matthew 10:16). In a parable He commended an unjust steward, not for being dishonest but for using his mind.

Ingenuity—St. Paul practiced it all the time, devising strategy in his mission work. He used the main roads and sea-lanes to reach key cities. He wrote, by way of explaining his approach to Israelites and Gentiles: "I have become all things to all men so that by all possible means I might save some. I do all this for the sake of the Gospel" (1 Corinthians 9:22–23). He knew how and when to use his Roman citizenship, his skill as a tentmaker, his knowledge as a scholar.

During the gold-rush days in the mid-1800s another tentmaker, Levi Strauss, observed that the prospectors needed strong, rugged clothes. So he conceived the idea to use rough tent material to make the Levi jeans. The idea worked, and in the course of time the Strauss company became the world's largest apparel maker.

God blesses rightly conceived and properly motivated ingenuity in His people, as He did the know-how of St. Paul in behalf of the Gospel. He blesses their efforts to spread His Word by person-to-person testimonies and by the use of the mass media. He doesn't want them to travel by oxcarts or in slow boats to China when they can use aircraft.

God Himself showed great ingenuity in the way He created us in body and soul, and especially in the way He provided for our salvation. He gave His Son, Jesus Christ, born of a woman, to redeem us by taking our place. What love and wisdom!

Prayer Suggestion

Thank your Creator for the powers of your mind, asking His help to use them for good and to the glory of Christ.

THE WONDERS OF GOD'S LOVE

O LORD, our Lord, how majestic is Your name in all the earth! Psalm 8:9

Thomas Moore, the Irish poet and songwriter—"The Last Rose of Summer" is one of his—visited Niagara Falls in 1804. He was so impressed that he declared, "I felt as if approaching the very residence of the Deity."

God's world is not only full of beauty, but it is also full of awe-inspiring sights that attest God's majesty and power: mountains, the redwood trees in California, the thundering cataracts.

Sometimes we feel so small by comparison. The psalmist had that feeling when he looked up into the sky. He exclaimed: "When I consider Your heavens, the work of Your fingers, the moon and the stars, which You have set in place, what is man that You are mindful of him?" (Psalm 8:3–4)

That question only the Bible can answer. It declares in one of the great Gospel declarations: "God so loved the world [so loved frail human beings] that He gave His one and only Son, that whoever believes in Him shall not perish but have eternal life" (John 3:16). Only God's love can explain why He bestowed on the human being—on so small a creature—a glorious mind such as the mighty elephants, the giant sequoias, or Pike's Peak, or even the sun in the sky do not have. The human mind can penetrate space, construct wonderful buildings, discover the powers of nature and harness them, as at Niagara Falls.

Only God's love can explain why He did a great deal more than give human beings mind and memory; He gave them immortal souls and hearts capable of being changed from the hardness of sin to the tenderness of love. In love God sent His Son, Jesus Christ, who not only showed the human family what goodness is, but also made us capable of it by giving His life for us and sending the Holy Spirit to make us God's children by faith. Here is a wonder that exceeds Niagara Falls.

Prayer Suggestion

Pray that the heavenly Father may open your eyes and minds to the wonders of His love in Christ Jesus.

When Facing Hard Tasks

Be strong and take heart, all you who hope in the LORD.
Psalm 31:24

Some things we have to do are hard. When General Robert E. Lee, his army in Virginia defeated, had to prepare to meet General Grant to surrender, he said: "I would rather die a thousand deaths."

What difficult tasks have you had to perform? Give up your home or business? Prepare for the death of a loved one? Submit to serious surgery? Break bad news to a friend?

Think of some heart-rending assignments that people of the Bible had to carry out. Moses had to leave his flocks and herds to assume the staggering task of leading the murmuring Israelites out of Egypt amid crisis after crisis. King David had to flee from the would-be usurper of his throne—his own son, Absalom. Someone had to bring him the news that Absalom was dead, and David mourned his death with outcries of grief. Someone had to tell Mary that Jesus, her son, had been arrested, and she gathered up all her strength to stand under His cross.

What a task confronted Jesus! In Gethsemane He felt the full force of the evil confronting Him: the arrest, the farce of a trial, the condemnation, the crucifixion. No wonder that He trembled and sweated blood! Yet our Lord went ahead with what He had to do. He knew it was the Father's will that He must suffer and die to redeem the sinful human race.

Because Jesus endured all for us, we are enabled to carry out what we know is God's will, difficult as it is. General Lee, a biographer tells us, considered for a moment the possibility of exposing himself to enemy fire so that he might be rendered incapable of going to Grant to surrender. But he dismissed that impulse quickly, saying: "It is our duty to live." Suicide, direct or indirect, is not the answer to our problems. What we all can do is place ourselves into God's hands, pray for strength, and then go forward to the unpleasant task.

Prayer Suggestion

Implore God, for Jesus' sake, to strengthen your heart, mind, and body to carry out hard tasks confronting you.

LASTING LOVE

I have loved you with an everlasting love; I have drawn you with loving-kindness. Jeremiah 31:3

Sometimes human love fails. In 1908, when he was 26 years old, the Hungarian musician Bela Bartok began to compose a violin concerto for his lady friend, a violinist. But by the time he had finished it, his beloved had married somebody else. She accepted the concerto as a gift but laid it away and never looked at it. It was not found until after her death in 1956.

Divine love is not like human love. God's love is not subject to changes—to whims, unstable emotions, or a change of heart. God declares through Jeremiah: "I have loved you with an everlasting love; I have drawn you with loving-kindness" (31:3). And through Isaiah, this: "Though the mountains be shaken and the hills be removed, yet My unfailing love for you will not be shaken nor My covenant of peace be removed" (54:10).

The apostle John follows through on these declarations of God's love, saying: "This is how God showed His love among us: He sent His one and only Son into the world that we might live through Him. This is love: not that we loved God, but that He loved us and sent His Son as an atoning sacrifice for our sins" (1 John 4:9–10). What gives God's love such validity is the permanence of it. What St. John wrote of God's love nearly 2,000 years ago is still true. We can rely on it.

After the example of God's love, we too remain steadfast in our love to God and to one another—that should be our concern. Love that changes with the wind is worthless. Abiding love is precious. Gifts of love—whether Bartok's violin concerto or any other expression of love—are to be appreciated and put to good use. That is what God wants. He desires that we pass on His love, and that we can do only if we cling to it ourselves.

Prayer Suggestion

Thank God for His lasting love to you in Jesus Christ, and ask His help for strengthening your love to Him and to people around you.

WE MAY BE WEAK, BUT GOD IS STRONG

God chose the weak things of the world to shame the strong.
1 Corinthians 1:27

People say "It's for the birds" to express the futility or unimportance of something. But these little creatures are not to be underestimated. In Salt Lake City stands a monument to sea gulls that in 1848 saved the crops of the new settlers by eating the crickets. We read in the Bible that God directed the ravens to feed the prophet Elijah during a famine. Jesus in the Sermon on the Mount points to the birds as teaching us not to worry, for the heavenly Father feeds them and us.

A great truth is involved here: God can do great things through weak beings. St. Paul writes to the Corinthians, who had demanded wise and powerful speakers as their spiritual leaders: "God chose the foolish things of the world to shame the wise. ... He chose the lowly things of this world and the despised things—and the things that are not—to nullify the things that are, so that no one may boast before Him" (1 Corinthians 1:27–29).

God chose to save the sinful human race through His Son, Jesus Christ, who became a man—a man whom the enemies could nail to a shameful cross. This Christ had chosen twelve very ordinary men to be His disciples, and they turned the world of the powerful Roman Empire upside down through the preaching of the simple Gospel of God's love. He chose also the apostle Paul, of whom it was said: "In person he is unimpressive and his speaking amounts to nothing" (2 Corinthians 10:10).

God still accomplishes His saving purpose that way—often through uninfluential people: little children whose faith in Jesus is an example to adults; through poor, and often poorly educated, people who possess the wisdom of God; through social outcasts whom God has accepted because they believed in Him. Through these He gets the job done.

"It's for the birds"? The situation is hopeless? Not if God has a purpose to fulfill. Perhaps you are living proof of this.

Prayer Suggestion

Pray that God in His grace may give you wisdom and strength to fulfill your tasks.

HIGH FIDELITY

It is required that those who have been given a trust must prove faithful. 1 Corinthians 4:2

In the recording industry, some years ago, "hi-fi" stood for high fidelity. Much enjoyment is derived from listening to music that is faithfully and accurately reproduced.

"High fidelity" is the mark of the children of God in the performance of their Christian calling. In this respect they are imitators—as children should be—of their heavenly Father, who faithfully keeps all His promises.

As "hi-fi" servants of God, we in life carry out and fulfill the Word of God which we hold in our hearts and confess with our mouths. We are stewards and caretakers of all that God has entrusted to us. We do credit to the high privilege that is ours when we are found trustworthy. When we are so found, then we, as the apostle Paul writes, are showing "all good fidelity; that [we] may adorn the doctrine of God our Saviour" (Titus 2:10 KJV). What sweet music it is to God—and in the ears of our fellow human beings—when with high fidelity we reproduce the Word of God in our lives!

In commending high-fidelity performance, and in encouraging us to continue, our Lord is not asking anything of us that He Himself was unwilling to render. All His words and works were marked by high fidelity. Of Him the writer of the book of Hebrews declares, "He was faithful to the One who appointed Him, just as Moses was faithful in all God's house" (3:2). Jesus was faithful to all the will of God, His heavenly Father, to the point of death, even death on a cross. All this was for us, that He might redeem us from sin and enable us to give all the sweet sounds of heavenly music in all of life.

Prayer Suggestion

Pray that the Holy Spirit through the Word may work His fruit in you, including the virtue of high fidelity.

THE BOLDNESS OF FAITH

Love is made complete among us so that we will have confidence on the day of judgment. 1 John 4:17

An unpretentious little plant found in woodlands, fields, and perhaps your own yard is the violet. Its delicate purple and blue flowers are not showy, like those of the peony or hibiscus. That may be the reason that poets refer to "the shy little violets," and in everyday speech we refer to some persons as "shrinking violets."

Usually this is not meant to be a complimentary term—not in an age when self-assertiveness is stressed. How are people to be, in the light of biblical teaching? Christian humility is stressed—a modesty not of weakness but of strength, not of self-contempt but of honoring what God has honored.

Our Savior Jesus Christ best exemplifies this kind of humility, this servanthood. "Learn from Me," He tells us, "for I am gentle and humble in heart" (Matthew 11:29). But this does not mean that Jesus was weak, for with His meekness went the might of His saving, enduring love, enabling Him to be obedient to death, even death on a cross, for our salvation.

Christians' humility is a reflection, a mirror, an image, of Christ's humility. It shows that they are genuine, not pretending to be what they are not, but demonstrating themselves to be what they are: God's redeemed children. As such they have courage and confidence not based on their own merits but on what they have become in Christ: new creations. This is not to say that they have reached perfection, but that they are growing in holiness, always more and more conformed to Christ's image.

What happens when people, who for reason of guilt or self-depreciation were like shrinking violets, have come to faith in Jesus? St. John writes that they "have confidence on the day of judgment" (1 John 4:17). Every day they may, with all boldness and confidence, come to God in prayer, for Christ has made them acceptable to the heavenly Father.

Prayer Suggestion

Pray that you may grow in the likeness of Christ and that you, by faith clothed with His righteousness, may boldly come before God in prayer.

YOUR SENSE OF VALUES

Do not worry about tomorrow, for tomorrow will worry about itself. Matthew 6:34

The owner of a Jaguar in New Jersey was so enraged over a $25 repair bill on his speedometer that he did $36,000 worth of damage—to his own car, to a police cruiser and other cars, and to the garage doors.

Yes, people do foolish and harmful things, even when they *don't* lose their tempers, because they have a false sense of values. Nowhere else does this become more evident than in the realm of spiritual choices, as the Bible amply demonstrates. The prodigal son in Jesus' parable was willing to exchange his home and a father's love for fleeting and deceitful pleasures. Judas Iscariot, a thorough-going materialist, betrayed his Savior for 30 pieces of silver. None of the rulers of this world, writes St. Paul, understood what salvation and eternal life were all about, for otherwise they would not have crucified the Lord of Glory.

In our age, people's sense of values needs a close look. Psychiatrist Frances C. Welsing, addressing herself to loveless parents, has written, "This culture has attempted to substitute material things for emotional needs, and it doesn't work. As a result, even children from well-to-do families are getting into all kinds of trouble with drugs and sex."

Of what use is wealth when children perish from spiritual poverty? What enjoyment can anyone find in worldly fame and fortune when it costs him or her their marriage, their health, their happiness?

God Himself proposes a set of values that assures peace with Him and with oneself. Jesus said that people do not live spiritually from bread but from the Word of God. He tells us of this priority: "Seek first His kingdom and His righteousness, and all these things [the things we need for everyday life] will be given to you as well" (Matthew 6:33).

When we love God above all things—love His Word, love the salvation He prepared for us all in the life, death, and resurrection of Jesus Christ—we bring our sense of values into clear focus.

Prayer Suggestion

Ask the Holy Spirit for a better understanding of the issues of life and for greater faith in Christ, your highest treasure.

PEACE IN THE REALM OF NATURE

The LORD God took the man and put him in the Garden of Eden to work it and take care of it. Genesis 2:15

A scientific team studying wildlife in the Kalahari Desert of Botswana, Africa, where people are rarely seen, reports that the animals are trustful. One wonders to what extent people make wild animals fearful and ferocious.

The fall of Adam and Eve into sin brought a blight on nature. The Lord said the ground was cursed and would bring forth thorns and thistles. If plants were affected, how about animals? Does man's wastefulness and mismanagement of the habitat of our fauna make them vicious, fighting as they do with tooth and claw for their survival? It gives us something to think about. Human greed has had a devastating effect on the environment—this we know for sure.

God appointed Adam the caretaker of the Garden of Eden. The fact that he could give "names to all the livestock, the birds of the air and all the beasts of the field" (Genesis 2:20) as God brought them to him indicates a good relationship. Regrettably, man the hunter, man the sportsman, man the commercial entrepreneur has changed that relationship, as witness, for example, the slaughter of the buffaloes in the early days of our nation.

God still looks to us to be wise stewards of all His creation. It is there for our wise use, but not for senseless abuse. As our heavenly Father, He wants to provide for us through what nature produces and through what we can grow. He gives us also animals for food—not for purposeless or profligate destruction.

God shows His love to an even greater extent in providing for our spiritual lives. He sent His Son, our Lord Jesus Christ, to be the Savior from sin and to nourish our souls as the Bread of Life. He brings us peace with God, and, as a result of it, peace with our fellow creatures. "The wolf and the lamb will feed together," writes Isaiah (65:25) in a symbolic reference to that peace.

Prayer Suggestion

Give thanks to God for His wonderful creation and ask for wisdom to treat it wisely and well.

GOD'S MESSAGE IN A "DOUBLE ENVELOPE"

These are the Scriptures that testify about Me. John 5:39

Engraved wedding invitations usually come in two envelopes: an inner one and an outer one. The first contains the message—the invitation—and the second is the medium or wrapper that brings the whole thing to you through the mail. May we say that God brings His message of salvation to us in a double envelope?

A European theologian has written: "Since Jesus is the revealed Word of God, He is the source of our knowledge of God." In another place, this: "Theology is to be drawn from the Bible."

Both statements are true, but they must be related properly to each other. Jesus is truly the personal Word through whom God speaks to us. The letter to the Hebrews, reflecting what St. John wrote in the prologue of his gospel ("The Word became flesh" 1:14), states in its own prologue: "In these last days He [God] has spoken to us by His Son" (1:2).

This does not mean that we may dispose of Holy Scripture as the source of divine revelation. Some theologians, claiming the Bible to be a human document with many errors, say in a cavalier fashion, "Don't worry about it. We don't have to rely on it, for God has revealed His saving love for us in Jesus, the personal Word."

However, apart from the written Word we wouldn't know anything about Jesus and what God tells us through Him. In Holy Scripture, which testifies of Jesus, God reveals fully and completely why He sent His Son into the world: to die for the sins of the human race and then to rise again. He invites us to believe in Him for our salvation.

The Gospel of Jesus Christ is in the nature of a wedding invitation, God bidding us, as Jesus declares in a parable: "Come to the wedding banquet" (Matthew 22:4). This invitation comes to us, we might say, in a double envelope: through Jesus, the personal Word, and through the written Word. The latter, like the larger, outer envelope, brings us the "Jesus message." The Bible is the "Jesus Book," on whose message concerning Jesus the Savior we can fully rely, for it is God's own revealed Word, altogether truthful.

Prayer Suggestion

Thank the heavenly Father for speaking the words of His forgiving grace through the Scripture's testimony concerning Jesus Christ, His Son.

PORTRAITS OF CHRISTIAN SPOUSES

While Pilate was sitting on the judge's seat, his wife sent him this message: "Don't have anything to do with that innocent Man." Matthew 27:19

There was a happy feeling in the St. Louis Art Museum when two portraits—those of a husband and wife—which had been separated for sixty years, were acquired and reunited as a pair. They had been painted by the 17th-century Dutch artist Franz Hals.

Sometimes in real life husbands and wives are not compatible. Take the example of Pontius Pilate and his wife. If they had ever had their portraits painted, the great differences between them would not have been glossed over. Pilate was cruel, tactless, and stupid as procurator of Judea. Aside from authorizing the crucifixion of Jesus despite his own conviction of His innocence, Pilate was guilty of other crimes. He had some Galileans slain in the temple, mingling their blood with that of their sacrifices. He had a whole Samaritan village wiped out on the mere suspicion of disloyalty. Little wonder that he was ordered to Rome where, according to the church historian Eusebius, he was ordered to "become his own murderer."

Pilate's wife, on the other hand, urged him to set Jesus free because of a dream she had. Tradition has it that her name was Procula and that she was a "proselyte of the gate," that is, a convert to Judaism who later became a Christian. The Greek Orthodox Church honors her as a saint and has set aside October 27 as her day.

In the Bible we find word-portraits of husbands and wives. How good it is when people in real life live up to them! To husbands St. Paul says: "Love your wives, just as Christ loved the church and gave Himself up for her" (Ephesians 5:25). The love of Christ is not just the model but also the enabling force for marital love. St. Peter has important words for wives, telling them to find their true beauty in the heart rather than in outward adornments. This purity and reverence of the heart God sees, and also unbelieving husbands may be moved thereby to become Christians.

How wonderful it is when husbands and wives reflect the image of Christ in what they say and do, especially in what they are! Piety and purity are their best portraits.

Prayer Suggestion

Pray that Christ may daily renew faith in your heart and with it Christian love as its main fruit.

THE PRIVILEGE OF LONG LIFE

Lord, You have been our dwelling place throughout all generations. Psalm 90:1

On February 21, 1986, a man in Japan, Shigechio Izumi, died at the age of 120 years. He was believed to have been the oldest person on earth.

Age is a relative thing; it varies from person to person. Moses lived to be 120 years old, and when he died, "his eyes were not weak nor his strength gone" (Deuteronomy 34:7). But he knew that not everybody would attain such an age with unabated strength. He writes in Psalm 90:10, "The length of our days is seventy years—or eighty, if we have the strength."

The gift of long life comes as a special favor of God, especially if it is attained in relatively good health. When giving the Ten Commandments, God said: "Honor your father and your mother, so that you may live long in the land the LORD your God is giving you" (Exodus 20:12). In writing to the Ephesians, St. Paul calls this "the first commandment with a promise—'that it may go well with you and that you may enjoy long life on the earth' " (6:2–3). The promise of long life to children who honor their parents bespeaks a reward of divine grace, not of human merit.

The aging among us are honored by God, and they should be honored by us also. In the book of Leviticus we read: "Rise in the presence of the aged, show respect for the elderly and revere your God" (19:32). The aging in our homes, churches, and communities have much to share with us of their wisdom, experience, and maturity.

It follows, too, that the aging honor themselves by regarding themselves not as excess baggage or useless beings, but as persons whom God loves and blesses. How wonderful is God's promise, spoken through the psalmist: "The righteous will flourish like a palm tree, they will grow like a cedar of Lebanon; planted in the house of the LORD, they will flourish in the courts of our God. They will still bear fruit in old age, they will stay fresh and green, proclaiming, 'The LORD is upright; He is my Rock, and there is no wickedness in Him' " (Psalm 92:12–15).

There is goodness and grace in God, who sent His Son, Jesus Christ, into the world to redeem with His life, death, and resurrection all people, both young and old.

Prayer Suggestion

Give thanks to God for your life, asking His help to make it fruitful to the glory of the Savior Jesus Christ.

MARY'S LAMB AND OURS

Look, the Lamb of God, who takes away the sin of the world!
John 1:29

"Mary had a little lamb," the children sing. Did Mary of Nazareth, as a girl or later in life, have a pet lamb? Perhaps she did, for sheep played an important part in the lives of the Israelites, who depended on them for wool and food. Mary, we can be sure, ate the Passover lamb with her family.

To Mary was given the privilege and responsibility to bear and care for someone far greater than a lamb, namely, Jesus, the Lamb of God, the *Agnus Dei.* John the Baptist gave this title to Jesus when, pointing to Him, he testified; "Look, the Lamb of God, who takes away the sin of the world!" (John 1:29)

John was repeating what Isaiah had said before him. The prophet had said as he drew a parallel between the offering of lambs and the sacrifice of the Messiah: "He was oppressed and afflicted, yet He did not open His mouth; He was led like a lamb to the slaughter" (Isaiah 53:7). It was on the basis of this text that Philip the evangelist told the Ethiopian official riding in his chariot "the good news about Jesus" (Acts 8:35).

Not only the spoken prophecies but also various rites and symbols pointed to Jesus as the Lamb of God. The perfect lamb offered up during the Passover festival was a type of Christ.

Yes, Mary had Jesus, the Lamb of God. She gave birth to Him, loved Him, brought Him up, and believed in Him as her Savior. She was present when He was offered up on the cross as the true Passover Lamb. She and other eyewitnesses saw Jesus after His resurrection. Then He ascended into heaven, where He is enthroned as the Lamb that was slain (Revelation 5:11–12).

Jesus, born of Mary, is our Savior just as He was Mary's. He has taken away all our sins. He now bids us come to Him with our burdens, and our response is that of Charlotte Elliott, the hymn writer: "O Lamb of God, I come, I come."

Prayer Suggestion

Pray for a stronger faith in Jesus, the Lamb of God, who was sacrificed for your salvation.

JESUS, COME OUR WAY

A blind man, Bartimaeus ... was sitting by the roadside begging. Mark 10:46

Bartimaeus, sitting by the roadside near Jericho, was both miserable and blessed—miserable because he was blind, lonely, and forced to beg, but supremely blessed to have Jesus, the Son of David, the promised Messiah and Savior, come his way to give him sight.

There is hardly a person today who in one way or another doesn't find himself or herself in a situation of distress. If it isn't blindness that handicaps him or her, it is something else: lack of education, poverty, failing health, sickness in the family, or the loneliness that usually accompanies misfortune. But such persons are also greatly blest to have Jesus, the Helper and Healer, come their way.

The Lord comes our way through the Word and the sacraments. Through these means He conveys all the blessings He gained for us on the cross: remission of sins, peace with God, a purpose for living, the promise of eternal life. He comes our way whenever the Gospel is applied to us through brotherly consolation and the pronouncement of forgiveness.

The Savior comes our way in the person of a friend, relative, neighbor, or fellow Christian in whose heart the love of God is working. Through such a representative He imparts many gifts of healing, including new perspectives, a clearer vision, eyes of the mind that now can see.

We are blest for our own good and to be a blessing to others. Jesus has brethren like Bartimaeus among us today. We find them in homes beset by hunger and other needs, in hospitals, in prisons, and in many other places. He has ascended into heaven and will not go physically in person to help them. But He has you and me as His delegates. Through us He still comes to the needy.

Prayer Suggestion

Think of persons in your congregation or community who are distressed. Pray for them and follow up your intercession with a personal call.

THE FATHER'S EMISSARY OF LOVE

He [Jesus] then began to speak to them in parables:
"A man planted a vineyard." Mark 12:1

The tenants of the well-stocked vineyard of which Jesus speaks in this text were more like thugs and murderers than grape growers. When on three different occasions the owner sent servants to collect the rent, the tenants not only sent them away empty-handed but also abused them. The owner then resolved to send his son, whom he loved, as the last emissary. "They will respect my son," he said. But he was wrong. The ungrateful tenants reserved their worst treatment for the son: They killed him and threw his body out of the vineyard.

Our Lord's telling of this parable was a part of the predicted passion history, the Lenten story. He narrated in advance the outcome of God's dealing with His covenant nation. God had richly endowed His chosen people for service, giving them a vineyard, so to speak, in which to be spiritually active. St. Paul writes, "Theirs is the adoption as sons; theirs the divine glory, the covenants, the receiving of the law, the temple worship and the promises. Theirs are the patriarchs, and from them is traced the human ancestry of Christ" (Romans 9:4–5).

But through the years Jerusalem killed the prophets and stoned those who were sent to remind its people of their obligation to yield the fruits of repentance and faith. The ultimate crime was the slaying of our Lord Himself as told by the four evangelists. God so loved the world that He gave His one and only dear Son, but the receiving nation—and all the rest of the world with it—hated Him so much that it sent Him to the cross outside Jerusalem ("outside the camp," Hebrews 13:13), throwing His body outside the vineyard, as it were.

But nothing that humanity has done changes the heavenly Father's loving intent: "Whoever believes in Him shall not perish but have eternal life" (John 3:16).

Prayer Suggestion

Tell the Lord Jesus that you will gladly and gratefully receive Him when, through the Gospel, He knocks on your heart's door.

LIFE'S TRUE RICHES

The love of money is a root of all kinds of evil.
1 Timothy 6:10

The writings of St. Paul readily yield one-liners on one's attitude toward money. "The love of money is a root of all kinds of evil" (1 Timothy 6:10), he writes. Further: "If we have food and clothing, we will be content with that" (v. 8). As for the dishonest use of money, this: "No one should wrong his brother or take advantage of him" (1 Thessalonians 4:6).

Recently, in an interview in the newspaper, James T. Bell, a black ballplayer of years ago who made hundreds while his counterparts today make millions—and was good enough to be belatedly voted into the Hall of Fame—said about his limited income: "I've got enough to eat and a roof over my head. I can pay my bills. I don't care what other people have. I don't want what other people have."

We do need money, and we do well to earn it honestly. But instead of doing that, many deceive themselves into thinking that they can get rich quickly through lotteries and other games of chance. One wrong attitude about gambling is that a person wants something he has not earned—money that really belongs to other people. Truly, "the love of money is a root of all kinds of evil" (1 Timothy 6:10).

While there is nothing morally wrong with riches properly and honestly acquired, it is good to bear in mind that material wealth is not life's highest good. Of far greater worth is our salvation in Jesus Christ. Our Lord divested Himself of His heavenly glory so that we might have it, as the apostle states: "You know the grace of our Lord Jesus Christ, that though He was rich, yet for your sakes He became poor, so that you through His poverty might become rich" (2 Corinthians 8:9). He refers to such riches as the full and free forgiveness he has earned for us, our place in the fellowship and family of God, our status as heirs of eternal life, our awareness not only of *who* we are but also *whose* we are, and inner peace which money cannot buy.

Be thankful if you have that, and never mind what other people have in the line of money!

Prayer Suggestion

Thank God for having enriched you in Christ with the blessings of peace, forgiveness, and eternal life.

LETTING GOD'S VOICE COME THROUGH

We are bringing you good news, telling you to turn from these worthless things to the living God, who made heaven and earth and sea and everything in them. Acts 14:15

Praying Christians are at times concerned about the seeming silence of God. "Why don't we hear His voice?" Perhaps He has been speaking to them all the while, even shouting, but they can't hear Him because they aren't tuned in properly.

An English writer commented that the Cistercian religious order kept silence, hoping to hear the voice of God speaking to them through silent days and nights. All the while they heard, says the writer, "the soft singing of the waters, the whisperings of the river grass, the music of the rushing winds." Is it not true that God speaks to us through the sounds and sights of nature? To Elijah, isolated in the desert, God spoke in a whisper, a thin, small voice, perhaps resembling a soft wind.

God speaks through His marvelous, majestic works in nature, as the psalmist exclaims: "The heavens declare the glory of God; the skies proclaim the work of His hands" (Psalm 19:1). St. Paul said: "The living God, who made heaven earth and sea and everything in them … has not left Himself without testimony" (Acts 14:15, 17). He states that God has revealed to us (in nature and in history) His "invisible qualities—His eternal power and divine nature" (Romans 1:20).

Does God still speak? The psalmist writes: "Day after day they [God's mighty works] pour forth speech" (Psalm 19:2). It is a speech in which God reveals Himself as the all-powerful, all-wise Maker of heaven and earth.

But God has much more to say to us. In Jesus Christ, His Son, He reveals His love and saving grace to sinners. God has once for all spoken to us through His Son, who is therefore called the Word, by St. John: "The Word became flesh and made His dwelling among us" (John 1:14). This Son, crucified for our sins, rose from the dead and ascended into heaven. But His message is still heard—the Gospel. It is proclaimed from the pages of Holy Scripture; whenever we hear it or read it, we hear the voice of God, who speaks to us through the prophets and apostles. Are you hearing this voice?

Prayer Suggestion

Ask God to open your ears and heart so that you may hear His Word and may rejoice in your salvation in Christ.

PERSONAL GROWTH

We pray this in order that you may live a life worthy of the Lord and may please Him in every way: bearing fruit in every good work, growing in the knowledge of God.
Colossians 1:10

A proper self-image is hard to attain when you are neither one nor the other—neither child nor adult, neither middle-aged nor old-aged. Gail Godwin has written in her novel *The Finishing School* that both the adolescent and middle-aged person are neither one thing nor another. "They are both in the process of molting," one of the characters declares, "of turning into something else."

For that matter, all of us are in a state of transition. We are always, however gradually, becoming what we were not last month and/or last year. We can put a positive face on change by calling it personal growth.

Christians are always in the process of becoming. According to St. Paul, people are by nature dead in trespasses and sins, lost in spiritual darkness. Then through the Gospel God called them to life and light. The apostle writes: "He [God] has rescued us from the dominion of darkness and brought us into the kingdom of the Son He loves, in whom we have redemption, the forgiveness of sins" (Colossians 1:13).

Being a Christian is not a static thing. To settle down to a status quo is to lose ground, to go backwards, as would people who do not eat, drink, rest, and exercise. So it is in our spiritual lives. Through a steady daily diet of God's Word we are nourished in our faith, and we grow. We leave the in-between stage of stagnation and become developing Christians, regardless of age or station in life.

No one need consider himself or herself locked into a bad situation. If deep in the hole of bad habits, alcoholism, loss of the will to live, and the like, you can climb out and make a transition to something better. But you need help for this—help from God through the Word and sacraments.

Be glad that you are in a state of transition if that is a change for the better.

Prayer Suggestion

Thank your Lord for raising you up to a higher life, asking His help for continued growth in Christian faith and life.

ARE WE IN SHAPE TO SERVE?

Strengthen your feeble arms and weak knees.
Hebrews 12:12

St. Paul compared life to a strenuous athletic contest. There are many points of comparison. For one thing, life as a whole, like participation in sports, requires the expending of great energy on a sustained basis. That's why we need to exercise ourselves spiritually—to be and remain in shape.

St. Paul writes, "Everyone who competes in the games goes into strict training. They do it to get a crown that will not last; but we do it to get a crown that will last forever. Therefore I do not run like a man running aimlessly; I do not fight like a man beating the air. No, I beat my body and make it my slave so that after I have preached to others, I myself will not be disqualified for the prize" (1 Corinthians 9:25–27).

It is not enough once to have lived in Christ. To keep on living in Him as members of His body and as branches connected to the vine, we need to stay in shape—we need to "throw off everything that hinders and the sin that so easily entangles" (Hebrews 12:1). We can get rid of excess fat and flabbiness and acquire a good muscle-tone of faith. We can cultivate good spiritual health so that these fruits of the Spirit may grow in us: "Love, joy, peace, patience, kindness, goodness, faithfulness, gentleness and self-control" (Galatians 5:22–23).

Alive in Him who died for us on the cross to redeem us from sin and who now lives in us, we do want to be in shape to serve Him with the strength that the Holy Spirit gives us. When we are diligent in the study of God's Word and in prayer, we acquire the spiritual vitality we need from day to day to live for Jesus Christ and to serve Him. In doing this, we shall live by faith in the Son of God, who loved us and gave Himself for us. It's our way of saying "Thank You" to God.

Prayer Suggestion

Pray that through spiritual exercise Christ may strengthen you for service to Him.

Why Jesus Came

The Son of Man did not come to be served, but to serve,
and to give His life as a ransom for many. Mark 10:45

Many come to Jesus, wanting to sit restfully and comfortably in His kingdom. But that was not what James and John had in mind when they said to Jesus: "Let one of us sit at Your right and the other at Your left in Your glory" (Mark 10:37). What they wanted was to sit with power and honor in Christ's government. According to Matthew's gospel, their mother also made this request (20:21).

That kind of ambition, Jesus said, was characteristic of pagan people as they jockey for position in state and society. Their preference is to be top person on the totem pole while others are cast in supporting roles. Our Lord reverses the order, saying: "Whoever wants to be first must be slave of all" (Mark 10:44).

The Savior does not ask anything of us that He Himself did not first perform, both as Exemplar and Enabler. He tells us, "The Son of Man did not come to be served, but to serve, and to give His life as a ransom for many" (Mark 10:45).

Through the ages people have asked: Why did Jesus Christ, the Son of God, come into this world? Was His mission one of social and political reform? Did He come to found a brotherhood on the basis of human love and justice? The answer is no. His was the role of the Servant who preferred others to Himself and who offered up His life on the cross for the redemption of all people. That is the Jesus in whom we believe and whom we serve.

The question occurs also to us as Christ's followers: Why are we here? Why has God created us? Why did Christ redeem us? Why did the Holy Spirit call us to faith through the Gospel? Surely that we, having been added to the family of God, might serve Him and serve one another.

Prayer Suggestion

Ask your Savior to show you human needs and opportunities that call for your service.

THE HOPE FOR THINGS TO COME

The desert and the parched land will be glad. Isaiah 35:1

It is the beginning of March, a time when in middle America the promises of spring are not yet fulfilled. A walk through the local park is uninspiring. The defoliated cypress trees stand like sentinels without uniforms along the lily pond now without lilies. The early blooming daffodils are still asleep. Later on the park will be filled with people playing handball, eating picnic lunches, or just strolling. Now it is empty and unappealing. But it gives promise of something better to come.

The above scene hints at the life of believers in Old Testament times. God's law, with all its restrictions, was in effect. Everywhere were signs of do's and don'ts—do be circumcised, do bring sacrifices, don't work on the Sabbath, don't step on the grass. Isaiah spoke of life then as "the desert and the parched land." The prophet Ezekiel writes about the haunting vision in which he compares "the whole house of Israel" to a valley filled with dry bones (Ezekiel 37:11). The many adverse experiences through which God's people had to pass—slavery in Egypt, a 40-year journey through the wilderness, the 70-year captivity in Babylon—all were parts of the dismal scene.

But there was hope. God Himself, through the prophets, gave promise of better things to come. Isaiah uses symbols of a new and joyful era to come. The crocus will burst with blossoms; refreshing water will gush forth to make the land fruitful; a highway, to be called "the Way of Holiness," will be built; ailing people will be healed (Isaiah 35:8). All these expressions point to the joy of salvation fulfilled in the New Testament era. Isaiah testifies clearly and cogently about the coming time of grace and forgiveness in the Messiah. In chapter 53 he dwells on Christ's suffering, death, burial, and resurrection for the salvation of all. Because of His atonement, the winter of discontent is turned into the springtime of God's fulfilled promises. What a joy it is for us to walk through the park—through the new Garden of Eden—of our fulfilled salvation in Jesus Christ!

Prayer Suggestion

Give thanks to God for fulfilling His promises and for giving us the joy of salvation in Jesus Christ.

HOW TO THINK ABOUT OURSELVES

Offer your bodies as living sacrifices. Romans 12:1

The Farmers' Museum near Cooperstown, N.Y., houses among its exhibits the stone image of a man more than 10 feet tall. It is known as the Cardiff Giant. The museum describes it as "America's greatest hoax." Unearthed in 1869, it was at first believed to be evidence that once "there were giants in the earth." It turned out to be a giant deception.

Satan often resorts to a hoax to get people to think wrong things about themselves, such as the delusion that they stand 10 feet tall because of their accomplishments and wisdom. In the Garden of Eden he told Eve that she would be "like God, knowing good and evil" if she ate the fruit of the forbidden tree (Genesis 3:5). Eve believed this overstatement about herself. The message to all is this: "Do not think of yourself more highly than you ought."

We are also taught the opposite: Do not think of yourself less than you ought. Some of God's people have at times done this. It was a great distortion—a hoax in the other direction—for the majority of the Israelite explorers of Canaan to come back to Joshua with the report: "All the people we saw there are of great size. ... We seemed like grasshoppers in our own eyes, and we looked the same to them" (Numbers 13:32–33). Fear and pessimism were speaking here, and surely it came about by Satan's prompting.

How are we to regard ourselves? As sinners indeed, but also as persons wonderfully created by God, totally redeemed from sin and death by Jesus Christ, and made saints when the Holy Spirit gave us the saving faith through the Gospel. This is God's work in every Christian, regardless of age, station in life, or physical stature. One need not be a "Cardiff Giant" to do the great things St. Paul urges: to offer our bodies and minds in devoted service "as living sacrifices, holy and pleasing to God" (Romans 12:1).

Prayer Suggestion

Ask the Holy Spirit to give you the right self-image as a person made great and strong in your service to Christ.

WHEN GOD BLESSES CITIES

Your country is desolate, your cities burned with fire.
Isaiah 1:7

The play *Brigadoon*, by Lerner and Loewe, is pure fantasy. It is about two New Yorkers on vacation who come to a most strange Scottish city. In the 18th century it vanished under a religious spell. But every 100 years it allegedly comes to life for a day, shows itself as it was then, and disappears again.

The Bible speaks of two cities that disappeared from the face of the earth by fire and brimstone: Sodom and Gomorrah. They will never appear again because the Dead Sea covers the sites. St. Jude writes in his epistle that they perished because of "sexual immorality and perversion" (Jude 7). St. Peter adds that God "made them an example of what is going to happen to the ungodly" (2 Peter 2:6). Unlike Brigadoon, they were not imaginary cities but were very real— real in their sinfulness, and real was God's judgment on them.

In a certain sense Sodom and Gomorrah live on, not only because the Bible, in both the Old and New Testament, makes mention of them but also because their sins continue in other cities. Jesus said of the cities of His time—Capernaum, Korazin, Bethsaida—that a greater judgment awaited them than did Tyre and Sidon, Sodom and Gomorrah, because they rejected the ministry of the very Son of God (Matthew 11:21–24).

St. Paul writes in his letter to the Corinthians that the Scriptures were written for our learning and warning. We are not to repeat the sins that displease God and arouse His anger. Sodom and Gomorrah are long gone, but some of their sister cities live in the same iniquities.

The Scripture teaches us, too, that communities where righteousness prevails and God is honored are blessed. All the truths written in the Bible give us endurance, encouragement, and hope because they bear witness to Jesus Christ, God's own sacrifice for the sins of all (Romans 15:4).

"O blest the land, the city blest, Where Christ the Ruler is confessed."

Prayer Suggestion

Ask for the power of the Holy Spirit to make you a wholesome influence and a faithful witness for Christ where you live.

A Sure Foundation for Life

I laid a foundation as an expert builder, and someone else is building on it. 1 Corinthians 3:10

If you had the beautiful blue Hope diamond—or the world's largest diamond, the 530-carat Great Star of Africa—you would be rich. But could you build your life on such wealth? Would it stand the test of time?

St. Paul writes: "If any man builds on this foundation using gold, silver, costly stones, wood, hay or straw, his work will be shown for what it is, because the Day will bring it to light" (1 Corinthians 3:12–13). St. Paul had no worry about the outcome of his work, for he had built on the foundation that is Jesus Christ—on His Gospel of the forgiveness of sins.

Our Lord Himself said: "Everyone who hears these words of Mine and puts them into practice is like a wise man who built his house on the rock. The rain came down, the streams rose, and the winds blew and beat against that house; yet it did not fall, because it had its foundation on the rock" (Matthew 7:24–25).

Jesus' words are recorded in the four gospels. His teaching is reflected also in the epistles which the apostles wrote, for He had instructed them: St. John, St. Peter, St. Paul, and the rest. St. John wrote these words of Jesus: "God so loved the world that He gave His one and only Son" (John 3:16). St. Peter stated: "You know that it was not with perishable things such as silver or gold that you were redeemed … but with the precious blood of Christ, a lamb without blemish or defect" (1 Peter 1:18–19). St. Paul, also one of Jesus' apostles, wrote: "You know the grace of our Lord Jesus Christ, that though He was rich, yet for your sakes He became poor, so that you through His poverty might become rich" (2 Corinthians 8:9).

This spiritual wealth we have in the Gospel, in value far exceeding that of the great diamonds of the world. When we take the Gospel to heart, we build on a solid foundation. It is precious, and it is permanent.

Prayer Suggestion

Include in your prayer that Jesus Christ and His Word and work may more and more become the basis of your life.

TRAVELING WITH THE LORD

After six days Jesus took with Him Peter, James and John the brother of James, and led them up a high mountain. Matthew 17:1

A short hymn stanza, by Joseph A. Robinson, that stays with us after we've sung it reads:

> How good, Lord, to be here!
> Yet we may not remain;
> But since you bid us leave the mount,
> Come with us to the plain.

Lutheran Worship 89, st. 5.

The reference is to Jesus' transfiguration on a mountain. When Peter saw Him glorified and in the company of Moses and Elijah, he exclaimed: "Lord, it is good for us to be here" (Matthew 17:4). He volunteered to put up shelters so that they all could stay on the mount. But Jesus had other plans. He must leave the mount through the valley of the shadow of death and ascend another mount, Calvary, to be offered up for the sin of the world. So He, with His disciples, descended to the plain below. Immediately He was confronted by the human need there. A father pleaded for his epileptic son (Matthew 17:14–18).

Many have been the times when we wished we could stay in a beautiful place where God's glory and beauty are revealed: a mountaintop overlooking verdant valleys, an inspirational worship service in God's house, or at a church convention, a fellowship visit with friends, a vacation trip. Jesus would say: "Fine! Enjoy yourselves. You need time to rest. But you can't stay here indefinitely. Come with Me into the valley below—into the plain where the sick people are and where your help is needed."

So we respond, "Yes, dear Lord, we will come with You into the everyday world. We cannot do miracles like You did, but we can show love. We can be the extensions of Your healing arms. We can be Your voice telling people the good news of salvation in You. We know we are not alone, for You are with us in the plain."

Prayer Suggestion

Thank Jesus for His promise that He will be with you as you go on errands of mercy.

WHO IS YOUR HERO?

Join with others in following my example, brothers.
Philippians 3:17

It is said that in Spain, notably in the Andalusia region, the great ambition of a boy is to become a great matador. Manolete, although killed by a bull at age 30, is still an idol to many.

Children in all lands have role models. It is important that they chose good ones, that is, persons who inspire them to pursue their dreams with upright moral characters.

The Bible presents men and women, also children, who are role models. These persons did not always win but what is noteworthy is that they, win or lose, stood for what is right. Joseph in Egypt would rather go to jail than sin against his God. A real heroine was the Israelite girl who was captured by Syrian soldiers and became the slave maid to the Syrian general Naaman. She was a heroine not only because she kept faith amid difficult circumstances but also because she advised her mistress to send Naaman to the prophet Elisha for a cure of his leprosy. A man of courageous faith was Daniel, who would not pray to idols even if he must be cast into a lion's den. We say today on the basis of his example, "Dare to be a Daniel, dare to stand alone," surely a good reminder to people who easily become copycats and followers of fads.

A child's hero needs to be more than a famous athlete, a glamorous bullfighter, a TV or movie star. There are qualities that make up a true hero, that is, one who doesn't compromise character, soil conscience, and ruin health with drink and drugs for the sake of fame. A true hero puts first things first: faith in Jesus Christ. His or her concern is to follow Jesus Christ, who put God's will above everything else, even if it meant death on the cross for our salvation.

Is Jesus a superstar? He is far more. He is our Savior, enabling us to be lights in the world and stars in His right hand.

Prayer Suggestion

Pray for courage and strength to follow the example of people who put Christ first in their lives.

FIRM FRIENDSHIPS

As the Father has loved Me, so have I loved you. John 15:9

Shortly before the outbreak of the Civil War, Secretary of State William H. Seward handed President Lincoln what a historian calls "the most remarkable memorandum ever submitted by a cabinet member to a President." He suggested that the United States declare war on France and Spain so that the North and the South would become united by facing a common foe. That would have been a very shaky friendship indeed.

Who is not reminded of what St. Luke writes about an incident in the trial of Jesus—how both Pilate and Herod opposed Jesus. "That day," writes St. Luke, "Herod and Pilate became friends—before this they had been enemies" (Luke 23:12).

But we all know that a so-called friendship based on shared hatreds or dislikes is negative in nature and cannot last. True friendships are based on positive truths that both parties are *for* rather than *against.*

Jesus tells us about the foundation of true friendship: love. He said that as the Father loved Him, so He loved His disciples. Because we remain in His love, we are empowered to observe His command to love one another (John 15:9). Our Lord declared: "Greater love has no one than this, that he lay down his life for his friends. You are My friends if you do what I command" (John 15:13–14).

Love is the basis of friendship; true friendship cannot exist on mutual hatreds. It is based on our mutual love for Jesus, who communicates the Father's love to us. Because we love Him, we can love one another and on that love build firm friendships.

How wonderful are such relationships, as between David and Jonathan, St. Paul and Timothy, Jesus and His disciples and with Mary, Martha, and Lazarus!

No, Herod and Pilate couldn't be true friends if all they had in common was their rejection of Jesus. And a war with France or Spain would never have united the North and South. To love one another— that is the foundation for firm friendships.

Prayer Suggestion

Thank the heavenly Father for the friend you have in Jesus, who bore all your sins and griefs.

WE ARE NOT ALONE

He [Jesus] looked toward heaven and prayed. John 17:1

Jesus led a rich prayer life. Some of His prayers are recorded, including the Lord's Prayer (Matthew 6:9–13), His prayer of thanksgiving (Matthew 11:25–26), His prayer at Lazarus' tomb (John 11:41–42), His Gethsemane prayers (Matthew 26:39–42), and His High Priestly Prayer (John 17), spoken on the night before His death.

Jesus' High Priestly Prayer divides into three major parts: (1) request for Himself, vv. 1–5; (2) request for His disciples, vv. 6–19; and (3) request for future disciples, that is, "for those who will believe in Me through their [the apostles'] message" v. 20. It is a sacerdotal prayer because as our High Priest Jesus not only offered up Himself on the cross as a sacrifice for our sins but also because He intercedes for God's people and for the world.

In behalf of all who will follow Him through the long corridor of time Jesus asks, "Father, I want those You have given Me to be with Me where I am, and see My glory, the glory You have given Me because You loved Me before the creation of the world" (John 17:24).

The prayer of Jesus is still in effect for us who live in this late age of the world. And the heavenly Father hears His Son's intercession. We are not alone; Jesus is with us and supports us with His prayer. And if that were not enough, also the Holy Spirit Himself "intercedes for us with groans that words cannot express" (Romans 8:26).

Prayer Suggestion

Open your hymnal and read the hymn "What a Friend We Have in Jesus" (*Lutheran Worship*, 516).

ON HAVING ONE'S OWN FAITH

The righteous will live by his faith. Habakkuk 2:4

Charles Dickens was a celebrated English author whose many works—*Oliver Twist, David Copperfield, A Tale of Two Cities*— include also the one everyone knows, *Christmas Carol*. At Moline, Illinois, in an obscure grave, rest the remains of his son, Francis. It is said that more people coming to the cemetery visit the grave of John Deere, the implement maker, than that of the famous novelist's son.

As with fame, so it is with faith, only more so. It is to each his own. We cannot be saved by another's faith, whether our parents', our spouse's, our children's, or anyone else's. "The righteous shall live by *his* faith," the Bible declares in several places.

It was futile for some of Jesus' contemporaries to say they were right with God because they had Abraham as their father. This physical connection did not help them. The question was: Did they have the faith by which Abraham was declared just before God? (Galatians 3:6, 9)

In His parable of the ten virgins Jesus has the five foolish virgins ask the five wise ones whether they could use some of their oil so that, with lamps burning, they might go forth to meet the bridegroom. They could not, of course. As good as sharing is, we cannot divide our personal faith in Christ as Savior and let someone else have a part of it. To each his own!

God tells us through the apostle Paul: "If you confess with your mouth, 'Jesus is Lord,' and believe in your heart that God raised Him from the dead, you will be saved" (Romans 10:9). This is God's wonderful promise, and one that He will keep. Far from trying to slip in by another's faith, you have the assurance that by faith you are in the right relationship with God for time and eternity.

Prayer Suggestion

Enlarge on this prayer of our Lord's disciples, "Increase our faith."

TRUTH IN MOCKERY

The soldiers twisted together a crown of thorns and put it on His head. John 19:2

It is often the nature of mockery that it affirms the truth it seeks to ridicule. During the trial of Jesus, for example, the soldiers put a purple robe on Him, a staff in His hand, and a crown of thorns on His head. They sought to make fun of Jesus' kingship.

But we have news for them. The purple robe points to the very real robe of righteousness in which Jesus is clothed and in which He clothes all who believe in His redeeming merit for them. The staff or reed symbolizes His scepter of divine authority, for to Him is truly given all power in heaven and on earth. The crown of thorns bespeaks the crown of glory that Jesus wears as the King of kings—the crown of everlasting life He shares with His own. So, unintentionally—and with opposite intent—the Roman soldiers proclaimed the true kingship of Jesus.

Also mockery directed at us, who are Jesus' followers, often has the effect of asserting the very truth it seeks to ridicule. Inadvertently, and by a reverse process, it proclaims and praises what it tries to deride.

It was at Antioch that Christ's followers were first called Christians, a nickname hung on them by their enemies, as if to say: What pitiable people, to follow in the footsteps of the humble, disrespected, crucified Christ! But the mockery backfired, and the term became one of honor. St. Peter writes to persecuted believers: "If you suffer as a Christian, do not be ashamed, but praise God that you bear that name" (1 Peter 4:16).

In your own life, keep in mind that mockery directed at you is very likely a reverse mirror image of a praiseworthy quality you have. Accept it calmly, even thankfully. An intended insult is really a compliment. If you are in the right, you—not they—will have the last laugh.

Prayer Suggestion

Thank Christ for having called you to be His disciple, to share both His honor and dishonor.

GOD KNOWS US AND OUR NEEDS

He [Peter] said, "Lord, You know all things; You know that I love You." John 21:17

The chairman of a large company in the data field announced that it had perfected "a new computer memory chip that can store more than a million bits of information." Undoubtedly by this time computer chips can store much more knowledge.

While this technological development is astounding, it still falls short of total knowledge, which only God possesses. God—and only God—is omniscient, all-knowing. He made the universe by His almighty power, and that power was guided by His total wisdom. Scientists, in their research, are trying to think God's thoughts after Him as they discover bits and pieces of God's total knowledge—what life is, how the atom is constructed, what lies beyond in outer space.

The total knowledge of God takes on personal meaning when we consider that He knows us—who we are, what our needs are, what hopes we harbor, from what evils we need protection, what opportunities we have for good. Hear what the psalmist declares: "O LORD, You have searched me and You know me. You know when I sit and when I rise; You perceive my thoughts from afar. You discern my going out and my lying down; You are familiar with all my ways. Before a word is on my tongue You know it completely" (Psalm 139:1–4).

As the Son of God, Jesus Christ is all-knowing. After the resurrection, our Lord asked Peter, who had repented over his denial, whether he loved Him. Peter replied: "Lord, You know all things; You know that I love You" (John 21:17). The same Lord, having redeemed us for eternal life because He loved us, can see into our hearts. He knows our failings that we confess to Him. He forgives us and reinstates us in His grace, as he did Peter. He knows that we love Him.

A computer memory chip with more than a million bits of information? God knows all of that and infinitely more—He knows all.

Prayer Suggestion

Declare your love for Christ, thanking Him for knowing your needs and providing for them, especially for your need for His forgiveness.

PRAYING THAT PLEASES GOD

*When you pray, go into your room, close the door and
pray to your Father. Matthew 6:6*

If people in Tibet are too busy to pray, they can have Buddhist
priests do the praying for them on a prayer wheel. This is a mechanical device, a revolving drum, containing written prayers that can be
ground out, so to speak, in behalf of others.

Christians do not use prayer wheels, but some come close to doing
that by praying mechanically or by rote.

Jesus gave us much instruction on the art of prayer. He knew how
the heathen prayed and how would-be pious people prayed—like the
Pharisee in the temple. Jesus said: "When you pray, do not keep on
babbling like pagans ["use not vain repetitions, as the heathen do"—
King James Version], for they think they will be heard because of their
many words." How the heathen pray was demonstrated on Mount
Carmel, where the prophets of Baal shouted for half a day: "O Baal,
answer us!" (1 Kings 18:26).

In the same connection—it was in the Sermon on the Mount—
Jesus spoke also of the way religious hypocrites prayed loud and long
in synagogues or on street corners where they would be sure to be
seen. Reciting prayers to impress others is not much different from
having them turned out on a prayer wheel.

Prayers, whether petitions or thanksgivings, are pleasing to God
when spoken from the heart under the impulse of the thoughts and
desires of faith. It is said of a baseball pitcher that he must not let himself be distracted, that he must keep his concentration. The same is
true of prayers, whether long or short, spoken freely or devoutly read
from a prayer book. God is pleased with our proper prayers because
we as persons are pleasing to Him. Jesus Christ, our Reconciler and
Redeemer, has made us acceptable to God by His obedient life, atoning death, and glorious resurrection.

Prayer Suggestion

Pray for greater sincerity and attentiveness as you approach God
in prayer, always confident that for Jesus' sake God hears you.

Seven Times Is Not Enough

If he listens to you, you have won your brother over.
Matthew 18:15

The number seven has sacred significance in the Bible. God made the universe in six days and rested on the seventh day. Naaman, the Syrian general, was to wash in the Jordan seven times to be cured of his leprosy. In a vision St. John saw "seven golden lampstands," and in their midst stood the exalted Christ; "in His right hand He held seven stars" (Revelation 1:12, 16). The gifts of the Holy Spirit are sevenfold.

It is understandable why Peter, brought up in the tradition of regarding the number seven as sacred, would ask: "Lord, how many times shall I forgive my brother when he sins against me? Up to seven times?" The question followed the instruction Jesus had given on what steps to take when "your brother sins against you."

When it comes to forgiving a brother, and surely if he or she desires forgiveness and reinstatement in our good graces, seven times is not enough. Jesus makes this plain as He replies to Peter: "I tell you, not seven times, but seventy-seven times." By making the figure that large, our Lord implies that you are to forgive your brother or sister, whether a blood relative or a relative in the faith, *every time* he or she sins against you.

And why? The parable of the unmerciful servant immediately following explains the reason. We are all like the servant who owed his lord ten thousand talents and was forgiven his debt. Not to forgive the neighbor would be like wanting to exact the trifling debt he owes us. In Jesus Christ, our Substitute, God has forgiven us a mountain of sins. We can do no less than to forgive our fellow Christians the molehill of offenses against us. The love of Christ, evidenced by the empty cross and empty tomb, compels us (2 Corinthians 5:14).

Prayer Suggestion

Ask for the help of God to be forgiving toward those who offend you. Also thank Him for forgiving you for Jesus' sake.

Unity in the Family

Do not suppose that I have come to bring peace to the earth.
Matthew 10:34

During the Civil War not only the country but many families were divided. Brothers fought one another in the bloody campaigns. This partisanship reached right up to the White House. A brother and three half-brothers of Mary Todd Lincoln, the president's wife, fought in the Confederate armies.

Sometimes civil war on a smaller scale breaks out in the home. The reasons can be many—perhaps over an inheritance, or over who is to take care of the aging parents, or how the children are to be raised. At times the clash occurs because of religion, specifically over loyalty to Christ. Our Lord Himself spoke of this: "I have come to turn a man against his father, a daughter against her mother, a daughter-in-law against her mother-in-law—a man's enemies will be members of his own household" (Matthew 10:35–36).

Yes, confessing Christ and believing in His Gospel can have this effect on a family. But it is not always so, and our Savior helps us prevent this, giving us peace and harmony instead. Great strength and staying power come to families united in the Christian faith. A golden chain is forged when parents, brothers, and sisters are linked with one another in their love for Christ. Affliction, sickness, losses, even death cannot break that strong bond.

The same Lord who said He came to bring a sword—His words do cut the sinner—also promises His peace, peace such as the world cannot give. His peace rests on His reconciling work when in our stead He atoned for sin by His death on the cross. Believing in Him, we have peace with God, peace with oneself, peace with others. Then, unlike the situation in the Civil War, all family members will be on the same side, loving and helping one another.

Prayer Suggestion

Ask for Christ's help to maintain peace in the family and to help you be a healer when the family bond is broken.

DOVE, LAMBS, LAMB OF GOD

*Joseph and Mary ... offer[ed] ... what is said in the Law
of the Lord: "a pair of doves or two young pigeons."
Luke 2:22–24*

"The cooing of doves is heard in our land," writes the author of the
Song of Songs (2:12). That cooing, as we hear it from our native
mourning doves, is plaintive, not like the lark's. Their plumage is by far
not as colorful as that of the cardinals or bluebirds.

But mourning doves have much to commend them. You usually
see them in pairs, prompting the poet to say:

> In constancy and nuptial love
> I learn my duty from the dove.

Doves represent an important event in the life of the infant Jesus.
Forty days after His birth the Holy Family went to the temple for
Mary's purification. The Law of Moses prescribed that a lamb be sacrificed for a burnt offering and a young pigeon or a turtledove for a sin
suffering. Those who could not afford a lamb could offer a substitute,
a turtledove, and that is what Mary did.

The sacrificial rites in the temple also involved the young Jesus. As
the firstborn He belonged to the Lord. This special relationship of the
firstborn son dated back to the time in Egypt when the blood of the
Passover lamb on the doorpost saved the firstborn sons from death. At
the presentation of the Child in the temple, Mary and Joseph released
their son, now subject to the Law of Moses, from His special responsibility as the firstborn.

Jesus was in due time to become Himself the Lamb of God that
takes away the sin of the world—also your sin and mine—by His sacrifice on the cross.

Back to the turtledoves. The members of their species countless
generations ago played a part in salvation history. They became substitutes for sacrificial lambs, and these lambs were a shadow of the
things to come, that is of the sacrifice of Jesus, the Lamb of God, as
our Substitute.

Prayer Suggestion

Give thanks to Jesus, the Passover Lamb, for having died for your
sins and then risen again.

IF YOU CAN'T BE AN OAK ...

He is like a tree planted by streams of water. Psalm 1:3

Oak trees are strong; their durable wood is preferred for certain types of construction. Some people are like that, sturdy and strong.

But what if you are like a lesser tree—like a cottonwood, for example? Many people, in fact, are like cottonwoods, which, like other members of the poplar family, are rather short-lived, and their wood is soft and light. While some other trees, like olive trees in the Garden of Gethsemane, may attain an age of several centuries, the cottonwood is old at age 75. The trunks of old trees are deeply furrowed, like the faces of people threescore and ten, and fourscore years old. When felled, they decay rapidly.

Yet cottonwood trees, like people, are valuable. As timber trees they yield wood for excelsior, for barrel staves, crates, and other wood products. Further, they are not without attractiveness and beauty. The leaves are two-colored: shiny and dark green above, and paler beneath. Attached to flattened leaf stalks, the leaves flutter and flicker in the slightest breeze.

The poet Joyce Kilmer, in his poem "Trees," speaks of trees as lovelier than his poems. He visualizes a tree—he doesn't say what kind—wearing a choice spring hat: a nest of robins in her hair. The cottonwood, too, has its millinery. Its seeds are thickly covered with cottony or silky hair. It is well dressed.

If God has chosen you to be like a cottonwood rather than an oak or an ornamental tree in someone's front yard, be content. God loves common people too; He made so many of them. What is more, He had His Son, Jesus Christ, nailed to the accursed tree of the cross to redeem us *all*. God has blessed us all richly, equipping us to serve Him with what we are and have.

Prayer Suggestion

Tell God you want to glorify Him and serve people around you with the gifts He gave you.

WHY TAKE THE LONG WAY AROUND?

You have hidden these things from the wise and learned, and revealed them to little children. Matthew 11:25

The daily press reports that scientists at the National Aeronautical Space Administration (NASA) lean to the theory that life originated with clay instead of, as others say, a primordial chemical soup. While this theory as phrased has its problems, it seems to come closer to what we read in the book of Genesis in the Bible: "The LORD God formed the man from the dust of the ground and breathed into his nostrils the breath of life, and the man became a living being" (Genesis 2:7). According to the Hebrew dictionary, the word for "dust" can be translated as "clay."

This may be another instance of going the long way around to establish scientifically what is really an obvious truth. Centuries ago people known as the scholastics tried to establish from philosophical reasoning that there is a first Cause: God. While they were doing this, mothers put their children to bed, telling them about God's love and teaching them to pray to Him. They needed no learned proofs for the existence of God. "From the lips of children and infants You have ordained praise," exclaims the psalmist (8:2).

What to the scholarly Saul the Pharisee seemed foolishness, he later regarded the highest wisdom. The message of the Christ, which he as St. Paul proclaimed, has the power to do what no force on earth can do: convert a sinner and bring him salvation.

We ourselves could conduct extensive and expensive experiments to show that sin doesn't pay, that hatred does much harm, that pornography corrupts character, that the love of money so evident in the lottery craze is the root of many kinds of evil. But this isn't necessary. We already have God's Word for it. So why take the long way around to arrive at simple truths?

Prayer Suggestion

Pray, that through His Word and Spirit, God may lead you into all truth.

FIGURING THE COST

Suppose one of you wants to build a tower. Will he not first sit down and estimate the cost? Luke 14:28

It could be discouraging. Here you bring a candidate for Christian discipleship to Jesus, expecting that He will welcome him or her and thank you for being a good recruiter. But what does the Lord say? He seemingly drives prospects away by telling them, "Anyone who does not carry his cross and follow Me cannot be My disciple."

What does Jesus have in mind? He wants everyone to figure the cost of discipleship before signing on. Counting the cost in advance is a good rule to follow in all of life. The trip we plan to take, the car or camper we are about to buy, the house we intend to build—how much will it cost?

The "cost" factor, of course, is not to be computed only in terms of dollars and cents because other considerations are involved. Before making a commitment, we ought to ask: How much of my time, talents, and attention will be required? Can I be a good spouse, a good parent, or anything else by giving less than my total self? How will additional responsibilities affect my priorities?

These questions apply especially to a Christian disciple. Jesus wants us to ask them so that we may be properly prepared for a life-long experience of serving Him and living in His kingdom.

What we give up to be Christ's disciples is greatly outweighed by what we receive: the outpouring of our Lord's love—the love that made Him go all the way to Calvary's cross to redeem us. It is a love that also today will go the limit to bless us and make us a blessing. When that love is ours, we have everything that goes with it: daily forgiveness and renewal, peace with God, a purpose in life, a strength to share. This we keep in mind when considering the cost of Christian discipleship. It makes us all the more thankful to be in the company of Jesus.

Prayer Suggestion

Add to this prayer: Lord Jesus, we are mindful of the fact that You became poor so that we might be rich in all that pertains to our salvation. Send Your Holy Spirit that He may ...

LOVE FOR GOD'S HOUSE

How lovely is Your dwelling place, O LORD Almighty!
Psalm 84:1

It is said that on March 19 the swallows, having wintered in South America, return to the ruins of a Spanish mission in San Juan Capistrano, California. In a way they are doing what the swallows did in Jerusalem: building their nests at the temple. We read in Psalm 84: "The sparrow has found a home, and the swallow a nest for herself, where she may have her young—a place near Your altar." The swallows frequented the temple vicinity as though they loved God's house.

The psalm begins with this exclamation: "How lovely is Your dwelling place, O LORD Almighty!" It is saying: God's house—the temple, the church—is a good place to be. Even the swallows loved it there for the sake of the serenity it offered. It is a place where we, too, can take our young, our children, to hear the Word of God and to gather about His altar to receive the Sacrament.

When attending worship in God's house, we confess our faith to one another. "I ... go about Your altar, O LORD," the psalmist writes, "proclaiming aloud Your praise and telling of all Your wonderful deeds" (Psalm 26). What greater deed did God perform than to send His own Son, Jesus Christ, among us, to give His body and shed His blood on the cross for the forgiveness of our sins? As we gather about the Holy Communion table, we not only commemorate this great act of Christ, but we also receive His body and blood as pledges of that great redeeming love.

It is true: One swallow does not make the summer. Also, one swallow at San Juan Capistrano or in the temple area of Jerusalem does not make a flock. It takes more. Similarly, it takes more than one Christian to make a congregation; it takes at least two or three—and preferably more—to make a church. When there are more, the mutual confessing of faith to one another, and the exercising of Christian fellowship in support of one another, can begin.

In Psalm 84, the "swallow psalm," the writer goes on to say: "Better is one day in Your courts than a thousand elsewhere." As Christians we join him in saying this.

Prayer Suggestion

In your prayer count the blessings coming to you through worship in God's house, and thank Him for them.

The Gospel, No Blushing Matter

If anyone is ashamed of Me and My words in this adulterous and sinful generation, the Son of Man will be ashamed of him when He comes in His Father's glory with the holy angels. Mark 8:38

"I am not ashamed of the Gospel," St. Paul writes to the Romans. According to a Latin translation he is saying: "I am not blushing—or turning red in the face—when I speak of or witness to the Gospel." He finds nothing to apologize for or to feel ashamed about, for the Gospel "is the power of God for the salvation of everyone who believes"— believes that it is the good news that Jesus Christ, God's Son, died for his sins and rose again (Romans 1:16).

The writer of the epistle to the Hebrews (2:11) stresses that Jesus is not ashamed to call us his brothers (and sisters). Later on he writes that the heavenly Father is not ashamed to be called our God, for we are His children who seek the heavenly home He has provided for us (2:13).

Ashamed of Jesus? No, says the hymn writer—"Sooner far Let evening blush to own a star." He goes on to say if blush he must, "be this my shame, That I no more revere His name." Another hymn writer states, "Am I a soldier of the Cross, A follower of the Lamb, And shall I fear to own His cause Or blush to speak His name?"

The apostle Paul knew whereof he spoke when he expressed his high appreciation of Christ's Gospel. He had experienced its power in his own life: He had witnessed the results when he said to the jailer of Philippi to believe in the Lord Jesus Christ. While he valued his Roman citizenship and made use of it on several occasions, he valued his heavenly citizenship in Christ's kingdom much higher. Christ was everything to him, and for Christ he was willing to suffer the loss of all things.

We, too, have known the power of Christ's Gospel in our lives; we have seen the wonders it works in human hearts. It is also for us no blushing matter—nothing of which to be ashamed. It increases our faith and thus draws us closer to Christ, our Friend and heavenly Bridegroom. It is true what Martin Luther said: "Faith is the engagement ring that betroths us to Christ." This faith comes from hearing the Gospel.

Prayer Suggestion

Ask the Lord Jesus to strengthen the bond of your faith in Him so you may courageously confess Him and His Gospel before others.

PETER: REED AND ROCK

Jesus replied, "Blessed are you, Simon son of Jonah, for this was not revealed to you by man, but by My Father in heaven."
Matthew 16:17

The Peter who was on occasion impetuous, restless, and unstable can be compared to a fragile reed. His worst moment was his denial of Christ despite his declaration: "Even if I have to die with You, I will never disown You" (Matthew 26:35).

But Peter was also a rock, firm and solid. When Jesus asked His disciples, "Who do you say I am?" Peter replied, "You are God's Messiah," or as St. Matthew reports his confession, "You are the Christ, the Son of the living God" (Matthew 16:16). On that point Peter was never to waver.

Peter was truly *Petros*, a Greek word meaning rock. He was a rock-man not because of personal strength but because the faith he confessed was firmly grounded on the *petra*, the stone foundation, of Christ's Word. Jesus said to him then, "You are Peter (*Petros*), and on this rock (*petra*) I will build My church."

In his first epistle St. Peter extends his teaching about the atoning work of Jesus as God's Messiah: "It was not with perishable things such as silver or gold that you were redeemed ... but with the precious blood of Christ, a lamb without blemish or defect" (1:18–19).

Through the Word, the Holy Spirit strengthens our faith in Christ. That changes us from reeds to rocks. We can be like John the Baptist, who firmly adhered to his mission as Christ's witness. Our Lord said of him that he was not "a reed swayed by the wind" (Matthew 11:7). We, too, can be firm in our faith because our "hope is built on nothing less than Jesus' blood and righteousness."

Prayer Suggestion

Ask God to bless your reading of His Word today so that you may grow strong in your reliance on Jesus Christ, your Savior.

TRAINED TO SERVE

[Teach] them to obey everything I have commanded you.
Matthew 28:20

The owners and managers of professional athletic teams know that the players they have drafted need further instruction in the fundamentals of the game. So they set up training camps in advance of the season.

The Christian church likewise stresses training and teaching. It is part of the evangelism outreach, for Jesus told His apostles, "Make disciples of all nations, baptizing them in the name of the Father and of the Son and of the Holy Spirit, and teaching them to obey everything I have commanded you" (Matthew 28:19–20). Christ wants His followers to be taught and then to teach others.

By nature no one knows Jesus Christ to be his Savior from sin and eternal death. People need to be told the truths and teachings of Christ, not only once or twice but over and over so that Christ becomes the center of their lives. Then they can relate this fact to all the other teachings of Christianity revealed in the Bible.

Who will do this teaching? In Christian day schools we have professionally trained teachers. For teaching in Sunday schools and in the home our Lord relies on volunteer teachers and on parents—on persons alive in Christ who are not only willing to teach but will also seek to become more proficient by regularly attending training sessions.

When we have rightly grasped what Christ teaches us and lays on our hearts, we will want to tell others as informal teachers. It is a great privilege to be recruited and trained for the Lord's service.

Prayer Suggestion

Pray that the Holy Spirit will open your heart and mind more fully to God's Word so that you can share it with others.

THE RIGHT WAY TO GO

Everything should be done in a fitting and orderly way.
1 Corinthians 14:40

Henry Thoreau, the naturalist-philosopher of Massachusetts, wrote, "If anything ails a man, so that he does not perform his function, if he have a pain in his insides ... he forthwith sets about reforming the world."

The other extreme in human behavior is complacency, smugness, an "I don't want to get involved attitude."

Jesus had a representative group of men following Him—His 12 disciples. At times they showed misguided zeal. Peter was impulsive, given to rash words and deeds. James and John were nicknamed "Sons of Thunder" because they toyed with the idea of burning a Samaritan village when the inhabitants were inhospitable. Another disciple, Simon, was known as the zealot or super-patriot. Others—and perhaps all at some time—were complacent, and Jesus had to stir them up. Of course, after the Holy Spirit came to them on Pentecost Day, they were properly motivated and guided by a better understanding of the truth.

How is it with us who are Christ's disciples today? Do we want to make radical, overnight changes in the church? Or are we seemingly unconcerned, claiming God's promises but sitting on the premises? What is the right way to go?

The Roman poet Horace spoke of the golden mean, that is, the happy medium, the prudent way that avoids extremes. As we go this way, we keep our commitment to Jesus Christ. We confess Him to be the Son of God and our one and only Savior, dying for our sins and rising again. In obedience to His will we proclaim the Gospel. We know of no other way of bringing people to the faith. We realize that spiritual growth is often slow. In this time of "instant this" and "instant that" we realize that instant Christianity of the perfect variety is not to be expected.

So we patiently but resolutely keep doing what our Lord has directed us to do. By going this way we avoid two extremes: mindless activism and do-nothingness.

Prayer Suggestion

Tell your Lord that you want to abide by your baptismal covenant to remain loyal to Christ no matter what comes.

FOR THE THIRSTY: GOD'S WORD AND PRAYER

"Sir," the woman said, "You have nothing to draw with and the well is deep." John 4:11

John Newton, author of "Amazing Grace" and other hymns, once wrote to a theology student: "The chief means for attaining wisdom and suitable gifts for the ministry are Holy Scripture and prayer. The one is the fountain of living water, and the other is the bucket with which we are to draw." This is good advice for all Christians.

The source of all truth is Holy Scripture. From it comes the refreshing Word. At Jacob's well near a Samaritan village Jesus spoke the Word of God to a woman. He said: "The water I give him [the receptive hearer of the Word] will become in him a spring of water welling up to eternal life."

The word of God that Jesus proclaimed does in turn proclaim Him as the source of all grace. St. John writes in his gospel that Jesus, the Father's one and only Son, was "full of grace and truth" (John 1:14). He added: "From the fullness of His grace we have all received one blessing after another" (v. 16). This is living water. The grace of Jesus, to which Holy Scripture bears witness, brings us salvation. St. Paul tells us how Jesus' grace applies to us: "You know the grace of our Lord Jesus Christ, that though He was rich, yet for your sakes He became poor, so that you through His poverty might become rich" (2 Corinthians 8:9). Jesus went into the desert of this world; He endured poverty and deprivation; He hungered and thirsted; He suffered death on the cross to bring us the refreshment of God's forgiving grace.

At Jacob's well the woman said that Jesus needed a vessel with which to draw water. All the blessings Jesus procured for us would do us no good unless we had faith in Him. Faith is the hand by which we receive God's gifts and make them our own. The cup of faith holds the water of life. In faith we approach the throne of God in prayer. The hymn writer states: "Thou art coming to a King, Large petitions with thee bring." And also bring along a large container! Bring a faith large enough to draw the water of life—grace and truth—from the fountain of God's Word!

Are you thirsty? Be refreshed! Come to the fountain of Christ's Gospel.

Prayer Suggestion

After you have read God's Word, pray that the Holy Spirit may refresh you by leading you closer to Christ.

TIPS FOR TIMID SOULS

Fear not, for I have redeemed you; I have summoned you by name; you are Mine. Isaiah 43:1

A part of wildlife in town and country is one of God's commonest creatures—the cottontail rabbit. It or its kin has entered folklore. In *The Tale of Peter Rabbit* Beatrix Potter tells about Peter's mischief-making—how he trespasses in Mr. McGregor's garden.

Rabbits are timid animals; they have reason to be when the hounds are on the loose. To survive, their Creator gave them good ears—their antennae—and fast legs. Joel Chandler Harris describes his Brer Rabbit as also brave, clever, and of a ready wit. When a tiger asks why he isn't scared of him, Brer Rabbit replies that the fleas on the tiger are much smaller than him, and they aren't scared, so why should he?

These are parables about people. Many stand their ground in the face of threats. But others are timid souls. Perhaps because of a bad conscience they are hiding from God, like a rabbit under a bush. In his poem "The Hound of Heaven," Francis Thompson narrates his efforts to flee from God. But no matter what his hiding place or escape, God would find him, wanting to save him.

Fear also can make people run—the fear of poverty, of being left alone, of becoming involved in situations they can't handle. Topping them all is the fear of death. But God is not like an overpowering hound chasing a hare. He is their Friend and Father who wants to help and heal. Adam and Eve and all their descendants don't have to run from God, for He has declared His love. He put this love into effect when He sent Jesus Christ, His Son, into the world to give His life for the salvation of all.

In His Word, God gives tips to timid souls. "Fear not," He assures them, "for there is nothing to fear. You are safe in My hands."

Prayer Suggestion

Consider for a moment what fears you may have, then take them to the Lord Jesus in prayer, asking for strong faith in Him.

FAITHFUL STEWARDS

Whoever can be trusted with very little can also be trusted with much. Luke 16:10

In His parable of a shrewd manager as recorded on Luke 16, Jesus is not advocating clever business practices bordering on dishonesty. He is discussing Christian life as faithful stewardship. He points to a certain amount of consistency in human behavior. He who has a reliable character will be honest regardless of his line of work and the amount of responsibility entrusted to him. He will run true to form no matter where he lives, whether in New York, Kansas, or California.

The same consistent pattern of conduct is evident whether the person in question administers temporal or spiritual treasures— whether it be money ("the unrighteous mammon") or things of intangible value such as knowledge, personal talents, gifts of the Spirit, God-given opportunities, and even the gift of salvation. Jesus declares, "If you have not been trustworthy in handling worldly wealth, who will trust you with true riches?"

The question of ownership, whether the goods belong to others or to ourselves, doesn't really matter. If we are good stewards of another's property, we will be good stewards of our own, and God, knowing this, will bless us and may increase what is ours. On the other hand, says Jesus, "If you have not been trustworthy with someone else's property, who will give you property of your own?" (Luke 16:12)

What makes for faithful stewardship? Daily renewal in the likeness of Jesus Christ, who was faithful to all His commitments in that He was obedient to death, even death on the cross for our salvation. Follow Him by faith!

Prayer Suggestion

Let your prayer focus on your various responsibilities. Ask the Lord Jesus for the wisdom and strength to follow faithfully in His footsteps as a wise steward.

THE LIFELONG STRUGGLE OF FAITH

Let us run with perseverance the race marked out for us.
Hebrews 12:1

The Word of God tells us time and again to persist in our faith, to adhere to the purpose for which God has called us. In His parable of the four soils Jesus speaks of a group of hearers who believe for a while but who, in the time of testing, fall away. He sought to prepare His disciples for such times of temptation. The apostles in turn urged their hearers and the readers of their epistles to stand firm when wave after wave of persecution passed over them.

The writer of the letter to the Hebrews lays great stress on spiritual persistence, telling his readers to run with perseverance the race marked out for them (12:1). St. Jude likewise urged early Christians to contend earnestly for the faith once for all delivered to the saints (v. 3).

It helps when the spiritual leaders set a good example. A Latin saying has it: *Qualis rex, talis grex*—as the leader or shepherd is, so is the flock. One of the qualities a leader needs is staunch and strong commitment to the task at hand.

In the Civil War, the two opposing generals in the final battles in Virginia were Grant and Lee. When, in May of 1864, the Union army was bogged down at Spottsylvania, Grant wrote to his superiors in Washington, D.C.: "I propose to fight it out on this line if it takes all summer." He was a man of determination.

In our spiritual battles we always have Jesus to look up to. As the captain of our salvation He endured the cross, refusing to be deterred by the shame and pain of the crucifixion. When in faith we look to Him, the Lamb of Calvary, we receive strength to pursue our spiritual goal in life until heaven itself is attained. We do this even if it takes a whole lifetime. The promise holds: "He who stands firm to the end will be saved" (Matthew 10:22).

Prayer Suggestion

Ask your Lord for patience, persistence, and steadfastness in the faith until you attain the goal: eternal life in heaven.

CHRIST IS FOR REAL

Christ has indeed been raised from the dead, the firstfruits
of those who have fallen asleep. 1 Corinthians 15:20

Accepted beliefs are often challenged, sometimes because of new evidence, sometimes simply to touch off controversies resulting in publicity for the challenger. Some have said that George Washington never chopped down a cherry tree, that Shakespeare did not write the plays attributed to him, that King Arthur was a legendary figure. And here comes someone who claims that Rembrandt never painted "The Golden Helmet"—somebody else did.

Of course, we know there are myths, some originating with real persons and real events, but in the course of time they become considerably embroidered by the imagination.

Could this have happened with the stories of Jesus? Is Christ for real? Is the Bible a book of myths, legends, and fairy tales? Some say that it offers moral lessons and kernels of truth in a sack full of chaff. Some say yes to that, adding that the task of the biblical expounder is to "demythologize" the Bible stories about Jesus.

As for the resurrection of Jesus, some believe that He was never dead but rose from a coma. Others claim that Jesus was dead all right and stayed dead; we must regard His "resurrection" as a spiritual event, as symbolic of the renewal of life that should occur in people. Some years ago a rebuttal of this claim came from an unexpected source—from the author John Updike, who stated in a poem published in *The Christian Century* that "either Jesus rose in the flesh, or He did not rise at all."

The resurrection of Jesus, His atoning death, as well as all that the New Testament teaches of Him, is solidly documented by competent eyewitnesses. There is no ground for anyone to contradict the witness that the Holy Spirit bears in the hearts and minds of hearers when the Gospel proclaims "Believe in the Lord Jesus, and you will be saved" (Acts 16:31). He is for real.

Prayer Suggestion

Pray that the living Christ may more and more become a reality in support of your faith in Him as your Savior.

THOSE COMFORTED BECOME THE COMFORTERS

Praise be to the God and Father of our Lord Jesus Christ ...
who comforts us in all our troubles, so that we can comfort
those in any trouble with the comfort we ourselves have
received from God. 2 Corinthians 1:3–4

The light of the sun is God's free public utility to all people. It is the same for everyone: for the sunbather resting on the beach, for the farmer tilling his fields, for the woman growing flowers in her yard. Since the sunshine is meant for all, those who are healthy can share it with the weak by taking them for walks; by letting more sunshine come into our dark city slums; by providing solaria, or sunshine rooms, for the sick and the institutionalized.

As is the Creator's sunlight, so is the comfort of our heavenly Father in Jesus Christ. It is free, and it is the same for all, as St. Paul writes: "Praise be to the God and Father of our Lord Jesus Christ, the Father of compassion and the God of all comfort, who comforts us in all our troubles, so that we can comfort those in any trouble with the comfort we ourselves have received."

God's comfort is the same for rich and poor, young and old, learned and unlearned, pastors and lay members in the church. Social standing, ethnic background, and skin color are no factors. In Jesus Christ, His Son, God loved and redeemed the whole world—all humanity—inviting everyone to accept the comfort of His forgiveness. Also with respect to God's compassion and consolation, in St. Paul's words: "There is neither Jew nor Greek, slave nor free, male nor female, for you are all one in Christ Jesus" (Galatians 3:28).

The apostle makes this important point: God comforts us not only for our own sakes but also to equip us for comforting others in their troubles. The comfort is the same. How wonderful and God-pleasing, when Christians who have experienced divine comfort take that same consolation and speak it to others in their distress! It is like sharing God's sunshine.

Prayer Suggestion

Tell God how grateful you are for comforting you with His forgiving love in Christ Jesus, and ask that He may help you bring comfort to others.

From Killing to Kindness

While they were in the field, Cain attacked his brother
Abel and killed him. Genesis 4:8

The many killings reported by the news media are not a modern phenomenon. In Shakespeare's *Hamlet,* the king is killed, and the uncle, Claudius, marries Queen Gertrude. Hamlet wants to kill Claudius but by mistake slays Polonius, the father of his beloved Ophelia. Her brother, Laertes, and Hamlet kill each other in a duel. Hamlet's mother dies of poison intended for her son.

We can go back to a much earlier source to see the killing instinct at work: the Bible. Cain, the first son ever to be born, killed Abel. Among Adam's other descendants was Tubal-Cain, "who forged all kinds of tools out of bronze and iron" (Genesis 4:22), some of them used for killing. Another descendant, Lamech boasted to his two wives, Adah and Zillah: "I have killed a man for wounding me, a young man for injuring me" (Genesis 4:23). As you read on in the books of the Bible you find many instances of individual and group killings, in peace and in war.

Some say the Bible shouldn't be read because it indirectly encourages people to shed human blood. But the opposite is true. Secular humanists and others who deny the reality of sin and claim an inborn goodness of human nature should read the Bible to convince themselves of the truth of this statement in Genesis: "Every inclination of his [man's] heart is evil from childhood" (Genesis 8:21).

Killings will not stop until there is a change of heart—a change that only the Holy Spirit can effect through the Gospel. He makes the individual a new creation in Jesus Christ. The Spirit creates faith in the Savior, and with faith He engenders love: love to God and love to fellow human beings, including enemies.

Strange as it may seem, only the death of Christ, brought on by His enemies, can keep people from killing each other. For it not only reveals the horror of hatred vented against the Innocent One, but more important, it sets people free from the power of sin. God is at work in converted human beings, enabling them to change hatred, anger, jealousy, and other motives for murder into love, patience, and forbearance. In Christians the killing instinct turns to kindness.

Prayer Suggestion

Pray for a constant renewal of your heart so that you may love Christ and those with whom you live.

FREE TO BE A DISCIPLE

*Through the obedience of the one Man the many will be
made righteous. Romans 5:19*

This is a paradox: As we make ourselves captives of God's Word,
we become free—free from everything that can make life a kind of hell
on earth: fear, guilt, self-service, and the "I have my heaven here on
earth" syndrome.

Martin Luther, the great Reformer, writes, "I do the will of God,
who sent Christ. To the Word alone have I listened; and I say, 'Dear
Lord Christ, I want to be Thy pupil and believe Thy Word, want to
close my eyes and make myself a captive of Thy Word.' Then He
makes me a free lord."

The Law makes humanity into a fear-filled, guilt-laden slave. It
demands, threatens, and condemns. No one can reach the moral perfection it demands. Therefore the pronouncement: "Cursed is everyone who does not continue to do everything written in the Book of the
Law" (Galatians 3:10).

Thank God for this: "Christ is the end of the Law so that there may
be righteousness for everyone who believes" (Romans 10:4). While the
Law condemns, the Gospel announces God's saving purpose in Christ,
creates and confirms faith in God's promise, and imparts all blessings
for which Christ went to the cross: divine favor, forgiveness, life now
and eternal life to come, membership in God's family, peace.

Only by faith in the Gospel are we made acceptable to God and
made free for discipleship. The Reformation gave new emphasis to
this truth. Hand in hand with freedom from the curse of the Law
comes the freedom to serve God. God's saving grace in Jesus Christ
does not compel us to discipleship, like a man being drafted and com-
pelled to serve in the army; it prompts Christians to *volunteer* for service under Christ's banner.

Prayer Suggestion

Thank your Savior, the Lord Jesus Christ, for all the blessings of
His saving grace, especially for the opportunity He gives you to be His
disciple.

WHAT THE HUMAN BEING CAN BECOME

[Give] thanks to the Father, who has qualified you to share in the inheritance of the saints in the kingdom of light. Colossians 1:12

What is the Human Being?

Shakespeare's Hamlet, in a moment of good feeling about the human being, exclaims in Act II, scene 2: "What a piece of work is man, how noble in reason, how infinite in faculties, in form and moving how express and admirable, in action how like an angel, in apprehension how like a god—the beauty of the world, the paragon of animals!" At first blush this seems ludicrous—like an All Fool's Day delusion.

Here someone will surely ask for equal time to say that the human being is not like an angel in thoughts, words, and actions. Attention will be called to sins and crimes reported in newspapers: robbery, killing, oppression, adultery, drunkenness. A paragon of animals? Sometimes it is the other way around: Animals show more sense. Male and female birds, like the cardinals, stay together permanently. Do human couples?

It is hard to place human beings. Surely they are neither animals nor angels. What are they? The Bible says: "God created man in His own image, in the image of God He created him; male and female He created them" (Genesis 1:27).

Adam and Eve were like God in holiness and righteousness, but when they sinned they lost this image or likeness. Sin had a way of growing, like cancer. Wickedness abounds in our world, in our present age as in all past ages. No uplifting measures designed by man can pull himself out of the mire. Only God could do it, and God *did*. He sent His own Son, whom we adore as our Lord Jesus Christ, to redeem us from sin. By faith in the Redeemer the human being becomes a new creation, a reconstructed being. He becomes the new person whom Jesus desires—and empowers—him to be: the salt of the earth and the light of the world.

Christianity holds that sinful humanity can be renewed in the image of God. We are neither angels nor animals. We are reborn persons, children of God, reborn when the Holy Spirit has done His work.

Prayer Suggestion

Pray for a rich measure of faith in the transforming Christ so that you may grow more and more into His likeness.

BEAUTIFUL FLOWERS, BAD FRUIT

The fruit of the Spirit is love, joy, peace, patience, kindness, goodness, faithfulness, gentleness and self-control.
Galatians 5:22

Along in April or May, no tree or shrub adorns itself with more beautiful flowers than the wild crab. The blooms, in clusters of three to six, range in color from white to pale pink to deep rose. As for the fruit, the apples it produces are small—often less than an inch in diameter—and sour. They are inedible.

The Bible takes note of an all-flower, no-fruit type of life. Some would-be religious people try to assume a decorative Christianity. Their speech is flowery, their prayers full of pious phrases, their behavior in church correct, their deeds eye-catching. The so-called electronic churches on television increase the temptation to practice a visual kind of religion. It is mostly flowers.

This is by no means a new development. The Old Testament prophets vehemently denounced external piety. Jesus exposed the false righteousness of the Pharisees. And St. James in his epistle took note of would-be worshipers "wearing a gold ring and fine clothes" (James 2:2)—not that it is sinful to be well dressed but because this externalism betrayed a so-called faith lacking the works of love.

God, who is the Creator of all things, can appreciate beautiful flowers, but He realizes that they don't provide food. The fruit does that. Good fruit is the test of a good tree, even as works of true love are the test of the true saving faith in Jesus Christ. The Holy Spirit, having through the Gospel brought us to faith in the Savior and His atoning work for us, makes us fruitful in all good works. He makes us like trees that bring forth their fruit in their season (Psalm 1:3). Not the flowers but the fruit of the Spirit are these: "love, joy, peace, patience, kindness, goodness, faithfulness, gentleness and self-control" (Galatians 5:22). These fruits, not empty words and deeds, are the Christian's adornment.

Prayer Suggestion

Implore the Holy Spirit to make you a fruitful Christian, out of love to Jesus, your Savior.

WHEN GOOD IS NOT GOOD ENOUGH

Come and hear the message that has come from the LORD.
Ezekiel 33:30

God said to the prophet Ezekiel: "My people come to you, as they usually do, and sit before you to listen to your words, but they do not put them into practice. With their mouths they express devotion, but their hearts are greedy for unjust gain" (Ezekiel 33:31).

Surely it is good to sit together in church to hear the Word of God. The hearers of the Word of God are distinguished from non-hearers—from those who turn away from God and refuse to hear what He has to say to them through His spokesmen.

It is likewise good when, with our tongues, we speak or sing the praises of God in His sanctuary. Many consider this "good" even when the performance is mechanical. They consider the mere doing of a thing a service to God.

What might be good—listening to the Word with our ears and praising Him with our mouths—can turn out to be displeasing to God. Ezekiel was told the reason: The hearers do not put God's Word into practice. They are, in the words of St. James, hearers but not doers of the Word. Obedience is missing. Further, worship or devotion, even when expressed eloquently, is meaningless—is in fact hypocritical—when piety and sincerity are lacking. Hearts that should be full of faith are filled with greed leading to unjust gain.

What is "good" will indeed be good enough, will in fact be excellent and gratifying to God, when the love of Christ prompts our hearing and worshiping. Jesus Christ came to us as God's great Prophet, and when He speaks the Word, our hearts are moved to receive that Word, believe it, and put it into practice. Our acts of devotion will be expressions of true faith and love, for they are prompted by our love for Him as our great High Priest, who offered Himself on the cross as the complete sacrifice for our sins.

So we say to our Lord: "Take my life and let it be Consecrated, Lord, to Thee." Take my ears to hear Your Word, my lips to praise You, my hands to do Your work, my feet to carry the Good News of salvation to the world. Then what is thought to be "good" will be good indeed.

Prayer Suggestion

Ask the Holy Spirit to open your heart to the Gospel of Christ that you may be both a hearer and doer of the Word.

I SERVE

Your attitude should be the same as that of Christ Jesus.
Philippians 2:5

The German origin of England's ruling house, Windsor—formerly Wettin—is evident from the German motto on the coat of arms of the Prince of Wales: *Ich dien*, "I Serve." While it is a tragedy that two related nations all but destroyed themselves in world war, there is a bright side to the ideal of serving to which England's rulers are committed.

Service is the word that describes the activity of Jesus in effecting our salvation, and it describes also what Christians do as the Lord's redeemed. *Ich dien* is the Christian's motto, as seen from a number of New Testament terms and titles.

1. **Doulos**: In the Philippians passage above, Jesus is, in the Greek, called doulos, a servant, or more literally, a slave. St. Paul chose that title also for himself (Romans 1:1). All Christians live under Christ in His kingdom and serve Him.

2. **Diakonos**: Jesus Himself says: "Whoever wants to become great among you must be your servant (diakonos)" (Matthew 20:26). Deacons and deaconesses—the word stems from diakonos—are not alone in serving Christ and His own. All Christians are, by the power of faith, made willing to gird themselves for service.

3. **Leitourgos**: Leitourgia, a Greek word that lives on in liturgy, or divine service, formerly described a public service performed by a citizen at his own expense. Biblical writers apply the term to Jesus' work as well as to the work of those who serve Him.

4. **Hyperetes**: The term meant a member of a ship's crew, specifically a rower. In the New Testament it stands for those who help their superiors, such as John Mark, who was chosen to assist Paul and Barnabas on the first missionary journey. The apostle speaks of himself and the others as "the servants (hyperetes) of Christ" and stewards of God's mysteries (1 Corinthians 4:1).

Is serving Christ a bore and a chore? Not at all. The hymn writer calls it so sweet a service "that angels well might envy me."

Prayer Suggestion

Pray for the increase of your faith and love so that you serve Jesus Christ and His brothers and sisters better.

THE GOLDEN MEAN

Godliness with contentment is great gain. 1 Timothy 6:6

In 1728 John Gay wrote *The Beggar's Opera* as a satire on moral conditions in the government and wealthy society of England. The theme is not far removed from Christ's parable of the poor beggar, Lazarus, lying at the doorstep of the rich man, "who was dressed in purple and fine linen and lived in luxury every day" (Luke 16:19).

Jesus had things to say to both rich and poor. He reminded the rich that it is easier for a camel to pass through the eye of a needle than for a rich man to enter God's kingdom. As for the poor, He did not urge them to start a revolution, but He had a heart for them. Both poverty and riches involve temptations.

The writer of this passage in the book of Proverbs in the Bible realizes the perils of both poverty and wealth: "Two things I ask of You, O LORD. ... Give me neither poverty nor riches, but give me only my daily bread. Otherwise, I may have too much and disown You and say, 'Who is the LORD?' Or I may become poor and steal, and so dishonor the name of my God" (30:7–9).

This believer wanted only his daily bread. His is a prayer for the golden mean, for a livelihood somewhere between poverty and riches. "Daily bread," of course, is more than bread baked in an oven. It includes the gifts of God we need from day to day: apparel, a home, income to pay for heating bills, a job, health, the opportunity for education, and always a little extra to share with the poor.

St. Paul writes: "Godliness with contentment is great gain. ... If we have food and clothing, we will be content with that" (1 Timothy 6:6, 8). And thankful for that!

All the while we are, above all, thankful for our spiritual riches in Jesus Christ, who became poor—poor to the point of death on a cross—to enrich us with forgiveness, peace with God, a purpose in life, and eternal life to come.

Prayer Suggestion

Thank God for giving you the necessities of life and for having enriched you in Jesus Christ, your Savior.

GOD KNOWS US AND OUR NEEDS

O LORD, You have searched me and You know me.
Psalm 139:1

The human individual, a complicated being, is hard to evaluate. This seems to be especially true of people with artistic temperaments and highly individualized dispositions. A case in point is the Dutch painter, Vincent van Gogh. During his stay in Arles, France, he was deemed insane and put into a cell. Once when he wanted to sell some paintings to the deputy mayor, he was told: "Take these to the market-place and get some money for a cup of coffee." As the 100th anniversary of his death approached, the city did all it could to acquire his paintings.

While human beings are often a puzzle to one another, God reads them like an open book. He searches and understands the heart. He knows all about us—has always known, even before we were born. "You know," says the psalmist, "when I sit and when I rise; You perceive my thoughts from afar. You discern my going out and my lying down; You are familiar with all my ways. Before a word is on my tongue You know it completely, O LORD" (Psalm 139:2–4).

God knows all our needs, even better than what we do. He is aware of what we need the most, and He has prepared the solution to our greatest problem: sin. God realized that human beings had fallen into sin, death, and Satan. So He sent His own Son, Jesus Christ, who did mortal combat, overcame them, and rose from the dead in proof of His victory.

Jesus knew the thoughts of people. "He knew what was in a man" (John 2:25), the Bible says. He is our Good Physician, who understood so complicated a person as Vincent van Gogh. He understands us. To Him we can go in confidence and with joy.

Prayer Suggestion

Open your heart to Jesus and ask Him to help you in all your needs. Tell Him you trust His promise to hear you.

BE WHAT YOU ARE

Shine like stars in the universe as you hold out the word of life.
Philippians 2:15–16

A worker at a New York state facility, it was learned, had stolen the chaplain's fountain pen. This seemed strange since the worker was illiterate. Why would he need a pen? He said he took it to wear in his coat pocket so that people would think he was able to write. He pretended to be what He was not.

There is much deceptive role-playing in life, also in religion. People in church circles who at heart are not what they outwardly seem to be—or what they want others to think they are—are called hypocrites. The classic examples of sham religion were the Pharisees of Jesus' time. Our Lord said to them, "You are like whitewashed tombs, which look beautiful on the outside but on the inside are full of dead men's bones" (Matthew 23:27).

Pretending to be what we are not is a temptation that comes also to us Christians. It came even to the apostle Peter, who on occasion would eat with the Gentiles. St. Paul goes on to say that when Jewish Christians came from Jerusalem, "he began to draw back and separate himself from the Gentiles because he was afraid of those who belonged to the circumcision group" (Galatians 2:12). But St. Peter knew also the right way—the way of truth and honesty he had learned from Jesus. He writes of Jesus, "He committed no sin, and no deceit was found in His mouth" (1 Peter 2:22).

St. Paul, stressing the same truth, writes to the Philippians that they should "become blameless and pure, children of God without fault in a crooked and depraved generation, in which you shine like stars in the universe" (2:15).

Christians are the children of God, and as such they conduct themselves in the world. People recognize them not only for what they are, but they see also the image of Jesus stamped on them. It cannot be otherwise. Jesus, the Holy One of Israel, bore their sins. Now in heaven, He through His Word and Spirit enables those still on earth to "die to sins and live for righteousness" (1 Peter 2:24).

Prayer Suggestion

Ask the Lord Jesus to continue His sanctifying work in you, enabling you to be, in private and in public, what you are: His disciple.

GETTING BACK ON COURSE

A wicked and adulterous generation asks for a miraculous sign! But none will be given it except the sign of the prophet Jonah. Matthew 12:39

In the fall of 1985 a 45-ton humpbacked whale, supposedly heading for warmer ocean water to the south, made its way into the San Francisco Bay, swam up the Sacramento River, and "landed" in a slough. A great deal of effort was required to get it back to its habitat. It seemed that the whale had come from the deep to deliver a message.

Human beings, too, at times go off course, and one who did so deliberately was the prophet Jonah, who had a message to deliver. God had called him to preach the Word in Nineveh, the pagan capital of the Assyrian Empire. But like the above whale, he got into the wrong channel. Instead of going east, to Nineveh, he boarded a freighter at Joppa and sailed west on a ship that was bound for Tarshish on the other end of the Mediterranean Sea.

But God put Jonah back on course. During a severe storm Jonah was cast overboard and was swallowed by a large fish. Preserved alive, the prophet heeded the second call from God and preached repentance in Nineveh. Jesus refers to Jonah's experience and applies it to Himself: "As Jonah was three days and three nights in the belly of a huge fish, so the Son of Man will be three days and three nights in the heart of the earth" (Matthew 12:40). By being crucified, buried, and raised from the dead, Jesus Christ put a lost and floundering humanity back on course—the course of salvation by faith in Him.

Although Christians have been put on the right course, they sometimes have difficulty staying on the course. They sometimes wander far from home, as did the whale on the West Coast, as did the prophet Jonah. But they can get back on course, for they have Jesus as the Captain of salvation; they have His saving Word. So they pray: "Chart and compass come from Thee: Jesus, Savior, pilot me."

Prayer Suggestion

In your prayer to Jesus, mention the special areas of your life where you need His direction.

WHEN WINNERS AND LOSERS BOTH BENEFIT

If anyone is in Christ, he is a new creation.
2 Corinthians 5:17

Sometimes, in court, not only the winner but also the loser benefits. In 1921 the composer Puccini brought suit against the publisher of the song "Avalon," claiming it was lifted from his opera *Tosca*. The court agreed and awarded him $25,000. But the defendant benefited, too, for the song became a best-seller because of the publicity.

On several occasions Jesus chided His disciples for lack of faith, for pride and rivalry, for quick tempers. The disciples lost every argument they had with their Master. But by this loss they were enriched. They learned valuable lessons.

Is it not so also among Christians today—in the Christian home? Brothers and sisters with differences of opinion go to their parents for a settlement. Sometimes accusations are made: "He took what is mine"—a toy, perhaps. Father or mother makes a ruling. The one declared to be in the wrong may be assessed a penalty. Then it is not for the winner to gloat, nor for the loser to pout. The loser has gained something. He has learned a valuable lesson. He has seen the parents' love and concern in action. The parent, noting the fondness for the thing in question, may present him with a similar thing for a birthday or Christmas. All have benefited.

Christ forgives those who turn to Him in repentance and faith, and always they are blessed, as St. Paul tells the Corinthians: "In Him [Christ] you have been enriched in every way" (1 Corinthians 1:5). Take the example of Peter. He denied his Lord, but he repented and was reinstated in his apostleship. He benefited from this experience, and we do likewise. Christ died on a cross that we, who also have sinned, might not be losers but winners. All who repent, accept God's forgiveness in Christ, and make a new start are winners.

Prayer Suggestion

Say thanks to God for taking you, a loser because of sin, and making you a winner in Christ.

Celebrating Victory in Advance

They took palm branches and went out to meet Him.
John 12:13

Palm leaves are the tokens of victory and peace. This is evident from two vivid scenes set in the Bible, one in the heavenly Jerusalem and the other in earthly Jerusalem.

As for the first, St. John sees in a vision "a great multitude … standing before the throne and in front of the Lamb. They were wearing white robes and were holding palm branches in their hands" (Revelation 7:9). The multitude sings this song: "Salvation belongs to our God, who sits on the throne, and to the Lamb" (v. 10). This is the celebration of Christ's victory and peace as it goes on forever in heaven.

The second scene, taking us to the streets of earthly Jerusalem, likewise shows people proclaiming victory and peace by carrying palms and singing: "Blessed is the King who comes in the name of the Lord! Peace in heaven and glory in the highest!" (Luke 19:38)

But there is a difference: On that first Palm Sunday in earthly Jerusalem, victory was yet to be won. The celebration, as it were, anticipated the great event of a week later when Christ rose from the dead as the openly established Victor and Prince of Peace.

Yet the palms are very much in place. What God had ordained in His eternal counsel must come to pass. It was as good as done already on that Palm Sunday.

As for us on earth, here and now, we have not yet reached our destination in heaven. For us the battle goes on. Yet we can be sure of our salvation because our saving faith is God's work in us. St. John writes, "This is the victory that has overcome the world, even our faith. Who is it that overcomes the world? Only he who believes that Jesus is the Son of God" (1 John 5:4–5).

Prayer Suggestion

Let your prayer request be that God, through the Gospel and the sacraments, may sustain your faith in Jesus to the end.

WHO "FARMS" ON YOUR SOUL?

My soul glorifies the Lord and my spirit rejoices in God my Savior. Luke 1:46–47

The St. Louis poet, Sara Teasdalea, was a troubled person. Two of her lines read, "My soul is troubled field/Plowed by pain." After moving to New York City, despair followed distress and she took her own life.

The psalmist also experienced pain when enemies "farmed" on him. He writes, "Plowmen have plowed my back and made their furrows long" (129:3). No one has the right to perform this kind of "agriculture" on another. In many cases the "plowing" on the soul is more painful than evil done to the body. God opposes it. He said, "You shall not murder" (Exodus 20:13), and that includes, as Martin Luther has taught us in the explanation of this commandment, not to "hurt nor harm our neighbor in his body"—and not in his soul, either.

Another young woman with poetical gifts was Mary of Nazareth. When informed by the angel Gabriel that she would become the virgin mother of the Messiah, she began her Magnificat with joyful thanksgiving: "My soul glorifies the Lord and my spirit rejoices in God my Savior" (Luke 1:46–47). No one is by nature such a believer. Mary had come to faith early in life because through her parents, relatives, neighbors, and teachers the Holy Spirit had carefully "farmed" her soul—her inner self, her heart, mind, and memory. He sowed the seed of God's Word as revealed by the psalmists and prophets. That instruction included the prophecy that the Messiah would come to bring salvation. Jesus, the son of Mary, was that promised Savior.

Who has "farmed" on us? Our Christian parents, assisted by pastors and teachers, under the direction of the Holy Spirit, have done so. Their plowing and sowing, sometimes accompanied by pain, give promise of a good harvest.

Prayer Suggestion

Pray for God's continued blessing on the seed of the Word sown within you.

EASTER'S THREE LITTLE WORDS

He has risen! Mark 16:6

"Three Little Words" was the title of a popular song years back. The Christian faith has its three little words which convey the greatest news ever told. They say: "He has risen!"

Had the Easter message been "Christ is dead," life would be a succession of most distressing facts, as St. Paul enumerates them in 1 Corinthians 15: preaching is in vain, faith is futile, we are still mired down in our sins, the dead will not rise, we will have no reunion with them (1 Corinthians 15:14–20).

But "He has risen!" That entirely reverses the terms, and life has made a turn of 180 degrees. From the gloom of the grave Christ, the Light of the world, has emerged alive. He has kept every promise—the promise that on the third day He would raise the temple of His body, the promise that He would see His followers again, the promise that they, too, would live and on the Last Day rise from the dead.

Christ's resurrection casts us Christians in entirely new roles. From mourning we proceed to rejoicing. Doubt and despair turn into faith. Truly, as St. Peter declares: "In His great mercy He [God the Father] has given us new birth into a living hope through the resurrection of Jesus Christ from the dead" (1 Peter 1:3).

Since Christ has risen, many are the consequences for us as Christ's church. The angel bids us: "Go quickly and tell … [that] He has risen from the dead" (Matthew 28:7), and the living Lord Himself issues this mission mandate: "Therefore go and make disciples of all nations" (Matthew 28:19). The Head of the church is alive, and from His throne at God's right hand He rules and guides the affairs of His kingdom of grace, eventually turning it into the kingdom of glory.

The three little words "He has risen!" describe an event that has changed life completely for us as members of Christ's kingdom.

Prayer Suggestion

Give thanks to Christ for His return to life as a seal on the completeness of His redeeming work.

WASTE NOT!

*He said to His disciples, "Gather the pieces that are left over.
Let nothing be wasted." John 6:12*

Ours is a time of carelessness and waste. Taxpayers' money is wasted when manufacturers overcharge the government for defense equipment. How different in the Civil War, when Commodore Foote told his riverboat gunners to make each shot count because, he said, each one costs the government eight dollars!

Wastefulness is common also in civilian life. We waste food when elsewhere many go hungry. Because of planned obsolescence, we throw away things still usable. Some people, even when on public welfare, waste what money they have by betting on horses or buying lottery tickets. Wastefulness leads to want.

Our Lord was opposed to wastefulness. After He had fed the multitude with a few loaves and fish, He told the disciples: "Gather the pieces that are left over. Let nothing be wasted."

Our daily bread comes from God, for He gives rain and sunshine for crops to grow. It would be unthankfulness on our part to waste food. A resourceful cook knows how to make tasty meals from leftovers. And what food we don't need for ourselves we can—and should—share with the hungry.

Much more serious is the waste of human beings who were made in the image of God—waste of their minds, waste of their skills, waste of the remaining talents of retired persons.

As there is misuse of goods that hurts people and dishonors God, so is there a right use of them—a use that glorifies God, the Giver. When Mary of Bethany anointed Jesus' feet with a precious ointment, Judas Iscariot called it a waste. But our Lord was pleased with this love offering. Soon He would be crucified and would give His life for the salvation of all. He gave the best He had: Himself. We honor Him when we, instead of wasting our goods, give them to the poor.

Prayer Suggestion

Thank God for His gifts to you, asking Him also to help you in using them wisely and well.

MAXIMUM CHRISTIANITY

Jesus said to him, "Today salvation has come to this house." Luke 19:9

It is said that a man who had knowingly underpaid his income tax was troubled in conscience and had difficulty sleeping. So he sent a check for $150 to the Internal Revenue Service with this note: "I hope this is enough. If I can't sleep now, I will send you the rest of the money."

We read in the Bible about another man who cheated on taxes: the publican Zacchaeus of Jericho. As a tax collector he charged people more taxes than what they owed, putting the surplus into his own pocket. Perhaps also his conscience bothered him, for he resolved to do more than make restitution for his thefts. He said: "Here and now I give half of my possessions to the poor, and if I have cheated anybody out of anything, I will pay back four times the amount" (Luke 19:8).

The first man had not really repented because he wanted to settle for the minimum amount—just enough to find peace and rest. Zacchaeus, on the other hand, practiced maximum Christianity. Little wonder that Jesus commended him highly!

Maximum Christianity means doing the most we can to serve Jesus Christ, who gave everything He had—His very life—to give us peace with God and eternal salvation. Maximum Christian faith gladly and freely goes the limit out of love to Christ. The lazy Christian will do the least he can. If anyone asks him to walk a mile with him, he will go a fourth or, at the most, half a mile. Jesus said: "If someone forces you to go one mile, go with him two miles" (Matthew 5:41).

Jesus might have reasoned: Isn't it enough if I earn half a salvation for people and let them work out the rest of it themselves? But He didn't think or act that way. He practiced maximum love. Shouldn't we do the same?

Prayer Suggestion

Ask the Lord to enlarge your heart so that you will serve Him and His own not with the least but with the most.

A People Prepared for the Lord

Many of the people of Israel will he [John the Baptist]
bring back to the Lord their God. Luke 1:16

On April 15,1912, the giant ocean liner *Titanic* sank, with the loss
of some 1,500 lives. This disaster at sea has been the subject of many
books. In the Library of Congress, only books on Christ and on the
Civil War (in that order) have exceeded those on the *Titanic.*
Attention is called to the lack of preparation for such an event. The
ship was considered unsinkable. Not nearly enough lifeboats were
available.

Adequate preparation for all of life's events and eventualities needs
to be made. Parents help us to prepare for school. We need to prepare
for the transitional time known as adolescence. As adults we prepare
for marriage, for family life, for our jobs. We can't run the risk of taking too much for granted.

The most important preparation we need to make is to be right
with God. Years ago crude signs along highways read, "Prepare to
Meet Your God." It was not altogether improper to post such signs
along busy roads, for there many motorists meet their God in fatal
accidents.

The need to prepare to meet God calls for more than a casual road
sign. It calls for a more complete context—for a setting of life in which
we are at peace with God as we travel or abide at home, as we work
or rest, as we fulfill our overall vocation as Christians.

We were put on good terms with God at the time of our Christian
baptism, when we were "implanted," so to speak, into the atoning
death and resurrection of Jesus Christ. The faith created by water and
the Word was nurtured through our reading and applying of God's
Word and through frequent participation in Holy Communion. Living in
a state of grace, we are always prepared to meet God, regardless of
when He calls us. Helping us are our pastors, whose calling it is, as
was John the Baptist's, "to make ready a people prepared for the Lord"
(Luke 1:17).

Prayer Suggestion

In your prayer give your reply to the questions in the hymn line:
"O Lord, how shall I meet You, How welcome You aright?"

THE FOUNDATION MUST BE SOLID

*Everyone who hears these words of Mine and puts them
into practice is like a wise man who built his house on the
rock. Matthew 7:24*

When excavations were begun for the historic Arcade Building in
downtown St. Louis in 1917, a bed of quicksand was discovered, and
no solid foundation could be built on it. The problem was solved when
caissons were driven 50 feet below the subbasement.

Jesus was not a building contractor in a physical sense. He built
human life and character, based on faith in His Word and redeeming
work. In a parable He calls attention to the folly of a man who built his
house on sand. He declares: "The rain came down, the streams rose,
and the winds blew and beat against that house, and it fell with a great
crash" (Matthew 7:27). The man who built his house on a rock had a
foundation that could withstand the elements.

The sayings of Jesus are like this rock. What our Lord said and
taught was the eternal truth. What He said about mankind lost in sin
was true. What He said about the love of God was true: He so loved
the world that He gave His only Son, Jesus Christ, to reconcile it by
the shedding of His blood.

What He said about living a life of wisdom and righteousness was
true and is true to this day. The wood, hay, and stubble of human opinion cannot serve as a foundation for life. Only the Word of God is the
abiding bedrock on which to build.

Christian education is based on the truths of the Law and the
Gospel. It is begun in the home, continued in Christian schools, and
applied in the day-to-day encounters of our world.

All persons—parents, children, teachers, business people—says St.
Paul, should be careful how they build. "For," he says, "no one can lay
any foundation other than the one already laid, which is Jesus Christ"
(1 Corinthians 3:11). Quicksand, as building contractors know, cannot
support a building, but solid rock can. In our spiritual lives Jesus
Christ is that rock.

Prayer Suggestion

Ask the Holy Spirit to guide you as you live your life according to
the truth of Jesus' words.

"ME FIRST" IS SOMETIMES IN ORDER

*He [Jesus] poured water into a basin and began to wash
His disciples' feet. John 13:5*

Geoffry Chaucer, in his *Canterbury Tales*, describes various persons who are on a pilgrimage. He says of a village priest that he taught others the teachings of Christ and the apostles, but adds: "First he followed it himself."

Jesus, although He was God's Son, took the lead in serving. On the eve of His death He girded Himself and washed the disciples' feet. He said, "I have set you an example that you should do as I have done for you" (John 13:15). Jesus was indeed the Servant who had come to serve and to give His life as a ransom for the redemption of us all.

The prophet Isaiah volunteered and said: "Here am I. Send me!" (Isaiah 6:8) He was a "me first" person and so was the apostle Paul, who applied the Word of Christ to himself, "so that after I have preached to others, I myself will not be disqualified for the prize," the crown of eternal life (1 Corinthians 9:27).

A "me first" person is one who expects of others only what he has first expected of himself. In the home, parents teach the children good manners and obedience to the Word of God. But they follow it themselves.

Those are good teachers who first do, then say. Otherwise they are involved in a contradiction, such as: "Do as I say, not as I do."

Spiritual leaders in the church know that they can lead only when they practice what they preach. Jesus, in His time, faulted the religious leaders who sat in Moses' seat as teachers but lived contrary to what they taught.

There are "me first" opportunities where you live and work—you first in showing love to Christ and to all whom He calls His brothers and sisters.

Prayer Suggestion

Tell your Lord you would be glad to serve as opportunities present themselves and that you need His help to set others a good example.

THE MEANING OF "CHRISTIAN"

If you suffer as a Christian ... praise God that you bear that name. 1 Peter 4:16

Active in Lebanon's civil war were military groups called "Christians." They did what is usually done in war: kill, burn, destroy. They massacred whole camps of refugees. One has to bear in mind that "Christian" here referred to a political party who may have had only the vaguest identity with the Christian faith. We ask, are these Christians? People find this puzzling.

Also in other lands the "Christian" label can be misleading. The United States is sometimes called a Christian nation, probably because many of the citizens make a Christian confession. But officially America is not a Christian nation.

What does "Christian" mean? Historically the name was given to Jesus' followers in Antioch around A.D. 43. Twice more they are called by this name in the New Testament writings: in the book of Acts, where King Herod Agrippa II is quoted as telling St. Paul that he questions whether to become a Christian (Acts 26:28), and in First Peter, where the apostle writes: "If you suffer as a Christian, do not be ashamed" (1 Peter 4:16).

Obviously, "Christian" is derived from the word "Christ." It designates persons who believe in and follow Jesus as the Christ, the Messiah, the Appointed One. Together they form the holy Christian church, the communion of saints. The creeds of Christendom—the Apostles, Nicene, and Athanasian Creeds—state what Christians believe, notably about the Triune God and about the person and saving work of Jesus Christ, God's Son.

Christian *life* is very important—what Christians say and do. This is what the outside world hears and sees. Christian life is based on the Ten Commandments, and the motive for it is the love that comes from Christ. It has been said that non-Christians do not read the four gospels—of Matthew, Mark, Luke, and John—but they do read the *fifth gospel*, that is, the gospel according to you as a Christian.

Prayer Suggestion

Let members of the family group pray for God's help to be "Christian" (Christ-like) to one another and to others in the larger circles of life.

What Is a Human Being Worth?

What can a man give in exchange for his soul?
Matthew 16:26

Several centuries ago, in his effort to modernize his country, the czar of Russia, Peter the Great, visited lands in western Europe. He saw in Koenigsburg, East Prussia, an instrument of torture that interested him. Himself a cruel man, he asked to see a man broken on it. The local authorities said they had no criminal on hand just then who deserved such a punishment. Peter was astonished at this. He exclaimed: "What fuss about killing a man!"

Human life, also in our times, is often regarded as cheap and worthless, or even as a hindrance to be removed, as shown by the destruction of millions of unborn babies. Thousands starve to death during famines. A related tragedy is the loss of human lives on highways because of drunken driving.

What is a human life worth? Is it thirty pieces of silver, the price of a slave in ancient times? Does its worth consist in the value of the chemicals in a human body, said to be worth something like ten dollars?

The Bible gives us the right standard of evaluation. Human life is precious because God gave it. He created the first human beings in His own image. Besides divine creation, our divine redemption by the blood of Jesus Christ makes every person most precious. Jesus said that you could give nothing, not even the worth of the whole world, in exchange for your soul. St. Paul tells us not to cause weak brothers and sisters in the faith to stumble because of our bad examples, for Christ died for them.

It is good to ask: In what light do I consider my own worth? Do I appreciate the fact that God made me, Jesus redeemed me, and the Holy Spirit made me a temple of God?

Prayer Suggestion

Thank God for giving you life, for redeeming you through Christ, and for sanctifying you through the work of the Holy Spirit.

CHRIST'S CHURCH—LIKE A SHIP

God waited patiently in the days of Noah while the ark was being built. 1 Peter 3:20

Before the Pilgrims, aboard the *Mayflower*, landed at Plymouth, Massachusetts, in 1620, permanent settlers had come to Jamestown, Virginia, in 1607. Their little known ship was the *Godspeed*. The name implied the much-needed prayer: "God speed you!" that is, "God give you a prosperous journey!"

Such a prayer was certainly in order when Noah and his family entered the ark to escape destruction in the great flood. In the New Testament mention is made of this unique vessel, the ark, and of the faith involved in building and entering it. We are told: "By faith Noah, when warned about things not yet seen, in holy fear built an ark to save his family" (Hebrews 11:7). Further, St. Peter in his First Epistle draws a parallel between Noah's salvation then and our salvation now in the church through the water of Holy Baptism (3:18–22).

From ancient times the church of Christ has been compared to a ship whose passengers are safe from the perils of life's journey. Jesus Christ is the captain of this spiritual vessel. He built and founded it when, in His great love, He gave His life for the church. After rising from the dead, He commanded His apostles to launch this ship by preaching the Gospel everywhere in the world.

The apostles then—and those following in their footsteps to this day—were to extend this invitation to all who were floundering in the sea of sin and death: "Come aboard! In the ship of Christ's church you are safe."

The church would well be named *Godspeed,* as was the ship of the first Virginia settlers, for in and through it God saves and blesses all who enter it and sail under the captaincy of Jesus Christ. Our individual response is: "Jesus, Savior, pilot me Over life's tempestuous sea; Unknown waves before me role, Hiding rock and treacherous shoal. Chart and compass come from Thee. Jesus, Savior, pilot me."

Prayer Suggestion

In your prayer mention special situations in which you need and want Christ's guidance.

LEARNING FROM GOD'S LESSER CREATURES

See how the lilies of the field grow. They do not labor or spin. Yet I tell you that not even Solomon in all his splendor was dressed like one of these. Matthew 6:28–29

Referring to a pair of Canada geese building their nests in metropolitan St. Louis, a newspaper article said: "Unlike many West County residents, Canada geese keep the same mate for life, forming new relationships only when widowed."

The Bible urges us to learn from lesser creatures—diligence, for instance: "Go to the ant, you sluggard; consider its ways and be wise!" (Proverbs 6:6) Gratitude can be learned, as Isaiah writes: "The ox knows his master, the donkey his owner's manger … but … My people do not understand" (Isaiah 1:3)—do not understand that God is the Giver.

As for caring about the young, is there a better example than a mother bear attending to her cubs? Animals are known to be faithful, like the Skye terrier of Edinburgh, Scotland, named Greyfriars Bobby, who for 14 years stayed at his master's grave, everyday bringing him lunch. The city built him a statue.

Faithfulness, diligence, gratitude are qualities we can learn from God's lesser creatures. Jesus bids us consider the lilies of the field, the birds of the air, even the lowly sparrows, learning from them to trust in God's providence. Some truths, however, God's lesser beings cannot teach us—truths about our spiritual well-being. For this we have to turn to the Word of God, to people who can teach us the Word. St. Paul tells Timothy that his mother, Eunice, and grandmother, Lois, had taught him the faith (2 Timothy 1:5). And where did they find this faith? In "the Holy Scriptures, which are able to make you wise for salvation through faith in Christ Jesus" (2 Timothy 3:15). Not only from adults but also from little children we can learn this truth: "Jesus loves me, this I know, for the Bible tells me so." It takes Christian humility to learn from God's lesser beings.

Prayer Suggestion

Ask God to help you to lay pride aside and to learn the truths to believe and to live by—from all He has said and done.

REMAINING FIRM AND FAITHFUL

Why are you downcast, O my soul? Why so disturbed within me? Put your hope in God. Psalm 43:5

School children learn of the bravery of Captain James Lawrence. During the War of 1812 he commanded the frigate *Chesapeake* in a sea battle with the English ship *Shannon*. While he, mortally wounded, was being carried below, he told the men: "Don't give up the ship." This has become the slogan of the U.S. Navy.

The spirit of persistence, supported by a strong sense of loyalty and devotion, comes from our spiritual lives. In fact, it has its roots in the Christian faith. "Don't give up!" is written in large letters in the message of the Bible. When the situation seems hopeless, many people are ready to throw in the towel. The psalmist admitted that he was downcast and disturbed. But he rallied his faith and declared: "Put your hope in God, for I will yet praise Him, my Savior and my God" (Psalm 42:5).

In the face of so many temptations from without, to say nothing of personal weakness within, it is easy to take the way which is usually the way of sin. But St. Paul encourages us not to yield to evil, but to "offer ourselves to God, as those who have been brought from death to life" (Romans 6:13). Jesus brought us to life by sacrificing His own life to redeem us from sin and to get us started in the new life in Him. It would be a great mistake to give up what Jesus provides, as people do when they surrender to sin.

The easy road is not usually the right one. Our Savior tells us: "Enter through the narrow gate. For wide is the gate and broad is the road that leads to destruction. ... But small is the gate and narrow the road that leads to life" (Matthew 7:13–14). The hard road of suffering led to Jesus' resurrection and to life for us.

Victory comes to those who stand firm and fast, trusting in God, as did the psalmist. When the little craft that is your life is greatly threatened, take to heart the captain's words: "Don't give up the ship!" Keep fighting!

Prayer Suggestion

Come before your risen Savior, asking His help to resist temptation and to choose what is right and good.

JESUS, OUR INTERCESSOR

"Sir," the man replied, "leave it alone for one more year."
Luke 13:8

Usually fig trees, when properly cultivated, yield fruit. "He who tends a fig tree will eat its fruit," states the writer of Proverbs (27:18).

In a parable Jesus speaks of a fig tree that for several years had disappointed its owner. No figs! So he ordered it cut down. But the vinedresser interceded for the tree, asking that it be spared for another year. In the meantime he would tend it carefully. If it then yields fruit, fine! If not, well, it will be soon enough then to remove it from the vineyard.

Jesus did not tell stories just for the sake of stories. His parables made a point pertaining to God's kingdom. Here the point is that for a long time God had expected His chosen people, whom He "planted" in the land flowing with milk and honey, to bear the fruits of obedience and faith. But such evidence of spiritual life was largely absent. He considered bringing His people under final judgment. In his time, Moses interceded, asking for more time and even offering to have his name expunged from the book of life if thereby Israel could be spared (Exodus 32:32). Then came Jesus at the fullness of time. He desired that the time of grace be extended. To His intercession He added intervention. He went all the way to Calvary's cross for the salvation of all. Then He rose from the dead, ascended into heaven, and sent the Holy Spirit as promised.

Jesus pleads for us today when we are unfruitful. St. John writes, "If anybody does sin, we have one who speaks to the Father in our defense—Jesus Christ, the Righteous One. He is the atoning sacrifice for our sins, and not only for ours but also for the sins of the whole world" (1 John 2:1–2). What is more, Christ has sent—and still sends—His Holy Spirit to intercede for us "with groans that words cannot express" (Romans 8:26). We have two intercessors, Jesus and the Holy Spirit, to give us prayer support. "Hear me, for Thy Spirit pleads; Hear, for Jesus intercedes."

Prayer Suggestion

Express your thanks to the Lord Jesus for having redeemed you and for extending the time for you to be a fruitful Christian.

GOD GIVES US WHAT WE NEED

I will remove from them their heart of stone and give
them a heart of flesh. Ezekiel 11:19

A serious error was made when a heart patient in a St. Louis hospital was given the wrong heart. The patient had Type A blood, but the transplanted heart was Type B. Fortunately the patient was able to survive the error.

God, our heavenly Physician, makes no such mistakes. When we pray: "Create in me a clean heart, O God, and renew a right spirit within me," God the Holy Spirit gives us the kind of heart we need. What we ourselves are unable to do to meet our spiritual needs—and we know our inability—God can and will do, as He has promised through the prophet Ezekiel: "I will give you a new heart and put a new spirit in you" (36:26). He replaces the heart of stone with a heart of flesh.

This new heart is not a physical organ, such as beats in our chests. It stands for the human mind, soul, and spirit by which we are enabled to harbor and hold the saving faith that God grants through the Gospel (and, as a result of it, a warm, living heart of flesh).

Having given us the right kind of heart—a heart that trusts in the life-giving, forgiving, sin-atoning death of Jesus—God grants also the other spiritual gifts we need. Jesus has promised that the Father in heaven gives good gifts to those who ask Him. He is unlike such fathers who give their children a stone when they ask for bread or a snake when they request a fish (Matthew 7:9). This would be a cruelty far beyond the nature of our good and gracious Father in heaven.

We are like our divine Father and perfect Physician when we share God's blessings with others who need them and when we exercise great care to supply them with the right things they need. It helps very little—it may hurt, in fact—when we give a Type B gift instead of the needed Type A. Worse still is the giving of empty words when loving deeds are in order, such as saying, to quote St. James, "Go, I wish you will; keep warm and well fed," but then doing nothing about it (James 2:16).

God blesses His children so that they can be a blessing to others.

Prayer Suggestion

Ask God to create in you a clean heart and to renew a right spirit within you, for Jesus' sake.

IT TAKES TIME TO GROW

Fathers, do not exasperate your children; instead, bring them up in the training and instruction of the Lord. Ephesians 6:4

There is a time schedule, a hurried one, that is strictly for the birds. A scientific bird-watcher learned how quickly a pair of mourning doves can raise a family. Eggs that were laid on April 18 hatched on May 1. By May 14 the fledglings had left the nest. A few days later the parents started a new brood.

How fortunate we human beings have a longer childhood, to have more time with our parents and they with us! Of the childhood of Jesus it is said: "The child grew and became strong; He was filled with wisdom, and the grace of God was upon Him" (Luke 2:40). Other Bible versions say that He increased also in favor with people. His was a well-balanced, fourfold growth: physical, mental, social, and spiritual.

Our children should develop that way, and all of this takes time. Parents have to take the time not only to provide for the physical, educational, and social needs of their children, but also for *spiritual* growth. Birds and other creatures of God have no need for a spiritual life, but human beings do. As children they learn that Jesus loves them and gave His life for them. He did this to redeem them from sin, to make them the sons and daughters of God. They learn to pray, to please God with their life, to serve one another at home, in school, in church, and in the community.

In fact, we need to grow spiritually all of life, as St. Peter bids us: "Grow in the grace and knowledge of our Lord and Savior Jesus Christ" (2 Peter 3:18). We do this through Bible study, family and personal devotions, worship in church, and the use of the sacraments.

There are no shortcuts to the Christian upbringing of children. There are no 90-day wonders. It takes time and effort, but these are richly rewarded, to God's glory and the joy of parents.

Prayer Suggestion

Whether you are a parent or a child, ask God for the faith and wisdom you need to follow Jesus Christ throughout life.

CLEAN WATER

Whoever drinks the water I give him will never thirst.
John 4:14

How concerned we would be if we discovered that a sewage stream had broken out of its channel and had run right through our basement! We would say: "We don't want this germ-filled filth in our house. It endangers our health."

Yet such a river of spiritual filth can flow right into our living rooms through television—cable and regular. Bad enough that the lyrics of some radio songs border on pornographic or pornophonic! Bad enough that spiritual sewage comes through the mail, through books and magazines, even anonymous telephone calls! Now the complete medium of sound and sight, television, has the potential of becoming a channel of immoral materials and motivation to immorality. Not only open sex but also violence is involved. Someone has found that in prime time there are 1.7 crimes per TV show. Add immoral philosophy. A woman in a soap opera justifies her illicit relationship by saying: "I wouldn't feel this good if it weren't right!" And it is before their TV screens that people spend thousands of hours—some young people more hours there than in school.

What to do? Mere deploring gets us nowhere. It helps, of course, to voice one's objection to program sponsors. And it helps a lot to exercise one's choice, to have the self-discipline to turn off offensive programs.

But needed most of all is to have a clean river flowing through one's house. The psalmist says: "There is a river whose streams make glad the city of God" (Psalm 46:4). This is the stream of clean, clear living water flowing from the Word of God. The Holy Scripture is such a fountain because it is, as our children sing, the "Jesus Book": "Jesus loves me, this I know for the Bible tells me so." From Jesus comes the water of life which refreshes, quenches our spiritual thirst, and edifies. Jesus opened up this stream, which flows into our hearts and homes, when He gave His life for our redemption from sin and for continued renewal of life in Him. Is this stream refreshing your home?

Prayer Suggestion

Pray for God's help to keep your heart and home free from moral filth through the use of His Word as the water of life.

THE TURNAROUND OF FAITH

We were therefore buried with Him [Christ] through baptism into death in order that, just as Christ was raised from the dead through the glory of the Father, we too may live a new life. Romans 6:4

The *USS Constitution*, the historic frigate called Old Ironsides, is berthed in the Boston harbor. Once a year a ceremony is made of turning it around so it will wear evenly on both sides.

Human beings, too, need turning around. To stay in one position all the time is like being in a rut, and a rut, as someone has said, "is a grave with the ends kicked out." We travel, read good books, and make new friends to attain and maintain a well-balanced mind and personality. We could say it is good for our constitution when we weather evenly.

The Bible speaks of a much more important about face. It is called conversion. Different from outward reform of undesirable habits, it is a thorough-going change of heart, a remaking of the person from an enemy to a friend of God. Such a turnaround is the doing of the Holy Spirit, who through the Gospel—including the Gospel made visible in the water of Holy Baptism—gives people a new heart. As converts they rely altogether on the atoning merit and resurrection of Jesus Christ for their salvation.

Also, after conversion, we need to turn daily from sin to a life pleasing to God. The prophet Jeremiah prays according to the King James Version of the Bible: "Turn Thou me, and I shall be turned; for Thou art the Lord my God" (Jeremiah 31:18).

A striking example of a complete turnaround is Saul the Pharisee, who became St. Paul the Apostle. That event took place when he was converted to the Christian faith near Damascus. He urges a daily turning to God. He tells us to do this every day as we rise with Christ from the grave of sin and death to the newness of the life in Him.

Prayer Suggestion

Let it be your petition to the Holy Spirit to daily renew your faith in Jesus Christ, your Savior and Lord.

THE GOSPEL: FACT, NOT FICTION

*We did not follow cleverly invented stories when we told
you about the power and coming of our Lord Jesus Christ,
but we were eyewitnesses of His majesty. 2 Peter 1:16*

Fact and fiction marked the life of Brigadier General Lew Wallace. As for historical *fact*, he was involved in bloody battles of the Civil War. The *fiction* came to expression in his books, particularly in the historical novel *Ben Hur*, a best-seller of all time.

While fiction has its place in historical novels, it is not found in the one Book God wrote: the Bible. St. Peter writes: "We did not follow cleverly invented stories when we told you about the power and coming of our Lord Jesus Christ, but we were eyewitnesses of His majesty" (2 Peter 1:16).

The great acts of God for our salvation of which the Bible speaks—the birth of the Lamb of God offered for everyone's sins, His resurrection—all are historical events attested to by eyewitnesses, of whom Peter was one.

How can we be sure that in Christianity we are dealing not with fiction but with fact? Arguments will be of little help. Jesus suggests a better method, saying: "If anyone chooses to do God's will, he will find out whether My teaching comes from God" (John 7:17). Someone asked Coleridge, the English author: "Is Christianity true?" His simple reply was: "Try it!"

Yes, try it! Do God's will as made known in the Bible! Read, study, apply, and inwardly digest God's Word! Tell Christ that you need Him! As He gave His life for you, so give your life to Him. Have the courage to do this. Then you will be convinced—convinced by the Holy Spirit—that Christ's Gospel is the truth. You will find peace. Your life will be richly blest. No one can argue about this fact.

Prayer Suggestion

Invite the Holy Spirit into your heart that He may strengthen your conviction that Jesus is truly God's Son and your Savior.

FROM DOUBT TO FAITH

Thomas said to Him, "My Lord and My God!"
John 20:28

Doubt is often close to faith, as is rust to the finest steel. The psalmist momentarily doubted God's goodness to him when he "saw the prosperity of the wicked" (Psalm 73:3). The father of a demon-possessed child confessed to Jesus that he moved between two opposite poles: "I believe; help my unbelief" (Mark 9:24 RSV). Doubt often shakes the confidence we should have when we pray. So St. Paul wants us to lift up our hands in prayer "without wrath and doubting" (1 Timothy 2:8 KJV).

Doubt, along with outright denial, is part of the Easter story. At the mountaintop meeting in Galilee the disciples worshiped the risen Christ present there, "but some doubted" (Matthew 28:17).

Doubt afflicted Thomas especially. Weighed down with grief, he said, "Unless I see the nail marks in His hands and put my finger where the nails were, and put my hand into His side, I will not believe it" (John 20:25). To lay down a condition ("unless") is to declare incipient unbelief. To predicate truth on the sight test and touch test is to leave out faith entirely.

The risen Lord changed the heart of Thomas by ministering to him. He conferred His peace on him. He urged him: "Be not faithless, but believing" (John 20:27 KJV). And Thomas confessed, "My Lord and My God!" (John 20:28)

Some who are Christians today had to make the transition from doubt to firm faith. They may have had problems with the miracles recorded in the Bible, or with Christ's virgin birth, or with His resurrection from the dead. But as they searched the Scriptures diligently, they gained new perspectives. Christ became real to them as one who lives today. The Holy Spirit entered their hearts and said, "Let Me introduce you to Jesus, your Friend and Savior. He is for real." Then they were convinced and exclaimed, each personally: "My Lord and My God!"

Prayer Suggestion

Thank the risen Lord Jesus for sending His Holy Spirit into your heart to grant you strong faith.

THE SPIRIT'S DESCENT WITH POWER

You will receive power when the Holy Spirit comes on you.
Acts 1:8

The Holy Spirit, imparted to the church and its members through Word and sacraments, comes with a power that does not always manifest itself in the same way.

In a Pentecost hymn the church prays: "O gentle Dew, from heaven now fall With power upon the hearts of all, Thy tender love instilling" (*The Lutheran Hymnal* 235, v. 7). Dewdrops form and gentle raindrops fall silently with no spectacular display. Yet they have the power to bring seeds to life and make plants fruitful. So it is with the Spirit. He enters quietly when an infant is baptized, when in the privacy of a home some person takes God's Word to heart, when Christians grow a little each day and yield the fruit of the Spirit: "love, joy, peace, patience, kindness, goodness, faithfulness, gentleness and self-control" (Galatians 5:22).

But the Holy Spirit can demonstrate His power in another way—in very audible, visible, and tangible forcefulness. On Pentecost Day He descended with the sound of a rushing, house-shaking, mighty wind, and there was the sight of tongues of fire as the disciples preached the Gospel in many languages. What power! Pictures of the Pentecost sometimes show the Spirit as a dove descending in a "power dive," and that is exactly how it was. The Holy Spirit keeps open His options to descend and work on the church in that way today.

In whatever way He comes, His purpose is the same. Through the means of grace He leads people to the one faith in the one Lord Jesus Christ, for there is "one Lord, one faith, one baptism" (Ephesians 4:5).

Prayer Suggestion

Pray for a renewal of the Holy Spirit's power in the Christian church and all its members.

A Changed Contest

The God of peace will soon crush Satan under your feet.
Romans 16:20

Second in command during the bombardment of Fort Sumter, where the Civil War began, was Captain Abner Doubleday, who set off the first cannon shot. The same man is credited with inventing the game of baseball, a much more peaceful pursuit. Baseballs replaced cannonballs.

In ancient times swords and spears were used in warfare. The prophets Isaiah and Micah foretold the conversion of these weapons into tools for peaceful pursuits: "They will beat their swords into plowshares and their spears into pruning hooks. Nation will not take up sword against nation, nor will they train for war anymore" (Isaiah 2:4; Micah 4:3).

The truth of the matter is that since these words were written nations have developed much deadlier weapons of war. Yet the words of the prophets are truthful. God's Word is never spoken in vain. The message of God's great love for the world is a positive influence within and among the nations. Who can say how much worse worldly hostilities would be if no Gospel had ever been proclaimed?

The Gospel begins with God's peace in Jesus Christ. The spiritual warfare between a righteous God and a sinful, disobedient human race has ended. In Christ, who atoned for sin, God and sinners are reconciled. All who accept this forgiveness are changed persons. They now strive to serve God and work for peace in the world. Think of Saul the Pharisee, who once used the sword to kill Christians. After his conversion to St. Paul the apostle, he used the Word of God, the sword of the Spirit, to bring people to Christ. He and many others are the fulfillment of the prophecy: "They shall beat their swords into plowshares."

Abner Doubleday has taught us to use bats for hitting baseballs, not as clubs for killing people. The world will be a better place when more such changes occur.

Prayer Suggestion

Ask Christ to bless the preaching of the Gospel in the world so that peace—peace with God and peace with fellow human beings—may prevail.

GOD WORKS THROUGH MEANS

Faith comes from hearing the message, and the message is heard through the Word of Christ. Romans 10:17

The psalmist tells God: "The eyes of all look to You, and You give them their food at the proper time. You open Your hand and satisfy the desires of every living thing" (Psalm 145:15–16). People may wonder about this. Does God really appear on the scene to feed His creatures—human beings, animals, birds?

God does indeed provide, but He generally does it through means. We can learn this from observing a pair of finches. While the female bird sits on the nest and incubates the eggs, the male brings her food. Later the nestlings will be fed by the parent birds. God has written this instinct into the birds so that they do His work in providing for each other.

In the book of Job the question is asked: "Who provides food for the raven when its young cry out to God?" (38:41) The psalmist (Psalm 147:9) gives this answer: "He [God] provides food for the cattle and for the young ravens when they call." God does it through the bounty of nature—through the grasses and grains and through His helpers: parents who provide for the young.

That is how God provides for you and me. He works through means. Yes, He could do it through astounding miracles, as when He fed the Israelites with manna from heaven or as when Jesus fed the multitudes miraculously. But even in the latter case our Lord used means: bread and fish.

In our lives God likewise provides for us by giving us sunshine and rain, strength and health so that we can work. He gives us fathers and mothers and other persons as His agents. They provide for us in His behalf: It is God who gives us daily bread and other blessings.

God works through means to feed also our souls. He nourishes us spiritually through His Word, through the Gospel of Christ's redemption. The Gospel is the power of God for salvation to all who believe it. God speaks through it. Are you listening?

Prayer Suggestion

Thank God for daily bread and all the blessings He provides.

THE NAZARENE IN NAIN

[Jesus] said, "Young man, I say to you, get up!"
Luke 7:14

Nazareth and Nain are only about five miles apart. Jesus the Nazarene may have been personally acquainted with the widow whose only son was being carried to his grave.

The Nazarene comes to Nain as a *true man*—one who in human compassion tells the mother, "Do not weep." Because of His true human nature He can "sympathize with our weaknesses" (Hebrews 4:15) because He in every respect experienced life's ups and downs, its joys and sorrows, even death itself. He differs from us only in that He is sinless.

The Nazarene comes to Nain also as *true God*. This means: He can do more than offer condolences because, to use William Cullen Bryant's expression, "a youth in life's green spring" has been claimed by death; He can remove the cause for sorrow by raising the widow's son from death, for Jesus Christ is the Lord of life and death.

Our Lord overcame death on that day when, outside Jerusalem's walls, another widowed mother, Mary, saw her Son taken away by death on a cross. But He was to rise again by the same power that raised the youth at Nain from death. Thus the Nazarene, who is true man and true God, "destroyed death and has brought life and immortality to light" (2 Timothy 1:10).

Jesus approaches us today in places small and great: in towns and townships, in cities and communities. He comes through the Word and the sacraments, sending also His Holy Spirit through them. And when He comes, He brings blessings, as He Himself declares, "I stand at the door and knock. If anyone hears My voice and opens the door, I will come in and eat with him, and he with Me" (Revelation 3:20).

Prayer Suggestion

Extend a prayerful invitation to Jesus to come into your heart and home with the gifts you need.

SOARING ON EAGLES' WINGS

*[God] satisfies your desires with good things so that your
youth is renewed like the eagle's. Psalm 103:5*

In certain times of the year people go to Clarksville, Missouri, on
the Mississippi River, to see the flock of bald eagles gathered there.
They bring along field glasses to see better. But the eagles, sharp-eyed,
need no such equipment.

Besides their good sight, the Bible ascribes other qualities to
eagles: the strength of their wings, the swiftness of flight, the renewal
of vigor, the attainment of old age. All this was known also to the
ancient Romans who chose the *aquila*, the eagle, as a symbol on the
standards of their legions.

Through Moses, God reminded His people: "You yourselves have
seen what I did to Egypt, and how I carried you on eagles' wings and
brought you to Myself" (Exodus 19:4). It was as though God had used
eagles as His air force to deliver His people from bondage.

The goodness of God to individual persons is described in Psalm
103 in these terms: "He satisfies your desires with good things so that
your youth is renewed like the eagle's" (v. 5). The reference is probably to an eagle renewing its life through molting.

What people have perhaps most admired about eagles is their ability to soar majestically at high altitudes. They rise high above the
earthly scene and direct our sight to heaven above. This may be the
reason why St. John's gospel is symbolized by an eagle. Someone has
said, "From first to last his gospel soars on eagles' wings to the throne
of heaven." With what loftier note and soaring power could St. John
have begun his testimony of Jesus than this one: "In the beginning was
the Word, and the Word was with God, and the Word was God" (John
1:1)? Grace and truth, the love of God bringing salvation, forgiveness,
eternal life—this comes to us through Jesus Christ, the Son of God
offered on Calvary's cross for our sins.

Believing in Jesus as God's eternal Word enables us to soar like
eagles on the wings of faith.

Prayer Suggestion

Ask the Holy Spirit to give you strong wings of prayer and faith in
Jesus so that you can soar above the problems of life.

LEARNING LIFE'S LESSONS

Let us love one another, for love comes from God.
1 John 4:7

In Harper Lee's novel *To Kill a Mockingbird* we admire little Jean Louise Finch, nicknamed "Scout," the six-year-old daughter of Atticus Finch, an attorney in a southern town. She learns that the larger world with its prejudices is not as innocent as her own little world.

We all make this discovery as we emerge from our childhood homes and enter the ever larger circles of life. Our parents help us make these almost daily adjustments to the world. We learn that we not only receive but also give, that friendliness will in most cases be rewarded with friendliness. We learn the lessons of sharing, of cooperating, or rolling with the punches, of having to live with people of different beliefs and backgrounds. In many of life's situations it is proper to yield, to go fifty-fifty, to be satisfied with half a loaf instead of having no bread at all.

But we learn also that in some issues we have to stand firm and not make concessions. These are the moral and spiritual things of which God has spoken in His Word. The Ten Commandments are our guide for a moral life. They do not budge, although many try to set them aside. As for our Christian faith, no compromise is possible. We cannot cut the Gospel in two, as though we could rely partly on Christ's redemption and partly on our good works to be right with God. We are expected to be consistent in our acknowledgment of Christ as our Savior, confessing Him not only before friends but also our enemies. As Christians we are called to be wholehearted in our love to Jesus, doing this not only in church on Sundays but also on weekdays. If we love Jesus, we also love our brothers and sisters, whom He loves and for whom He died.

The world in which we live is not consistently good. It often does worse than to kill a mockingbird. So it is up to Christians to walk a straight mile in a crooked world.

Prayer Suggestion

Ask God for the courage to stand up for what is true and for the strength to confess Jesus before the world.

RIGHT THOUGHTS, RIGHT DEEDS

When He, the Spirit of truth, comes, He will guide you into all truth. John 16:13

In a Sunday prayer the worshipers ask God that "by Your holy inspiration we may think the things that are right and by Your merciful guidance accomplish them" (Collect for the Third Sunday after Pentecost).

We have always known that in everyday life right doing follows right thinking. If you think you must go ten miles west and five miles north to reach your destination, then that is what you are going to do. If a golfer has wrong ideas about the game, he will make wrong shots.

Terrible things have been done in the name of religion because people had the wrong thoughts. "A time is coming," said Jesus to His disciples, "when anyone who kills you will think he is offering a service to God" (John 16:2). An example of this is St. Paul, who as Saul the Pharisee persecuted Christians because he thought this was God's will.

How necessary that we, led by the Holy Spirit, devote ourselves to right learning, right knowing, and right thinking so that there can be Spirit-led believing, followed by right doing! Knowledge and faith go together like horse and carriage. We need to know that in love for all mankind God gave His Son, Jesus Christ, as an offering for sin and then to believe that God so loved *me*.

Right knowing and believing then result in right doing. True faith always bears fruit: good works. God's people acknowledge that the weakness of sin is still in them, that often there is a slip between the cup and the lip, that wanting to do the right thing doesn't always lead to doing it. So they ask for God's help, namely, that by His guidance they may accomplish their God-pleasing thoughts, plans, and resolutions. God answers that prayer. He strengthens His people through Word and Sacrament to do His will. The kingdom of God grows when right thoughts are translated into right deeds.

Prayer Suggestion

Implore the Holy Spirit to implant His truth in your heart and mind and then to help you carry it out.

THE WAY TO LIFE

The wages of sin is death, but the gift of God is eternal life in Christ Jesus our Lord. Romans 6:23

A construction company repairing bridges and roads at Arcadia, Missouri, put up a sign of its own that said: "Slow Down or Die." The state highway department called it "irregular," that is, different from the kind of warning signs it puts up.

It is all too true that many highway deaths are caused by excessive speed and the lack of caution.

In all of life some people die because they don't slow down in their work, their energy-draining lifestyle, or their use of alcohol and drugs. The message to them, in plain words, is: "Slow Down or Die."

The same applies to our spiritual life, so often beset by sin. The prophet Ezekiel states: "The soul that sins shall die" (18:20 RSV). Nothing is said that it is not only accelerated sinning that brings death; slow, infrequent sinning does the same. This includes all of us. The warning sign of God's law is very plain on this.

So we need another sign—the sign of the Gospel. It declares: Because Jesus died, you live. Because He rose again, you can rise daily from the tomb of spiritual sin and death, and you will on the Last Day take part in the bodily resurrection. Because the Holy Spirit comes to you through the Gospel, you have faith. That is good news, and how you rejoice to hear it, see it, and read it as you journey through life!

Someone traveling on a highway saw a sign at a church that read: "The wages of sin is death." He mused to himself that such a church message was incomplete—it could give people the wrong impression of Christianity. On his return trip he read what was written on the other side of the sign, namely: "But the gift of God is eternal life." This was the second part of the quotation from Romans 6:23. This is the message of the Gospel.

As we travel through life, we need both signs—the one that says: "If you keep on sinning, you'll die," and the other one, too: "Believe on the Lord Jesus Christ and you will live."

Prayer Suggestion

Thank the Holy Spirit for giving you the life in Christ and for keeping you in the faith through the Gospel.

Running the Race of Faith

Let us run with perseverance the race marked out for us.
Hebrews 12:1

The Bible compares day-by-day living of the Christian faith to an endurance race. The apostle Paul writes: "Do you not know that in a race all the runners run, but only one gets the prize? Run in such a way as to get the prize" (1 Corinthians 9:24). Elsewhere in the New Testament we read: "Let us run with perseverance the race marked out for us" (Hebrews 12:1).

There is a right and a wrong way to run the religious race. The right way includes that we prepare for it, be aware of the obstacles and overcome them, and run with persistence to the finish line. The wrong way is to make a good start but then drop out. Also, it doesn't help if one gets into the wrong lane—one in which one's spiritual life is foolishly endangered by spills and thrills.

In the world of sports there are races like that—perilous, purposeless, dangerously opportunistic. There are contests such as the running of the bulls in Pomplona, Spain. Men and boys run with the bulls through the streets. Many get hurt. The occasion for this mayhem, San Fermin's festival, began in 1591. Since then 52 men have been gored to death.

In the race of Christian faith and life it is to no purpose—it is hazardous, in fact—to expose oneself foolishly to Satan and the temptations of a sinful world. It is asking for trouble.

But it is asking for and receiving divine assistance when we look to Jesus, the Author and Finisher, the Pioneer and Perfecter of our faith. In our behalf He finished His course all the way to Calvary's cross. When we believe in Him as Savior and ask His help, we will receive strength to stay in the race until its victorious conclusion. The Spirit of Pentecost keeps us in the faith through the means of grace: Word and Sacrament.

Prayer Suggestion

Make your plea to God to strengthen you through His Word so that you may complete the race of faith in Jesus, your Savior.

GETTING A SECOND LIFE

I have been reminded of your sincere faith, which first
lived in grandmother Lois and in your mother Eunice.
2 Timothy 1:5

When a three-year-old boy from the Ukraine had received normal vision through a cornea transplant in the United States, his mother exclaimed, "My son was given a second life, and I with him."

It is not a surprising statement since, under normal circumstances, the lives of parents are closely linked to those of their children. Whatever brings true joy and hope to children is of utmost delight to the parents also. The reverse is also true: Fathers and mothers suffer when evil befalls their offspring.

We find examples of mothers in the Bible who rejoiced over their sons—Hannah, for example, was happy to bring young Samuel to God's house that he might learn to serve the Lord (1 Samuel 1:21–28). And those two widows whose sons were restored to life—the mother in Zarephath with whom Elijah stayed (1 Kings 17:17–24) and the one in Nain whose son Jesus raised to life (Luke 7:11–17)—surely felt that they, too, had received a second life.

Perhaps the prime biblical example of a close union between mother and son is that of Eunice and Timothy. The apostle Paul tells Timothy that his sincere faith "first lived in your grandmother Lois and in your mother Eunice" (2 Timothy 1:5). Later in his letter he declares that young Timothy had known the Holy Scriptures from infancy. Who had taught him? Not his father, for he was an unconverted Greek. Yes, the grandmother helped, but it was mostly Eunice. She began early to instruct him in what the Scriptures taught—that salvation comes through faith in Jesus Christ, the promised Messiah, who died for our sins and rose again. In later years St. Paul further taught Timothy, but the initial credit goes to Eunice, an otherwise unknown woman living in an area that is now Turkey.

It remains true: When anything good comes to children, mothers rejoice with them. It is as though both had received a second life.

Prayer Suggestion

Speak words of thanks to God for the gift of your mother and, if she is still living, thank her also.

PRAYING PARENTS

*In the course of time Hannah conceived and gave birth to
a son. 1 Samuel 1:20*

By an act of Congress in 1988, the first Thursday in May was
declared as National Day of Prayer. Traditionally the second Sunday in
May is observed as Mother's Day. The two occasions are close together, not only on the calendar but also as to content and intent. Prayer
and parenthood are related topics.

Hannah, the mother of the prophet Samuel, is well known for her
prayers, both for her petition and her thanksgiving. In the temple she
asked God for a son, and God gave her one. After the son was born,
Hannah was back in the temple, where she spoke a prayer of thanksgiving as recorded in chapter two of 1 Samuel. It was a prayer that
surely served as a model for the Magnificat, the prayer of praise Mary
spoke when the angel Gabriel announced that she would be the virgin
mother of the promised Christ.

Fervent payer and faithful motherhood go together like a hand and
glove. One can speak of the two topics in the same breath. Hannah
and Mary were good mothers, largely because they were diligent in
prayer and taught their sons how to pray, one of them, the Son of God,
had become a human child. Again, St. Paul told young Timothy, "I want
men [people] everywhere to lift up holy hands in prayer" (1 Timothy
2:8). Timothy was able to teach his parishioners how to pray because
he himself had learned prayer from his mother Eunice and his grandmother Lois.

Mary's Son, nailed to a cross as a sacrifice for the sin of the world,
died with a prayer on His lips: "Father into Your hands I commit My
spirit" (Luke 23:46). He had previously committed His mother to the
care of the apostle John. He is our Exemplar on both counts: prayer
and parental concern. We follow in His footsteps when we honor
father and mother and when we faithfully cultivate the art of prayer.

Prayer Suggestion

After Hannah's example, ask God for blessings you need and thank
Him for those already granted.

THE CLAY THAT COUNTS
FOR SOMETHING

We have this treasure in jars of clay to show that this all-surpassing power is from God and not from us.
2 Corinthians 4:7

Clay, as the expression "feet of clay" indicates, is a material not as permanent and precious as gold, silver, bronze, or other metals. Yet much can be done with it, depending on the artist or artisan who works with it.

Often mentioned in the Bible is the potter, a follower of an ancient craft and the creator of vessels, both artistic and practical. St. Paul asks: "Does not the potter have the right to make out of the same lump of clay some pottery for noble purposes and some for common use?" (Romans 9:21) The apostle's point is this: We cannot dictate to God, nor quarrel with Him, for the way He has made us.

Human beings, on the physical side, are creatures of clay, for they are the descendants of Adam, whose body God formed from the dust of the ground. To bodies of clay God added living souls, minds that think, hearts that love. These talents of mind and spirit God, the divine Potter, did not distribute to each in the same quantity and quality. As Creator He reserves the right to provide us with personal gifts as He wills. The result is that God created a human race for multiple, mutual service.

We know that clay has many uses. Known as kaolin in China, it is used for exquisite chinaware, for pottery, and for porcelain. But it is also used in rubber, plastics, textiles, paper, pencils, insulation, medicine, paints, and so forth. How versatile it is! And so are human beings because God has so variously endowed them.

This principle of varied usefulness especially applies to Christians, who are the eyes, ears, tongues, hands, feet, and other members of the body of Christ. By serving one another, they serve Christ, who, by His shed blood, redeemed them.

Should we despise common clay? Not for a minute, for look what God has done with it and still does!

Prayer Suggestion

Praise your Maker for the talents and opportunities He has given you to serve Jesus Christ, your Savior.

HELP FOR OUR PRAYERS

The Spirit helps us in our weakness. We do not know what we ought to pray for, but the Spirit Himself intercedes for us. Romans 8:26

Christians have the Father in heaven to care for them. They have also the Son of God to make intercession for them, as St. John writes: "We have one who speaks to the Father in our defense—Jesus Christ the Righteous One. He is the atoning sacrifice for our sins, and not only for ours but also for the sins of the whole world" (1 John 2:1–2).

There is still another, the Holy Spirit, who not only prays *for* us but also *with* us. While Christ intercedes in heaven, the Spirit intercedes in our hearts.

Someone has written: "You might say the Holy Spirit performs a type of editing service on prayers." In a publishing house an editor helps the author in making the message of his manuscript more effective and clear. An editor doesn't do the work for the author; he *helps* him or her.

We learn from Holy Scripture that the Holy Spirit intercedes for us "with groans that words cannot express" (Romans 8:26). A hymn stanza explains: The Spirit "can plead for me with sighings That are unspeakable to lips like mine; He bids me pray with earnest cryings, Bears witness with my soul that I am Thine."

St. Paul declares: The Spirit is in prayer partnership with us. He takes hold on the other end. The picture is of someone who helps us carry a heaven burden or move a piece of furniture by taking hold on the other end.

Often we don't know how to pray and for what to ask. The Spirit teaches us. He whispers the answer in our heart. Our prayers may be weak; the Spirit, like a booster station, sends them on. He takes our groans, sighs, brief prayer fragments, our "Abba, Father" (Galatians 4:6), and conveys them to the heavenly Father in our behalf.

Prayer Suggestion

Implore the Holy Spirit to teach you what to pray for and to lend support to your petitions in Jesus' name.

GOLD IS WHERE YOU FIND IT

When Jesus had entered Capernaum, a centurion came to Him, asking for help. Matthew 8:5

An artist has pictured the Roman centurion of Capernaum with his helmet under his arm to indicate his humility. He is humbly asking for Jesus' help in behalf of his sick slave.

A centurion was an officer in the Roman army, normally commanding 100 men. Four centurions are referred to in the New Testament: the one stationed in Capernaum, the centurion under Jesus' cross, Cornelius of Caesarea, and Julius, who conducted St. Paul and other prisoners to Rome. The first three were believers, and of Julius it is said that he "treated Paul kindly" (Acts 27:3 RSV), gave him special privileges, and later saved his life. He, too, may have been—or later became—a Christian. It may strike us as unusual to find officers of the Roman army as followers of Jesus.

It is not possible to predict who will or will not accept the Gospel of salvation in Christ. Sometimes faith is found in the most illogical, unexpected persons: the thief on the cross, the jailer in Philippi, Saul the Pharisee, who was "breathing threats and murder against the disciples of the Lord" (Acts 9:1 RSV). The gold of faith, like the precious metal, is where you find it—in unusual persons, often in surprising places.

So the Christian church preaches the Gospel "to every creature" (Colossians 1:23) without distinction, leaving it to the Holy Spirit to perform the miracle of conversion. It is not necessary to look for outstanding examples of persons who came to the saving faith. You and I are cases in point. While we were yet sinners—while we were dead in sin—Christ died for us. We are all walking miracles of the grace of God.

Prayer Suggestion

Declare your gratefulness to God for having found you and brought you to the saving faith in Christ.

WINNING FOR JESUS

Do you not know that in a race all the runners run, but only one gets the prize? 1 Corinthians 9:24

What is Christian preaching when stated in gymnastic or athletic terms? Someone has said, "It is a spiritual locker-room address in which a spiritual coach asks a spiritual team to be ready to go out there and win one for Jesus."

One's first impression might be that it is improper to drag in sports when referring to religion. Yet this is the very thing the apostle Paul did in chapter 9 of 1 Corinthians. There he discusses the length to which he will go—and to what extent he will exercise his Christian freedom—to win people for Christ. He writes, "I have become all things to all men so that by all possible means I might save some" (v. 22). He says it is his desire to "win those not having the Law [Gentiles]" (v. 21), as well as those under the Law—Jews.

For the apostle to be all things to all people for the sake of the saving Gospel of Jesus Christ requires considerable effort. He has to exercise and train. In this connection he comes to speak of himself as an athlete getting ready for the Greek games. He proposes to run and to box for a purpose: to "share the prize," namely the crown of everlasting life with all who will believe the Gospel. He knows that his own efforts will not accomplish this. But he will get it done nevertheless, for God's powerful and appealing grace is made perfect in Paul's human weakness.

As Christians we are members of Christ's church. We are all His disciples and witnesses, His performers in the arena of Christian living. With St. Paul—and with the person quoted at the beginning—we want to go out there and win one for Jesus. We keep our eyes fixed on Jesus, "who for the joy set before Him endured the cross, scorning its shame, and sat down at the right hand of the throne of God" (Hebrews 12:2).

Prayer Suggestion

Prayerfully request the Holy Spirit's guidance to gain souls for Christ through the Gospel.

FRUITBEARING CHRISTIANS

You also died to the law ... that you might belong to another, to Him who was raised from the dead, in order that we might bear fruit to God. Romans 7:4

Fig trees are often mentioned in the Bible. Quite frequently they are used as illustrations of people. For one thing, young fig trees have to be carefully cultivated if they are to develop properly and bear fruit. So it is with human beings. Careful, Christ-centered training of children is necessary if they are to mature into fruitbearing Christians.

In a well-known parable Jesus speaks of a man who had planted a fig tree in his vineyard, expecting it to bear fruit. Our Lord was acquainted not only with orchards but also with vineyards, where grapes were grown. In John 15:5, again with emphasis on fruitfulness, He declares the source: "I am the Vine; you are the branches. If a man remains in Me and I in him, he will bear much fruit."

In Jesus' Sermon on the Mount mention is made of a fig tree as illustrative of people. There our Lord referred to a consistency: Figs grow on fig trees, not on thistles. He declared that the fruit of a tree is consistent with its nature, saying: "Every good tree bears good fruit" (Matthew 7:17). Applying this principle to people, He said: Know the prophets, preachers, and religious teachers by their public teachings and actions, checking whether they are consistent with the written Word of God. Know also other people—preachers or not—by their fruits, for they are the index to character.

The Holy Spirit enables us to be fruitbearing Christians. Through the Gospel He calls us to faith in Jesus Christ, causing us to rely entirely on His atoning sacrifice for salvation. He enables us to be like good trees yielding the fruit of the Spirit: love, joy, peace, righteousness, and whatever else is truly good.

Prayer Suggestion

Request that the Holy Spirit may deepen your faith in Jesus Christ and thus make you a fruitbearing Christian.

THE ANGELS WERE IN ON IT

They were looking intently up into the sky as He was going, when suddenly two men dressed in white stood beside them. Acts 1:10

In 1992 Eric Clapton won the Grammy Award with his recorded song *Tears in Heaven*. He composed it after his 4-year old son had fallen to his death from an apartment building in New York City.

Christian parents who lose children through accidents or sickness can assuage their grief with the assurance that their little ones, on earth and in heaven, have "their angels" (Matthew 18:10) to attend to them—high-ranking angels, so Jesus stresses, who "always see the face of My Father in heaven."

Not tears but great joy attended the heavenly homecoming of God's own Son, the exalted Jesus. Participating in the joyful celebration were angels and archangels with all the company of heaven, also with the throne angels (the cherubim and the seraphim). They rejoiced because the Son of God, become man, had fulfilled His mission on earth and could now return in triumph. All along, when in all eternity the heavenly Father planned the salvation of sinful mankind, and also when at the fullness of the time the Son came to earth to die and to rise again, angels were concerned. The apostle writes that with the preaching of the Gospel "by the Holy Spirit sent from heaven," angels had longed "to look into these things" (1 Peter 1:12). The Greek verb implies that they leaned forward and strained themselves to catch a glimpse of what God was doing to save mankind.

There was joy also on earth when Jesus ascended into heaven. St. Luke reports that the disciples "worshiped Him and returned to Jerusalem with great joy" (Luke 24:52). For Jesus it was "mission accomplished"; for them it was "mission to be accomplished." And not only the angels and apostles but also we rejoice at the Son's heavenly homecoming. In heaven Jesus intercedes for us and with His grace governs His church.

Prayer Suggestion

Address the Son of God with words of praise and thanksgiving for having completed His work of redemption and for His intercession.

GOD WANTS YOUNG AND OLD

I write to you, dear children, because you have known the Father. 1 John 2:13

Sometimes a public notice—or any statement for that matter—can imply more than what is intended. At the entrance of a park in St. Louis is a sign that says: "Bicycles and dogs not allowed." Since bicycles and dogs cannot read, the message is obviously addressed to people—to the youngsters who ride bicycles and to the elderly who walk their dogs.

What a pity it would be to ban the young and the elderly from any part of our world—not only parks but other parts of the community as well! Could this ever happen? Some think a beginning has been made on this score. Millions of children are annually banished when they are denied birth and become the victims of abortion. And in some societies, mostly primitive ones, the next in line to yield their places to other, more productive persons are the elderly. It can happen nowadays in socially advanced lands. The gas furnaces in concentration camps of a once cultured and civilized country testify to what can be done to unwanted people when merciless tyrants gain control.

When a country considers babies and senior citizens superfluous, it is on its deathbed. Without children, the population has no future. Without the elderly, it has no past, no memory, no wisdom on which to build the present.

God wants all people to be His people. His Son, Jesus Christ, gave His life so that all may have life: the young, who have many years ahead of them; the aging with many years behind them; and those in the middle. This Savior declares: "Let the little children come to Me"(Matthew 19:14)—come to Him through Holy Baptism and kept with Him through instruction in the Gospel. God says to those on the other end of the rainbow: "Even to your old age and grey hairs I am He, I am He who will sustain you" (Isaiah 46:4). And to all Jesus says: "Come to Me, all you who are weary and burdened, and I will give you rest" (Matthew 11:28).

Back to the sign: "Bicycles and dogs not allowed." There have to be regulations, and these should be observed. But you, children and the elderly, come one and all! Come to Christ!

Prayer Suggestion

Ask God to make you an instrument to befriend young and old, and to be the middle person to lead them to Christ.

CLOSING THE COMMUNICATION GAP

Faith comes from hearing the message, and the message is heard through the Word of Christ. Romans 10:17

Thanks to our highly efficient news media, we are living in an age of instant communication. Events abroad can be televised and seen locally by means of communication satellites stationed in space. The world has become an intimate whispering gallery. And yet much information does not get through. We call it a communication gap.

Communication gaps are a hindrance to the propagation of the Good News. Somehow the Word does not get around as it once did. "You have filled Jerusalem with your teaching" (Acts 5:28), said the members of the high council accusingly to the apostles. No communication gap there! Time and again the book of Acts reports at key points in its mission story, "The Word of God grew and multiplied" (Acts 12:24 RSV).

Yet beyond Jerusalem, Judea, and Samaria lay a big world where millions of heathen lived, and most of them had not heard the Gospel of Jesus Christ crucified and risen again for everyone's redemption from sin and death. St. Paul did his utmost to close this communication gap as he traveled through the Roman Empire as a messenger whom the Lord had sent "far away to the Gentiles" (Acts 22:21). But a gap remained.

In Romans chapter 10 St. Paul asks a series of questions bearing on the communication gap in the Gospel proclamation: "How, then, can they call on the One they have not believed in? And how can they believe in the One of whom they have not heard? And how can they hear without someone preaching to them? And how can they preach unless they are sent?" (vv. 14–15)

To take the apostle's questions in reverse order, the communication gap in the telling of God's Good News is closed when we send missionaries into all the world, when these missionaries faithfully preach the Gospel, when the Holy Spirit leads believers to call on the name of the Lord. Locally, there may be a communication gap because we do not witness to our Lord at home, in school, at work, and in our communities. We begin to close that gap when we, in St. Peter's words, are "ready always to give an answer to every man that asketh you a reason of the hope that is in you" (1 Peter 3:15 KJV).

Prayer Suggestion

Ask God to help you lead a godly life so that your example may prompt people to inquire about the Christian faith.

Skills for Christian Service

Huram was highly skilled and experienced in all kinds of bronze work. 1 Kings 7:14

A man who was trained as a bookbinder stated that 41 steps were involved in binding a book. Every vocation calls for special skills. Technology cannot entirely replace handcrafts.

In person-to-person relationships special social skills are still necessary. No machine can render the human touch. Science cannot invent a surrogate mother, for example, an automaton or robot, that can do what a loving mother so skillfully does: give tender, loving care to a baby, help keep the family together, and take an interest in what her children do.

To be an effective Christian requires skills. In His love God grants talents to us, and in His wisdom He gives them to each one, "Just as He determines" (1 Corinthians 12:11). Several times St. Paul enumerates such special talents and endowments that Christians have. These skills are to be used for the good of all, for the edification of Christ's body, the church.

God wants us to develop the talents He has given us. They are a good foundation on which to build a life of service to God's glory and the good of others. The shepherd boy, David, practiced his skills as a musician and poet, and he became a great psalmist. Helping to build Solomon's beautiful temple was a man named Huram-Abi, who was "trained to work in gold and silver, bronze and iron, stone and wood, and with purple and blue and crimson yarn and fine linen" (2 Chronicles 2:14). Also gifted for performing skillful Christian services was Dorcas of Joppa (now part of Tel-Aviv), who sewed garments for the poor.

What skills can you sharpen to become a more competent Christian servant?

Prayer Suggestion

Ask the Lord's help to refine and sharpen your skills and to grant you spiritual graces for service.

THE HOMECOMING THAT PRECEDES OURS

While [Jesus] was blessing them, He left them and was taken up into heaven. Luke 24:51

Homecoming is usually a happy occasion. It is that for college alumni returning to their alma mater, for family members reunited after an absence, for persons who completed their assignments and can come home again. A well-known song from the Civil War era expresses happiness at the thought of a soldier's homecoming. A hearty welcome awaits him: "The church bell will peal with joy; the laurel [wreath] is ready now to grace his loyal brow."

There was joy when the Son of God, having completed His work on earth, returned home in triumph. Jesus' ascension, 40 days after His resurrection, marked His heavenly homecoming. St. Paul wrote of it: "He who descended is the very one who ascended higher than all the heavens, in order to fill the whole universe" (Ephesians 4:10). He, the Maker of all things, now resumed His throne in heaven to rule the universe. Sitting at the Father's right hand, He especially governs and protects the church, of which He is the Head.

But our Lord's ascension was more than a homecoming. This event was to have a sequel. Before He left, He promised to return, saying: "If I go to prepare a place for you, I will come back and take you to be with Me that you also may be where I am" (John 14:3). That place, He explained, is His Father's house of many rooms. On the mount of the ascension the angel repeated the promise: "This same Jesus, who has been taken from you into heaven, will come back in the same way you have seen Him go into heaven" (Acts 1:11). That "same way" is not only a visible return, but also one in power and great glory. The Savior's homecoming occasioned joy both in heaven and on earth. We are told that the disciples "returned to Jerusalem with great joy" (Luke 24:52). They continually praised God, both at the temple and in the Upper Room, awaiting the coming of the Holy Spirit. For us, too, the ascension is a festival of joy. We are happy over Jesus' triumph and for His promise to come back to take us home.

Prayer Suggestion

Thank the Lord for the home in which you now live. Thank Him also for your eternal home that has been prepared for you by Christ.

CHRIST'S PEOPLE, LIKE ROSES

A servant girl named Rhoda came to answer the door.
Acts 12:13

A far cry from the celebrated "roses of Picardy," mentioned in a popular song of yesteryear, are the wild roses found in fields and pastures. Yet they have a natural beauty of their own. The American composer Edward MacDowell was moved to name a piano solo after them.

To some, the wild rose is a weed. It grows low to the ground. Its stem is prickly, its thorns reminding us of what God said to Adam after the fall into sin: "It [the ground] will produce thorns and thistles for you" (Genesis 3:18). Of course, the curse of sin was really a curse on the sinner, for disobedience of God draws punishment, the ultimate wages of sin being death.

Human beings are by nature like wild roses. Totally sinful, they still retain some of the qualities that are good and useful for life in this world. The person of dissolute character may have talent for the arts and sciences. Then you say: "Think what such a person could be and do if moral and spiritual uprightness went along with talent! He would be a wild rose become an American Beauty!"

As a matter of fact, that is what God has in mind when He causes the Gospel to be proclaimed in the world. For the Gospel is "the power of God for the salvation of everyone who believes" (Romans 1:16). Those who have come to faith in Jesus Christ as their liberator from sin and the fear of death are an entirely new creation. They are like prickly weeds turned into lovely roses.

Such changes have taken place in Christians from earliest times. It took place in the servant girl in Jerusalem named Rhoda, or Rose, who recognized Peter's voice and let him into the house. Yes, also servants can be beautiful roses in God's sight. They can, in Isaiah's words, cause the desert to rejoice and "blossom as the rose" (Isaiah 35:1 KJV)—this by the power of Him who has been called the Rose of Sharon, our beautiful Savior, Jesus Christ.

Prayer Suggestion

In prayer seek Christ's help to grow more like Him in the beauty of life.

DESTINATION AND DIRECTIONS

I have told you these things, so that in Me you may have peace. John 16:33

In His farewell conversation, John 14–16, Jesus is preparing His disciples for His imminent departure through death's door. He speaks words of comfort to them. For the orphaned disciples, life would be like a difficult journey traversing "field and fountain, moor and mountain" and finally leading through the valley of the shadow of death.

But the journey is worthwhile, for it has a glorious *destination*. The goal toward which they are striving is not anything in this world. It is not what man's hands can build—the kind of houses people want today and already wanted in the time of Amos (3:15): "winter house," "summer house," "houses adorned with ivory," "mansions." The destination is the Father's house of many mansions. To come face to face with our Father in heaven—that is also our goal.

But it would be purposeless for Jesus to point to the destination if He didn't also give us the *direction* for getting there. What road must His disciples follow to reach their destination? Jesus is specific: "I am the Way and the Truth and the Life" (John 14:6). This is one of many "I am" passages in John's gospel, showing that Jesus equated Himself with the Lord who revealed Himself to Moses as "I AM WHO I AM" (Exodus 3:14). Jesus is the Way, the only road leading to the Father, and all who believe in Him have found the way. He is the Truth, the Revealer of the true God and of His good and gracious will for our salvation. He is the Life, the Giver of eternal life beginning here and now and reaching its fullness in heaven.

Destination and direction for getting there—heaven and faith in Christ—that is why the Savior came.

Prayer Suggestion

Express your gratitude for Christ's coming to be our Savior.

"Chasing" the Good Life

*I do not understand what I do. For what I want to do
I do not do, but what I hate I do. Romans 7:15*

Sometimes children, because of language problems, recite their own versions of Bible passages. In a confirmation instruction class a boy said, "There is one God and one equator between God and men, the man Christ Jesus"—his version of 1 Timothy 2:5. (He substituted "equator" for "Mediator.") A little girl quoted Romans 8:31 as follows: "If God isn't for us, we are up against it." A third gave Martin Luther's explanation of the Sixth Commandment: "lead a chaste and decent life" as "chase a decent life." In all three instances, truth was told, although with garbled texts.

As for the third instance, it cannot be stressed enough that real effort has to be put forth to lead a pure sexual life inside and outside of marriage. It has to be pursued and "chased." The psalmist (34:14) urges, "Turn from evil and do good; seek peace and pursue it."

Even so dedicated a Christian as St. Paul had all he could do to "chase a decent life," saying: "What I want to do I do not do, but what I hate I do" (Romans 7:15). This came about because an evil force, aided and abetted by the Law, was at work in him. It opposed the "new self" engendered in Him by the new birth in Christ. In another passage (Philippians 3:12) he confesses, "Not that I have already attained all this [the total renewal in the likeness of Christ], or have already been made perfect, but I press on to take hold of that for which Christ Jesus took hold of me."

So you can see that the children were correct: If God is not for you, helping you through His Word and Spirit, you are up against it. And also the boy was right: There is an "equator" between God and sinners, one who equates and mediates for you before God—Jesus Christ. His redeeming merit saves you when you fail to "chase a decent life." The children told the truth despite improperly rendered texts. God speaks to us also through children.

Prayer Suggestion

Look in prayer to Jesus, the Author and Finisher of your faith, for strength to lead a God-pleasing life and for forgiveness when you fail.

ABOUT PAYING DEBTS

He [God] forgave us all our sins, having canceled the
written code, with its regulations, that was against us …
nailing it to the cross. Colossians 2:13–14

"The wicked borrow and do not repay" (Psalm 37:21), says the
Bible. The reference is not to unfortunate ones who want to but are
unable to repay. It rather means those who borrow money or anything
else without any sense of moral obligation. So they run off without
paying their bills, pay with checks that bounce, or use credit cards in
an irresponsible way. People are being robbed as though held up with
a gun.

Two prominent Americans set us examples to the contrary. When
Mark Twain lost every penny and was saddled with a debt when a
printing firm he partly owned went bankrupt, he, at age 60, began to
travel, lecture, and write vigorously until the debt was paid. The second man who went heavily into debt when an investment firm went
broke was Ulysses S. Grant. Although ailing, he rented a cottage in
New York State to write his memoirs. He completed his work three
days before dying of cancer on July 23, 1885. He, too, paid his debt.

The Bible speaks of debt-paying people—like Zacchaeus, who
repaid everyone fourfold. The Bible cites examples of persons who
considered themselves indebted because of solemn promises made.
The psalmist states that he will go to God's house to fulfill his vow.
The woman, Hannah, paid her debt when she took her son, young
Samuel, and returned him to God's service in the temple, for she considered him a loan from God.

We need motivation and power for leading honest, Christian lives,
and this comes from faith—from our appreciation that God "loaned"
His Son, Jesus Christ, to redeem us. Although Himself sinless and
without debts of His own, He paid our debts. He atoned for our sins.
In love to Him we pay our earthly debts, thankful that our spiritual
debts before God are paid in full.

Prayer Suggestion

Thank the Lord Jesus for paying all your debts before God, asking
Him also to help you to be a good steward of your possessions.

ANARCHY IS NOT FREEDOM

I urge ... requests, prayers, intercession and thanksgiving
be made for everyone—for kings and all those in authority.
1 Timothy 2:1–2

In the 1920s world attention was focused on the conviction and execution of Nicola Sacco and Bartolomeo Vanzetti for the payroll theft and murder of a guard in Braintree, Massachusetts. Because they were anarchists, some thought they were being victimized because of politics. However, recent laboratory tests give evidence that the men had indeed committed these crimes.

Anarchism is a dangerous philosophy. It holds that all forms of government unjustly infringe the rights and freedoms of the individual. It represents the ultimate in individualism. It turns liberty into license. At its worst it leads to acts of terrorism. Personal liberty is one thing and must be defended against tyranny. License is something else. It is like a river leaving its banks and becoming a rampaging flood.

Government at local, state, and federal levels enables citizens, in the words of St. Paul, to "live peaceful and quiet lives." For this reason he urges "that requests, prayers, intercession and thanksgiving be made for everyone—for kings and all those in authority." The government is there to protect the people, not only against foreign enemies but also against homegrown criminals. And private citizens are a force for good when, on the basis of righteous laws, they assist the governing authorities to maintain peace and decency in the land.

Jesus said: "Give to Caesar what is Caesar's" in other words, give to the government what it has the right to ask: loyalty, obedience, payment of taxes. Then Jesus added: "and [give] to God what is God's" (Matthew 22:21). God asks of us a higher love—a love that exceeds the love we owe our fellow human beings. This love is our response to His great love that granted us a Savior from sin in the person of His Son, Jesus Christ. This love, once for all, shuts the door to anarchism and opens the door to a God-pleasing life here and now, and in the world to come.

Prayer Suggestion

Give thanks to God for peace and order in the land as maintained by responsible government He has ordained.

HOW GOD SETTLES A STRIKE

About that time there arose a great disturbance about the Way. Acts 19:23

Nowadays most labor-union strikes are conducted peacefully. Those out on a strike realize that gains are made at the conference table, not by engaging in riotous behavior.

Quite different was the strike in Ephesus. After St. Paul had evangelized the city and had induced many to give up the worship of idols, the business of making idolatrous objects dropped off sharply. This fact prompted Demetrius, a silversmith, to call a meeting of craftsmen who made silver shrines in honor of Artemis. The "sympathy" protest soon degenerated into a first-class riot. The town clerk called the attention of the unruly crowd to peaceful ways in which their differences could be settled.

Without realizing it, many people go out on strike against God. They have a grudge against their Maker. Some refuse to work for Him any longer because they think He has been unfair to them in the way He distributes money and goods to them. So they walk the streets, as it were, with sandwich boards accusing God of being an unfair employer.

Others walk out on God because life out there in the world seems so much more attractive. So they say, "God give us everything we have coming to us, all our back pay, and take our names off the books. We are not going to work for You anymore. We are going to enjoy ourselves."

The reason why still others go out on a strike against God may be the bitter experience of grief at the loss of property or of a person dear to them. Then resentment sets in. They say, "Why should we continue to serve God if that is the way He treats us? He has taken away our possessions, our livelihood, and all our fringe benefits."

God invites all striking sinners to gather around the conference table. He says, "Come now, let us reason together" (Isaiah 1:18). He says there is no need to be at odds. His love extends to all. He plays no favorites when He extends equal forgiveness to all. "There is no difference, for all have sinned ... [They] are justified freely by His grace through the redemption that came by Christ Jesus" (Romans 3:22–24).

In Christ Jesus God and sinners get together. The strike is settled.

Prayer Suggestion

Say a prayer of intercession for people whom you know to be at odds with God.

IN THE END, IT'S THE SAME

After this I looked and there before me was a great multitude that no one could count. Revelation 7:9

Sometimes two processes may differ greatly but have the same effect. In past years France had a penal colony on Devil's Island off French Guiana in north Africa. The prisoners' treatment, often leading to death, was called the "dry guillotine."

After Christ's ascension and the outpouring of the Holy Spirit, the evangelistic activity of the twelve apostles began. The treatment accorded them by their enemies varied. The first to become a martyr was James, the brother of John. Around 44 A.D. King Herod had him "put to death with the sword" (Acts 12:2). John however, as far as we know, died a natural death in high old age circa 98 A.D., nearly a century old. This did not mean, however, that John had a relatively easy life. He likewise suffered for his faithful witness to Jesus. In the year 95 the Roman emperor Domitian banished him to the lonesome, barren, and rocky island of Patmos in the Aegean Sea. There he was divinely inspired to write the book of Revelation, or the Apocalypse.

Who of the two brothers shines with greater glory in heaven? Is it James, who felt the sharp edge of a hand-held "guillotine," or is it John, who, among other sufferings, languished on the Aegean version of a devil's island? It is not for us to say what measure of glory Christ will bestow on any of His followers. Suffice it to say that both, James and John, in the prophet Daniel's words, "shine like the brightness of the heavens … like the stars forever and ever" (Daniel 12:3).

Short life, long life—a long service career or a deathbed conversion (like that of the penitent thief on the cross), our salvation is altogether by God's grace. In all eternity each one of us will glorify Jesus, the Lamb of God, who was sacrificed for us and rose again in glory.

Prayer Suggestion

Finish this prayer: "Lord Jesus, receive my thanks for … "

TO VOW OR NOT TO VOW

Praise awaits You, O God, in Zion; to You our vows will be fulfilled. Psalm 65:1

The ancients knew that one should not make foolish vows or rash promises. They told about a king of Crete who had fought in the Trojan War and who, on his return voyage, was caught in a severe sea storm. He vowed to Poseidon, the sea god, that he would sacrifice to him the first living being he would meet on landing, should his life be preserved. The first person he met was his own son. He kept his false vow and sacrificed him.

People make wrong vows today when they try to bargain with God: "Lord, let me win this money, and I'll give You half of it," or "Lord, make me well, and I'll enter a holy order and devote the rest of my life to You," or "Lord, help me make this sale, and I'll never miss a Sunday in church from now on."

What is wrong about this is that we cannot bargain with God; we cannot earn His favor, which comes only as a free, undeserved gift. It is unwise to vow or promise anything that may exceed our ability. Further, the temptation arises to change one's mind and not do what has been pledged. Jesus tells us we need not vow or swear in the everyday things of life. He says: "Simply let your 'Yes' be 'Yes,' and your 'No,' 'No'" (Matthew 5:37).

Vows are in place in the church: baptismal vows, confirmation vows, marriage vows, ordination vows. In public life we administer the oath of office to an elected official. "So help me God" is part of the formula. This is proper, for our Lord says, "Apart from Me you can do nothing" (John 15:5).

This saying applies especially to our salvation. No one can save himself or earn God's favor and a place in heaven by good works. The Bible is very clear on this: "It is by grace you have been saved, through faith" (Ephesians 2:8)—through faith in Jesus Christ as one's personal Savior from sin and the fear of death by His own death and resurrection.

Foolish vows? No. God-pleasing vows based on His help? Yes.

Prayer Suggestion

Ask for God's guidance so that you may avoid false vows and promises, and ask for His strength to fulfill proper ones in Jesus' name.

BETTER WHEN USED

There are different kinds of gifts, but the same Spirit.
1 Corinthians 12:4

Some experts claim that musical instruments, like grand pianos, stay in better condition when played than when stored unused in a museum. The wood stays more sensitive to sounds when the piano is played.

As for human talents, it is generally held that we either use them or lose them. The great Polish pianist Ignace Paderewski was quoted as saying, "When I don't practice for one day, I notice it; when not in two days, my friends notice it; when not for three days, everyone does."

God has given each of us personal endowments—if not musical talents, then perhaps mechanical; if not for painting pictures or writing poetry, then perhaps for speaking cordially to visitors at church services.

On top of natural talents God has given us spiritual gifts. Some gifts of the Holy Spirit once given to early Christians seem to be discontinued now in the Christian community: speaking in tongues, miraculous healing, prophesying. But other spiritual gifts are distributed to each of us as God wills: comforting, counseling, exhorting, teaching, expressing faith through friendships, and the like.

So, whether we speak of natural talents or of spiritual gifts, a good principle to follow is this: Use them to the glory of God and for the well-being of others and ourselves. By using them, we keep them; by "spending" them, we enhance them.

Christians have every motivation for using their gifts. In that way they show their appreciation for what the Triune God has done for them. The Father "thought" (planned) our salvation back in all eternity; the Son, Jesus Christ, "wrought" it on the cross; and the Holy Spirit "brought" it into our hearts through the Gospel. We say our thank-You to God when we serve Him with our gifts.

Prayer Suggestion

Complete this prayer: "Dear Lord, I thank You for granting me gifts … Help Me to use them to Your glory and for serving …"

RELIVING OUR YESTERDAYS TODAY

I remember the days of long ago; I meditate on all Your works. Psalm 143:5

Soren Kierkegaard, a Danish philosopher and lay theologian, wrote: "It is not worthwhile remembering the past if it cannot become the present."

On Memorial Day, also known as Decoration Day, we remember the deceased members of our military forces, especially those who gave their lives for their country. The observance becomes meaningful as we, the living, follow their example, serving in the present as they did in the past. When we remember the loyalty and devotion of those who have preceded us, we honor them and keep their memory alive for good purposes by emulating them as we carry out our civil and military duties and complete the tasks that remain.

The time of sacrifice for our country—for its government and people—is not past. There is much for us to do. We have battlefields of one kind or another in our midst, if not of a military nature then certainly of a civil nature. Our enemy, if not foreign, is domestic and lurks within. Vices vie with virtues. Laws are flouted, dishonesty is practiced, people are robbed and killed on the streets, drugs are misused and lead to crime. It is time for all citizens today to rise to the heights of patriotism so that the faithful service rendered in the past will be repeated in the present.

Memorial Day also prompts us as Christians to remember our departed parents, teachers, pastors, and missionaries. These veterans of the cross were the servants of Jesus Christ, whose salvation they embraced and proclaimed. Truly, "the memory of the righteous will be a blessing" (Proverbs 10:7). Holy Scripture bids us, "Remember your leaders, who spoke the Word of God to you. Consider the outcome of their way of life and imitate their faith" (Hebrews 13:7). The writer adds the reason for such constancy: "Jesus Christ is the same yesterday and today and forever" (Hebrews 13:8). When we honor our Lord, as did those who preceded us, we cause the past to become the present.

Prayer Suggestion

To your prayer of thanksgiving for past leaders, add a petition that God may help you set a good Christian example for others.

A CONVERT IN PRISON

He [the Jailer] then brought them out and asked,
"Sirs, what must I do to be saved?" Acts 16:30

With so much unrest in our regular life as citizens—minority groups wanting more freedom, more opportunities, more rights—it is not surprising that also those in prisons and penitentiaries should express their protests or demands in outbreaks of violence. A prison riot, usually accompanied by fire, wanton destruction, and death, is a terrifying experience.

In Phillipi, Paul and Silas were in prison because an uproar ensued when Paul freed a slave girl from a spirit of divination and thus deprived her owners of income. When at midnight a sudden earthquake shook the prison to its very foundations, opened the doors, and unfastened every prisoner's fetters, all the elements were present for a prison panic. With the prisoners free, a riot might easily have followed, with the inmates turning on the jailer and the jail guards.

But such an outbreak—and breakout—never took place. The reason was that two prisoners were exerting an unbelievably great Christian influence on their fellows. At midnight Paul and Silas "were praying and singing hymns to God, and the other prisoners were listening to them" (Acts 16:25). After the earthquake this was not forgotten. The other prisoners were willing to take their cue from Paul, this time not only hearing him but also heeding him. They made no attempt to escape.

Seeing the effects of the earthquake—and believing that all the prisoners had fled, as they would normally do—the jailer was about to commit suicide. But Paul called out loudly from the darkness to restrain him: "Don't harm yourself! We are all here!" (Acts 16:28)

In the darkness of that prison Paul and Silas were letting their light shine as witnesses of Jesus Christ, the Light of the World. Their influence extended also to the jailer, for when he asked, "Sirs, what must I do to be saved?" (Acts 16:30), the Christian missionaries replied, "Believe in the Lord Jesus, and you will be saved—you and your household" (Acts 16:31).

Everywhere in our world people are sitting in the darkness of sin and in prisons of their own making: selfishness, fear, anxiety, doubt, unbelief. What is needed is the message of Christ's salvation which sets them free. The Gospel does "proclaim freedom for the captives and release from darkness for the prisoners," as Isaiah 61:1 declares.

Prayer Suggestion

Say a prayer, asking the Lord Jesus to bless the ministries of prison chaplains.

FAMILY MEMBERS AS JEWELS

The gifts you sent … are a fragrant offering, an acceptable sacrifice, pleasing to God. Philippians 4:18

Emperor Shah Jahan of Agra, India, must have loved his wife very much. When the empress died, he built her a magnificent mausoleum, the Taj Mahal. It is made of marble, trimmed with precious stones: jade, agate, jasper, onyx, and diamonds. Completed in 1645, it is one of the most elegant structures ever built.

Not every man can pay such an architectural tribute to his wife. What is more, it is not necessary. Love can express itself in less pretentious ways. True love can turn a humble cottage into a sparkling castle. A popular song in the 1920s was "My Blue Heaven." It described a small home with a fireplace, a cozy room, "a little nest that's nestled where the roses bloom." There was also the smiling face of Molly, the wife, and the happy baby when the husband and father came home from a day's work.

Faithful spouses don't need jeweled tombs, for they themselves are jewels. The writer of the book of Proverbs declares: "A wife of noble character who can find? She is worth far more than rubies" (31:10). The same can be said of a loving, loyal husband. And children are precious to the parents and vice versa. According to a story in a school reader, a Roman mother refused to be embarrassed for her lack of rings and bracelets. When asked, "Where are your jewels?" she called in her children and said, "These are my jewels."

Love is the prime ingredient of a happy home and family. Happiness results when spouses love each other as Christ loved the church and gave Himself up for her. That was love expressed not in mere words but in a deed—in the deed of sacrificing His life for the salvation of all.

Human beings are not perfect. Consequently misunderstandings will arise. Then it is time to ask for forgiveness, as St. Paul writes: "Be kind and compassionate to one another, forgiving each other, just as in Christ God forgave you" (Ephesians 4:32).

Prayer Suggestion

Pray for God's help to grow in love and in appreciation of the members of the family.

HOPE FOR ALL CREATION

*The LORD God took the man and put him in the Garden
of Eden to work it and take care of it. Genesis 2:15*

A magazine article states why measures have to be taken in behalf
of the bighorn sheep in the mountains of British Columbia: "They have
to be protected from disruption and disease brought on by the
encroachments of man." Human enterprises, especially of thoughtless
greed, tend to pollute land, water, and air, thus endangering many
species of animals and plants.

The plaintive voices heard in nature, if combined into a chorus,
would add a very distressing stanza to Gustav Mahler's *Das Lied von
der Erde* ("The Song of the Earth"). St. Paul has given us the substance of it: "We know that the whole creation has been groaning as in
the pains of childbirth" (Romans 8:22). It groans because man's sin has
placed it under bondage and added many burdens.

The beginning of nature's distress goes back to man's fall into sin.
To Adam God said: "Cursed is the ground because of you…. It will produce thorns and thistles for you" (Genesis 3:17–18). The once beautiful
Garden of Eden is gone. Instead we have an earth whose spontaneous
fruitfulness is greatly reduced. Sinful man aggravates the curse resting
on it. To the existing Sahara Desert man adds new deserts by his mismanagement of soil and water. Devastating floods result from this.
Flora and fauna suffer because of it, making conservation efforts necessary.

The great conservationist is God Himself—the Creator who wants
to enlist our help for the preservation and restoration of what He
made. He starts with the sinner, seeking to regain him for his role as
the crown of creation, "Joy to the world, the Lord is come," we sing in
a well-known song. God's own Son came in the person of Jesus Christ
to break the power of sin and to bring the blessings of redemption, as
the refrain has it, "far as the curse is found." Through His death and
rising again He effected freedom for sinners and enabled them to
become the children of God. Those who believe in the Son as the total
Liberator are freed for every God-pleasing service, including the care
of nature's environment. Now hope begins, even for God's creation.

Prayer Suggestion

Ask for God's help in the exercise of your stewardship in His created world.

IF TREES COULD WEEP

To this you were called, because Christ suffered for you,
leaving you an example, that you should follow in His steps.
1 Peter 2:21

In nature we see God's handiwork, including the trees. The poet Joyce Kilmer, author of "Trees," would call them God's lovely poems. The weeping willow is one of these trees. It is not universally admired because of its habit to "weep" its sticky sap on your car, especially the windshield, if you park underneath it. Then you have trouble seeing, tears always blur vision. But willows have both utility and beauty. They yield their flexible twigs for basket weaving; their gracefully drooping branches rank it with ornamental trees.

The weeping willow goes under the scientific name of *salix babylonica*, perhaps because of its mention in Psalm 137: "By the waters of Babylon, there we sat down and wept, when we remembered Zion. On the willows there we hung our lyres [harps]" (vv. 1–2 RSV).

What would there be for a willow to weep about if it had feelings and the facility to shed real tears? It might be sorrowful because some trees, like the fig tree in Christ's parable, do not bear fruit in their season. Or it could weep because forests are ravaged because of people's carelessness with campfires or their eagerness to obtain lumber. There would also be reason to shed tears of joy because, as the Holy Communion liturgy so strikingly puts it, Satan, who by a tree overcame our first parents in Eden, was himself overcome by a tree—the tree of the cross on which Jesus died to atone for sin. St. Peter writes: "He Himself bore our sins in His body on the tree, so that we might die to sins and live for righteousness" (1 Peter 2:24).

St. Paul tells us that "the whole creation has been groaning" (Romans 8:22), not only because human sin lays a heavy load on it but also because it awaits its liberation (Romans 8:21), along with that of God's people, when Christ will come again and bring us to final glory. The weeping willow, a part of creation, joins in this expectation.

Prayer Suggestion

Express your gratitude to God for sending His Son to the tree of the cross to effect your salvation and turn your weeping into joy.

NO LONGER FOREIGNERS

You are no longer foreigners and aliens, but fellow citizens with God's people. Ephesians 2:19

A story of doubtful origin has it that a man from an English-speaking country was visiting the city of Rome. He enjoyed seeing the many interesting, historical sights but added, "What I don't like is that there are so many foreigners here."

People have had problems with foreigners, both justified and unjustified. In the early United states, the Federalist Party in 1798 passed laws through Congress to stem the tide of incoming aliens. The Naturalization Act sought to provide that people had to live 14 years in this country before they could become citizens. Think of it: If generations ago people with problems had been barred from North American countries, many of us would not be here.

As far as the Christian religion is concerned, there is a common bond—a spiritual brotherhood and sisterhood—that supersedes racial differences. The first century saw tensions developing in Christian circles. The main problem centered in the question: Should the ceremonial laws of Moses, including circumcision, be binding on Gentiles coming into the church?

St. Paul and others sought to keep a rift from becoming a divisive gulf. In his letter to the Ephesians the apostle stresses that Christ, by His obedience to the Law and by His suffering and death fulfilled and removed "the Law with its commandments and regulations" (Ephesians 2:15). He became our Peace—our Peacemaker—by abolishing the circumcision issue and thus uniting Christians of Jewish and of Gentile origins. He tells the Ephesians, "You are no longer foreigners and aliens, but fellow citizens with God's people and members of God's household" (Ephesians 2:19).

In Christ, east and west, north and south are united. Here, too, the truth holds: "What God has joined together, let man not separate" (Matthew 19:6).

Prayer Suggestion

Pray for peace in our nation and for Christ-centered unity in the church.

Satan's Charges Are Futile

On another day the angels came to present themselves before the LORD, and Satan also came with them to present himself before Him. Job 2:1

The book of Job tells us: When the angels presented themselves before God for worship, Satan was present. The New Testament gospels report that Jesus attended the synagog in Capernaum. Present there was a man possessed by a demon, who said through his victim: "What do You want with us, Jesus of Nazareth? Have You come to destroy us?" (Mark 1:24)

What possible reasons could Satan have for going to church, a place so many people find unattractive? A partial answer may be found in a fresco painting in Roskilde Cathedral, Copenhagen. It shows a grotesque figure of the devil, with an inscription that says he "writes down the names of those who are late or loiter about with idle talk." Why would the devil want to do that? He considers the church a good place to get a line on people, a good place to find prospects for greater temptations.

Take the case of Judas Iscariot. Satan must have noted Judas' fondness for the collection money in the treasury of that little congregation. That gave Satan a hint of how vulnerable Judas was for the betrayal of his Master for 30 pieces of silver.

The devil keeps his own records of people, even of church people. The story is told of a time when Satan confronted Martin Luther with a long list of his sins. Asked if this was the total list, the devil replied: "Oh, no, I have other even longer lists." Luther asked that he bring them all, and when this was done, he wrote these words across them: "Paid for by the blood of Jesus Christ."

You and I can do the same thing when the evil accuser confronts us with his notes of our spiritual delinquencies. Then his church-going to spy on us will do him no good.

Prayer Suggestion

Give thanks to God for marking all your spiritual debts as paid for by Christ's redeeming blood.

THE GREAT AWAKENING

The Lord Himself will come down from heaven, with a loud command, with the voice of the archangel and with the trumpet call of God, and the dead in Christ will rise first.
1 Thessalonians 4:16

An English hunting song says that the baying hounds and the horn of the morning hunter, John Peel, bring the foxes from their hiding places, rouse people from their beds, and are loud enough to "awaken the dead."

A trumpet to awaken the dead—is there such a thing? Yes says St. Paul. He writes, concerning the order of Christ's action on the Last Day: "The Lord Himself will come down from heaven, with a loud command, with the voice of the archangel and with the trumpet call of God, and the dead in Christ will rise first" (1 Thessalonians 4:16). Again, when referring to the glorified resurrection bodies, he states, "The trumpet will sound, and the dead will be raised imperishable, and we will be changed" (1 Corinthians 15:52).

We can't imagine what that will be like—what kind of trumpet sound will be heard around the world, how those who have died so long ago and with their bodies now turned to dust can hear that call. And what is the nature of the changed, glorified, and imperishable bodies? But we can catch a glimpse of that future scene—how a tree or shrub, barren in the winter, blooms in spring; how a caterpillar becomes a beautiful butterfly; how an eagle or other bird molts and then renews itself; how a patient, near death's door, overcomes his ailments and again achieves glowing health. If such changes occur in our natural world, should it be impossible for God to do the greater miracle of awakening the dead to a new life?

In a sense we are already raised from the dead—from being spiritually dead in trespasses and sins. Jesus Christ, having died for our sins and conquered death, rose again from the dead. Believing in Him and baptized into His name, we live in Him and have even now a foretaste of eternal life to come.

Yes, Christ's trumpet call will be heard! Are we ready for it?

Prayer Suggestion

Ask the Holy Spirit to deepen your faith in Jesus' promise to come again and raise you from the dead.

A TIME FOR EVERYTHING

As long as it is day, we must do the work of Him who sent Me.
John 9:4

While Jesus was preaching and healing in Galilee and Samaria, a Pharisee warned Him: "Get away from here, for Herod wants to kill You" (Luke 13:31 RSV). It is not clear why men who were opponents would say this; perhaps their intent was to get Jesus to leave, for He was gaining many followers.

Our Lord refused to be intimidated. Until the time came for Him to suffer and die for all mankind, He had His work cut out for Him, and no one, not even King Herod, could stop Him. Further, Jesus foreknew that it would be in *Jerusalem*, not in a Galilean or a Samaritan town, that He would be arrested and killed. He said, "It cannot be that a prophet should perish away from Jerusalem" (Luke 13:33 RSV). He was right.

We are thankful for Christ's commitment to His work in our behalf. He said on another occasion that he must "work the works of Him who sent Me, while it is day; night comes, when no one can work" (John 9:4 RSV). Preaching, teaching, healing—this is what Jesus did during His three-year prophetic ministry. At the appropriate time He would also be our High Priest, offering up Himself on the cross for our sins.

Also for our lives it is true: "There is a time for everything, and a season for every activity under heaven" (Ecclesiastes 3:1). What Longfellow says of the village blacksmith applies to most of us: "Each morning sees some task begun: Each evening sees its close." This was certainly the case with Jesus.

Prayer Suggestion

Ask the Lord Jesus to direct you in selecting and doing the work He wants you to do today.

JESUS STILL LEADS ON

Jesus began to preach, "Repent, for the kingdom of heaven is near." Matthew 4:17

Daniel Boone, a frontiersman, has been called "the Columbus of the woods." A painting by George Caleb Bingham shows him leading settlers through the Cumberland Gap in east-central United States.

Spiritually speaking, Adam and Eve and all their descendants were lost in the woods, unable to find their way out of the encumbered land of sin. But God had mercy. He promised to send His own Son to lead the way out of "the land of the shadow of death" (Isaiah 9:2) into the realm of light and life eternal. That Son was, at the "fullness of time," born of the virgin Mary and was called Jesus, meaning Savior. He was in every respect—by His Word and divine works—revealed as the promised Messiah of whom Isaiah and the other prophets had spoken. When Jesus of Nazareth opened His preaching and healing ministry in Galilee, the evangelist Matthew pronounced Isaiah's prophecy fulfilled.

Our Lord did more than show us the way to life; He Himself was—and still is—the Way, the only way, to the Father. He became that when He, as the Pioneer and Perfecter of our faith, endured the cross to atone for our sins and then rose again to assure us of the resurrection of our bodies to life eternal.

Human beings are limited in what they can do. Christopher Columbus and Daniel Boone could open up parts of the world for human habitation, giving economically depressed people a new lease on life. But saviors from sin and givers of eternal life they could not be. Only Jesus Christ is both Giver and Guide as we wend our way through this world, en route to the "better country—a heavenly one" (Hebrews 11:16).

Prayer Suggestion

In your own words add to these lines: "Heavenly Leader, still direct us, Still support, control, protect us."

Finding the Lost

The Pharisees and the teachers of the law muttered, "This Man welcomes sinners and eats with them." Luke 15:2

We hear a lot these days about lost children—children who are kidnapped or who mysteriously disappear. The parents are broken-hearted.

United States history knows of other disappearances. In 1587, on Roanoke Island off the coast of North Carolina, Sir Walter Raleigh founded the third of his colonies. Belonging to that group was Virginia Dare, said to have been the first white child born in the new world. Three years after the founding, a ship came to bring supplies, but no trace of the colonists could be found.

Earlier in history an entire people disappeared: the lost ten tribes of Israel that were carried away into the Assyrian captivity in 722 B.C. They were undoubtedly absorbed into the general population and lost their identity. Missing children, missing tribes, missing people represent a human tragedy, especially if foul play was involved.

The Bible testifies to the greater tragedy of Adam and Eve and all their descendants lost in sin and subject to eternal death. But God wanted the missing to be found and to be restored to fellowship with Him. He sent His only Son, Jesus Christ, to be the Good Shepherd seeking the lost sheep. That was the purpose of His mission as the Savior Himself said: "The Son of Man came to seek and to save what was lost" (Luke 19:10).

By laying down His life, Jesus paid the price for everyone's salvation. He loved the world—the total human race of all times and places—and for it He died. It is therefore a matter of great concern to Him when one person goes astray. He wants to have a one-on-one relationship with each one of us. His love is not impersonal, not an en masse concern, although it is all-inclusive. He loves each person and wants each one to love Him. He searches for individuals. There is joy in heaven and on earth when the missing person is found and has returned home.

Prayer Suggestion

Request your Savior to lead you to a lost soul and to give you the right words to speak and the right things to do toward restoration.

THE KIND OF CHILDREN WE WANT

Children, obey your parents in the Lord, for this is right.
Ephesians 6:1

An impressive sight in Copenhagen, Denmark, is Anders Bundgaard's massive fountain of the Nordic goddess Gefion, who according to a myth turned her four sons into four oxen to plow a portion of land away from Sweden and add it to Denmark. Imagine, turning sons into oxen!

Long ago, before child-labor laws went into effect, children were made to do hard work in factories and on farms, almost as though they were oxen. In our time many children are abused in other ways—by inflicting bodily injury. In other homes children are neglected, or they are brought up to be self-centered individuals who turn out to be little monsters—and not so little monsters when they become users of drugs and alcohol. Some parents want to make status symbols of their children by pushing them into all kinds of glamour roles at school and elsewhere.

It is a good question for parents to ask: What kind of children do we want? Are we turning them into oxen? Are we fashioning sparrows and sending them out to fight hawks? It is no small task to be molders of children. Parents, teachers, and youth leaders need all the help they can get.

Such help comes from the Bible—from Jesus Christ, who is the center of the Bible. He Himself, we are told, "grew in wisdom and stature, and in favor with God and men" (Luke 2:52). This points to mental, physical, spiritual, and social growth. We bring up our children to be like Christ when we teach them to love the Lord their God and to love one another. Such love comes as the Holy Spirit-induced response to the prior love of God, who gave His Son to expiate our sins, to reconcile us to God as His forgiven sons and daughters.

We should not turn our children into human animals, and we cannot bring them up to be angels, but we can guide them to be persons in whom the love of God dwells.

Prayer Suggestion

Ask God for wisdom and love so that you fulfill your role as a discerning parent or an obedient child.

JESUS IS THERE

Where two or three come together in My name, there am I with them. Matthew 18:20

A Christian congregation has great power. As bearer of the Office of the Keys it has the power to retain and forgive sins, as Jesus says, "Whatever you bind on earth will be bound in heaven" (Matthew 18:18). The members of the church exercise this power as they follow the three steps of brotherly and sisterly admonition which Jesus outlines at the beginning of today's Bible reading.

But how large must a congregation be to have the power of the Keys? Must it be housed in a cathedral-size edifice and served by a high-ranking clergyman? Must it have a hundred, five hundred, or a thousand members? Is it required that it be organized into a legal corporation recognized by the state?

None of this is necessary. Our Lord does not condition the church's power on large numbers. In fact, as He goes on to speak of Christians coming together for prayer and for fellowship in His name, He uses the words "two or three." Then He ascribes to so small a group the highest honor possible: "There am I with them" (Matthew 18:20).

What a promise! When Christians assemble to fulfill the purposes for which Christ's church exists—to praise the God of their salvation and serve Him, to hear His Word and administer the sacraments, to instruct young and old in Christ's teachings, to admonish and exhort one another, to share the Gospel with the unchurched—Christ is in their midst.

Whether God's people worship in a little white church on the prairie or in an inner-city storefront building, Jesus is there. It is important that you and I be there, too.

Prayer Suggestion

Join hands with those in your group and ask Jesus to join the prayer chain with His blessing.

FREEDOM WITH MEANING

It is for freedom that Christ has set us free. Galatians 5:1

It has been said, "Freedom so often means that one isn't needed anywhere." So employees no longer needed at work are given their freedom with the proverbial pink slips of dismissal. Such "freedom," in many cases, leads to bondage—to the obligation to find another source of income.

Freedom *from* something, to be meaningful and enjoyable, had best be accompanied by freedom *for* something. Freedom in a vacuum can be boring. Here is a child, when asking its mother, "What can I do?" was told, "Do whatever you want to do." The reply to that was, "I am tired of doing what I want to do."

Freedom has a distinct meaning when considered in the light of the Gospel. St. Paul lays much stress on freedom in his letter to the Galatians. False teachers had trailed him into the area, claiming that the law of Moses which demanded certain good works, especially Sabbath observance and the practice of circumcision, was still in effect for New Testament Christians. This demand, according to the apostle, was "a different gospel" (Galatians 1:6). In fact, it was no Gospel at all, for the true Gospel proclaims that Jesus Christ has freed us from the curse of the Law by Himself bearing its curse: death. Now, freed from the Law and justified through faith in Jesus' merit, we have forgiveness, peace with God, and the guarantee of a foretaste of eternal life now and the full enjoyment of it in heaven.

We are free in Christ, with St. Paul bidding us: "Stand firm, then, and do not let yourselves be burdened again by a yoke of slavery" (Galatians 5:1).

Free *from* something, we are free *for* something—free to leave life's cares and burdens behind and to seek the higher good in Christ, free to leave the slavery to sin and serve the living God, free to enjoy all the blessings of God's grace and to share the Good News with the people around us. It is wonderful to be free in this sense.

Prayer Suggestion

Pray for a faith that fully grasps your freedom under Christ's Gospel and for willingness to translate it into daily life.

LOVE CANNOT BE MEASURED

These three remain: faith, hope and love. But the greatest of these is love. 1 Corinthians 13:13

A publishing firm had the custom of sending its retirees calendars printed on felt. When these were not delivered, it was found that the postal workers, finding the mail bags so light, put them away because they thought they were empty. Weight is not a reliable basis for judging the value or non-value of things. A load of coal is far heavier than a diamond but not nearly as valuable.

Weight, size, bulk—these are not the important factors in one's Christian experience. What about being "cumbered with a load of care," as the hymnal line says? What would ordinarily be a heavy burden becomes light when Christ helps us carry it. St. Paul speaks of the Christian's suffering as being "momentary," adding that they work "for us an eternal glory that far outweighs them all" (2 Corinthians 4:17).

Weight, volume, mass—these are not the qualities by which we judge God's blessings. Gold and silver were once estimated by weight, and the heavier the bags containing these precious metals, the wealthier the owners. Yes, God blesses us also with this world's goods, perhaps even abundantly as He did Abraham. But His spiritual gifts are greater. You cannot weigh them on the scales. You cannot estimate the worth of His love nor fully determine its dimensions. Who can grasp "how wide and long and high and deep is the love of Christ, and to know this love that surpasses knowledge" (Ephesians 3:18–19)? Beyond our understanding are all God's gifts flowing from His love: forgiveness, peace, eternal life in Christ.

Your gifts to God and to one another don't go by weight or price tags, either. What counts is the love that prompts giving and serving. A cup of cold water given in faith is more precious in God's sight than a river of gifts people don't need. Parents know—should know—that the giving of themselves to their children is worth more than material gifts offered as substitutes for personal love.

In your house are meters or devices for measuring gas, water, and electricity. But love in your home cannot be metered, cannot be put in bags, cannot be bought. But how valuable it is!

Prayer Suggestion

Thank your Savior for His love to you, asking Him to increase your love to Him and to His own.

A LETDOWN CAN BE A LIFT

Every day He [Jesus] was teaching at the temple. But the chief priests, the teachers of the law and the leaders among the people were trying to kill him. Luke 19:47

Often the passage to a useful life leads through one or more doors marked "Failure." The biography of John James Audubon tells how he left his studies in France to become a merchant in America. He ran a store and a grist mill but failed in both. Then he became a naturalist, especially a well-known painter of birds. The Audubon societies are named after him.

"Failure" was a word written in large letters in the life and labors of St. Paul. Converted to the Christian faith, he wanted to do mission work in Damascus and then in Jerusalem, but he failed in both places. Then Barnabas took him along to Antioch, where his ministry could begin. But even in later years the apostle encountered failure. In some places all the doors were locked, and he could do nothing, for the handles were on the inside.

When you receive a setback in your plans, think not only of Audubon or St. Paul; think of Jesus. In many towns people would not listen to Him. Even the people of Nazareth, where His home had been, literally ran Him out of town. His acceptance in Jerusalem wasn't any better, and we hear Him say: "How often I have longed to gather your children together, as a hen gathers her chicks under her wings, but you were not willing" (Matthew 23:37).

Perhaps God wants to lead you from smaller to greater things. So He lets you experience setbacks and failures in these smaller things. Or He may force you to spend time on a sickbed, giving you the opportunity to think things through and to make plans for a more useful and satisfying life. He may lead you on unfamiliar roads, to strange cities in strange lands, so that your life will be fulfilling, to God's glory and the good of all concerned.

We can live with disappointments if we keep in mind where we are, why we are here, and where we are going. We have the assurance of God's loving-kindness, which He expressed to the full extent when He redeemed us and made us His own through His Son, Jesus Christ our Lord.

Prayer Suggestion

Request God's guidance so that you may under any circumstances live to His glory and the good of all.

THE CALL TO FAITHFULNESS

You have been faithful with a few things; I will put you in charge of many things. Come and share your master's happiness. Matthew 25:23

Christians are called to be "imitators of God, as beloved children" (Ephesians 5:1 RSV). We are to let the family resemblance show and be like our heavenly Father. Of course, some of God's attributes are beyond our attainment. We can never be like God in faithfulness. God is faithful; He keeps His Word and covenant. St. Paul writes, "God, who has called you into fellowship with His Son Jesus Christ, our Lord, is faithful" (1 Corinthians 1:9).

Like the father, so also the Son is faithful and therefore is called, as St. John writes, "the Amen, the faithful and true Witness" (Revelation 3:14).

Like the Father, so also His sons and daughters are called to be faithful in the discharge of their stewardship, faithful in all of life. "Faithful" is the key word in Jesus' parable of the talents. The "man going on a journey" (Matthew 25:14) did not demand of his servants that they be business geniuses or be given to high intellectual attainment. What he did require was that they be faithful in managing the property he entrusted to them. The servants who gained five talents and two talents were commended alike: "Well done, good and faithful servant! You have been faithful with a few things; I will put you in charge of many things. Come and share your master's happiness" (Matthew 25:21, 23).

"It is required that those who have been given a trust must prove faithful," writes St. Paul in 1 Corinthians 4:2. Whatever it is that God has given us—our moments and days, our hands and feet, our voice and lips, our silver and gold, our intellect and all our powers, our will and heart, above all, our life and love—He calls us to administer faithfully every entrusted talent. That's all He asks.

Prayer Suggestion

Express thanks to God for the opportunities He has given you to work for Him, asking also that through faith in Christ you may remain faithful.

CHRISTIANS ARE NEW BEINGS

Because of His great love for us, God, who is rich in mercy, made us alive with Christ even when we were dead in transgressions. Ephesians 2:4–5

A well-known television pastor has stated, "Sin is a condition before it becomes action." This is a helpful statement, for it distinguishes between what a person is by nature—sinful, that is—and what outward behavior results from it in words and deeds. The latter include words and works of commission, and also of omission, that is, the failure to say and do what is right. The time-honored, still helpful and still valid, distinction is original sin and actual sin.

People going about to solve human problems or improve society often fail to take human sinfulness into consideration. They assume that everyone is good, or potentially good, by nature; they are apt to overlook original sin. Their fond belief is that people, essentially the good ones, need only be shown or taught what is good and they will do it. Every system, whether in economics (socialism, for example) or in education, based on the supposed innate goodness of people will eventually stagger to failure. Its promoters fail to take sin into account—our tendency toward selfishness, pride, greed, laziness, sexual impurity, and all kindred vices.

Original sin is a fact, and likewise is actual sin, flowing from this condition. Both are well documented in the Bible. Both are there described as leading to the wars and woes of mankind. Both are clearly revealed as leading to God's displeasure and as barring a person's right relation to God for time and for eternity.

But God acted in grace and mercy. His saving act is briefly summed up in the sending of His Son, the holy and innocent Jesus, to atone for our sin, both original and actual. His sin-forgiving merit is imparted to us through faith, which the Holy Spirit creates through the Gospel and Holy Baptism, sustaining it through the same Word and the Sacrament of Holy Communion.

This is how we are freed from sin and re-created into new beings who love God and their neighbor.

Prayer Suggestion

Confess to God that you have sinned often, and ask Him to help you become more like Jesus, your Savior.

GOD MENDS BROKEN PEOPLE

A broken and contrite heart, O God, You will not despise.
Psalm 51:17

Eugene O'Neill, the American dramatist, is hardly known for great statements of faith. But he did write this: "Man is born broken. He lives by mending. And the grace of God is the glue."

Every human being is born broken in sin, so the Word of God teaches. Here we think not only of criminals—killers, thieves, cheaters—but people wearing blue collars, white collars, or none at all. Included are all people, also those who profess faith in God. King David declares: "Surely I was sinful at birth, sinful from the time my mother conceived me" (Psalm 51:5). Again, St. Paul, the great missionary: "Nothing good lives in me. ... The evil I do not want to do—this I keep on doing" (Romans 7:18–19). It is as the playwright said, "Man is born broken."

When a doll is broken, the little girl tries to mend it. Many things in everyday life need mending: valuable plates and dishes, clothes, the screen door, the back fence. The broken human being, too, needs mending. In fact, he needs more than a little repair here and there, a little outward reform, a little cosmetic renovation. He needs a complete overhaul, a conversion, a new birth. God the Holy Spirit takes broken people and through the Gospel converts them into new persons—persons who repent of their sins and believe in Jesus Christ as the one who died for them and now forgives them.

To stay mended, it is necessary to stay close to Christ, love Him, pray to Him, serve Him, and do the kinds of good things He wants done in the world and in the church. We stay mended when we by faith adhere to the promises of the Word of God, for this is the Word of divine love and grace. It is as O'Neill said: "The grace of God is the glue." "It is by grace you have been saved," writes St. Paul in Ephesians 2:8. What wonderful grace! No wonder that John Newton wrote in a hymn: "Amazing grace! How sweet the sound that saved a wretch like me! I once was lost, but now am found, was blind but now I see!" You can say the same.

Prayer Suggestion

Express your desire for the Holy Spirit's help to amend your life where and when it falls short of Christ's expectation.

Baptism Links Us to Christ

I will ransom them from the power of the grave; I will redeem them from death. Where, O death, are your plagues? Where, O grave, is your destruction? Hosea 13:14

What do newspaper obituaries say about the dead? Some say that they "entered into rest." Others say that the departed (usually Roman Catholics) were "fortified by the sacraments of the church." Refreshingly different is this statement about one who was likewise a Roman Catholic: He "was baptized into the hope of Christ's resurrection."

In the above text Hosea makes no mention of the link between baptism and Christ's resurrection. It is plain, however, that St. Paul refers to this text when he writes, "Death has been swallowed up in victory. Where, O death, is your victory? Where, O death, is your sting? … Thanks be to God! He gives us the victory through our Lord Jesus Christ" (1 Corinthians 15:54–57).

The benefits of Christ's victory become ours when we are baptized into His name. This is clearly taught by St. Peter when he writes in his first epistle: "In His great mercy [God] has given us new birth into a living hope through the resurrection of Jesus Christ from the dead" (1 Peter 1:3). In linking up our baptism with salvation in Christ, he states, "It saves you by the resurrection of Jesus Christ" (1 Peter 3:21). The merit Christ gained for us through His death and resurrection is imparted through baptism. The Christian's faith in life and in death is riveted to the good news of Easter morning: "He is risen!"

Death is defeated, and life—the life in Christ—flourishes. On the dedicatory page of his novel *War and Remembrance* Herman Wouk (of the Jewish faith) quotes these words from Isaiah 25:8 in memory of his deceased firstborn son, "He (God) will destroy death forever." Our Savior died and rose again to destroy death and to bring life and immortality to light through the Gospel. That's why we rejoice on Easter Day and all other days.

Prayer Suggestion

Baptized into Your name, Lord Jesus, I have the sure hope of the resurrection and of life eternal. Amen.

THE CHOICE OF PEOPLE
FOR PUBLIC OFFICE

The authorities that exist have been established by God.
Romans 13:1

The Bible has the allegory or parable of the trees wanting to choose a king over them. They approached the olive tree, the fig tree, and the vine. When these said no, the offer went to the bramble and was accepted.

The parable is about the people of Israel who no longer wanted to be ruled by judges but sought a sole ruler from among Gideon's descendants. The choice went to Ahimelech, one who was the least qualified, a human bramble. It happens often in politics that thorn-bushes make themselves available, while good people, who are like the olive trees or fig trees, want to stay in private life.

As you walk through the woods today, ask: What kind of trees best represent the type of persons we want in public office? Oak, hickory, and walnut trees are strong, and people of strong moral character are always needed in government. Also the sycamore is a hardwood tree, but its use in construction is limited because of its tendency to warp. People who easily succumb to temptation are not good candidates. The cypress tree stands tall and symmetrical. Qualities of good balance and lofty ideals stand political people in good stead. Then you come to the evergreen family: cedars, pines, blue spruces. You admire their constancy. In summer or winter they are the same.

Voters should select the best available men and women for public office. Then, as citizens, they should follow through and cooperate with the elected officials and obey the laws. In that way both the governed and those who govern fulfill God's will. St. Paul teaches that Christians are to uphold good order for conscience' sake.

God desires our total good, also our spiritual welfare, our salvation. This is beautifully stated under a "tree" theme in the church liturgy: "We give thanks to You, holy Lord. … Who on the tree of the cross … gave salvation to all mankind that, whence death arose, thence life also might rise again and that he [i.e. Satan] who by a tree once overcame likewise by a tree might be overcome, through Christ, our Lord."

Prayer Suggestion

Thank God for all faithful persons who serve in public office. Ask Him for help so that you can support them.

What Christ's Love Is All About

Love one another. 1 John 4:7

Sometimes, with good intentions, Christ's love is presented as an entirely unstructured, formless, even mushy sentiment comparable to the feeling of a doting grandfather. So it behooves us to consider the Savior's love as something that has body to it—that it is very real and has functioning power.

The love that Jesus has, and that He wants us to share with one another, has a *source* and therefore a great force. Christ's kind of love is not limited. It went all-out. It went the total distance in that He laid down His life so that He might restore us to fellowship with God, our heavenly Father.

The love Jesus wants us to exercise among ourselves needs a *standard* of comparison. Previously the commandments on the second table of the Law had said, in summary: "Love your neighbor as yourself." Jesus explains this in its fullest sense when He states in His "new command": "As I have loved you, so you must love one another" (John 13:34). That means: Let your love go all the way!

The love Jesus has, and which He wants us to practice as we live day by day in intimate human fellowship, particularly in the family, needs an *object*. Far from loving abstract beings, it concerns itself with flesh-and-blood persons. Where but in the close marriage and home relationships does such love find its immediate—and very real—object?

In his first epistle, St. John has more to say about the love lessons learned from Jesus. He knows how love welds parents and children together as they live under Christ's love. This love, because it is love, must sometimes be "tough." If it were lax, ignoring what is right in the sight of God, it wouldn't be love. The motivation for true love comes from Christ's love as the source. St. John states, "I write to you, dear children, because your sins have been forgiven on account of His name. I write to you, fathers, because you have known Him who is from the beginning" (1 John 2:12–13). The sum of it all is this: "Love one another" (1 John 3:11).

Prayer Suggestion

If a family group is present at this devotion, let the members take turns asking for Christ's help to love one another.

HUMAN ACORNS

*They will be called oaks of righteousness, a planting of
the LORD. Isaiah 61:3*

This is a parable about oak trees and acorns representing people.
What happens to their seed? Some acorns drop on the sidewalk, to be
carried away by squirrels or to be crushed under people's feet. Other
acorns fall into the street gutter, but they have no chance there—
because underneath the thin layer of dirt is solid concrete. Others
drop on the parkway where they must compete with other plants.
People run lawn mowers over them. Fortunately, at the end of the
sloping street is a tree nursery. Acorns landing there are picked up by
the owner, who plants them, nurses them along until he can sell them
as little trees that will become big ones.

Imagine a home on that street where parents, like oak trees, have
offspring—human acorns. Much can happen to the children. They can
become the victims of all kinds of street events. In the city park is
equipment for physical exercise, but that does nothing for mental or
spiritual growth. Down the street are places called "joints," where children can play electronic games or see cheap movies, and the older
ones smoke pot. These are not places where human acorns can
become sturdy oak trees.

But at the end of a downhill street is a school. Here children learn
the three R's. They learn about the world and how to be good citizens
in it. A part of their education is to learn respect for teachers. They
learn how to get along together, how to respect the rights of others. If
it is a Christian school, the children learn the greatest truth of all:
Jesus Christ, God's Son, loves them. He gave His life for their salvation. He wants them to love others.

You will agree: There are human acorns that get crushed in streets,
that have no future in the gutters, that can't develop in parks whose
grass is cut by mowers. Those in the fourth group are the ones who
will become what the Bible calls "oaks of righteousness."

Prayer Suggestion

Thank God for homes, schools, and churches where children learn
God's Word and come to love Jesus, their dearest Friend.

WHAT IS MONEY FOR?

What good is it for a man to gain the whole world, yet forfeit his soul? Mark 8:36

It is not *money* that is the root of all evil, but the *love* of it. Money is not evil in itself. We need it. Money is God's gift to us, to be administered by us as good stewards.

In modern times, with the emphasis on material goods, we see something emerging that raises questions about our sense of values. Games of chance are on the increase. They are the focus of tremendous interest, aided and abetted by wide-spread publicity. The sad part is that the people who can least afford it buy the most tickets, spending money on a wish and a dream—money they need for food, clothing, and fuel. They read stories of ordinary people hitting the jackpot, and they begin to reason: "If they can do it, so can we." Not mentioned in these news stories are the millions who did not win anything.

It's no fun being poor. So there come visions of what life could be like if you were suddenly a millionaire. You ditch your job, go traveling, build a big house, drive a limousine-length car. But that is only a vision. The cold facts are that the chance of getting rich by chance are so remote that you can forget about it.

Underneath the lottery fever is a philosophy that says you can get a great deal for very little—you can get wealth without working for it. This is a delusion. Satisfaction comes from acquiring what you need in the old-fashioned way: earning it!

The Bible has a good suggestion for those who hang around games of chance with money burning holes in their pockets: "Do something useful with his own hands, that he may have something to share with those in need" (Ephesians 4:28).

We cannot repay Jesus Christ for having redeemed us—redeemed us not with gold or silver but with His holy, precious blood. But we can show our thankfulness by being faithful stewards of all He has entrusted to us.

Prayer Suggestion

Start with the hymn verse: "Take my silver and my gold," giving thanks to Jesus for redeeming you, not with money but with His blood.

THE LORD'S INVITATION

The kingdom of heaven is like a king who prepared a
wedding banquet for his son. Matthew 22:2

A well-laden table is a symbol of the abundant grace God offers in His kingdom. Such a festive board reminds us of the plentitude of the gifts of forgiveness, life, and salvation in Jesus Christ. Our Lord said, "The kingdom of heaven is like a king who prepared a wedding banquet for his son" (Matthew 22:2). The invitation did not only say, "Come to the wedding banquet," but also made reference to the sumptuously prepared dinner: "My oxen and fattened cattle have been butchered, and everything is ready" (Matthew 22:4).

God prepares a feast for us whenever and wherever the means of grace, Word and Sacraments, are dispensed. This generally occurs in church, supplied as it is with pulpit and lectern, baptismal font, and the Lord's Table. Faith comes through hearing the Word and through the use of the sacraments. Faith is created in Holy Baptism and confirmed and strengthened in Holy Communion—saving faith in the Savior Jesus Christ.

This is how the Lord states His invitation:

- "Come, all you who are thirsty, come to the waters; and you who have no money, come, buy and eat! Come, buy wine and milk without money and without cost" (Isaiah 55:1).
- "Come to Me, all you who are weary and burdened, and I will give you rest. … I am gentle and humble in heart, and you will find rest for your souls" (Matthew 11:28–29).
- "The Spirit and the bride say, 'Come!' And let him who hears say, 'Come!' Whoever is thirsty, let him come; and whoever wishes, let him take the free gift of the water of life" (Revelation 22:17).

The Spirit extends the invitation and transforms our hearts to accept it. It's that simple.

Prayer Suggestion

Give thanks for food and drink, especially for Christ's Gospel, which is food and drink for the soul.

HELPING THE HELPERS

After this the Lord appointed seventy-two others and sent them two by two ahead of Him. Luke 10:1

This human drama, enacted in St. Louis, has been repeated in many other cities and communities: A workman was buried when the ground in which he was working collapsed. For 17 hours firefighters and paramedics worked to free him, and free him they did. During those working hours women from the Red Cross and the Salvation Army served the rescuers with food and drink. They helped the helpers.

Something similar took place when Jesus sent out 72 disciples to preach and heal in the towns where He Himself would come. The people in these towns were, spiritually (and physically) speaking, in a desperate situation—like the man under the collapsed ground. Jesus sent this large group of disciples as a rescue team. They were helpers of the needy. Helping the helpers were the families who welcomed them into their homes, giving them not only food and drink but also gracious hospitality and expressions of peace. This meant much to the evangelizing disciples.

To this day God provides both the evangelists and the people who give them support. The latter back up Christ's workers with prayers and gifts, with hospitality and spiritual support. These are necessary and appreciated by our Lord's rescue forces. One wonders how much free hospitality the early settlers in this country gave the horseback missionaries who came to them on the prairies and forests primeval. Without such help, the pioneer pastors and teachers could not have done their work. Also the small favors count when done in faith. Jesus said to His workmen: "Anyone who gives you a cup of water in My name because you belong to Christ will certainly not lose his reward" (Mark 9:41).

Christ's love always constrains and prompts us to help those who help the spiritually lost. It is that love that brought God's Son down from heaven to give His life for the salvation of all: the people in need, the helpers, and those who help the helpers.

Prayer Suggestion

Pray for a missionary family known to you, following up your prayer with such assistance that you can give.

GETTING INVOLVED

Love your neighbor as yourself. Luke 10:27

Several years ago a young woman in New York City, Catherine Genovese, was twice attacked on the street and then killed. All the while, 38 persons in surrounding apartments heard her screams, but not one did so much as call the police. The onlookers did not want to get involved.

One sometimes wonders how cold and impersonal people can become in our large cities. The fault doesn't lie in the surroundings but in human nature. Jesus spoke of this in His parable of the Good Samaritan. Long ago, not on a busy city street but on a country road from Jerusalem to Jericho, a traveler was robbed and nearly beaten to death. Two men who knew better, a priest and a Levite, passed by on the other side, failing to help the victim. They, too, didn't want to get involved. It was up to the Good Samaritan to cross cultural and racial barriers to come to his rescue.

Sometimes it is fear and not knowing what to do that keeps people from helping. Sometimes another factor enters in—we are in a hurry to do something or get somewhere. So we pass on and leave it to someone else to lend a hand.

Emergency situations are hard to predict or to prepare for. But some things can be kept in mind. For one thing, we should know what number to call to summon the police, the fire department, or an ambulance. Another minimal effort is to stay with the victims and comfort them until professional help arrives.

Christians know why they want to do these things, not only because human decency requires it but also—and primarily—because our Savior, Jesus Christ, chose to become involved in our behalf. He did for us in a spiritual way what the Good Samaritan did for his victim: He took proper measures to heal us from the wounds of sin, save us from death, and make us well. We cannot repay Jesus for this, but we can show our thankfulness by helping others in need.

Prayer Suggestion

Ask God, for Jesus' sake, to give you a compassionate heart toward people in distress and willing hands to help them.

A HUMILITY THAT EXALTS

Everyone who exalts himself will be humbled, and he who humbles himself will be exalted. Luke 14:11

When there is an official dinner for government heads or their representatives, the guests are seated according to rank. It would not only be an infringement on established protocol but folly as well for someone to occupy a high place by his own choice. He would run the risk of being demoted and thus lose face with the assembly.

Jesus, once a guest in the home of a prominent Pharisee, noted how the pride-prone guests sought out places of honor for themselves at the table. It drew from Him a parable with this good advice: "When someone invites you to a wedding feast, do not take the place of honor, for a person more distinguished than you may have been invited. If so, the host who invited both of you will come and say to you, 'Give this man your seat.' Then, humiliated, you will have to take the least important place. But when you are invited, take the lowest place, so that when your host comes, he will say to you, 'Friend, move up to a better place.' Then you will be honored in the presence of all your fellow guests" (Luke 14:8–10).

Our Lord's major concern is not proper table manners but the virtue, or fruit of faith, underlying good behavior in general: humility. The pride displayed among people is often a symptom of pride before God. That is shown to us by the Pharisee praying in the temple: "God, I thank You that I am not like other men" (Luke 18:11). He recites his good deeds: fasting and tithing.

Before God, none can be declared just on the basis of good works or excellence of character. We are acceptable to God only if we take off the spotted garment of the flesh and of our own righteousness and are, by faith, adorned with the merit credited to us because of Christ's shed blood. Trust in Jesus Christ makes for true humility—the kind that exalts.

Prayer Suggestion

Petition the Holy Spirit to work in you the fruit of humility that exalts Christ Jesus, to whom all glory and honor are due.

NOW IS THE TIME

Today, if you hear His voice, do not harden your hearts.
Hebrews 3:7–8

In a burned-out house, where a little boy lost his life, two unused smoke detectors were found on a closet shelf. Had they been installed, they might have sounded the alarm, and the boy's life might have been spared. Perhaps the parents wanted to install the smoke detectors at some vague, future time.

A tragedy is all the more painful when we have reason to think it might have been avoided. So it is in our spiritual lives. The Lord doesn't want anyone to perish. It is His good and gracious will that all people be saved and come to the knowledge of the truth (1 Timothy 2:3–4). To that end He took measures to prepare salvation for all. He sent His Son, Jesus Christ, among us to give His life to save us all from sin and its consequences. Salvation is a gift God wants every person to have. He wants the Gospel proclaimed—the Good News that is "the power of God for the salvation of everyone who believes" (Romans 1:16).

But God's gift of salvation does us no good if we refuse to accept it or let it function in our lives—like those smoke detectors left lying on a closet shelf. Look what we are missing when we pass up so great a salvation! We forfeit peace with God, a good conscience, the assurance of God's presence in our hearts and homes, the daily access to God in prayer.

God's blessings are like a delicious, nourishing banquet meal. The sumptuous wedding dinner has been prepared, and the heavenly Host declares: "Everything is ready. Come to the wedding banquet" (Matthew 22:4). What a pity that many go spiritually hungry or even starve to death when all this soul food is available without cost!

There is an urgency about all this—the need to act now, as the Scripture says: "Now is the time of God's favor, now is the day of salvation." Now is the time to let Christ direct our lives so that the power of His love might bless us.

Prayer Suggestion

Thank God that He has led you to say yes to His promise of full and free salvation in Christ Jesus, His Son.

LIFE'S WHEAT AND WEEDS

We know that in all things God works for the good of those who love Him. Romans 8:28

An author who wrote interestingly about the struggles of early settlers in Nebraska was Willa Cather. *O Pioneers!* was one of her novels. In her poem "Prairie Spring" she wrote about the opposites that made farming difficult: "The growing wheat, the growing weeds." Early Nebraskans, fighting blizzards, dust storms, droughts, and grasshoppers, knew that also weeds had to be controlled if there was to be wheat. They understood what God meant when He told fallen Adam concerning the ground: "Through painful toil you will eat of it all the days of your life" (Genesis 3:17).

Good and evil—the proverbial wheat and weeds—are encountered in all vocations and walks of life. The businessperson has profits and losses. Salespersons hear yes and no from the buying public. Teachers have bright pupils and dullards. Life in the home is similarly marked by ups and downs, by many a plus and many a minus.

Christians put up with "the growing wheat, the growing weeds." They put all of life, including occupational, domestic, and personal affairs, into God's hands. They do the best they can, leaving it to God to add His blessing—to give the increase to their sowing. Their trust in Him is supported through the use of God's Word and prayer.

What gives us confidence, speaking specifically, is a certain "logic" of faith. St. Paul refers to this in a beautiful passage in Romans. In chapter 8 (verse 32) he confronts us with the great truth of the Gospel and then lets us draw our own conclusions with regard to the everyday affairs of life. He writes, "If God is for us, who can be against us? He who did not spare His own Son, but gave Him up for us all—how will He not also, along with Him, graciously give us all things?"

We are reminded: Not only our spiritual well-being—that is, our sure salvation in Jesus Christ—but also our daily activity is covered by God's promise to provide.

Prayer Suggestion

Tell your Lord that you can cope with life because you have His promise to grant you daily bread.

THE HOLY SPIRIT: HEAVENLY DEW

May the LORD bless his [Joseph's] land with the precious dew from heaven above. Deuteronomy 33:13

According to the Nicene Creed, the Holy Spirit "proceeds forth from the Father and the Son." Jesus Christ, God's Son, often emphasized that the Father had sent Him. He layed equal stress on the fact that both He and the Father were to send the Holy Spirit. The Father is God, the Son is God, and so is the divine Emissary, the Holy Spirit.

Our Lord teaches that the Spirit of truth would bear witness to Him. The medium through which the life-giving Spirit speaks is the Word. The Spirit and the Word always go together, as Jesus said, "The words I have spoken to you are Spirit and they are life" (John 6:63). The Spirit quickens, gives life, and renews us as He creates and confirms what the hymn line calls "the true faith, which we need the most," the faith that relies altogether on the redeeming merits of Jesus Christ.

Nothing so refreshes our world like water. Because the Holy Spirit gives new life to the arid desert of human hearts, He is called a heavenly Dew. A Pentecost hymn declares:

> O gentle Dew, from heaven now fall
> With power upon the hearts of all,
> Your tender love instilling.

When the seed of God's Word is sown in us, and the Holy Spirit is given as refreshing rain, there is every promise of an abundant yield of the Spirit's fruit.

Prayer Suggestion

Speak from your heart a prayer, asking the Father and the Son to send the Holy Spirit into your heart and home.

Two Types in the Temple

Two men went up to the temple to pray, one a Pharisee and the other a tax collector. Luke 18:10

In His parables Jesus often places two figures side by side to show contrast. Sometimes, as we all know, such opposites are found in the same family. Jesus spoke of two sons, the one saying yes to the father's wish but failing to act on it while the other first said no, then changed his mind and obeyed. In another parable, the prodigal son who repented and returned home and his resentful brother are similar opposites.

The Pharisee and the publican are two distinct types. The Pharisee typifies those who are confident of their own righteousness and look down on everybody else. Their self-trust was based mostly on what they were not—not crooks, adulterers, or the like—as well as on self-chosen deeds that exceeded God's requirements. Inevitably their church going was a cover-up, and their prayers were long recitals of gilded vices passing for virtues.

The publican represents Christ's type of person. It is not that our Lord approves of cheaters, such as most publicans were. The emphasis is on repentance, on a change of heart and mind, not on who the person is. Also of a penitent Pharisee Jesus would have said: He prayed humbly for God's mercy, he received it, he went home with the peace of God. That was the life story of Saul the Pharisee, who, after his conversion, believed in the Crucified One as Savior and bore witness to Him.

With the believing publican we, too, can go on our homeward journey and sing for joy because God has forgiven us in Christ and given us a new lease on life.

Prayer Suggestion

Give thanks to God for forgiving all your sins and raising you up in Christ, your Savior.

THREE STEPS IN DISCIPLESHIP

The next day John was there again with two of his disciples. When he saw Jesus passing by, he said, "Look, the Lamb of God!" John 1:35–36

Our Lord's first two disciples were Andrew and John. From their example we note several stages in the process of becoming a more understanding and committed disciple.

First, Andrew and John were *discoverers*. With the help of their former teacher, John the Baptist, they became aware of Jesus as "the Lamb of God, who takes away the sin of the world!" (John 1:29) On the basis of John's testimony, and their personal association with Jesus, they became convinced that they had discovered the promised Redeemer of whom the Scriptures speak. They exclaimed, "We have found the Messiah" (John 1:41).

Andrew and John proceeded to step two in their discipleship: They became *followers* of Jesus. They stayed in His company to share the experiences of His life and ministry, to learn from Him, to grow in faith through the Word He proclaimed, and to serve Him. Those who have come to know Jesus as the Christ can't help but make the proper response. From being discoverers they go on to become followers.

Third, Jesus' first two recruits, Andrew and John, proceeded to fulfill another important aspect of their discipleship: They in turn became *recruiters*—and among persons right in their own midst. Both had brothers with whom they started: Andrew with Peter and John with James. They told them: "We have found the Messiah" (John 1:41). As recruiters we follow in the footsteps of Christ's first disciples when we tell people near and dear to us: "Come with us to Christ; He will do you good."

Discovering Christ (that is, being found by Him), doing what He says, and sharing His Word with people near and dear to us—these are three important stages in discipleship.

Prayer Suggestion

Tell Christ in your prayer that you want to be a disciple after His own heart.

Our "Project Trinity"

*May the grace of the Lord Jesus Christ, and the love of
God, and the fellowship of the Holy Spirit be with you all.*
2 Corinthians 13:14

At Alamogordo, New Mexico, on July 16, 1945, the first atomic
bomb was exploded, ushering in the nuclear age. The venture was
known as Project Trinity. The physical power released was beyond
belief. Later the atomic bomb was used for real. The pilot of the U.S.
plane, on seeing the mushroom cloud level a Japanese city, exclaimed,
"My God, what have we done!"

Project Trinity is a term we can apply to the peace mission of the
Gospel—the mission intended to give spiritual life to people living in
the darkness of sin and death. Jesus Himself gave His disciples for all
time this mission when He said: "Go and make disciples of all nations,
baptizing them in the name of the Father and of the Son and of the
Holy Spirit" (Matthew 28:19).

Through the centuries Christ's church has engaged in Project
Trinity. It did this at Christ's command and also because of His
promise of salvation to all who believe in Him as the Lamb of God
slain for their sins and raised again to secure their eternal life. Project
Trinity brings into play the power of the Gospel to do what no physical
power can do: convert sinners and make of them the sons and daughters of the heavenly Father. It brings into our lives, in St. Paul's words,
"the grace of the Lord Jesus Christ, and the love of God, and the fellowship of the Holy Spirit" (2 Corinthians 13:14).

Project Trinity is at work in you as a Christian. The Holy Trinity—
Father, Son, and Holy Spirit—has participated in your salvation, for
the Father *thought* it (He planned and ordained it), the Son *wrought* it
when He redeemed you, and the Holy Spirit *brought* it to you through
the Gospel.

As Christians we pass on what we have received. That's why we all
participate in Project Trinity—in Christian missions.

Prayer Suggestion

Praise Father, Son, and Holy Spirit for adopting you into the family
of God through Holy Baptism and the Word.

THE GOSPEL—GOD'S LIBERTY BELL

It is for freedom that Christ has set us free. Stand firm,
then, and do not let yourselves be burdened again by a
yoke of slavery. Galatians 5:1

The metallic medium used on July 4, 1776, to announce the
Declaration of Independence in Philadelphia was the Liberty Bell. It
was cracked several times and now serves as a patriotic symbol.

The medium God uses to declare our independence from sin,
Satan, and servitude to the fear of death is the Gospel. Whenever it is
preached it proclaims spiritual liberty "throughout the land to all its
inhabitants." Although it has done this for so many centuries, it has
not cracked or broken; it is still in use and its message is circulating
wider than ever before.

How precious and powerful is the Gospel! St. Paul said he was not
ashamed of it "because it is the power of God for the salvation of
everyone who believes" (Romans 1:16). Jesus tells us what the Gospel
is. Briefly, it is the good news that "God so loved the world that He
gave His one and only Son, that whoever believes in Him shall not perish but have eternal life" (John 3:16). The Gospel is the good news that
through Jesus' crucifixion and resurrection we are set free to serve the
living God, the heavenly Father, whom we love and who loves us.

The thirteen colonies had to fight to gain and retain their freedom.
Christians must do the same to keep the liberating Gospel of Christ.
St. Paul writes to the Galatians: "It is for freedom that Christ has set us
free. Stand firm, then, and do not let yourselves be burdened again by
the yoke of slavery" (Galatians 5:1), that is, the slavery of trying to
establish one's salvation by doing the works of the Law. Freedom is
best preserved when it is used—when the freeing Gospel is believed,
lived, and proclaimed.

Prayer Suggestion

Praise God for the good news of your salvation in Jesus Christ—
for the freedom of the Gospel.

RIGHTEOUS RULERS, RIGHTEOUS CITIZENS

Righteousness exalts a nation, but sin is a disgrace to any people. Proverbs 14:34

When shifting through the oratory of political campaigns one occasionally comes across a worthwhile statement—like finding a kernel of truth in a bushel of chaff. One candidate for the United States presidency said, "The moral test of government is how it treats those who are in the dawn of life—the children; those who are in the twilight of life—the aged; and those who are in the shadows of life—the sick, the needy, and the handicapped." One wishes the speaker had referred also to the government's concern for human beings in the pre-dawn of life—the unborn infants.

Generally speaking, the moral tone of government reflects that of the citizens. If in private life people don't care about one another, they need not be surprised if the government is likewise indifferent. The men and women who represent us in government are an image of ourselves.

It has been said, "A rising tide raises all boats," not only the yachts of the rich but also the crafts of the poor. The proper place for righteousness to become a rising tide is where the people live, move, and have their being—in their homes and local communities. Righteousness exalts a nation when its people want good local schools, improved opportunities for honest work, and an atmosphere in which legitimate business can flourish. Also exalted will be the righteousness of government at all levels, in keeping with the God-given role of rulers: to be "God's servant to do you good," as St. Paul writes in Romans 13:4.

Jesus looked for righteousness in a country's citizens when he said, "Give to Caesar what is Caesar's" (Matthew 22:21). This refers not only to paying taxes but to fulfilling all of one's civic duties.

Christians are rightly motivated to be a righteous people. The love of God is at work in them—the love that came to its highest expression when God's own dear Son, our Lord and Savior Jesus Christ, gave His life for the salvation of us all.

Prayer Suggestion

Ask God to guide the citizens of our nation to seek His righteousness, beginning with you.

PRIVILEGE AND RESPONSIBILITY

We maintain that a man is justified by faith apart from observing the Law. Romans 3:28

Liberty, freedom, civil rights, and other issues can be compared to a two-wheeled cart. The two wheels are privilege and responsibility. Both are necessary.

It is the same with Christian freedom. First, what a *privilege* it is! St. Paul writes: "It is for freedom that Christ has set us free. Stand firm, then, and do not let yourselves be burdened again by a yoke of slavery" (Galatians 5:1). Christians in the New Testament have been set free from ceremonial laws demanding circumcision, the observance of Sabbath rules, and the distinction between foods. What is more, they are free from the curse and penalty of the moral law. For Jesus observed it perfectly for them and in their stead endured the punishment for their disobedience. By faith in this Savior we are at peace with God, reconciled, set free from the vain effort of meriting God's grace by our good works. Good works are to be done, not *in order* to be saved but *because* we are saved.

With the wonderful privilege of being set free by Christ goes *responsibility*. Christian freedom can be abused, and this often happens because we forget about the second wheel: responsibility. Christian freedom entails not only a privilege but also the responsibility to act in Christian love in all situations of life, as St. Peter declares: "Live as free men, but do not use your freedom as a cover-up for evil" (1 Peter 2:16).

St. Paul cites an instance of how Christians will at times suspend their freedom because they want to act in love toward those who are weak in faith. He says that no distinction needs to be made as to food. Christians have freedom. But they will gladly refrain from exercising this right if it offends another, that is, causes him to sin. He writes: "Do not by your eating destroy your brother for whom Christ died" (Romans 14:15).

As we stand firm in the privilege of Christian freedom, so we are mindful of its responsibility. Then our freedom is like a two-wheeled cart.

Prayer Suggestion

Thank God for the privilege of Christian freedom, asking Him for guidance to use it responsibly.

ETERNAL LIFE—BY GRACE

*Then the King will say to those on His right, "Come, you
are blessed by My Father; take your inheritance, the kingdom prepared for you since the creation of the world."
Matthew 25:34*

The above reading from Matthew, particularly our Lord's self-iden-
tification with the needy as "the least of these brothers of Mine"
(Matthew 25:40), is readily understood and deeply appreciated. Jesus
calls for good works in a most appealing way. Some have sought to
find support here for their belief that acceptance with God rests not
only on faith but also on good works. They claim that Jesus made no
mention here about salvation by faith in His redeeming merits, but that
He posits it on a person's own merits—on what he has done in the
area of Christian service.

It is good to remember that the Bible doesn't say everything that
needs to be said in one verse or in one group of verses. In other connections Jesus said often enough: "Your faith has saved you" (Luke 7:50).
The gospel reading for today has to be understood in light of Jesus clear
words in John 3:16, "Whoever believes in Him [the Son of God] shall …
have eternal life."

While it is true that *faith alone* saves, it is equally true that the saving faith is *never alone.* The living faith is always accompanied by
works of love—also words and thoughts of love, prayers, and the like.
A faith without works is dead, St. James declares. Jesus points to good
works as the *evidences* of the saving faith.

Eternal life comes by God's grace, not as a reward for deeds. This
is emphasized when Jesus says, "Take your inheritance" (Matthew
25:34). An inheritance is a gift, not wages for services performed.
Because salvation is God's free gift, we have all the more reason to
thank and praise Him by doing works of love. Are these works a burden? Not at all. The closing stanza of a hymn reads: "And then for
work to do for Thee, Which shall so sweet a service be That angels
well might envy me …"

Prayer Suggestion

Ask the Lord Jesus to lead you to persons who need your help,
your friendliness, and your smile.

THE EASY YOKE

Take My yoke upon you and learn from Me, for I am gentle and humble in heart. Matthew 11:29

Ordinarily the yoke stands for subjugation (from the Latin *sub-jugere*, to bring under the yoke) and bondage. Oxen on whose necks the yoke was laid were subjugated, that is, placed under the *jugum*, or yoke, so that they could be controlled as heavy draft animals.

In the Bible the term "yoke" is sometimes used figuratively, representing a person's oppression under sin. In Lamentations 1:14 Jeremiah declares, "My sins have been bound into a yoke ... They have come upon my neck." In a messianic prophecy Isaiah envisions the coming of the Deliverer to free God's people from "the yoke that burdens them, the bar across their shoulders, the rod of their oppressors" (9:4).

Jesus Christ has broken the yoke of sin and has freed us from every burden of guilt and punishment that the Law threatened. St. Paul writes, "It is for freedom that Christ has set us free. Stand firm, then, and do not let yourselves be burdened again by a yoke of slavery" (Galatians 5:1).

Obviously it is another kind of yoke that Jesus has in mind when He tells us, "Take My yoke upon you" (Matthew 11:29). He emphasizes that His yoke is easy and His burden is light. Christ's yoke is not forced on anyone; it is willingly and gladly assumed. It is the yoke of service to Him and to those who need our love. It is the yoke that links us to our Savior, who is "gentle and humble in heart" (Matthew 11:29). In His presence we find rest for our souls. It is a yoke that unites us with our family and our church to get adventuresome things done.

A pious legend has it that Joseph and Jesus in Nazareth had a woodworking shop in which they made yokes for oxen. They supposedly made their products so well that they did not chafe the necks of the oxen. If true, we could well understand why Jesus would later speak of the yoke of discipleship under Him as easy. Try it, and you will find it so.

Prayer Suggestion

Thank the Lord Jesus for freeing you from the yoke of sin and the Law's condemnation and for giving you rest for your soul.

SEEKING SAFETY IN OUR WORK

I have labored and toiled and have often gone without sleep; I have known hunger and thirst and have often gone without food; I have been cold and naked.
2 Corinthians 11:27

A highway patrolman was wounded and his partner was killed by a motorist they had stopped to question. He was asked how he felt about going back to work. He replied: "I'm a Christian. I know if something happens to me, I'll see my wife and family again—in heaven."

Some occupations are more dangerous than others. Yet they need to be filled. We need officers of the law who, at great risk to themselves, protect us.

Some might consider the Christian ministry a very safe profession. But it also is beset by perils, both physical and spiritual. This is especially true of missionaries who go into pagan lands and into countries where an anti-Christian philosophy prevails in government and society. It was true of the apostle Paul, who in the performance of his calling was beaten, stoned, involved in shipwrecks, and endangered by bandits. In the end he suffered a martyr's death in Rome. He said that Christ had loved him and had given His life for him. In gratitude he gave his life for Christ.

When it comes to work that needs to be done, and we are especially qualified to do it, the threat of danger need not deter us. All due caution should, of course, be exercised. And training should be sought to increase one's competence to cope with hazards. Christian workers deem trust in God as especially important. They implore the presence and protection of His guardian angels. Each day, as they go to work, they can commit themselves into God's hands.

What the highway patrolman said—about his belief in heaven—is of the greatest importance to Christians. It expresses belief in the life to come. Death comes to all of us sooner or later. While we live, we have the assurance of reunion with our loved ones in heaven. This assurance removes fear about the risks of our everyday work. Life is safe for those who are at peace with God through faith in Jesus Christ.

Prayer Suggestion

Ask the Lord Jesus to grant you the protection of His Holy angels as you do your work.

FOUR IMPORTANT "RE" WORDS

He [God] has rescued us from the dominion of darkness
and brought us into the kingdom of the Son He loves.
Colossians 1:13

Our Christian faith rests largely on truths expressed in "re" words. The syllable "re" means back to the original, retracing one's steps, doing something again. Sin led the human race away from God, who in His Word of the Gospel bids sinners to return to Him.

The return to life with God was made possible by the atoning work of Jesus Christ called *re*-demption. By this act our Savior brought us back, yes, brought us back with a price. "In Him [Christ] we have redemption through His blood, the forgiveness of sins" (Ephesians 1:7).

The sinner's restored relationship with God is presented in Holy Scripture from many points of view, but the truth on which it focuses is always this: *re*-storation to God. Human enmity, which separated mankind from God, is ended, and so is the wrath of God ended, thanks to Jesus' mediation. This is expressed in the "re" term *re*-conciliation. Through Christ we are made friends with God. "God ... reconciled us to Himself through Christ" (2 Corinthians 5:18).

The validity of Christ's redeeming, reconciling work is established by another "re" word: *re*-surrection. His deity is thereby attested. Jesus "was declared with power to be the Son of God by His resurrection from the dead" (Romans 1:4). What is more, His atoning work bears the seal that suffices for our salvation. "He was delivered over to death for our sins and was raised to life for our justification" (Romans 4:25).

To have the benefit of Christ's obedient life, redeeming death, and verifying resurrection, it is necessary to believe. St. Paul tells the jailer at Philippi: "Believe in the Lord Jesus, and you will be saved" (Acts 16:31). The coming to faith and the ensuing new life in Christ are covered by another "re" word: *re*-generation. It is the act of the Holy Spirit through the Gospel to make us a new creation in Christ. "[God] saved us ... by the washing of regeneration and renewal in the Holy Spirit" (Titus 3:5 RSV).

What other "re" words do you find in the Bible as pertaining to your salvation?

Prayer Suggestion

Give thanks to God for His acts whereby you have been brought back to Him.

THE VALUE OF QUIET TIME

When he came to his senses, he said, "How many of my father's hired men have food to spare, and here I am starving to death!" Luke 15:17

The prodigal son at long last came to his senses. It happened after the tumult and shouting of his riotous life. He had come to his senses, with quiet moments to commune with himself and with his God. Watching the swine in the field, he evaluated his life.

Out of his reflection grew this resolve, "I will set out and go back to my father and say to him: Father, I have sinned against heaven and against you." God used this resolve, although painful to carry out, to change the young man's life. A former prodigal son was now a penitent son. His merciful father forgave him and joyfully reinstated him as his son.

There is a time for action and a time for quiet meditation. The poet Goethe has said, *"Es bildet ein Talent sich in der Stille, sich ein Charakter in dem Strom der Welt"* (Talent is shaped in quietness, but character in the world's stream). Character is not formed in a vacuum but, given moral guidance and training, in the give and take of life. Talent, on the other hand, is largely perfected in silence and solitude.

Quiet time is valuable for other reasons. We need uninterrupted moments with ourselves, with those near and dear to us, with our God. "Be still, and know that I am God," the Lord tells us through Psalm 46:10. We can come very close to God in hours spent alone on the seashore or on peaceful mountaintops. There is opportunity in the presence of God to sort things out, to rethink our lives, to resolve to amend what has been amiss. The still, small voice calls us to return to our heavenly Father and to rededicate ourselves to Him. Then we turn to God's written Word, which speaks more explicitly to us.

God speaks to us most explicitly through His Son, who is the personal Word. Jesus Christ came to seek and save the lost, to give His life as a ransom, to invite all sinners to a joyful homecoming to His Father's house. We can hear the strains of the song, "Softly and tenderly Jesus is calling." He is calling to all of us.

Prayer Suggestion

Pray to God to open your ears, heart, and mind so that you may hear the voice of Jesus, the Shepherd.

GOD'S WORD—OUR GREAT HERITAGE

I am the Good Shepherd. The Good Shepherd lays down His life for the sheep. John 10:11

Motion picture actor Gregory Peck declared after he had recorded the New Testament on 16 cassettes, "I've always been a reader of the Bible." The traditional King James Version is, he said, "the most majestic and beautiful of the translations." He stressed the content—"the teachings and doctrines"—not only the great literacy and poetic value.

The Holy Scriptures are our great heritage. They are available to us in the beautiful language of the King James Version as well as in the updated language of more recent translations. The words are not an end in themselves; if they were, we would still have to use the original Hebrew and Greek words. What is important is God's message that these words convey. In all translations that are faithful to the original text the message is the same.

What is the message God conveys in this unique, divinely inspired book? It goes far beyond offering golden rules for morally upright living, although it does have moral guidance. It is not human philosophy, or essentially ethical wisdom, or aesthetic expression of great thoughts, or only a road map for life's journey. What good the Bible conveys in these areas comes as a result or fruit of something far greater, that is, of God's message of salvation by faith in Jesus Christ, God's Son and our Redeemer. Through this message of the Gospel the Holy Spirit brings people to Christ, to the one who for our sakes died on a cross and was raised.

God makes Himself perfectly clear in the Bible's message written by inspired authors. The message is good news. It can be discoursed upon at great length, or it can be briefly stated in "bumper sticker" length statements, such as: "God so loved the world that He gave His one and only Son" (John 3:16). Again: "Here is a trustworthy saying that deserves full acceptance: Christ Jesus came into the world to save sinners" (1 Timothy 1:15). Or in Jesus' own words: "I am the Good Shepherd. The Good Shepherd lays down His life for the sheep" (John 10:11). This is God's message in the Bible.

How blessed we are to have God's Word as our great heritage!

Prayer Suggestion

Ask God's blessings on your reading of the Bible so that you may be drawn closer to Christ.

GIVING LATE BLOOMERS A CHANCE

Blessed is the man who trusts in the LORD ... He will be like a tree planted by the water. Jeremiah 17:7–8

In the fall of the year, when most of the yard flowers have bloomed out, we notice the chrysanthemums coming into their own. Called mums for short, their name in Greek means "golden flowers." During the summer no one pays much attention to the uninteresting plants. The other eye-catching flowers disappear and the multicolored, full-blossomed chrysanthemums brighten the scene. It is their nature to bloom in late summer and fall.

The Bible compares people to flowers and teaches us lessons. One truth we can learn from flowers is that they have their proper seasons, and so it is with human beings. People do not grow and mature at the same rate. Some are like early spring beauties, while others, like the chrysanthemums, are late bloomers. Psalm 1 compares the righteous person to a plant "which yields its fruit in season" (v. 3).

There is for each Christian a proper season for blossoming out, maturing, and bearing fruit. It is a wise parent who knows what to expect from children at the time proper for them. Those are wise teachers who can discern the right growth and fruit-bearing season of their pupils. Those are wise spiritual leaders who can recognize the "chrysanthemums" in their congregations—people who come into their own when their time has come: retired persons, senior citizens, and many others who have individual talents and their own built-in schedules, calendars, and clocks of personal development.

Jesus, our Lord, found many late bloomers, that is, persons who came to Him relatively late in life, believed in Him, and served Him. He gladly accepted the ministrations of Peter's mother-in-law, whom He had healed. He welcomed a late bloomer in Jericho: Zacchaeus the tax collector, who became a follower of Jesus. He promised heaven to so late a comer as the penitent thief on the cross.

Are you like a chrysanthemum, like a fall flower? For you, too, Christ died and He wants you in His flower garden.

Prayer Suggestion

Thank God, your heavenly Gardener, for planting you in Christ's kingdom and giving you a chance to bloom.

HELPING THE REAPERS

The harvest is plentiful, but the workers are few. Ask the
Lord of the harvest, therefore, to send out workers into His
harvest field. Luke 10:2

Jesus compared the ingathering of people into His kingdom to a harvest. He said as He sent out the 72 disciples as missionaries: "The harvest is plentiful, but the workers are few. Ask the Lord of the harvest, therefore, to send out workers into His harvest field" (Luke 10:2).

In answer to the church's prayers, God sends His workers out into the world to proclaim the Gospel of forgiveness and grace with God, thanks to the redeeming work of Jesus Christ. It remains for us to follow up our prayers with every possible assistance we can give the Lord's reapers.

A man who did this in an effective way was Cyrus H. McCormick. He had invented the self-binder, or grain-reaping machine. It made him a wealthy man, a man who ushered in a new era in the method of harvesting grain. Being a Christian man, he did much to help also in the harvest of souls. He gave liberally toward founding a theological seminary in Chicago bearing his name. Through the years thousands of men have been trained there for ministry and mission. McCormick helped the Lord's reapers in bringing in the sheaves.

Most of us are not able to do what this man did. But God gives us other opportunities to participate in the harvest of souls. We have such opportunities as Christian parents in the home, as church members who support world missions, as persons who, at work and elsewhere, witness to their faith in the Lord Jesus Christ.

All the while we keep on doing what our Lord told us to do—to pray, "Thy kingdom come," to pray that He would send more pastors, teachers, medical missionaries, and the like into His harvest field. We sing along with Mary Maxwell in her hymn: "Saints of God, the dawn is bright'ning, Token of our coming Lord; O'er the earth the field is whit'ning; Louder rings the Master's word: Pray for reapers, Pray for reapers, In the harvest of the Lord!"

Prayer Suggestion

In your own words repeat the prayer in the above hymn verse.

KNOWING THE GOOD LIFE AND LEADING IT

Since we live by the Spirit, let us keep in step with the Spirit.
Galatians 5:25

The *Kansas City* (Missouri) *Star* has stated editorially that for many children "the sense of morality is a combination of 'Dallas' [a long-running TV program] and the pop music chart." Neither the named television program nor the popular songs set high moral standards. The emphasis is on greed, lust, sex, and all the other sins that have plagued the human race through the ages, as St. Paul mentions them in his epistles. They are the fruit of the flesh.

We have, thank God, a much higher moral standard set in the Ten Commandments. This standard is not a kind of a golden rule which people might attain by their natural powers. It is absolute; it demands perfection. To reach the high level of Christian morality, we need the power of the Holy Spirit working in us. Through the Gospel and the sacraments the Spirit first plants the tree. For without the tree no fruit is forthcoming. This tree is the faith He creates in us—faith in the Lord Jesus Christ, whose redeeming merit is credited to our account. This faith is more than the acceptance of a set of facts, although right knowledge is important. You can't believe unless you know what to believe. What is involved above all is a change of heart, a new spiritual birth, a new outlook on life, full trust in God. Faith makes a person a new creation in Christ.

The Holy Spirit, having kindled faith, doesn't then walk away, as a carpenter does when he has finished building a house. The Spirit continues to enlighten, nourish, sanctify, and keep us in the faith through the Gospel. He causes the faith to go beyond the ABCs; He makes it grow farther and farther into the alphabet of Christianity. The XYZ of perfection is attained only in heaven.

It helps children live moral lives if they have the good example of Christian parents to follow. So it is in our Christian growth. The heavenly Father sets us the perfect example. The triune God is active here. The Father is our example, the Son is the enabler, in that He took away our sins, and the Holy Spirit leads us to a new life in Christ.

Prayer Suggestion

Ask the Lord Jesus to send His Holy Spirit into your heart through the Word that He may make you more and more like the Father in heaven.

JESUS OUR RELIABLE PROVIDER

If a liar and deceiver comes and says, "I will prophesy for you plenty of wine and beer," he would be just the prophet for this people! Micah 2:11

Bo Giertz, when bishop of Gothenburg, Sweden, once said that these were the three great lies in the area of religion: There is no God, there is no devil, and everyone can be saved in his own way.

False prophets not only teach lies but also make deceiving promises—promises of things people crave for an enjoyable life. Besides the drinks Micah mentions, these things are also luxuries: large homes, miraculous cures, and sudden riches. If people want religious leaders who ignore God's Word and instead promise sensuous and materialistic things, they will have such prophets. These will come, not as a promise but as a punishment, in keeping with the words of St. Peter, "Judgment must begin at the house of God" (1 Peter 4:17 KJV). People get the kind of leaders they deserve.

Lies, falsehoods, distortions, unfounded accusations, false hopes—all these marked the trial of Jesus before the Sanhedrin and the tribunal of Pontius Pilate. The devil, who is a murderer and the father of lies, was certainly at work, as our Lord said to His enemies: "This is your hour—when darkness reigns" (Luke 22:53). All that the Swedish bishop mentioned was fulfilled here: the denial of the divine sonship of God (and thereby also the denial of God as such), the rejection of His way of salvation in preference for works righteousness, and without realizing it, full obedience to Satan.

Carnally minded people had rejected Jesus long before His final trials. They had wanted an earthly messiah capable of enriching them and serving them as a bread king. Our Lord would have found a great welcome if He had promised full tables and cups overflowing with wine. But His was not that kind of kingdom, not that kind of earthly rule.

We thank God that Jesus Christ, His Son, was not sent to be this kind of a provider. He had come to supply abundantly what we so desperately need—the bread of life and the living water of salvation. He had come to give His life a ransom for us, and this is what He did when He went to Mount Calvary to be crucified.

Prayer Suggestion

Ask the Savior to keep on supplying His church with faithful leaders.

THE EDUCATION OF THE HEART

Everyone who hears these words of Mine and puts them into practice is like a wise man who built his house on the rock.
Matthew 7:24

Credit for opening the first kindergarten in the United States goes to Susan Blow, who formed one in St. Louis, Missouri, in 1873. At that time the children of workers living in tenements usually went to school only three years—from age 7 to 10. The kindergarten enabled them not only to get an earlier start but also to associate enjoyment with learning.

Many dedicated men and women have contributed to perfecting the educational system. The education of the total person is like the construction process of an exquisite building. A good foundation has to be laid. The architect's plans are followed as the structure takes shape. The walls go up as stone is laid on stone. The roof is put on. The proper utilities provide heat, fresh drinking water, and communication facilities. The house acquires a soul when the family moves in. It becomes a home when people live, work, rest, play, and serve one another. A home cannot be built overnight, nor is the education of a person completed in a matter of days. It takes years, even decades. Many people like Susan Blow are involved in it.

It has been said: The heart of education is the education of the heart. The heart is where the person really lives, what he or she truly is. By nature the heart is the source of much evil. Jesus said that evil thoughts and desires, words and deeds, proceed from it. What is needed is a new heart, a heart not of stone but of flesh, a heart capable of faith and love. Such a heart the Holy Spirit creates in children as they are baptized and given Christian instruction. The converted heart becomes functional as it influences conscience, will, and mind. What the heart believes, that it prompts the hands to do. In the Christian's heart dwells Jesus Christ, who in love gave Himself for the salvation of every person and who through His Word enables Christian growth to continue.

Prayer Suggestion

Thank God for revealing Christ to you as the basis of true wisdom.

HOLY SCRIPTURE LEADS US TO CHRIST

The Word is near you; it is in your mouth and in your heart. Romans 10:8

Several years ago Dr. Nelson Glueck, then president of Hebrew Union College—Jewish Institute of Religion, Cincinnati, stated that the copper mines of King Solomon in the Negev (southern part of Judea) had been found and that a copper-mining industry had been established there. He said that the presence of metals was indicated in Moses' words that the Promised Land was "a land where the rocks are iron and you can dig copper out of the hills" (Deuteronomy 8:9). This statement, he said, was verified, adding, "I have always gone on the assumption that the historical statements of the Bible are true."

The biblical scholars at the time of Jesus' birth (Matthew 2:3–6), as well as the Old Testament prophets, went on the assumption that the prophetic statements of the Bible were true. The purpose of the Bible is not to serve as a textbook on history or science, although its statements also in these areas are true. The purpose of divine revelation in the prophetic and apostolic Scriptures is to lead us to Jesus Christ so that, believing in Him as the Redeemer from sin and death, we may obtain eternal salvation. In our time no special star, no angelic song in the sky, no great miracle in nature leads us to Christ. So we rely on the "prophetic Word" of the Old Testament Scripture, confirmed by the New Testament Word of fulfillment.

In His love and wisdom God stated the truths of His Word in plain language. What we need to know and believe to be saved He stated in simple speech—not in mysterious prophecies, not in wisdom buried in philosophy, not in truths attainable only in the depth of the earth or in the clouds above. St. Paul says, "The Word is near you; it is in your mouth and in your heart" (Romans 10:8). And right now it is in your hand as you read this devotion.

Prayer Suggestion

Thank God for giving us His holy Word that brings us Christ, our only Savior.

GOD'S PATIENCE: IT HAS LIMITS

God waited patiently in the days of Noah while the ark was being built. 1 Peter 3:20

Thomas Paine, a free thinker and declared enemy of Christianity, gives us something to think about in making this distinction: "Toleration is not the opposite of intolerance, but is the counterfeit of it. Both are despotism."

Tolerance is not the same as toleration. Tolerance implies patience and forbearance. When weighing or measuring things, we generally allow for a degree of variation, calling it tolerance. A tolerant person endures a situation for a while, working toward correcting it. On the other hand, toleration, while recognizing error, accepts it and does nothing about it.

God has shown Himself tolerant in the sense that He exercises great patience with sinners. He gave the people of Noah's generation 120 years to repent. When granting a time of grace, He continually and earnestly urges repentance. In being tolerant or patient for a season, God does not compromise His holiness. He is never given to toleration concerning the evil people do. If His proffered salvation in Christ is rejected, He brings people into judgment. In dealing with delinquent members, the church takes a page out of God's book in that it practices patience but never extends the toleration of error.

Thankful that God is patient, long-suffering, and always willing to forgive those who repent and believe in Jesus, it is also our concern not to tempt God by an attitude of indifference. This is important: "Now is the time of God's favor, now is the day of salvation" (2 Corinthians 6:2).

Prayer Suggestion

Express your thankfulness to God for having been patient with you in times when your faith was weak and when sin threatened to gain the upper hand. Ask Him, for Jesus' sake, to create a new spirit in you—a spirit of continual repentance and faith.

FINDING REFUGE IN GOD

Come to Me, all you who are weary and burdened, and
I will give you rest. Matthew 11:28

In his poem "The Hound of Heaven" Francis Thompson, an opium user, gives an account of his futile attempts to avoid God, who is portrayed as pursuing him relentlessly amid his problems. He describes five "refuges" he tried to take in his desire to escape God: self (ego), mind, knowledge of nature, children, and unconsciousness. But always God in His love found him in his "hiding places."

Many today seek to evade God, turning to many escapes, subterfuges, and substitutes for Him. But as Adam and Eve learned in Eden, they cannot give God the slip. The hymn writer declares, "Other refuge have I none; Hangs my helpless soul on Thee." And St. Augustine: "Thou hast made us unto Thyself, and our souls are restless until they rest in Thee." Jesus, having gained rest and respite for us by His atoning work, bids all who labor to come to Him.

The fact that God is everywhere may alarm the person who tries to run from God, but to Christians it is a great comfort. God is where we are: at home, at work, on the road, or wherever we are. The psalmist declares, "Where can I go from Your Spirit? Where can I flee from Your presence? If I go up to the heavens, You are there; if I make my bed in the depths, You are there. If I rise on the wings of the dawn, if I settle on the far side of the sea, even there Your hand will guide me, Your right hand will hold me fast" (Psalm 139:7–10). This is a great comfort!

Prayer Suggestion

Finish this prayer: "Heavenly Father, You are my Refuge and Strength. Today I ask You to help me in these situations ..."

SPEAKING THE TRUTH IN LOVE

*Speaking the truth in love, we will in all things grow up
into Him who is the Head, that is, Christ. Ephesians 4:15*

Sociologist John Hutchinson, of Columbia University, has written, "By the time word reaches the fourth person, a message is likely to contain no more than five percent of the whole story."

Truth was terribly distorted at the trial of Jesus, where it was said He wanted to destroy the holy temple in Jerusalem. As a matter of fact, He was speaking of the resurrection of the body. False rumors are apt to start when a statement is misunderstood or wrongly interpreted. The English courts distinguish between truth as it is spoken and truth as it is heard. Because we are fallible human beings, we ought always to speak plainly and listen carefully, lest we do someone an injustice.

In love we refrain from uttering untruth. So also in the same love we speak the truth—the truth of correction—when the situation requires it. Jesus is the Truth personified. He not only spoke but also *did* the truth, fulfilling the work the heavenly Father had given Him to do. He is more than our Exemplar; He is the Enabler of truth-speaking, giving us the willingness and power to speak the truth in love.

Speaking the truth in love, of course, has a reverse side, and that is to speak untruth in malice. It is especially sinful to do this behind a brother's or sister's back. St. James (4:11) reminds us, "Brothers, do not slander one another." Speaking the truth in love is an essential part of the fulfillment of our Lord's Word, "Love your neighbor as yourself" (Matthew 19:19).

Prayer Suggestion

Ask for God's help to avoid speaking evil to and against your neighbor, but to speak the truth in love.

Forgiveness: The Breath of Life

If you forgive anyone his sins, they are forgiven.
John 20:23

Truth is often written in headstone inscriptions. Mount Olivet Cemetery at Hannibal, Missouri, is a case in point. It is the resting place of John and Jane Clemens, the parents of Mark Twain. An inscription there records this grim fact:

> Leaves have their time in Fall
> And flowers to wither at the north wind's breath;
> And stars to set, but all—
> Thou hast all seasons for thine own, O Death.

Another headstone expresses this confidence:

> And when thou are refreshed in death,
> Christ will give thee back thy breath.

In a tomb in Joseph's "lovely garden" our dead and buried Lord was given back His breath. His presence was living proof of His victory over sin and death. At His reunion with His disciples He breathed on them and said: "Receive the Holy Spirit. If you forgive anyone his sins, they are forgiven" (John 20:23). To forgiveness is linked the promise of life and salvation—the promise of eternal life. Forgiveness is the breath of life. It brings peace, hope, and joy. For He who pronounces it is Himself the Resurrection and the Life.

Before ascending into heaven, our Lord entrusted to His church—and all His disciples constitute His church—the Office of the Keys, that is, the power to remit and retain sins. Those who live in repentance and faith have the burden of sin lifted off their chests and are free to breathe in Christ's assurance of forgiveness. It brings peace.

Prayer Suggestion

Thank the risen, ascended Christ for the privilege of having the church of disciples speak His forgiveness to you.

SPIRITUAL MEALS ARE INCLUDED

My God will meet all your needs according to His glorious riches in Christ Jesus. Philippians 4:19

A man who had booked passage on a ship sailing for England did a foolish and unnecessary thing. Thinking that he could not afford to pay for the meals in the ship's dining room, he had taken along a suitcase full of canned food. At meal times, when his cabin mate found him eating from his suitcase, he said, "You foolish man! Don't you know that the meals are included in the price of your ticket?"

Jesus Christ paid the price of our redemption. His salvation is total. The one price He paid is all-inclusive. It not only effected our release from sin, the fear of death, and the power of the devil; it also assured us of free passage to heaven. Along with this our Lord also provides for the full sustenance of our faith while we are en route to eternal life. He gave us His Word, which is "spirit and life." He instituted Holy Baptism and Holy Communion for the creation of faith and its preservation. It would be a foolish and futile thing to try to depend on man-made means to sustain spiritual life. The prophet asks: "Why spend money on what is not bread, and your labor on what does not satisfy?" (Isaiah 55:2)

Why try to rely on our own good works, wisdom, and resources, often at great cost to ourselves, to sustain the saving faith during life's voyage to the heavenly shores? Why try to supply what we need when our Lord has provided for our spiritual sustenance fully and freely? St. Paul assures the Philippians and us, "My God will meet all your needs according to His glorious riches in Christ Jesus" (Philippians 4:19).

Prayer Suggestion

To your thank-You to God for food and drink, add a statement of thanks for all that He provides in Christ for life's spiritual needs.

THE REBUILDING OF PERSONS

If anyone is in Christ, he is a new creation.
2 Corinthians 5:17

In his book *Peace of Mind* Joshua Liebman states a very obvious truth: "No reconstructed society can be built on unreconstructed individuals." By the same token, you cannot have a strong chain that has weak links, a good forest without good trees, a productive farm with unproductive fields.

At the level of civil righteousness, reconstructed individuals are those who from high motivation keep the laws and do more than what the civil laws demand. They set good examples. Their vision of the public good exceeds that of private gain.

But rebuilt persons in God's sight—that is, at the level of righteousness that meets His approval—are individuals born anew by water and the Spirit—by the Gospel that has brought the Savior Jesus Christ into their hearts and keeps Him there. Their hearts and lives have been cleansed by the shed blood of Christ. They are the temple of the living God. In them the Holy Spirit has found a home. Now a new community consisting of such persons can begin. This is the holy Christian church, the communion of saints. It is in itself the good spiritual society, and it is the only true prop for the society surrounding it.

Spiritually reconstructed persons constitute a community worthy to be called the body of Christ. St. Paul writes of the church built on Christ as the chief cornerstone: "In Him the whole building is joined together and rises to become a holy temple in the Lord" (Ephesians 2:21). Spiritually rebuilt persons make for a perfectly constructed church. Christ's church is without stain or wrinkle or any other blemish.

Prayer Suggestion

Pray for the spiritual welfare of Christ's church, asking that its forward progress in a sinful world may begin with a stronger, more active faith in you.

GOD'S FOREKNOWLEDGE AT WORK

The Scripture foresaw that God would justify the Gentiles by faith. Galatians 3:8

Some 70 years ago the head of a large electrical appliance company was shown a crude television camera and picture tube developed by one Vladimir K. Zworykin in the laboratory. The chief executive, seeing no future use for such devices, ordered, "Put that guy to work on something useful." Human vision of the future is limited, even for experts in their fields.

Omniscience—total foresight and knowledge of all things, including the future—is only to be found in God. The psalmist declares, "Before a word is on my tongue You know it completely, O LORD" (139:4).

As the Sovereign Lord of history, God is able to declare, "I make known the end from the beginning, from ancient times, what is still to come" (Isaiah 46:10). St. Paul tells the Galatians "Understand, then, that those who believe are children of Abraham. The Scripture foresaw that God would justify the Gentiles by faith, and announced the Gospel in advance to Abraham: 'All nations will be blessed through you'" (Galatians 3:7–9).

God foresaw the fall of the human race into sin, and from eternity He planned its salvation. At the fullness of time He sent His Son to be the world's Redeemer. He, the Messiah, was born of God's chosen nation, to whom belonged "the adoption as sons; theirs the divine glory, the covenants, the receiving of the law, the temple worship and the promises" (Romans 9:4). Yet God provided for the Gospel to be proclaimed also to the Gentiles, desiring them also to be justified by faith in Christ, the same as Abraham and his descendants. To this foreknowledge and foreordination of God the Scripture testifies.

Prayer Suggestion

Thank the God of Abraham for including Israelites, Gentiles, and you in His plan of salvation in Christ.

SHEPHERD AND SHEEP: THEIR RELATIONSHIP

I am the Good Shepherd; I know My sheep and My sheep know Me. John 10:14

In John chapter 10, Jesus spoke of His relationship to the sheep, and the sheep's relationship to Him. It is a close union.

Jesus declares what He, as the Good Shepherd, does and has promised to do. First, He has a most effective knowledge of the members of His flock. He *knows* us personally, individually, by name. This is more than an acquaintance with a few vital statistics. Christ's is an effective knowing—a knowing that is equal to a complete inventory of our needs together with a love-prompted know-how, ability, and willingness to help us.

As already implied, the Good Shepherd's knowing leads to *giving*. He states, "I give them eternal life" (John 10:28). He laid down His life on the cross that we might receive forgiveness, have the joy of living in Him and serving Him, and even now enjoy the foretaste of life everlasting.

What is our response to the Good Shepherd's knowing and giving? As His sheep we *hear* and *heed* His voice as it resounds in and through the written Word. Quite often others who know this Word speak to us informally. Our Lord addresses us "through the mutual conversation and consolation of the brethren" (Martin Luther). All who take Christ's Word and work to heart are spiritually enriched. "Blessed," said Jesus, "are those who hear the Word of God and obey it" (Luke 11:28).

The above points to a further aspect of our relationship with the Good Shepherd; hearing, as a first step of obedience, leads to *following*, as sheep follow their shepherd. This is the characteristic mark of true Christian discipleship. We accede to the Savior's call to walk in His footsteps, to come after Him as obedient followers. It means that we believe in Him for our salvation and then do His works.

Prayer Suggestion

Say to your Savior that you are blest indeed to have Him as your Good Shepherd. Say also from the heart that you will try to keep His Word.

WHAT WE CAN EXPECT FROM GOD

My grace is sufficient for you, for My power is made perfect in weakness. 2 Corinthians 12:9

Russian cosmonauts exploring outer space during the Communist regime came back to testify to their atheistic training by saying they had not encountered God. That was the prevailing philosophy of the time: Expect nothing from God, for there is no God; you must do everything yourself.

Another man who knew outer space, the astronomer Copernicus (1473–1543), came to a different conviction. He confessed his Christian faith in the epitaph he chose for his grave. It reads in translation: "I require not the grace that was given to Paul; I demand not the kindness which was given to Peter. But as You gave to the thief on the cross, I pray, give also to me." What he expected from God—forgiveness—was not something minor, but the greatest blessing God can give.

We can ask—and expect—of God what He Himself has promised in His Word. We know He has not promised to give us great riches, not a life of ease and pleasure, not worldly honor, not even escape from sickness and suffering. St. Paul, true and faithful that he was to Christ, had his thorn in the flesh to go with all the other deprivations he endured. But God had promised that His grace and His power are made perfect in weakness.

To be at peace with God, to have His forgiveness thanks to the atoning merit of Jesus Christ, to enjoy—even in this life—a foretaste of eternal life, to be strong by the divine power of Word and Spirit working in us, this God has promised. This we may expect from God. This we may boldly and confidently ask when we pray. Our Lord Jesus has promised, "Peace I leave with you; My peace I give you. I do not give to you as the world gives. Do not let your hearts be troubled and do not be afraid" (John 14:27). What a wonderful gift to expect of our Lord as we work or as we rest!

Prayer Suggestion

Tell your needs to God, asking Him to grant you freely and abundantly what He has promised to give you for Jesus' sake.

JESUS VALUES THE INDIVIDUAL

There will be more rejoicing in heaven over one sinner who repents than over ninety-nine righteous persons who do not need to repent. Luke 15:7

Julia Ward Howe, a prominent woman in Civil War Times—and author of "The Battle Hymn of the Republic"—one time interceded with an "eminent senator" in behalf of someone in need. But the senator replied that he "was so busy saving the human race that he couldn't be bothered about an individual."

Jesus often taught large multitudes. But He never overlooked the importance of an individual. The sermon of Jesus that we have on record in the New Testament in John 4 is the one He addressed to an audience of one—the Samaritan woman at Jacob's well. Another discourse rich in instruction was delivered to a class of one—Nicodemus—in John 3. The New Testament gospels report many instances when Jesus interrupted His journey to help someone by the wayside.

Heavy in its emphasis on the value and importance of the single person is the instruction Jesus gives in His three lost-and-found parables in Luke 15: the recovery of the lost sheep, the finding of the lost coin, and the reinstatement of the lost son. In each instance joy prevailed at the end. The shepherd arranged for a party with his friends and neighbors, the housewife did the same, and the forgiving father in the parable of the prodigal son likewise arranged for a celebration when the son returned. Jesus said there is "rejoicing in the presence of the angels of God over one sinner who repents" (Luke 15:10).

Our Lord stresses that we must not let individual persons disappear in nondescript, faceless crowds—not fail to see individual trees, as it were, because of the forest. It is good for us that Jesus sets a high value on each single person. It is good, for when He gave His life on the cross, it was for *you* and for *me*. In Holy Baptism He brought us, one by one, into fellowship with Him. He sends His Holy Spirit into our individual hearts. He hears our prayers, One on one.

Prayer Suggestion

Thank the Lord Jesus for thinking of you and providing for your salvation long before you were born, and for dealing with you Person-to-person.

Going God's Way

How can a young man keep his way pure? By living according to Your Word. Psalm 119:9

William E. Gladstone (1809–1898), who served as England's prime minister into a ripe old age, declared: "The problem of statesmanship is to find out which way God is going and to go that way."

Not only persons in public life but all people do well to go God's way throughout life. Where do we pick up the signals directing us in the right way? We find them in Holy Scripture. St. Paul declares, "Everything that was written in the past was written to teach us, so that through endurance and the encouragement of the Scriptures we might have hope" (Romans 15:4). Again, the apostle writes, "All Scripture is God-breathed and is useful for teaching, rebuking, correcting and training in righteousness, so that the man of God may be thoroughly equipped for every good work" (2 Timothy 3:16–17). Earlier in his letter St. Paul reminds Timothy that "from infancy you have known the Holy Scriptures" (2 Timothy 3:15).

The Holy Scriptures, as the apostle testifies in this connection, make us "wise for salvation through faith in Christ Jesus" (2 Timothy 3:15). In keeping with the Father's will, Jesus Christ went the way of the cross to take away sin. We follow in the footsteps of Jesus and go God's way when we, empowered by the Holy Spirit and by the faith He creates in God's promises, find pleasure in doing the will of the heavenly Father. With the hymn writer we say, "Your way, not mine, O Lord!"

How good it is when young people, like Timothy, go God's way throughout life. The psalmist in the above text has a short catechesis. He asks the question, "How can a young man keep his way pure?" The answer: "By living according to Your Word" (Psalm 119:9). He explains that one is to have this Word hidden in his or her heart. Then it will serve us as a true and reliable compass.

Prayer Suggestion

Ask the Lord to plant His Word firmly in your heart and mind so that you may live according to it to the glory of Jesus Christ.

STAYING CLOSE TO CHRIST

I am the Vine; you are the branches. John 15:5

During the disastrous retreat of Napoleon's army from Russia in the dead of winter (1812–1813), many soldiers perished. Out of the 600,000 men only 10,000 able-bodied soldiers remained. At night the men would huddle close to one another around the fire. That was their only chance for survival. On the following morning it was found that those on the outer fringes had frozen to death.

Jesus bids us to stay close to Him. He declares, "I am the Vine; you are the branches. If a man remains in Me and I in him, he will bear much fruit; apart from Me you can do nothing" (John 15:5). If we stay in close fellowship with Him, we experience the strength and warmth of His love to sustain us.

Close fellowship with Christ is the basis for close fellowship among His followers. They become brothers and sisters in the faith to one another. Christian fellowship is like a bed of glowing coals. When one coal is separated and lies by itself, it grows cold. The disciple Thomas grew weak in his faith when he was separated from the others after Christ's resurrection. But he rejoined the group a week later and was richly rewarded. The risen Savior singled him out and restored not only his faith but also his commitment to the other disciples. Of the first Christians it is said, "They devoted themselves to the apostles' teaching and to fellowship, to the breaking of bread and to prayer" (Acts 2:42).

The religious teacher Hillel gave this advice to his students: "Do not separate yourselves from the community." St. Augustine said of the first Christians, "That they might not be frozen with fear, they burned with the fire of love." This is our response to the warm embrace of Christ's love: "As Thou hast died for me, Oh, may my love to Thee Pure, warm, and changeless be, A living fire!"

Prayer Suggestion

Rephrase the above hymn lines in your own words as you pledge your love and loyalty to Jesus Christ, your Lord and Savior.

GOD LOOKS ON THE HEART

Man looks at the outward appearance, but the LORD looks at the heart. 1 Samuel 16:7

In Peter De Vries' story *The Glory of the Hummingbird*, one of the characters declares, "There has been enough of personality; it is time for character." Indeed, the cult of personality, the preoccupation with good outward appearance and skin-deep beauty, the good-image projection, the greater emphasis on style than on substance—we've had enough of these; it is time for upright character, truth, and reality.

People are often misled by what they see. So it was with the prophet Samuel, whom God sent to Bethlehem to anoint one of the sons of Jesse as king. Samuel was impressed by the imposing stature of Eliab, the oldest son. But he was not God's choice, for the "LORD does not look at the things man looks at. Man looks at the outward appearance, but the LORD looks at the heart" (1 Samuel 16:7). This is to be a warning, as Jesus said to and of the Pharisees: "You clean the outside of the cup and dish, but inside they are full of greed and self-indulgence" (Matthew 23:25). A superficial piety is not pleasing to God, for He looks on the heart.

The fact that God examines the heart is also a comfort, for God, who searches our hearts, truly knows us and provides for all our needs. He especially sees the saving faith in Jesus Christ, as well as the love we have toward our Savior and His needy brothers and sisters. He looks on our hearts and sees our needs.

God knows our hearts better than we do. St. Paul writes that the Holy Spirit knows our needs and intercedes in our behalf. The heavenly Father understands the Spirit's plea: "He who searches our hearts knows the mind of the Spirit, because the Spirit intercedes for the saints in accordance with God's will" (Romans 8:27).

Prayer Suggestion

Pray that God may for Jesus' sake create a clean heart in you and give you the right spirit.

IN THE LIKENESS OF CHRIST

Those God foreknew He also predestined to be conformed to the likeness of His Son. Romans 8:29

What did Jesus look like? We have no photographs or portraits of Him. The earliest representation we have of Jesus in Christian art shows a beardless youth clad in a tunic and carrying a lamb on His shoulders. Early paintings depicting events in the life of Jesus were found in a Christian chapel at Dura-Europos in southeast Syria. These undoubtedly date back to a time before A.D. 250, when the site was abandoned. But these pictures are certainly not photographic likenesses of Jesus. The fact simply is that we do not know what He looked like.

Although we do not know what Jesus' physical likeness was, we can nevertheless be like Him. St. Paul, in Romans chapter 8, speaks of a series of God's acts whose ultimate purpose was to fashion us after Christ. God foreknew, set aside, chose, or predestined, and in due time called certain ones to faith through the Gospel for a reason: God wanted them "to be conformed to the likeness of His Son" (Romans 8:29). How can we become like Jesus, the Son of God? He is righteous and holy. To be reconstructed in His image or likeness means to be renewed in His righteousness and holiness. When the image of Christ is renewed in us, we know Him and believe in Him as God's Son and our Savior. By faith in Him, God declares us righteous, taking away our sins for which Jesus died. What is more, Christians grow in righteousness and holiness, which the Holy Spirit works in them. Sanctification follows justification.

Growth in our likeness to Christ goes on for life. The nature of Jesus was characterized by humility and compassion. His earliest followers took on that likeness and became more and more like Him. When Peter and John were apprehended in Jerusalem for preaching Jesus' atoning death and resurrection, the religious authorities saw more than just Peter and John before them. They saw Jesus reflected in them, for we are told that "they took note that these men had been with Jesus" (Acts 4:13). The family resemblance showed.

How wonderful when, as persons baptized into Christ, we are perceived to be disciples of Christ—when our words and works, attitudes and actions, conform to those of Jesus!

Prayer Suggestion

Thank God for declaring you just and righteous for the sake of Christ and for granting you His Holy Spirit so that you can grow in holy living.

WORDS AND DEEDS THAT COME BACK TO BLESS

A man reaps what he sows. ... The one who sows to please the Spirit, from the Spirit will reap eternal life.
Galatians 6:7–8

During World War I an army would release poison gas against the other when the wind blew in that direction. Sometimes the wind would reverse itself during an attack, with the result that the lethal fumes were blown back upon the sender.

Evil words can come back to haunt and hurt those who first spoke them, as Jesus said: "With the judgment you pronounce you will be judged, and the measure you give will be the measure you get" (Matthew 7:2 RSV). So it is also with evil works, which contrary winds can blow back with a vengeance. A case in point is wicked Haman in the book of Esther, who was hanged on the gallows he had erected for the execution of Mordecai.

By way of contrast, God's blessing rests on those who speak well of the neighbor and befriend him with deeds of love, as described in Ecclesiastes 11:1: "Cast your bread upon the waters, for after many days you will find it again"—find it increased and multiplied by the grace of God. Those who sow to the Spirit will from the Spirit receive God's greatest gift of grace: eternal life. They sow to the Spirit because of their faith in the fulfilled redemption of Jesus Christ.

Words and deeds have consequences, just as though there were a kind of retributive principle at work—like a cause-and-effect law that operates in nature. St. Paul writes, "A man reaps what he sows. The one who sows to please his sinful nature, from that nature will reap destruction; the one who sows to please the Spirit, from the Spirit will reap eternal life" (Galatians 6:7–8). Eternal life is never earned; it is always the free gift of God. And whatever other blessings God bestows, these are rewards of His grace.

Prayer Suggestion

Request in your prayer that the Spirit of God will always give you pause to consider the weight of your words and works before you speak and do them.

THE SOURCE OF LOVE

Dear friends, let us love one another, for love comes from God. 1 John 4:7

The great and first commandment, said Jesus in reply to a question, is this: "Love the Lord your God with all your heart and with all your soul and with all your mind" (Matthew 22:37). A second commandment, following from it as a corollary, reads: "Love your neighbor as yourself" (Matthew 22:39). Loving God and loving human beings whom He has made and placed in our midst, while we can distinguish between the two, are really of one piece. Reduced to one word, God's expectation of His people is LOVE. What is the source of love?

"God is love," writes St. John in 1 John 4:16. As our heavenly Father is, so we, His children, are expected to be. Our response to Him and all His saving acts in our behalf is to be love. But something has to happen before there is such a response in human beings. Our love to our Father and to a brother or sister in Christ is not self-generating. Love does not proceed out of the hearts of people as they are by nature, for sin has deadened and dried out the heart and made it a desert from which no streams of love can flow.

Our love to God and to man represents God's workmanship. It is the Holy Spirit's accomplishment in us through the Gospel and the sacraments as He creates and sustains faith in Jesus Christ. Love is God's great gift. The tide of divine love, cresting in the sending and sacrificing of His Son for our salvation, is the source of our love to God.

The apostle whom Jesus loved and who loved Jesus puts it very plainly: "We love because He first loved us" (1 John 4:19). And for that reason we love our brothers and sisters, even when they are less than perfect.

Prayer Suggestion

Ask God to increase your faith in Jesus, your Savior, and with it an increase of love to Him and to one another.

TURNING POVERTY TO RICHES

Every Word of God is flawless; He is a shield to those who take refuge in Him. Proverbs 30:5

It is said that the painter and sculptor Pablo Picasso passed through various periods, or extended moods, including the optimistic "rose period" of youth followed by the "blue period" of mental depression. The latter was for him also a time of poverty, even of hunger. Consequently at this time, it is said, he seemingly got vicarious satisfaction out of depicting people in the act of eating and drinking.

Poverty, with all its overtones and undertones, is the plight of many people in this world. Poverty is often beset with temptations—to be envious, to steal, to despair of God's mercy, to harbor the fantasy that riches can be gained through gambling.

Christians, too, can be born—or fall—into poverty. What to do? The apostle Paul urges that they stay productive through work, "doing something useful" (Ephesians 4:28) with their hands. Honest manual labor is no disgrace. If necessary, they can ask for help. To fellow Christians who are better off the apostle says, "We want you to know about the grace that God has given the Macedonian churches. Out of the most severe trial, their overflowing joy and their extreme poverty welled up in rich generosity" (2 Corinthians 8:1–2).

For Christians, earthly poverty loses its sharp edge when they reflect on their riches in Christ Jesus, their Lord and Savior. The apostle goes on to tell the Corinthians that Jesus, God's own Son, for their sakes became poor so that through His poverty they might become rich. He writes to the Ephesians, "In Him we have redemption through His blood, the forgiveness of sins, in accordance with the riches of God's grace" (Ephesians 1:7).

Keeping this in mind prevents us from passing through "blue periods" when we don't have everything the neighbors have. And it helps when we, like the Macedonian Christians, seek to enrich others by our prayers, words, and works of faith. Then we come under this category: "poor, yet making many rich" (2 Corinthians 6:10).

Prayer Suggestion

Tell God that, having food and clothing, you are content. Thank Him especially for the spiritual riches in Jesus Christ.

WHAT WE CAN DO ABOUT POVERTY

*God said to him, "You fool! This very night your life will
be demanded from you." Luke 12:20*

"You can't abolish poverty, but you can abolish some of the consequences of poverty," said Dr. Albert Sabin, wanting to make his anti-
polio vaccine available to poor people, especially those in the Third
World.

Poverty, not an evil in itself, often brings with it numerous evils:
untreated illnesses, insufficient diet, poor housing, and, on the spiritual side, loss of hope and the temptation to steal.

When Jesus said, "The poor you will always have with you" (Mark
14:7), He did not express His approval of poverty, nor did He imply that
His followers need not be concerned about it. At other times Jesus
spoke words of concern about the poor. His words to the righteous are:
"I was hungry and you gave Me something to eat, I was thirsty and you
gave Me something to drink, I was a stranger and you invited Me in, I
needed clothes and you clothed Me, I was sick and you looked after
Me, I was in prison and you came to visit Me" (Matthew 25:35–36).

On many occasions Jesus showed His compassion for the poor. All
the while He was well aware of the sinfulness of human nature that
directly or indirectly causes poverty. The prodigal son caused his own
poverty by his wastefulness. In another parable Jesus underscored the
greed and callousness of a rich man toward poor Lazarus. Our Lord
did not propound a system to eliminate poverty. But He certainly aided
and advocated the abolition of "some of the consequences of poverty,"
of which Dr. Sabin spoke.

And that is what Christians are doing to this day. Their concern is
essentially, as Christians, to make a beginning of this by dealing with
spiritual poverty, that is, the great need of people who do not know
the love of God in Jesus Christ. Faith in the Gospel of Christ's redemption from sin enriches people with forgiveness, peace with God, a new
purpose in life, and the promise of eternal life.

Prayer Suggestion

As you pray, "Give us this day our daily bread," consider how you
can share the gift of love with the needy.

A PROPHET WHO PROFITS

The LORD your God will raise up for you a prophet like
me from among your own brothers. Deuteronomy 18:15

Moses, like a gem of many facets, had many talents. Although not an orator ("Lord, I have never been eloquent. ... I am slow of speech and tongue" [Exodus 4:10]), he was a national leader, lawgiver, psalmist (Psalm 90), and prophet. He spoke of the Messiah as the great Prophet of whom he was a type.

Not only Moses but others as well had prophesied of the ransom, the redemption, the forgiveness of sins that was to come through Him who was not only David's descendant but his Lord as well. God revealed this, said Zechariah, the father of John the Baptist, in his Benedictus song, "through His holy prophets of long ago" (Luke 1:70). This revelation was recorded in the sacred writings of the Old Testament.

As the New Testament opened, we find Zechariah the priest adding to the messianic prophecies by saying that his newborn son John "will be called a prophet of the Most High; for you will go on before the Lord to prepare the way for Him" (Luke 1:76).

In fulfillment of all prophecies, Jesus Christ came into the world as the great Prophet of whom Moses spoke. By word and deed He proclaimed Himself as the promised Messiah who had come to redeem sinners and reconcile them to God. This redemption is ours, as the Scripture teaches, "through faith in Jesus Christ" (Galatians 3:22). He truly is the Lamb of God sacrificed for us.

Because this Prophet profits us so greatly, both in this life and in the life to come, we can join in the heavenly chorus: "Worthy is the Lamb, who was slain, to receive power and wealth and wisdom and strength and honor and glory and praise!" (Revelation 5:12)

Prayer Suggestion

As your own prayer of thanksgiving read Zechariah's exultation in Luke 1:68–79.

ROME: CITY OF SINNERS AND SAINTS

I am obligated both to Greeks and non-Greeks, both to the wise and the foolish. That is why I am so eager to preach the Gospel also to you who are at Rome. Romans 1:14–15

Rome is an ancient city, supposedly founded in 753 B.C. It probably began earlier than that as villages on the Tiber River grew together into the city on the seven hills.

Whatever its history, there was never a lack of sinners in Rome, as in every city: thieves, murderers, adulterers. Its heathen temples—and whatever religion was practiced—only added to the sins committed. In fact, idolatry was the fountainhead of all evil, as St. Paul writes to the Romans: "They exchanged the truth of God for a lie, and worshiped and served created things rather than the Creator. ... Because of this God gave them over to shameful lusts" (Romans 1:25–26). One of the great sinners in Rome was the emperor Nero, who persecuted the Christians and, very likely, also ordered the execution of the apostles Peter and Paul about A.D. 64.

But God also had His saints in Rome. St. Paul addresses his epistle to "all in Rome who are loved by God and called to be saints" (Romans 1:7). In chapter 16 the apostle mentions some of them: the deaconess Phoebe; Aquila and Priscilla, who assisted St. Paul in Corinth during their stay there; Mary, "who worked very hard for you" (v. 6); Epenetus, "the first convert to Christ in the province of Asia" (v. 5); Onesiphorus, who searched hard in Rome to visit St. Paul and was not ashamed of his chains; many others, including Rufus (or "Red"), who may have been the son of Simon, the bearer of Christ's cross.

The Gospel, probably first proclaimed in Rome by Christians in advance of the apostles, had the power to change sinners into saints. Also in the capitol of the mighty Roman empire, the Gospel drew people to Christ who confessed Him as Savior and as the Lord mightier than Caesar.

Also today the Gospel is God's power for the salvation of all who believe. It is the power that leads them to faith and keeps them in it. It is that power in our hearts and lives, too, keeping us in fellowship with our beloved Savior. It is the power God still releases as we proclaim His Word in this world.

Prayer Suggestion

Give thanks to God for the wonders He has worked in human beings in making them saints who are declared righteous by their faith in Christ.

OUR FOOD: INVITATION TO FAITH

*The Bread of God is He who comes down from heaven
and gives life to the world. John 6:33*

God revealed the glory of His love when, in Old Testament times, He fed His people with heavenly manna and caused water to flow from a rock.

No less did Jesus reveal loving concern when at Cana He performed His first miracle by turning water into wine. Later He was to feed thousands by miraculously multiplying a few barley loaves and fishes. By all these acts He manifested His grace and glory.

The Lord reveals the glory of His love even when no apparent miracle accompanies our eating and drinking. Three times a day we sit down to meals to eat and drink what we bought in the supermarket or raised in our garden. Our own earnings and efforts, we think, have provided all this.

Yet, is there not a chain of divine acts of love involved? God gives rain and sunshine so that crops can grow. God sustains our life through these means. God gives wisdom, strength, and health so that we can work for our food and drink. These are daily occurrences, but they speak just as eloquently of divine providence as do astounding miracles.

Above all our Lord and Savior revealed His love by coming into our world to die that we might live. He came to be the Bread of Life and the Living Water. Jesus did not become this by simply speaking the words. He had to do the works the heavenly Father sent Him to do. He rendered obedience to the Law that humanity had transgressed, endured the consequences—suffering and death—and rose again in demonstration of His victory. What is the result for us? Our souls are nourished and refreshed with the bread and water of life—with forgiveness and peace with God.

Prayer Suggestion

In your prayer, change the petition "Give us this day our daily bread" into a thanksgiving for God's gifts.

CHRISTIAN ETHICS, BASED ON LOVE

*Love must be sincere. Hate what is evil; cling to what
is good. Be devoted to one another in brotherly love.
Romans 12:9–10*

"Repay kindness with kindness, but evil with justice," said Confucius, the Chinese philosopher and ethics teacher of some 15 centuries ago.

Confucius was a pagan, but what he said in the above statement is an acceptable principle in an area we call "civil righteousness." Civil government exists to maintain law, order, and a level of decency in life as we lead it in community, state, and nation.

Jesus rises above that minimal righteousness as enunciated by Confucius and as practiced by us as citizens. Shall we repay "evil with justice" in our private lives as Christians? Jesus has a different formula. He tells His followers, "Love your enemies and pray for those who persecute you" (Matthew 5:44). In these words He sets aside the eye-for-an-eye and tooth-for-a-tooth principle as improper in our private Christian lives. Instead, He wants us to pray for and do good to our enemies. St. Paul follows through by likewise enunciating the higher Christian ethic: "Bless those who persecute you. ... Do not repay anyone evil for evil. Be careful to do what is right in the eyes of everybody. If it is possible, as far as it depends on you, live at peace with everyone. Do not take revenge, my friends, but leave room for God's wrath, for it is written: 'It is Mine to avenge; I will repay,' says the Lord" (Romans 12:14, 17–19).

Personal Christian ethics are based on love—love that conquers and endures, love that supersedes feelings of revenge, love that does not repay evil with punishment but with prayer. Such love has its source in the redeeming love of Jesus Christ. To the Ephesians St. Paul writes, "I pray that you, being rooted and established in love, may have the power, together with all the saints, to grasp how wide and long and high and deep is the love of Christ" (3:17–18).

We keep in mind that Christian love must at times be "tough." It does not want to aid and abet evildoers, perhaps even encourage them, by covering things over with a declaration of love. True love, to be helpful and healing, must occasionally serve as a corrective.

Prayer Suggestion

Do what Jesus says. Pray for your enemies—both personal and those who oppose Christ and His church.

A GOOD CONSCIENCE: GOD'S GIFT

[Keep] a clear conscience, so that those who speak maliciously against your good behavior in Christ may be ashamed of their slander. 1 Peter 3:16

We have undoubtedly, at one time or another, thanked our Creator for our healthy bodies, sound minds, creative emotions, and memories that bless. Should we also thank God for the moral voice in us: our conscience?

St. Paul writes that people not under the influence of God's Word also have consciences "bearing witness" and causing their thoughts to either "accuse" or "defend" them. This says that conscience, even in the unconverted, is a moral monitor. It functions as a judge. The basis on which conscience either accuses or excuses people is God's moral law "written on their hearts" (Romans 2:15). Also in pagan societies, where the Ten Commandments in written form were never taught, there remains a trace of moral awareness. Conscience and the moral law tell them that it is wrong to kill, wrong to steal, and the like. The ancient Inca people of Peru had three rules: 1) Don't steal, 2) Don't lie, and 3) Don't be lazy. This shows that conscience and the internally inscribed moral law are imperfect and incomplete in the unconverted.

The Bible speaks also—and especially—of the Christian's conscience. It acts on the basis of God's Word in the heart renewed by faith. St. Paul speaks of it as properly related to faith and its fruits, writing to Timothy about "love, which comes from a pure heart and a good conscience and a sincere faith" (1 Timothy 1:5). St. Peter asks his readers to give witness to their faith "with gentleness and respect, keeping a clear conscience" (1 Peter 3:15–16).

It is often said, "Follow your conscience!" This is good advice, provided that it is not an erring conscience but one correctly lined up with God's Word.

Thank God for a good conscience? Indeed, for it goes with the "whole package" of being a Christian, completely redeemed by the blood of Christ and completely equipped "to do good works" (Ephesians 2:10).

Prayer Suggestion

Ask God, for Jesus' sake, to give you a clear conscience to live with a pure heart.

LIFE'S SURPRISES

God chose the foolish things of the world to shame the wise.
1 Corinthians 1:27

There are surprises in the business world. A company in the computer field was going broke. It began to make millions when it switched to making something else—the homely Cabbage Patch Dolls.

From a human viewpoint, there are surprises in the way God deals with us. His sense of values seems so different from ours. This is what St. Paul writes, "Since in the wisdom of God the world through its wisdom did not know Him, God was pleased through the foolishness of what was preached to save those who believe" (1 Corinthians 1:21). He asks, "Has not God made foolish the wisdom of the world?" (1 Corinthians 1:20) What a surprise that the foolishness of God is wiser than human wisdom and that God's weakness is stronger than the sum total of human power!

It is true: God chose the weak things of this world—and often weak people—to accomplish His purposes. His plan for our salvation was different from any plan we might have devised. Not in a royal palace but in Bethlehem's stable lies a weak little baby, Jesus. He is the Son of God, and through Him we are redeemed—not by a mighty ruler or a wise scholar. The first messengers sent out to preach the Gospel were twelve ordinary men. They were not highly educated; they were not equipped with mass communication; they were not backed by an army, navy, or air force. Yet they set the world upside down for Christ.

You can apply God's surprising sense of values to your own life. You learn not to despise what is small and weak: your child, your limited talent, your lack of a college education, your limited possessions, your fleeting moments and your days. In the hands of God, great things can come about through you. Think of the company that couldn't make it with computers but succeeded with rag dolls.

Prayer Suggestion

Ask God for the wisdom to discover and then to use the important little things in your life to God's glory and the good of all.

REDEEMING THE TIME

Be very careful, then, how you live—not as unwise but as wise, making the most of every opportunity, because the days are evil. Ephesians 5:15–16

Moses writes in Psalm 90, "The length of our days is seventy years—or eighty, if we have the strength" (v. 10). A proper question for Christians is: "What are we doing with our years?" A person attaining the age of 75, it has been estimated, will have spent 24 years in bed. This is necessary, since we need sleep and rest. More on the questionable side are the 13 years this person will have spent watching television, although some daytime recreation is necessary.

Does the Bible say anything about our use of time? In a general way, it tells us to be faithful stewards of all gifts God has entrusted to us, and time is certainly such a gift, along with our talents and treasures.

In writing to the Ephesians, St. Paul urges his readers to live circumspectly and wisely, "redeeming the time, because the days are evil" (5:16 KJV). The New International Version renders this as "making the most of every opportunity." The Greek verb St. Paul uses has *agora* (market place) in it, thereby implying a business transaction that can be translated as "buy from" or "redeem." A purchase involves an exchange, usually money for a product needed. This idea is not foreign to the use of time. In appreciation for the time God has given us we render service to Him. We put time to good use when we give part of our day back to Him for worship services in church, for prayer and study of His Word at home, for work faithfully performed, for needed rest, for giving "our moments and our days" to share the Gospel with our neighbors—always for the reason given by the Apostle: "the days are evil," and the days are short.

"Redeem" the time is a good term, fitting in with the overall "redemption" theme of the Gospel of Christ. Our Savior gave His time to redeem us; we are bought with a price. In gratitude we give Him back as much of our time as we can so that we might serve Him.

Prayer Suggestion

Express gratitude for the time God has given you for living, working, serving, resting, and enjoying His creation.

DOES THE GOOD LIVE ON?

Blessed are the dead who die in the Lord from now on.
Revelation 14:13

A touch of pessimism and cynicism is inherent in what Shakespeare has an actor say, "The evil that men do lives after them; the good is often interred with their bones" (*Julius Caesar*, act 3, scene 2).

It is true: Deceased evildoers have successors who carry on evil designs—sometimes their own sons. Ahab, the evil king of Israel, was succeeded by his son Ahaziah, who likewise "did evil in the eyes of the LORD" (1 Kings 22:52). Evil is perpetuated because all people are sinners. It is easy for children to walk in the sins of their parents. And so the evil done by people lives on.

What about the second part of Shakespeare's statement? Is the good that people do buried with them? Sometimes, yes, but not always, depending on what it is. The good that people do in the expression of their faith is work that God blesses; it remains in one form or another. Jesus told His disciples that, if they lived in Him, they would be fruitful in their work, and their fruit "will last" (John 15:16). How true! The Twelve left this world almost 20 centuries ago, but their message and mission continues to this day. Jesus Christ is still being proclaimed as the crucified Savior who rose from the dead for the salvation of the world.

Coming closer to home, we ask: What about our own Christian work, our purposes, our influence? Will they be "interred with our bones"? Of course, some things we stood for will cease when we die. The psalmist says of important people—the mortal princes of this world—when they die: "On that very day their plans come to nothing" (146:4). This statement does not apply to those who followed God's plan. The good done by Christian parents, teachers, pastors, missionaries, and rank-and-file Christians lives on. This is true: "Blessed are the dead who die in the Lord from now on. Yes … they will rest from their labor, for their deeds will follow them" (Revelation 14:13).

The above has to be added to put Shakespeare's statement into proper perspective.

Prayer Suggestion

Thank God that His "solid foundation stands firm, sealed with this inscription: 'The Lord knows those who are His' " (2 Timothy 2:19). Also thank God that your good work will last.

PERSONAL RESPONSIBILITY

The man said, "The woman You put here with me—she gave me some fruit from the tree, and I ate it." Genesis 3:12

A prominent political leader once said, "We must live with the consequences of our judgments." Put into another form, the statement says that people must assume personal responsibility for what we do or leave undone.

In our time it is quite common to shove the axioms of life aside and to seek refuge in excuses. You have heard the attempted dodges of personal accountability: "I can't help it. I am what I am—it is because of genes inherited from my parents." Again: "My so-called vice is a sickness." Further: "I only did what the majority of people would do." Or: "I beat up on my children severely because that is what my parents did to me." Sometimes the blame is not only placed on other people but also on unfavorable environments.

Alibis may work in society, sometimes even in courts of law. But all forms of pretense and all attempts of self-delusion don't "wash" with God, who is just, all-knowing, and always beyond deception. The psalmist prays, "Judge me, O LORD, according to my righteousness, according to my integrity, O Most High. O righteous God, who searches minds and hearts, bring to an end the violence of the wicked and make the righteous secure" (7:8–9).

The futility of trying to avoid responsibility is vividly portrayed in the aftermath of the fall in Eden. Adam said it was "the woman You put here with me" (Genesis 3:12). (It was really your fault, God!) Eve said, "The serpent deceived me" (Genesis 3:13).

There is only one thing to do when we are confronted with our wrongdoings—acknowledge personal responsibility. Here is everything in a nutshell: "If we claim to be without sin, we deceive ourselves and the truth is not in us. If we confess our sins, He is faithful and just and will forgive us our sins and purify us from all unrighteousness" (1 John 1:8–9). God forgives, because "the blood of Jesus, His Son, purifies us from all sin" (1 John 1:7).

Prayer Suggestion

Tell the heavenly Father your faults and ask His forgiveness for Jesus' sake.

THE OBEDIENCE OF FAITH

Submit yourselves for the Lord's sake to every authority instituted among men. 1 Peter 2:13

A revolution can be a frightful thing. In Russia, on July 17, 1918, the rebels killed Tsar Nicholas II and his family and threw their bodies into a mine shaft. When private citizens arm themselves and over-throw a properly constituted government, the action is usually like a rampaging flood or a devastating forest fire, destroying everything in its path, including innocent people.

A nation that resorts to peaceful means when it is necessary to replace an unfit government is a nation truly blessed. It makes neces-sary changes with ballots instead of bullets. Likewise, a country is blessed when its citizens on every level live righteously, deal honestly, and obey the laws they themselves have enacted through their duly elected representatives in government. The Proverbs writer (14:34) states, "Righteousness exalts a nation," adding that "sin is a disgrace to any people." In many instances, corruption in high places of govern-ment is a reflection, or projection, of a preceding corruption in the low places of the citizenry.

Christians are under a dual responsibility, rendering obedience to God and to government in the proper spheres. Jesus said, "Give to Caesar what is Caesar's, and to God what is God's" (Matthew 22:21). St. Peter, in the above indicated reading, and St. Paul in Romans 13:1–7, tell us what we should render to Caesar. And what is it that we gladly render to God? It is praise and thanksgiving for His marvelous works, especially for sending the best Representative possible, His own dear Son, Jesus Christ, to give His life for our eternal salvation.

When there is gratitude in our hearts and praise on our tongues, there will also be services our hands will perform. This is "the obedi-ence that comes from faith" (Romans 1:5).

Prayer Suggestion

Ask God to grant you, with the increase of faith, also growth in obedience to His Word, for Jesus' sake.

AIDING THE AGING

I was young and now I am old, yet I have never seen the
righteous forsaken or their children begging bread.
Psalm 37:25

Research has indicated that, of persons over 85 years of age, some 20 percent are in nursing homes. Where do we find the other 80 percent? They are everywhere. Some live with their children in what is called three-generation families. Others live in their own houses or apartments, with or without assistance from others. Good health care has enabled many of the aging to care for themselves as they attain longer life spans.

Although the elderly, perhaps more today than in previous times, are better provided for, one has to keep in mind that their needs are more than physical. Their total well-being includes the social and spiritual aspects of life. Nothing can ever take the place of Christian love—love that the elderly receive and can extend to others. If involved in the exchange of love, they have the feeling that they are still in on things—in family circles, in community affairs, and in the mission of Christ's church.

The Bible has much to say on the subject of showing consideration to people on the sidelines. What was said in the Old Testament still applies: "Rise in the presence of the aged, show respect for the elderly and revere your God" (Leviticus 19:32). Again: "Listen to your father, who gave you life, and do not despise your mother when she is old" (Proverbs 23:22). And to the aging and ailing, God declares, "Even to your old age and gray hairs I am He, I am He who will sustain you" (Isaiah 46:4).

Certainly also the elderly, especially those in need, are our Lord's brothers and sisters. When we serve them, we perform a ministry to Jesus Christ, who came among us to minister and to give His life as a ransom for us all.

Prayer Suggestion

Give thanks to God for giving you life through your parents. Ask His help for showing love and respect to them as Jesus' representatives.

"REMEMBER LOT'S WIFE"—WHY?

Lot's wife looked back, and she became a pillar of salt.
Genesis 19:26

Jesus said we should remember Lot's wife. It would be helpful if we first remembered Lot, Abraham's nephew. He was a prosperous cattleman on "the whole plain of the Jordan" (Genesis 13:11), who retired to Sodom. There, when two angels came to visit him, he was sitting by the gate, in an area where legal and commercial business was transacted. Lot was an active man in an active city. Jesus said its "people were eating and drinking, buying and selling, planting and building" (Luke 17:28). Lot, very likely, had a spacious home, with extra rooms where guests could be accommodated.

Lot's wife was involved in the busy life of a busy city, especially in social affairs, perhaps a matronly type. She had two virgin daughters engaged to men in Sodom. Entrenched in a favorable position and blessed with the things money could buy, she would be extremely reluctant to leave the city and flee to the primitive hills.

The context in which Jesus tells us to "remember Lot's wife" (Luke 17:32) shows that her motive for looking back on the burning city was not curiosity to see a spectacular sight. It was the faint hope to go back to recover something from her house. It cost her life. We remember Lot's wife for the wrong choice she made.

The Bible tells us of other wives well worth remembering. In the Old Testament we read of a wealthy woman in Shunem called "the Shunammite," who showed hospitality to the prophet Elisha as he came by that way. In the New Testament we come across Salome, the mother of James and John, who was among the last to leave Christ's cross on Mount Calvary and among the first to come to the empty tomb. We also remember Pilate's wife, who interceded with her husband for Jesus and who reportedly became a convert to Christianity. Most of all, there was Mary, the mother of Jesus; her faith shines through in her Magnificat.

Remember Lot's wife for her folly and the other wives for their faith? Yes, but most of all, we go with what St. Paul writes, "Remember Jesus Christ, raised from the dead" (2 Timothy 2:8), who was "delivered over to death for our sins and was raised to life for our justification" (Romans 4:25).

Prayer Suggestion

Complete this prayer: "Lord Jesus, I remember Lot's wife because ..."

WHAT GOD HAS PROMISED

I know that my Redeemer lives, and that in the end He will stand upon the earth. Job 19:25

It is hard to imagine a greater shock than the one that came to a couple in the Missouri Ozarks when they learned that someone had wiped out their family by killing their four children. Christian faith sustained the parents. They relied on the Word of God. The message that sustained them was the assurance of God to them: "Your children are in My hands." Their life continued. God gave them a second family of three children.

That man of great faith, Job of the Bible, had a similar experience. He lost his possessions, his health, the support of his spouse. But even more, he lost his sons and daughters who perished when a severe storm destroyed the house where they were assembled. On hearing this, Job felt thoroughly stripped of everything. He tore his robe, fell to the ground, and exclaimed, "Naked I came from my mother's womb, and naked I will depart. The LORD gave and the LORD has taken away; may the name of the LORD be praised" (Job 1:21).

Job survived in his faith, confessing, "I know that my Redeemer lives" (Job 19:25). It meant that he, too, would rise again from the grave. But even more! Job was to live many more years. God gave him a second family and enabled him to see "his children and their children to the fourth generation" (Job 42:16).

God has not promised that He would replace lost families, but He has solemnly declared, "I will strengthen you and help you; I will uphold you with My righteous right hand" (Isaiah 41:10). Also this: "My grace is sufficient for you, for My power is made perfect in weakness" (2 Corinthians 12:9). This grace is given to us in its fullness in Jesus Christ, His Son, who gave His life for our salvation.

Prayer Suggestion

Say to God in your own words that you trust in Him to give you strength to sustain you amid your weaknesses.

CHRIST'S CHURCH WILL ENDURE

You are Peter (Petros), and on this rock (petra) I will build My church, and the gates of Hades will not over-come it. Matthew 16:18

In the early centuries of the Christian era, Santa Sophia in Constantinople (now Istanbul) was one of the great churches in Christendom. When, in 1453, the city fell into the hands of Islamic forces, the church was turned into a mosque. Today it is a museum.

Changes like this do not contradict the assertion in the hymn line "The Church shall never perish," nor do they deny what Jesus said of the church, "The gates of Hades will not overcome it" (Matthew 16:18). Christ's church of believers, the communion of saints, will endure, as another hymn writer states, "even when steeples are falling." Church *buildings* may be destroyed by fires and floods, or be converted into other kinds of structures as they were in Russia, but the church proper—people, believers—lives on.

In our times of great neighborhood changes in our cities, many once-beautiful church edifices are all but abandoned. This fact we regret, but we are consoled by the conviction that the church invisible continues, and even thrives, in other communities.

The true church, that is, the sum total of all Christians the world over, lives on because it is built on Jesus Christ. He is the "chief Cornerstone" in the solid "foundation of the apostles and prophets" (Ephesians 2:20). The apostles—and the prophets before their time—did not build Christendom on the flimsy ground of human opinion—not "on wood, hay, or straw," not even on the more solid things: "gold, silver, costly stones" (1 Corinthians 3:12), but on the Gospel truth that Christ Jesus, God's true Son, came into the world to save sinners.

The truth of salvation through faith in the redeeming merit of Jesus Christ stands firm, and so does the church based on it. You and I, as believers, are integral parts of that structure.

Prayer Suggestion

Complete this prayer: "Lord Jesus, I believe that Your church will endure because ..."

HONORING THE LIVING

Children, obey your parents in the Lord, for this is right.
Ephesians 6:1

W. H. Auden, in one of his poems, speaks of the human tendency to speak more favorably of "horizontal" people than of "vertical" ones. By the former he means persons lying in their graves, while the latter refers to the living ones who are still up and about. Usually more flowers, in a literal and figurative sense, are given to the dead than to the living.

In the "table of duties" section of his Ephesian letter, St. Paul reminds children to honor their parents by obeying them. Faithful obedience honors fathers and mothers while they are still alive.

To speak words of commendation and to do deeds of kindness to faithful Christians is always in place. St. Paul has words of praise in his epistles for the living "saints" in the congregations he addresses. In his words to the Philippians he recognizes an unnamed "loyal yokefellow," probably the spiritual leader. Euodia and Syntyche, temporarily on the "outs," nevertheless drew the compliment that they "contended at my side in the cause of the Gospel" (Philippians 4:3). He said they did this "along with Clement and the rest of my fellow workers, whose names are in the book of life" (Philippians 4:3). Are we following the apostle's example with regard to recognizing and thanking faithful church members, teachers, pastors, and officers? Let us not wait with our commending words until it is time to write the obituaries.

Sometimes it is hardest to give deserved compliments to those nearest to us in the family. In the last chapter of his Romans epistle St. Paul does not hesitate to give cordial greetings to several of his relatives who "were in Christ before I was" (Romans 16:7).

Giving honor to whom it is due is a good principle to follow. This is especially true in our relationship with the living Christ, whom we honor equally with the Father and the Holy Spirit, and to whom we owe special gratitude for giving His life that we might have eternal life, now and in the life to come.

Prayer Suggestion

Ask the Holy Spirit to help you find words of commendation for those who faithfully serve Christ and His church.

QUOTING ALL OF GOD'S WORD

I have not hesitated to proclaim to you the whole will of God.
Acts 20:27

The stern, 18th-century Puritan clergyman in Northamton, Massachusetts, Jonathan Edwards, is often criticized for saying in a sermon that God holds the sinner over "the pits of hell much as one holds a spider, or some loathsome insect over the fire." Usually not quoted is what Edwards went on to say: "Yet it is nothing but His hand that holds you from falling into the fire every moment."

A good point to make is this: When you quote someone, quote accurately, fairly, and completely. Satan can quote the Bible when he thinks it is to his advantage. But he leaves out what does not serve his purpose. During the wilderness temptations Jesus quoted Scripture to good effect. So Satan tried to do the same, citing Psalm 91. But he left out the important words: "in all your ways." It is also for the dishonest use of the Word of God that the devil is called the father of lies.

Let's be careful how we quote the Bible and pay close attention to the context. The Bible can be made to say that there is no God when one leaves out what goes before, namely, that it is the fool who says this (Psalm 14:1).

It is of greatest importance to note the distinction between the Law and the Gospel. Jonathan Edwards was preaching the Law when he said that God was angry with sinners, and he was implying the Gospel when he said that God's hand keeps us from falling. St. Paul made a similar dual statement: "The wages of sin is death, but the gift of God is eternal life in Christ Jesus our Lord" (Romans 6:23). This is Law and Gospel. To preach only the Law is legalism. To preach only the Gospel of God's love in Christ to people who refuse to repent is declaring a half-truth.

In His Word, God declares to us His whole counsel of our salvation. To this revelation we add nothing nor take away anything.

Prayer Suggestion

Pray that the Holy Spirit may lead you into all truth concerning sin and concerning salvation from sin through Jesus Christ.

GOD'S SWORD VERSUS MAN'S SWORDS

Take the helmet of salvation and the sword of the Spirit, which is the Word of God. Ephesians 6:17

In Victor Hugo's novel *Les Miserables* Jean Valjean was imprisoned for 19 years for stealing a loaf of bread. After his release he was relentlessly pursued for years by Inspector Javert for being a parole breaker. In some societies lawbreakers are excessively punished. In our time, however, the opposite seems to be true.

Crime should draw its due penalty. St. Paul writes that the government "is God's servant, an agent of wrath to bring punishment on the wrongdoer" (Romans 13:4). Justice is not served when the victims of crime suffer while the perpetrators go free. Peace and tranquility in the community are endangered when unauthorized private citizens carry dangerous weapon with evil ends in mind, such as robbing and stealing. Jesus told Peter in the Garden of Gethsemane, "Put your sword back in its place … for all who draw the sword will die by the sword" (Matthew 26:52). It is a safe prediction that killing others by any kind of lethal weapon will sooner or later find killers to be the victims of their own preoccupation.

The great deterrent or preventive of sinful swordsmanship is not the sword or punitive power of the government but, in the words of the apostle, "the sword of the Spirit, which is the Word of God" (Ephesians 6:17). This Word includes God's law, which declares, "You shall not murder" (Exodus 20:13). It includes, above all, what St. Paul in this connection calls "the Gospel of peace" (Ephesians 6:15). This Word is effective because it changes hearts, for it is out of unchanged hearts—according to Jesus in Matthew 15:19—that murder proceeds.

The Word of the Gospel fills hearts with love that replaces hatred, greed, or whatever else drives people to hurt or harm their neighbor. This love has its source in the love of the Father who sent His Son, Jesus Christ, as our Savior. This same loving Father continues to send the Holy Spirit to strengthen us in the saving faith and to grant us peace on the basis of sins forgiven. God's sword prevails where man's sword fails.

Prayer Suggestion

Give thanks to God for changing your heart through the Gospel of peace and for filling it with love for the neighbor.

REASON TO CELEBRATE

When he finds it, he joyfully puts it on his shoulders and goes home. Luke 15:5

To celebrate means to rejoice together over an event—perhaps a victory, a birthday, a wedding, or a family reunion. Perhaps someone long absent has come home. The return is celebrated with a party.

The recovery of a lost sheep was an important event among Palestinian shepherds. At stake had been the loss of a living being—a beloved lamb, perhaps a ewe with a broken leg, or a sheep that the shepherd knew by name. To find it and restore it to the flock marked the triumph of the shepherd's love and concern. Here was the truly human touch so easily lost in the age of machines.

To be sure, there is joy in heaven over all the faithful members of Christ's church, over the so-called ninety-nine who remain true to their Savior. The Lord and His angels are happy over their constancy and consistency, their spiritual growth, and their service in and to the flock to which the Good Shepherd ministers. But there is also joy—exceedingly great joy—over one sinner who repents and returns to Christ's church of believers.

Why this great joy? It means the recovery of a human soul worth more than all the material wealth of the world. It means the reinstatement of a person for whom Jesus Christ shed His precious blood. It means the restoration of an essential link in the golden chain of Christian fellowship. It means regaining a lost jewel in the crown of the King of kings, Jesus Christ, whom God brought back from the dead "through the blood of the eternal covenant" (Hebrews 13:20).

If a sinner's repentance occasions great joy in heaven, shouldn't we on earth likewise rejoice and renew our efforts to bring straying sheep into Christ's fold?

Prayer Suggestion

Turn to the Lord in prayer on behalf of a straying person of your acquaintance, seeking His help in your effort to bring him or her back to Jesus.

SIGNS IN THE SUN

There will be signs in the sun, moon and stars.
Luke 21:25

On May 10, 1994, people in mid-America, for the first time in 200 years, saw a complete eclipse of the sun over the noon hour. They experienced an eerie feeling as they saw the sun darkened. The mountains on the moon appeared as notches at the edge of the moon as it passed across the sun. In ancient times some people believed that a large giant had bitten a piece out of the sun. Nowadays astronomers can predict when eclipses will appear.

Although eclipses are natural phenomena, they nevertheless are signs with a message to Christians. Jesus said, in this respect: "There will be signs in the sun, moon and stars" (Luke 21:25). These signs, even when they result from natural causes, remind us of the coming of the Son of Man on Judgment Day. Then "the sun will be darkened, and the moon will not give its light; the stars will fall from the sky" (Mark 13:24–25). These future events mark the end of the world as we know it, ushering in, according to St. Peter's words, "a new heaven and a new earth, the home of righteousness" (2 Peter 3:13). The apostle prefaces this saying by reminding us that we look forward to this great change as God's fulfillment of His promise. That promise pertains to our reception in the Father's heavenly home of many rooms which Jesus prepared for us.

Eclipses of sun and moon, as well as the other signs of Christ's second advent—the sea roaring under the lashing of hurricanes, the land convulsed by earthquakes, the increasing distress of nations, the coming of false christs and false prophets—are not to terrify us. We are at peace, knowing that God is in control of His universe and that the gates of His kingdom of glory are always open to us. The gates of hell cannot prevail against the holy Christian church, the communion of saints, of which Jesus Christ is the solid cornerstone. Sun and moon, heaven and earth, will eventually pass away, but the Word and redeeming work of our Savior abide forever. In His hands we are safe.

Prayer Suggestion

Ask the Holy Spirit for wisdom so that you may rightly discern the signs of the time and always be prepared for the coming of the Lord.

PATIENCE SUSTAINED BY HOPE

We have this hope as an anchor for the soul, firm and secure. Hebrews 6:19

Sometimes one's patience reaches a breaking point when failure follows failure. When things continually go wrong in one's vocation, the following questions are in place: What is God telling me? Does He want me to do something else? Such questions must have occurred to Anthony Young, a major-league baseball pitcher who made the record book by losing 27 straight games. Patience, while it is a virtue that the Bible greatly extols, needs to be practiced with persistence and discretion.

To be sure, Christian patience is in place without qualification in matters where God has clearly spoken. The writer of the epistle to the Hebrews makes this point with regard to Abraham, the father of the believers. God had promised him a son from whose offspring would come the Savior of the world. But the possibility of having an offspring seemed remote to Abraham because of the advanced age of both Abraham and Sarah. The son God had promised seemed slow in coming, with Abraham 85 years old and Sarah, 75, when Isaac was born. But Abraham had patience, as St. Paul observes, "He did not waver through unbelief regarding the promise of God, but was strengthened in his faith and gave glory to God, being fully persuaded that God had power to do what He had promised" (Romans 4:20–21).

It is from strong faith that patience and perseverance spring. Faith rests on God's promises—in our time on the *fulfilled* promises—that He would send His own dear Son to give His life for the reconciliation of us all. That Son was Jesus of Nazareth. Faith adheres to the Word of God even when one's outlook on life is dim. What God has promised is sure, for He cannot lie. It is therefore with unswerving patience we grasp and hold fast to the hope of salvation offered us in the Gospel. "We have this hope as an anchor for the soul, firm and secure," the writer to the Hebrews assures us in chapter 6 verse 19.

Prayer Suggestion

Pray for the strengthening of your convictions in all areas of life where God gives you His clear promises.

HEALING THROUGH THE CROSS

The leaves of the tree are for the healing of the nations.
Revelation 22:2

In his visions set in heaven, John saw many wonderful sights. On one occasion the angel showed him "the river of the water of life, as clear as crystal. ... On each side of the river stood the tree of life" (Revelation 22:1–2). This tree yielded fruit, and its leaves were "for the healing of the nations" (Revelation 22:2). Some trees, even in our sin-cursed world, provide help for healing. For example, from the Pacific yew tree comes taxol, a drug used in the treatment for cancer.

Trees played important parts in our *spiritual* lives, both in the fall of the human race and in its redemption. This dual truth is recalled in the Preface for Lent in the Holy Communion service. The Lord is praised because on the tree of the cross He gave salvation to mankind. He turned death into life. He also overcame Satan, so that "he who by a tree once overcame likewise by a tree might be overcome."

The two truths balance out beautifully. In the Garden of Eden the devil succeeded in tempting Adam and Eve to eat the forbidden fruit of the tree of knowledge of good and evil. For the time being the tempter Satan truly overcame our first parents by deceiving them to sin. Then came the Second Adam, Jesus Christ, who by the tree of the cross overcame Satan in our behalf. St. Paul writes, "Christ redeemed us from the curse of the Law by becoming a curse for us, for it is written: 'Cursed is everyone who is hung on a tree' " (Galatians 3:13).

When the Gospel of Jesus Christ is proclaimed and practiced in the world, the once rugged cross becomes a tree of life whose leaves yield spiritual medicine for the healing of the nations. This is what our risen Lord wanted when He said, "Go and make disciples of all nations" (Matthew 28:19). Faith in Him brings, as the hymnist writes, "sight, riches, healing of the mind."

Prayer Suggestion

Take all your problems to the Lord Jesus in prayer, thanking Him for being the Good Physician.

EACH PERSON COUNTS

I know you by name and you have found favor with Me.
Exodus 33:12

Individual citizens sometimes say, "Why should I go to the polls? My vote, pro or con, doesn't make a difference." But it does! In 1649 King Charles I of England was beheaded on the strength of a 68 to 67 vote of a special high court. In 1869 the impeached President Andrew Johnson escaped being ousted by one vote in the United States Senate. A larger lesson one may draw from this is that not only each vote but also each person counts.

How important is each person in the sight of God? Very important! God told Moses, "I know you by name" (Exodus 33:17). God's awareness of us as individuals is stressed throughout the Bible. According to Genesis, Adam and Eve counted for much, for they were the fountainheads of the human race. They were important to God also after their fall into sin, for He promised them a Savior. In Revelation we read that Jesus Christ is the Lamb of God slain for people of all ethnic groups, making the individual believers "priests to serve our God" (Revelation 5:10).

Open Holy Scripture anywhere and you find reference to God's relation to us on an I/you or person-to-person basis. David, in Psalm 139, declares that God knows everything about him—his coming and going, his thoughts and his words. Even stronger testimony in behalf of God's awareness comes from Jeremiah, to whom the Lord said, "Before I formed you in the womb I knew you, before you were born I set you apart; I appointed you as a prophet to the nations" (Jeremiah 1:5).

As each person was individually created and was individually redeemed with the price of Christ's blood, so each believer is through the Gospel personally called to faith by the Holy Spirit. Each person counts; each Christian has the promise of personal forgiveness and life eternal.

Prayer Suggestion

Continue this prayer: "Lord Jesus, my Savior, I thank You for thinking of me when You ..."

BEING WHAT WE ARE

If anyone else thinks he has reasons to put confidence in the flesh, I have more. Philippians 3:4

A St. Louis, Missouri, man, who gave music lessons, left the impression that he was poor. He wore shabby clothes; he went to places where he could get free food. After his death it was revealed that he was a wealthy man. On the good side, he gave a large sum of money for a public library.

The world is a stage where people play roles. Some are genuine performers, while others put on an act. Some who are rich pretend to be poor and vice versa. They are hypocrites. The word comes from the Greek *Hypokrites* and means one who plays a part, an actor, a pretender.

Jesus was aware of people who pretended to be what they were not. In Matthew 23 He upbraids the Pharisees, calling them hypocrites and pronouncing seven woes on them. He was especially critical of the outwardness of their religion. "Everything they do is for men to see," He declared (v. 5).

The apostle Paul had been a Pharisee, and not a run-of-the-mill kind but a very zealous one. As a former insider he could—and did—speak very authoritatively about self-righteousness, which is a form of pride and pretense. He urged the readers of his epistles to avoid sham, declaring: "Provide things honest in the sight of all men" (Romans 12:17 KJV). Again, "Let us behave decently, as in the daytime" (Romans 13:13).

An opponent of self-righteousness, St. Paul tells the Philippians how true righteousness is attained, and that is "not having a righteousness of my own that comes from the Law, but that which is through faith in Christ" (Philippians 3:9). Jesus Christ fulfilled the Law in our stead. He endured the penalty for our sins, which is death, by dying on the cross and then rising again.

Now there are no grounds for sham, hypocrisy, or self-righteousness. We can be what we are: Sinners declared righteous in the sight of God because of faith in Christ. We are clothed in the splendid robe of Christ's righteousness.

Prayer Suggestion

Declare your intention that, by the power of the Holy Spirit, you will lead a truthful life to Christ's glory.

IN BUT NOT OF THE WORLD

Do not love the world or anything in the world.
1 John 2:15

Two persons can say or write practically the same thing but have altogether different reasons for doing so.

In 1759 the French satirist Voltaire wrote the short novel *Candide* in which his main character by the same name found out how corrupt the world was (at a time when the church itself was corrupt). His purpose was to ridicule Christianity. The apostle John also states that the world is evil, but for a different reason: to keep Christians from participating in the evil ways of the world.

What is there to think or say about the surrounding world of our time? Is it as evil as many say it is? Many concerned people are of the opinion that moral conditions are getting worse. One thing to keep in mind is that the news media nowadays are more frank to report what people do in their private lives, especially public figures.

Allowing for this greater openness, the world of our time is still evil. We have no reason to disagree with the 12th-century hymn "The World Is Very Evil." Going back still farther, we have to agree with the red alert of St. John: "Do not love the world or anything in the world" (1 John 2:15). The world is what composite human nature is. The apostle tells us what its marks are: "the cravings of sinful man, the lust of the eyes and the boasting of what he has" (1 John 2:16). Human nature is still that way today.

How do we as Christians show concern? In His High Priestly Prayer in John 17 Jesus tells the Father to leave His disciples in the world. He does not want them to flee from the world, for they are to be His witnesses in it. They are to be the salt of the earth and the light of the world. They are to proclaim the Gospel of the forgiveness of sins through Christ and to back up their proclamation with Christian living.

Christians are *in* the world but not *of* the world. This, in short, indicates our role.

Prayer Suggestion

Say a short prayer, asking Jesus to help you be a good Christian witness in this world.

THE CORRECT "GRAMMAR" OF FAITH

Evidently some people are throwing you into confusion and are trying to pervert the Gospel of Christ. Galatians 1:7

A mother wanted to teach her son the correct use of the verb "see" when used in the past tense. She said he could either say "I saw" or "I have seen." But the boy didn't get it. He was next heard to say, "I have saw."

Some people have trouble with the "grammar" of Christian teaching. They fail to distinguish between salvation by faith and salvation by good works. They try to combine the two, like the boy did with "have saw." They end up with salvation by faith *and* good works. This mistake was once for all corrected by St. Paul: "It is by grace you have been saved, through faith—and this not from yourselves, it is the gift of God—not by works, so that no one can boast (Ephesians 2:8–9). But then he goes on in the next verse to say that God wants us to do good works, not to be saved but *because* we are saved. Good works are the fruit of faith.

Another case of mixed-up doctrinal "grammar" pertains to the nature of Christ's kingdom. Is it temporal-social-political or is it spiritual? Even the apostles had trouble with this, asking Jesus shortly before His ascension, "Lord, are You at this time going to restore the kingdom to Israel?" (Acts 1:6) Thanks to the coming of the Holy Spirit on Pentecost, the apostles correctly understood that the kingdom Jesus came to establish by His death and resurrection was basically spiritual; it dealt with the forgiveness of sins and the promise of eternal life.

Already in the first century some people got the articles of faith mixed up mostly because they had not studied God's Word. So the writer of the epistle to the Hebrews tells his readers that they "are slow to learn." He goes on, "Though by this time you ought to be teachers, you need someone to teach you the elementary truths of God's Word all over again. You need milk, not solid food!" (Hebrews 5:11–12)

When we diligently study the Scriptures and ask the Holy Spirit to guide us into all truth, we will have the correct "grammar" of the Christian religion.

Prayer Suggestion

Complete this prayer, "Holy Spirit, lead me into all truth so that I may grow closer to Christ and ..."

BAD NIGHTS, GOOD NIGHTS

The LORD will keep you from all harm—He will watch over your life. Psalm 121:7

Many a story promising an eventful plot has begun with the line, "It was a dark and stormy night." The Bible narrates many night events, all relating to God's story of our salvation.

It was a dark and eventful night that the trembling Jesus spent in the Garden of Gethsemane. He prayed fervently, was strengthened by an angel, and bravely yielded Himself to His enemies to begin His suffering for our salvation.

Previously Jesus had at times carried on His healing and teaching ministry at night. In Capernaum He healed the sick and the demon-possessed "that evening after sunset" (Mark 1:32). It was a dark but revealing night when He conversed with Nicodemus concerning His kingdom, bringing His teaching to a climax with the Gospel in a nutshell: "God so loved the world that He gave His one and only Son, that whoever believes in Him shall not perish but have eternal life" (John 3:16).

The apostle Paul did much of his teaching and testifying at night. It was a dark and painful night when he and Silas, with their backs beaten and their feet in stocks, sang hymns in a Philippian prison. It was a dark but enlightening night when the apostle "kept on talking until midnight" (Acts 20:7) to assembled Christians at Troas. There the young man Eutychus, sitting in a window, went to sleep and fell to the ground. St. Paul brought him back to life. It was a dark and tearful night—but one filled with love—when he met with the elders of Ephesus, who "wept as they embraced him and kissed him," knowing they would not see him again.

We all have nights that may be described as "dark and stormy," as certainly St. Peter had when he denied his Lord. But God is with us in dark nights, just as He is on calm, sunlit days, as Psalm 121 declares. He gives hope and joy. The closing lines of a hymn say it well: "And soon the night of weeping Shall be the morn of joy."

Prayer Suggestion

Tell God that you are confident that your times—your days and nights—are in His hands, thanking Him for the words and work of Jesus, His Son.

WHEN FACTS ARE CAMOUFLAGED

Repent therefore! Otherwise, I will soon come to you and fight against them with the sword of My mouth.
Revelation 2:16

The Canary Islands off northwestern Africa can be a beauty-versus-beast setting. We think of yellow songbirds and the sweet madeira wine made there. However, the name comes from the Latin *canis*, a dog, because of the large dogs the early owners kept to control the plantation workers.

Names can hide grim facts. Nain was a town meaning beauty because of its site in the Mount Hermon vicinity. The birds sang there. But the cruel hounds of death came there, too, for a certain woman. First her husband was taken, and then her only son, whom Jesus raised from the dead.

For the third temptation in the wilderness Satan showed Jesus "all the kingdoms of the world and their splendor" (Matthew 4:8). You could visualize beautiful palaces, pleasure gardens, and whatever appeals to human ambition. But it was a deluding picture, a sample of satanic magic. To receive all this, Jesus would have to bow down and worship the devil. And that would have been the end of our salvation. No paradise with beautiful birds, only the realm of the hounds of hell, would have awaited us.

We next go to Pergamum to which St. John wrote one of his seven letters in the book of Revelation. Satan was there with his human agents: the Balaamites and the Nicolaitans. Both put on a religious front camouflaging their advocacy of sexual immorality. The second group said that the way to subdue the sinful flesh was to exhaust it. People were led to believe that sainthood comes through sinning, through the misuse of sex. We are right back on the Canary Islands. What was offered as sweet madeira wine was in fact a deadly poison.

The same St. John writes: "Dear friends, do not believe every spirit, but test the spirits to see whether they are from God" (1 John 4:1). Those who plainly teach and confess that Jesus Christ is God's true Son, who came to die for our sins and then rose again, are telling the truth. These friends we follow.

Prayer Suggestion

Thank the Lord Jesus for not only speaking the truth but also for being the Truth, the Life, and the only Way to the Father.

CHRISTIAN YOUTH: A SOUND INVESTMENT

How can a young man keep his way pure? By living according to Your Word. Psalm 119:9

Someone has described teenagers as "the generation now in escrow." The reference is to funds held by a third party which then become available when the intended payee has met certain conditions.

Young people are the future. They are a precious possession, a human asset and resource to be drawn on for leadership in coming years. The Christian church values teenagers highly.

Parents have the responsibility and privilege of helping young people mature. They set good examples and back them up with Christian teaching. As children become adolescents, then young adults, they gradually learn to take responsibility for their lives. This calls for spiritual growth through the study of God's Word. The psalmist asks: "How can a young man [person] keep his way pure?" He replies, "By living according to Your Word" (119:9).

Christian living results from Christian believing, from being in right relation to God through faith in Jesus Christ, the Savior. This relationship—this living in Christ and Christ in us—normally begins with holy baptism in infancy. This "washing with water through the Word" (Ephesians 5:26) cleanses from sin, breaks the power of death and the devil, and conveys the eternal salvation procured by Christ. This one-time performance is in effect for life. The faith engendered by the sacrament is kept alive and strengthened through instruction in God's Word.

What a blessing it is to the individual, to the family, to church and nation, when teenagers, "the generation now in escrow," mature into full Christian adulthood! The apostle commends them: "I write to you, young men, because you are strong, and the Word of God lives in you" (1 John 2:14).

Prayer Suggestion

In your prayer request the Lord of the church to safeguard and nurture children and teenagers.

CHRIST IS THE CENTER

God raised Him from the dead, freeing Him from the agony of death, because it was impossible for death to keep its hold on Him. Acts 2:24

Jules Verne gave free play to his imagination when he wrote his novel *Journey to the Center of the Earth.* To get to the center of things—to the heart and core of matters in life—is the concern of many people, sometimes for selfish reasons.

Isaiah deplores the greed of people who put themselves at the center of their world, leaving no room for others. They join house to house, field to field, that "they may be placed alone in the midst of the earth" (Isaiah 5:8 KJV).

There is a right way—and a right reason—for penetrating to the center of a situation. We find Jesus doing this when He tells His hearers not to get lost in trivia to the neglect of the weightier matters of God's Word. He Himself represents the very center of God's revelation for our salvation. The same Isaiah points to Him as the redeeming Messiah, saying, "The punishment that brought us peace was upon Him, and by His wounds we are healed" (53:5).

The twelve apostles kept the sin-atoning, risen Christ and His cross at the center of their preaching. St. Peter did this in his Pentecost sermon. At the heart of St. John's testimony is this: God loved us and sent His Son as "the atoning sacrifice for our sins" (1 John 2:2).

Certainly the thirteenth apostle, St. Paul, knew what was the heart and core of the Gospel he proclaimed, writing to the Corinthians, "I resolved to know nothing while I was with you except Jesus Christ and Him crucified" (1 Corinthians 2:2). The time came when he as a prisoner was taken on a journey to the center of the world: Rome, the imperial capital. There he "preached the kingdom of God and taught about the Lord Jesus Christ," as St. Luke states at the end of the book of Acts (28:31).

We are at the center of the Gospel when we believe, teach, and confess with St. Paul: "Christ the power of God and the wisdom of God" (1 Corinthians 1:24).

Prayer Suggestion

Pray that throughout life's journey the Holy Spirit may keep you close to Christ, the heart of the Gospel.

CHOSEN IN CHRIST

You are a chosen people, a royal priesthood, a holy nation,
a people belonging to God. 1 Peter 2:9

The ancient Greeks had a strong sense of fate. They believed life's events unfolded exactly as the gods had ordained them—there was no escape. The legend of Oedipus is an example. Oedipus was a king's son, destined someday to slay his father and, as usurper of his throne, to marry the queen, who was his mother. The tragedy destroyed the lives of all concerned.

As far as the Christian religion is concerned, there is no blind fate. No one will ever go down into eternal perdition because this was divinely ordained. St. Paul teaches that God has a good and gracious will toward all people. He "wants all men [persons] to be saved and to come to a knowledge of the truth. For there is one God and one Mediator between God and men, the man Christ Jesus, who gave Himself as a ransom for all men" (1 Timothy 2:4–5).

To strengthen Christians, particularly when they are in great affliction, God tells them that He will not fail them. He promises them that the crown of life is theirs. So long as they continue faithfully in the use of His Word and the sacraments, their salvation is sure—sure, not because of anything they do but because of divine grace and because the Gospel "is the power of God for the salvation of everyone who believes" (Romans 1:16). God's acts of grace provide a firm foundation: "Those God foreknew He also predestined to be conformed to the likeness of His Son. ... Those He predestined, He also called; those He called, He also justified; those He justified, He also glorified" (Romans 8:29–30).

This teaching is not to be misunderstood or misused as if to say salvation is an absolute cinch regardless of how a person believes or lives, on the false assumption that election saves. The Bible teaches, "Whoever believes and is baptized will be saved, but whoever does not believe will be condemned" (Mark 16:16). It was Jesus who said this, the same who declares for our comfort concerning believers, "No one can snatch them out of My Father's hand" (John 10:29).

Prayer Suggestion

Let your prayer intention be, through Word and Holy Spirit, to abide faithful to the end.

WORK, YES—WORRY, NO

If a man will not work, he shall not eat.
2 Thessalonians 3:10

Ants can be a bother at picnics and at other times and places. But that should not keep us from doing what the writer of Proverbs states: "Go to the ant, you sluggard; consider its ways and be wise! It … stores its provisions in summer and gathers its food at harvest" (Proverbs 6:6–8). The fact is: While people are enjoying an outdoor picnic, the ants are working, gathering food.

The instruction is given to sluggards, lazy persons, those who sleep when they should work. They need to hear that it is through work, physical and mental, that God provides our daily bread. Jesus set us a good example of being diligent in work. Even on a day of rest He performed a work of love—He healed a lame man at the pool of Bethesda, saying: "My Father is always at His work to this very day, and I, too, am working" (John 5:17). Again, He said: "As long as it is day, we must do the work of Him who sent Me. Night is coming, when no one can work" (John 9:4).

In implying that we should work and look ahead to the future, Jesus is by no means contradicting what He said about not taking thought for tomorrow and worrying about what we will eat, drink, and wear. He is warning us against sinful worrying in that passage.

In urging us to diligence, both the writer of Proverbs and Jesus are addressing themselves to the able-bodied, not to those who are poor and needy because they are unable to work. The Proverbs author writes also this: "A generous man will himself be blessed, for he shares his food with the poor" (22:9). And on Judgment Day Jesus will commend the righteous for giving bread to the hungry. He does not criticize the hungry, as if to say: "Why aren't you working to earn your daily bread?" He is speaking of those who are hungry through no fault of their own.

Jesus Himself labored diligently and hard. The prophet speaks of "the suffering of His soul" (Isaiah 53:11). Through His work we are redeemed from sin and death and set free from every kind of worry. Thanks be to God for such a Savior!

Prayer Suggestion

Ask God to bless all people who do honest work.

IT DOESN'T GO BY SIZE

"Not by might nor by power, but by My Spirit," says the
LORD Almighty. Zechariah 4:6

Mount Calvary, described in a hymn verse as a "mournful mountain" and in another as a "green hill," is not noteworthy because of size. Its height cannot compare with that of Mount McKinley in central Alaska, which is 20,300 feet high, the highest mountain in North America. Yet Calvary towers above McKinley in importance. It was once crowned by a cross on which Jesus Christ died to redeem the world from sin.

In God's plan of salvation, the effectiveness and final outcome does not depend on size—not on the dimensions of things He employs, not in the importance of people He engages, not in the number of people involved. In the Old Testament, Gideon and his 300 men routed the hordes of Midianites. This made plain that it was God, not human beings, who effected the deliverance.

As little as God depends on *quantity*, so little does He depend on the *quality* of people He chooses to do His work. Jesus turned to a dozen ordinary men to evangelize His kingdom. God gave the treasure of His saving Gospel to frail men, to vessels of clay, to people who by all outward appearance were average, ordinary people. Yet troublemakers in Thessalonica had to say this of Paul and Silas: "These [are] men who have turned the world upside down" (Acts 17:6 RSV).

Also in our lives it is true that God gets His work done, as He said to and through Zechariah, "not by might nor by power, but by My Spirit" (4:6). This is the Holy Spirit who does His wonders through the simple Gospel we preach. As with Elijah (1 Kings 19:9–18), so also to us may come the experiences that impress us: strong wind, earthquake, fire. But God's messages often come to us in a "gentle whisper" (1 Kings 19:12), and His good gifts in small packages. All in all, as Jesus said, "a man's life does not consist in the abundance of his possessions" (Luke 12:15). It consists in being rich toward God with the blessings of forgiveness, peace, and a purposeful life lived to Christ's glory.

Prayer Suggestion

Pray for courage and strength to continue your life's work when difficulties confront you. Let Jesus show you the way.

LASTING LETTERS

Then He opened their minds so they could understand the Scriptures. Luke 24:45

A well-known author has stated, "When an old person dies, it is like a library burning." Much valuable knowledge is lost, except for what the deceased may have recorded or transmitted orally.

However, misconceived "wisdom" is not worth saving. After the three friends of afflicted Job had cited his wrongdoing as cause of his suffering, he replied, "Wisdom will die with you" (Job 12:2). Much of what they said was beside the point and should be buried.

It is different when people speak the wisdom of God. When they pass away, as all of them will, their truth abides. In His love God saw to it that Old Testament teachings given to Moses, the psalmists, and prophets, as well as the teachings given to the New Testament evangelists and apostles, were preserved in Holy Scripture. All was written for our learning so that, in St. Paul's words, "we might have hope" (Romans 15:4).

St. John was an apostle who lived to ripe old age. He may have reached age 90 or beyond. When the Lord finally did call him home, John had left a small library of writings: the fourth gospel, the three epistles, and Revelation. Reduced to one sentence, St. John's testimony was that Jesus Christ "is the true God and eternal life," as stated at the close of his first epistle (5:20). Our salvation rests in Jesus Christ alone, the Son of God crucified for our sins and raised again from the dead.

Our passing away in old age need not resemble the burning of a library. Even if we leave no books—no biographies or diaries—those near and dear to us will be our living libraries. They will be to us what the Corinthians were to St. Paul, "our letter, written on our hearts, known and read by everybody" (2 Corinthians 3:2). These are lasting letters, living libraries, Christ's continuing witnesses in this world.

Prayer Suggestion

Give thanks to God for revealing the Gospel of Christ to you and for preserving it through all generations.

OVERTAKEN BY THE WORD

We cannot help speaking about what we have seen and heard. Acts 4:20

It is said that the Old Testament prophets "were called by God and overtaken by the Word." The divine call to them was followed by obedience, by captivation, and by full immersion in God's Word.

Jeremiah was called in early youth. He said to the Lord, "I do not know how to speak; I am only a child" (Jeremiah 1:6). However, when God's message came to him, he was overtaken by it in complete obedience. How great was his absorption! He said to God, "When Your words came, I ate them; they were my joy and my heart's delight" (15:16). Jeremiah inwardly digested the Word, sometimes with joy, sometimes with tears.

Also in the New Testament persons called by Jesus were overtaken by the Word. The Savior's call to Peter and Andrew to follow Him drew this immediate response, "At once they left their nets and followed Him" (Matthew 4:20). The same is said of James and John. Throughout their ministry the apostles revealed their full commitment to the Gospel. St. Peter declared, "We cannot help speaking about what we have seen and heard" (Acts 4:20). They testified to the truth of Christ's crucifixion and resurrection of which they had been eyewitnesses.

The Holy Spirit through the Gospel has called you and me to faith in Jesus Christ as Lord and Savior. An important question, following our call, is this: "Have we been overtaken by the Word?" Has it taken hold of us? Does it prompt us to serve the Lord gladly in the various vocations we find ourselves? Can we say with the psalmist that the Lord's teachings "are more precious than gold, than much pure gold; they are sweeter than honey, than honey from the comb" (19:10)?

How blest we are that God's call to faith and service has come to us and we are overtaken by the Word! Jesus, the Good Shepherd, always seeks and finds us when we stray from His redeeming love. He calls to us in His familiar voice. His Word overtakes us.

Prayer Suggestion

Begin by saying, "Lord Jesus, I thank You for continually renewing me through Your Gospel. Help me share Your Word with …"

AN ACCEPTABLE YEAR OF THE LORD

*The Spirit of the Sovereign LORD ... has sent Me ... to
proclaim the year of the LORD's favor. Isaiah 61:1–2*

Because of the divorce of a daughter and the marriage separations
of two sons, the Queen of England, Elizabeth II, pronounced 1992 "a
horrible year." Heartaches, for many other reasons as well, invade the
homes of the rich and the poor, the mighty and the weak.

God provides help and comfort so that we can endure the distress-
ful years. The Israelites, who experienced horrible years in Egypt and
during their 40-year journey to their homeland, also had years of
divine favor. Every 50th year was a year of jubilee. It was the acceptable year, or the year of the Lord's favor, for then the land would
revert to its original owners, and everyone obligated in any way to
another was set free. The sound of the trumpet would announce the
jubilee year. It was such a joyful occasion that Isaiah speaks of it as a
pledge and foretaste of the spiritual freedom the Messiah would bring.

In the synagogue of Nazareth Jesus announced His Messiahship,
using Isaiah's words to proclaim the year, yes, the entire New
Testament era, as the time of the Lord's favor. Jesus, the Son of the
Highest, came to earth to make common cause with us, render obedience for us, bear our burdens, heal our souls, make full restitution for
our sins, and grant us a charter to our heavenly home.

With Jesus at our side, we can make it through the year no matter
how "horrible" it may be, for He supports us all the way. Through Him
the heavenly Father, in the psalmist's words, "crown[s] the year with
... goodness" (65:11 KJV). Whatever our station in life, whether the
queen of England, a working wife, a patient in a hospital, or an aged
person, God causes goodness to follow all the days of our life. He is
there for us, especially in times of trouble.

Prayer Suggestion

Turn to Psalm 50:15. Base both your petition and your giving of
thanks on verse 15.

SPIRITUAL TASKS, SPIRITUAL TOOLS

Though we live in the world, we do not wage war as the world does. 2 Corinthians 10:3

People visiting the museum of the United States Military Academy, West Point, New York, see the exhibited weapons of war divided into two classes: small weapons and large ones. The small weapons include handheld clubs, axes, and swords; the large ones, such powerful machines as tanks, but also the beloved, all-purpose vehicle for peacetime uses: the Jeep.

St. Paul considered himself engaged in warfare of a spiritual kind. He was fighting the Evil One, whom he considered to be a very powerful opponent. He writes to the Ephesians, "Our struggle is not against flesh and blood, but against the rulers, against the authorities, against the powers of this dark world and against the spiritual forces of evil" (Ephesians 6:12).

The struggle against spiritual enemies requires spiritual weapons. Taking us away from West Point, as it were, the apostle points out: "We do not wage war as the world does. The weapons we fight with are not the weapons of the world" (2 Corinthians 10:3–4). Then what are the spiritual tools with which we work? In Ephesians 6:13–17 he mentions them. The two main ones are "the shield of faith" and "the sword of the Spirit, which is the Word of God." Faith is trust in Christ's redeeming, forgiving, life-giving merit. It is our best protection against the devil's flaming arrows. The only effective spiritual weapon with which to overcome sin and Satan is the Word of God, here also called "the Gospel of peace" (v. 15).

Today as perhaps never before we must distinguish carefully the tools we use to build Christ's kingdom. None of the hardware on display at West Point, small or large, will do. Only the Gospel has the power to bring us salvation, to reconstruct lives, to convey wisdom and light, to open the door of heaven. God's Word is our armory.

Prayer Suggestion

Ask God to make wars cease so that we can wholeheartedly concern ourselves with the peaceful upbuilding of Christ's kingdom.

WHAT WE HAVE IN HEAVEN

*He carried me away in the Spirit to a mountain great
and high, and showed me the Holy City, Jerusalem, coming down out of heaven from God. Revelation 21:10*

What things does a person need for life in the world to come? The ancient Egyptians believed that the people needed there what they need here. When Queen Nefertiti was buried in the Valley of the Queens, her tomb was made to contain food, clothing, furniture, boats, and the like.

However, in the afterlife we have no need for such things, for it is a totally different world. Job declares that we brought nothing with us into the world, and when we leave, we can take nothing with us—no money, no fine clothes, no food, and, thank God, no pills or medicine. Also the crutches and canes will not be needed.

It is hard for us to visualize the situation in heaven. In Revelation St. John draws back the draperies, as it were, and gives us a glimpse into heaven. He calls it the New Jerusalem, the celestial city. It does not need what earthly cities find necessary. It does not need sun or moon, much less electric lights, for God gives it light. No edifices for worship are needed, for "the Lord God Almighty and the Lamb are its temple," he writes (21:22). Also not found in the heavenly city are stores and food kitchens, for there is no hunger or thirst. Absent, too, are hospitals and mortuaries, for heaven knows neither sickness nor death.

What heaven has to offer we will have in abundance. Much of this is told in picture language. The river of life flows there, as clear as crystal. Present, too, in all its beauty and fruitfulness is the tree of life. Jesus adds to our conception of heaven when He says, "In My Father's house are many rooms" (John 14:2). This is comforting and assuring: Heaven is like a beautiful home where there is room for everyone.

If the question of what we need is heaven is unimportant, there is, however, a question of utmost importance: How do we get there? The Bible clearly and fully answers it. Jesus said He is the Way to the Father above. He reconciled us to God. He removed every obstacle; He paved the way. Believing in Him as the Savior, we have eternal life.

Prayer Suggestion

Give thanks to God for His gifts you will take with you into heaven: joy, love, and a peace that transcends our human understanding.

FINDING REST IN CHRIST

Since the promise of entering His rest still stands, let us be careful that none of you be found to have fallen short of it. Hebrews 4:1

Early Christians chose the first day of the week as their worship day. They called it the Lord's Day, for on it the Lord Jesus rose from the dead.

The Old Testament believers also had their Lord's Day, the seventh day of the week. It was called the Sabbath, which meant rest. Freed from daily work, the Israelites had the opportunity on this day to meditate on God's Word, individually and as an assembled congregation. It was on the seventh day that God rested after creating the world.

The Sabbath of rest gave promise of God's goodness in providing not only bodily gifts but also of the perfect peace and rest for the soul through the Messiah. God had made provision for what the epistle to the Hebrews calls the "Sabbath-rest." This peace or rest consists of all that Jesus Christ has earned: forgiveness of sins, salvation, peace with God, and eternal life. This eternal, heavenly peace is still available, for the writer urges that his readers heed God's invitation and enter into God's rest.

To accept God's Sabbath-rest invitation does not require that we still keep Saturday as our day of spiritual rest. The laws of the Sabbath and the other once-prescribed holy days in the Old Testament have been fulfilled with the coming of Jesus as the Messiah. St. Paul states that these days and occasions were "a shadow of the things that were to come; the reality, however, is found in Christ" (Colossians 2:17).

In fact, then, Christ is our true Sabbath-rest. Through Him God conveys freedom from the Law, release from the many do's and don'ts of the Old Testament ceremonial law. St. Paul explains to the Colossians how this release came about, for in Christ "we have redemption, the forgiveness of sins" (Colossians 1:14). As the Israelites were delivered from bondage in Egypt and were given promise of eternal rest in heaven, so God "has rescued us from the dominion of darkness and brought us into the kingdom of the Son He loves" (1:13). It is fitting for the Son to invite us, who are troubled, to find our rest in Him.

Prayer Suggestion

Bless the Lord for granting you rest and peace in Christ, now and for eternity.

ON BEING READY

Be dressed ready for service and keep your lamps burning.
Luke 12:35

Someone has described negligence as the lack of preparation or
the failure to anticipate an event. The result is apt to be that a sudden
development finds the individual unprepared and at a very serious disadvantage to cope with it.

In the time before the great deluge the people were negligent.
Instead of making preparation, they were neglectful or preoccupied
with other things. They were, as Jesus said, "eating, drinking, marrying
and being given in marriage up to the day Noah entered the ark" (Luke
17:27). It was the same with the people of Sodom and Gomorrah prior
to the great destruction. And the situation will be no different in the
days preceding our Lord's Second Coming.

To be prepared means to be ready to make the most of opportunities that present themselves. As Christ's disciples and witnesses it is
well for us to be prepared to testify to our faith in Jesus Christ. St.
Peter tells us, "Always be prepared to give an answer to everyone who
asks you to give the reason for the hope that you have" (1 Peter 3:15).
The apostle could write this with a poignant recollection of that fateful
night at the high priest's palace when and where he was not ready to
give truthful answers to the questions he was asked. Instead, he
denied Jesus.

St. Paul seemed always to be ready, always prepared, to capitalize
on opportunities to witness to the Gospel. He was ready with an
answer when the shaken jailor in Philippi asked how he could be
saved: he was to believe in Jesus as his, and his household's, Savior.
Further, He liked to have his congregations do things in order—for
example, to be ready with the offerings so that, when he came that
way, he could pick them up and deliver them to the starving saints in
Jerusalem.

For all of life it is true, opportunity favors the prepared person.

Prayer Suggestion

Ask God's help to be ready to share His love wherever necessary.

LOVE, NOT LUST

Be kind and compassionate to one another, forgiving each other, just as in Christ God forgave you. Ephesians 4:32

A nationally syndicated columnist has written, "Gambling inflames the lust for wealth without work."

The normal way to acquire the things we need is to work for them, manually and mentally. The Bible speaks on the subject of honest work. Adam was not to be an idler but was to "rule over the fish of the sea and the birds of the air and over every living creature that moves on the ground" (Genesis 1:28). After his fall into sin, his work became considerably harder. But it was still to be his way of earning daily bread.

People through all ages have tried to acquire wealth in ways other than honestly earning it. Some thieves lived in the city of Ephesus. "Stop it!" St. Paul is in effect saying. Let the one who steals work, "[do] something useful with his own hands" (Ephesians 4:28). This is important for two reasons: to have the wherewithal for their own support and to have something extra "to share with those in need" (4:28).

Another way that people, past and present, have tried to get their hands on more money is by engaging in games of chance, or gambling. The Roman soldiers under Christ's cross cast lots to determine who would get our Lord's seamless coat. Rolling dice was a common pastime in the Roman army. Julius Caesar, about to cross the Rubicon and march on Rome, declared, *Alea jacta est* ("the die is cast").

What lies at the root of gambling is hardly sportsmanship. It comes much closer to being what the above columnist said it is: sinful covetousness, I-want-it-all, I-don't-care-about-the-neighbor *lust*. Lust lies in the heart, where love ought to be. It is from the sin of lust that Christ redeemed us. In place of lust He has implanted in us love for Him and for one another. What a grand conclusion to this reading: "Be kind and compassionate to one another, forgiving each other, just as in Christ God forgave you" (Ephesians 4:32).

Prayer Suggestion

Give thanks to God for your ability to earn your daily bread with work. If you are chronically ill and can't work, thank God for generous givers.

St. Luke, a Careful Witness

Our dear friend Luke, the doctor, and Demas send greetings. Colossians 4:14

St. Luke was a man of many talents, author of the third gospel and the book of Acts. He was a missionary assistant to St. Paul, who refers to him as "our dear friend Luke, the doctor" (Colossians 4:14). He has the distinction of being closest to the apostle when the latter needed him the most. "Only Luke is with me," St. Paul wrote when his fatal captivity in Rome drew to a close (2 Timothy 4:11).

St. Luke is best known to us through his gospel in which he records the highlights of Jesus' birth (his account of Christ's nativity is a classic), life, ministry, crucifixion, resurrection, and ascension. Under the inspired direction of the Holy Spirit he set forth these events for a definite purpose—not as a mere biography but as an account of what God did to effect the salvation of sinners through the redeeming, sin-atoning merit of His Son.

People who in ignorance, or out of intellectual pride, dismiss the sacred writings as carelessly thrown together, and therefore full of inconsistencies, even contradictions, should examine St. Luke's prologue to his gospel. They should note how carefully he proceeded. He investigated, he interviewed eyewitnesses, he arranged his material in proper order—all for the purpose of presenting a clear Christian witness to his friend Theophilus. All the while the Holy Spirit was at work in the author to make sure that only the truth—the truth of Christ Jesus as Savior and Lord—was set forth.

God's great blessing rested on this Gospel. As St. Luke, a Gentile, was gained for the Christian faith through the testimony of others, so he was God's instrument for bringing in many more converts from the Grecian world.

Prayer Suggestion

Let your prayer for today express your appreciation to God for St. Luke's witness to Jesus, your Savior.

GOING TO COURT

*If any of you has a dispute with another, dare he take it
before the ungodly for judgment instead of before the saints?
1 Corinthians 6:1*

What does "litigiousness" mean? The word occurred in a catechism years ago to describe the tendency of some people to litigate, to
sue one another when disputes arise.

Some of St. Paul's readers in Corinth ventilated their problems
before pagan judges. The apostle much preferred that they settle their
problems among themselves with the help of their spiritual leaders. In
the latter settings, Christian principles, especially Christian love, can
prevail to the satisfaction of both parties. "Litigiousness" over trivial
cases gives Christianity a bad name in a pagan society. The apostle
considers it inconsistent with the high spiritual role Christians have to
"judge the world" and to "judge angels" (1 Corinthians 6:2–3).

"Litigiousness" tends to reflect greed, a contentious spirit, a preoccupation with selfish interests to the neglect of responsibility toward
the neighbor. In our times, court cases are not only numerous but
sometimes border on the humorous. For example, a New Hampshire
college student, having had an unpleasant, unwanted encounter with
her date, initiated a lawsuit, not against the young man but against his
parents "for having done such a rotten job in raising their son." While
the complaint might have been justified, the procedure for personal
redress was ill-advised.

As citizens, Christians are entitled to the protection of the courts
when righteous issues are at stake. St. Paul, a Roman citizen, availed
himself of the imperial courts, in the end appealing his case as a witness of Jesus Christ all the way to Caesar in Rome. The book of Acts
closes with this account of the apostle as a litigant in Rome: "Boldly
and without hindrance he preached the kingdom of God and taught
about the Lord Jesus Christ" (Acts 28:31).

Before taking a case to court, a Christian will "take it to the Lord
in prayer," considering all aspects of the matter in the light of Christ's
redeeming love.

Prayer Suggestion

If you have a grievance against anyone, ask the Holy Spirit for love
and wisdom to guide you in accordance with God's Word.

PERSONAL COMMITMENT

I beat my body and make it my slave so that after I have preached to others, I myself will not be disqualified for the prize. 1 Corinthians 9:27

Jesus pointed out a serious inconsistency in the lives of the spiritual leaders of His time, saying, "The teachers of the Law and the Pharisees sit in Moses' seat. So you must obey them and do everything they tell you. But do not do what they do, for they do not practice what they preach" (Matthew 23:2–3).

Geoffrey Chaucer, an English poet of old, gives a better testimony of the village parson in his *Canterbury Tales*:

> But Cristes lore, and his apostles twelve,
> He taught, and first he folwed it him-selve.

It was the concern of the apostle Paul to subject himself to the same truths of God's Word that he was teaching to the members of his young congregations. He wrote, "I beat my body and make it my slave so that after I have preached to others, I myself will not be disqualified for the prize" (1 Corinthians 9:27).

This is the concern of every faithful pastor and teacher in Christendom. Christ's representatives in the church realize that they teach by personal example as much as by their words. What they *are* is often more eloquent than their spoken words. Their Christian life is important. It expresses the personal obedience of those who teach us to accept God's Word, both the Law and Gospel promises. Also St. Peter writes, "To the elders among you, I appeal as a fellow elder … not lording it over those entrusted to you, but being examples to the flock" (1 Peter 5:1, 3).

Parents also, like Chaucer's village parson, are to be commended when they themselves follow the teachings of Christ which they seek to impart to their children. Little children—also the older ones—are known to be imitators. What a blessing it is in the home when parents and children, in their Christian faith and life, are committed to Jesus Christ, who in love redeemed them and made them His own in Holy Baptism!

Prayer Suggestion

Express your gratitude to Christ for all servants of the Word and for all parents who personally profess and follow His Word.

CITIZENS OF HEAVEN

It is by grace you have been saved, through faith.
Ephesians 2:8

The Bible tells us how the Israelites entered the Promised Land. It wasn't easy. The meandering journey took 40 years. They encountered many hardships in the desert. The greatest challenge came when the fortress city of Jericho had to be taken. Then the land had to be conquered.

The "promised land" for many Europeans and other peoples was the United States of America. Between the years 1892 and 1924 some 16 million foreigners entered through Ellis Island. It wasn't easy for them, either. They had to pass physical examinations and meet other conditions. The fortunate ones were issued a "landing card" and were told through which door to pass to enter the new world.

The real "promised land" for God's people is not Canaan nor the United States of America. It is the heavenly country toward which they are striving and in which they are citizens already. St. Paul declares, "Our citizenship is in heaven." He said it is the home from which "we eagerly await a Savior ... the Lord Jesus Christ" (Philippians 3:20).

The key question has always been: How do we get admitted into heaven? Do we have to pass all kinds of tests and have a "landing card"? Must we make an arduous journey through the wilderness of this world before we can gain entrance? Those who believe in salvation through good works—through human effort and merit—say yes. But this is not what Holy Scripture teaches. St. Paul clearly states, "By grace you have been saved, through faith" (Ephesians 2:8). He means the faith by which we rely completely on the saving merit of Jesus Christ. And what is the blessed result? This: "Therefore, since we have been justified through faith, we have peace with God through our Lord Jesus Christ" (Romans 5:1).

Spiritually speaking, there is for us no wilderness to cross, no Jericho to conquer, no Ellis Island to pass through. Our citizenship is in heaven. Our names are already recorded in the book of life.

Prayer Suggestion

Pray for continued strong faith in Jesus Christ, who is the only Way to the Father in heaven.

THE RIVER OF SALVATION

Jesus replied, "Let it be so now; it is proper for us to do this to fulfill all righteousness." Then John consented.
Matthew 3:15

Rivers play a prominent part in the lives of people. In the United States, the Mississippi River was, and still is, the principal waterway in middle America. Originating with springs in Lake Itaska in Minnesota, it flows a length of 2,340 miles before it enters the Gulf of Mexico.

The most noteworthy river in the Holy Land is the Jordan. From its several sources in the north, it twists its way some 350 miles until it empties into the Dead Sea.

The Jordan enters frequently into the history of salvation as God planned the Promised Land. It plays so great a part that one writer takes what he calls "a sacramental view of the waters of the river." In it Naaman of Syria, at the prophet Elisha's command, bathed and was cured of leprosy. The water of the river truly became "sacramental" when, by the power of God's Word, it healed people of the leprosy of sin as John the Baptist performed his baptism of repentance.

The Lord Jesus, who later replaced John's baptism with His own (Matthew 28:19), was Himself baptized by John in the Jordan. With Him it was not a matter of washing away sin, for He was without sin. He was baptized not only to set an example but to do something for our good. By submitting to this sacramental act He fulfilled for us "all righteousness" (Matthew 3:15). In all His life He was our substitute as He kept the Law, rendered full obedience for our disobedience and, in the end, endured the penalty of death for our disobedience.

We are saved to this day "by the washing with water through the Word" (Ephesians 5:26), regardless of whether such water comes from the Jordan, the Mississippi, or any other source. As baptized Christians, our concern is to fulfill our Lord's directive to baptize all nations and teach them the Gospel. In a hymn line we pray that the "blest river of salvation" may pursue its onward course and flow to every nation until Jesus returns in glory.

Prayer Suggestion

Give thanks to the Triune God that the Gospel of Christ, like a river of salvation, has brought faith and peace to many.

THE HUMAN BEING: CROWN OF CREATION

Oh, the depth of the riches of the wisdom and knowledge of God! Romans 11:33

Near St. Louis, Missouri, is an area where the skeletal remains of mastodons were unearthed. It was made into a park, where a museum shows these large, elephant-like creatures, now extinct. The skull of one still contains a spear by which an early man slew the animal. The mastodons, it is estimated, date back some 10,000 years.

How old is the world, and when did human beings first appear? Nobody knows, and the Bible doesn't say. Through Job (38:4), the Lord asks, "Where were you when I laid the earth's foundation? Tell Me, if you understand."

The Bible asks and answers questions more closely related to our salvation. In doing this, it underscores the wisdom, knowledge, power, and love of the Creator: the triune God, Father, Son, and Holy Spirit. It penetrates to the question: Who and what is man, whom God created on the sixth day? It reveals that he was created holy but fell into the sin of disobedience and was doomed to die eternally. But the God of majesty, might, and glory is also the God of all grace. Through His Son, who became man and is designated as the Second Adam, sinners are redeemed. This divine Redeemer is Jesus Christ. By faith in Him, which the Holy Spirit creates through the Gospel, believers are renewed in the image of God. They are restored to their original position as the crown of creation.

While everything connected with the earth, including its age, is of importance, it must not distract our attention from the age-old question posed to the human being in Latin: *Dic cur hic:* Say why you are here. The reading from Romans 11 tells us to give all glory to Him, to praise Him for His wonderful works, here on earth and in space above—all "the work of Your fingers," as the psalmist declares (8:3). We are here, as the Bible goes on to say, to serve God where we are and have our being—in our daily work, in regular worship, and in our witness to Jesus Christ, whose saving love surrounds the world.

Prayer Suggestion

Finish this prayer: "Lord God, You have not precisely told us how old the universe is, but You have told us to serve you by ..."

SIDE BY SIDE: RICH AND POOR

They sell the righteous for silver, and the needy for a pair of sandals. Amos 2:6

Many world travelers say they know few places where the rich and the poor live in such obvious contrast as Hong Kong. The rich, more than anywhere else, stand off from the rest by their jewelry and dress. They drive Rolls Royces and drink cognac. The poor, not far away, live in boats amid abject poverty.

Utmost prosperity and grinding poverty are portrayed also in the Bible, sometimes as existing side by side. The prophet Amos speaks of the rich as stretching themselves on ivory beds and dining on choice meats while the poor are being sold for a pair of sandals.

Jesus draws attention to Dives, the rich man, dressed in expensive clothes and faring luxuriously every day. At his door lies poor, sick Lazarus, clothed in rags and living from crumbs and food scraps thrown out to the dogs.

The great contrast has its roots in sin—in greed, indolence, and negligence. Many of the rich are born into wealth, while many poor are locked into poverty from generation to generation. Christianity seeks to improve life for the poor by urging the wealthy to give them food and clothes. But the difference remains. Jesus said that we would always have the poor with us. Apparently we will always have the rich with us also. Christians can improve conditions, but because of sin we cannot eradicate socio-economic problems. Private efforts in the past on this score have failed. Christianity has first of all to do with the salvation of sinners, rich or poor.

The truths of the Bible establish the basis for a hope that transcends all earthly wealth. It speaks of "riches"; these are spiritual but very real. The full enjoyment of eternal life and all that it includes awaits us in heaven. St. Paul reminds the Corinthians how the wealth of faith came about: "You know the grace of our Lord Jesus Christ, that though He was rich, yet for your sakes He became poor, so that you through His poverty might become rich" (2 Corinthians 8:9). How rich? Again, St. Paul, "In Him [Christ] we have redemption through His blood, the forgiveness of sins, in accordance with the riches of God's grace" (Ephesians 1:7).

Prayer Suggestion

Praise God for all His blessings, especially for the gift of full forgiveness in Christ Jesus.

HAVING GOD IN OUR HEARTS

*If anyone loves Me, he will obey My teaching. My Father
will love him, and We will come to him and make Our
home with him. John 14:23*

A favorite, frequently used word, in the secular world and in the
church, is "enthusiasm." A salesperson needs to have enthusiasm for
the product he or she sells. In the church we need enthusiasm for missions such as Christ's apostles had. Interestingly enough, the word is
derived from the Greek *entheos*, which means to have God in oneself
and thus to be inspired by Him.

To say that we sinners have God in us in a pagan sense, or to go so
far as to say, as oriental religions do, that we are a part of God and
that He is a part of us, is blasphemy. It erases the distinction between
Creator and creature.

Yet Christians do have God in them. Jesus promised the believer
that He and the Father "will come to him and make Our home in him"
(John 14:23). St. Paul told the Romans that "the Spirit of God lives in
you" (8:9). He explained to the Corinthians that they, in body and in
soul, are the temple of the Holy Spirit (1 Corinthians 6:19). Biblical
scholars call this indwelling of God "the mystical union."

How does God's indwelling in Christians come about? He is in
them because they have faith in God's Word. Through the Word the
Holy Spirit enters human hearts, creating and confirming the saving
faith in them. Christians rely altogether on the atoning death of Jesus
Christ and His resurrection. They have God not only in their hearts but
also in their minds. He enters into their thinking. It can therefore be a
proper prayer to say with the song writer in the title of his anthem,
"God, Be in My Head."

God is in us when we keep His Word in good and honest hearts
and bring forth the fruits of faith. God is in us when we love Him who
first loved us and when we love one another, as our Savior bids us.
Thus understood, we can put right meaning into the word "enthusiasm" and express it as we joyfully and hopefully fulfill God's Word and
work.

Prayer Suggestion

Tell your Savior in prayer that, thanks to the Holy Spirit active in
you, you will receive Him when He stands before your door and
knocks.

LIFE'S HIGHEST CHOICE

Mary has chosen what is better, and it will not be taken away from her. Luke 10:42

"Choose something like a star" is a line from the poet Robert Frost. He encourages us to set our ideals high and to select our activities accordingly. A great loss occurs when people use their talents to gain only whatever glitters here below. The glamour soon vanishes, and what people consider a great gain often turns out to be fool's gold.

A star stands for hope. This is especially true of the Christian faith. Christ Jesus is the promised Star who was to rise out of Jacob. He is, in the words of St. John, "the bright Morning Star" (Revelation 22:16). The Wise Men saw His star in the East and in a very literal sense chose to follow it until it brought them to Christ, Himself the Star of hope.

Our Lord blesses all who by faith choose His Word as the polestar of their lives. In the town of Bethany He upheld Mary for regarding His teaching as the one thing needful, saying to busy Martha: "Mary has chosen what is better, and it will not be taken away from her" (Luke 10:42). Mary believed—and so did Martha as she revealed at the tomb of Lazarus—that Jesus was the promised Messiah. In Him is salvation, for by His atoning offering on the cross we have the forgiveness of sins. He is the Resurrection and the Life.

To this day the message goes out into the world and, in the words of St. Peter, we "do well to pay attention to it [the prophetic Word], as to a light shining in a dark place, until the day dawns and the Morning Star rises in [our] hearts" (2 Peter 1:19).

At a huge gathering of people at Shechem the aged Joshua in effect told the Israelites to choose the Star. "Throw away the foreign gods" (Joshua 24:23), he said. He told them not to worship the hosts of heaven—sun, moon, and stars—but to choose the true God, adding, "As for me and my household, we will serve the LORD" (24:15). This is our resolve as well.

Prayer Suggestion

Ask for the guidance of the Holy Spirit as you make choices in life and as you resolve to grow closer to Christ.

TWICE A CHILD

No one can see the kingdom of God unless he is born again.
John 3:3

In *Hamlet*, Shakespeare has one of the actors declare, "They say an old man is twice a child." The reference, of course, is to a man's early childhood and his return to childish ways in old age. The latter we call senility.

As far as Christians are concerned, Christians of all ages and genders are twice children. They have their natural childhood and they have a spiritual one. They are the sons and daughters of their parents and they are the children of God, their Father. The latter status is achieved through conversion. This is their second birth brought about through the water of baptism and the Word of the Gospel. Jesus said to Nicodemus, "No one can see the kingdom of God unless he is born again" (John 3:3). He explained it as a rebirth through "water and the Spirit" (3:5). St. Paul likewise links up our childhood under God with baptism: "You are all sons of God through faith in Christ Jesus, for all of you who were baptized into Christ have clothed yourselves with Christ" (Galatians 3:26–27).

The truth of being a child for a second time is explained as a relationship established by divine adoption. "In love," writes the apostle Paul, "He [God] predestined us to be adopted as His sons through Jesus Christ ... In Him we have redemption through His blood, the forgiveness of sins" (Ephesians 1:4–5, 7). Here the apostle also points to the benefit of being God's adopted children. If we are His spiritual offspring, His true sons and daughters, we are then His heirs and heirs of eternal life.

How greatly blessed and enriched we are to be "twice a child"! We owe a debt of gratitude to our parents for bringing us into the world and giving us a Christian upbringing. Yet we are especially thankful to God for bringing us into His family. Be glad that you are "twice a child"!

Prayer Suggestion

Speak to your heavenly Father in a glad and grateful way for all the blessings He grants in Christ for your double childhood.

LOOKING IN THE MIRROR

I became a servant of this Gospel by the gift of God's grace given me through the working of His power. Ephesians 3:7

God sent the prophet Samuel to Bethlehem to anoint one of the sons of Jesse as king of Israel. The prophet was impressed by the size and outward demeanor of the firstborn. But he was not God's choice. The Lord said, "Man looks at the outward appearance, but the Lord looks at the heart" (1 Samuel 16:7).

What if we could see ourselves as we really are? This is hard to do. The Scottish poet Robert Burns said in his quaint English, "Oh wad some power the giftie gie us to see ourselves as others do." We may not actually be what we seem to be in the eyes of others. Some emotions as expressed in one's face can be misinterpreted. Fear is easily misread as anger. Shyness can be confused with pride or self-centeredness. If we could see ourselves through the eyes of others, we could make improvements in our outward appearance.

It is much better, however, to try to see ourselves as God sees us. God's Word is a mirror in which we can see a true image of ourselves. The Law reveals us as sinners, but the Gospel assures us that through faith in Jesus Christ as Savior, God forgives us and accepts us as His beloved children. To be loved by God and to love Him in return makes us changed people, a people of a pure heart. This is how we should be able to see ourselves. God looks on us as His forgiven children.

St. Paul realized that he had no personal merit before God. He had formerly persecuted Christ's church. In great humility he considered Himself "less than the least of all God's people" (Ephesians 3:8). That was the self-image he saw in the mirror of God's law. But he saw himself also in the light of the Gospel. God gave him the grace to preach the Gospel of salvation totally in Christ. It was the same grace by which he was also saved and at peace with God. This faith gave him inner strength. Never mind that some said, "In person he is unimpressive and his speaking amounts to nothing" (2 Corinthians 10:10). He saw himself not as unfriendly people did, but as God saw him.

The Gospel enables us also to see ourselves through the eyes of God.

Prayer Suggestion

Pray for the grace of God in Christ so that you may see yourself as a person fully forgiven and as a walking witness of God's peace.

THE RIGHT KIND OF ETHICS

Love does no harm to its neighbor. Therefore love is the fulfillment of the law. Romans 13:10

Business, government, and the professions seek to hold their members to ethical codes. The subject of ethics has to do with moral do's and don'ts. Ethics can be systematized and taught as a subject. But much more is necessary. You can, for example, outline on paper how the game of baseball is to be played. But if the individual has neither the desire nor the ability to play the game, very little is accomplished.

There is a right way to motivate, teach, and enable people to lead ethical and moral lives. It is the Christian way, the way of the Bible. It begins with God's moral law drawn from the Ten Commandments. The moral law is like a mirror. It shows us our sins and condemns us for them. It calls for love to God and the neighbor but does not give us the power to fulfill it. But God does not leave us in this predicament. In His grace He comes to us in the Gospel and makes us new people. He grants us faith in Jesus Christ, His own perfect Son, so that we trust in Him for the forgiveness of our sins. Our coming to faith was accompanied by a change of heart. We are His new creation in Christ. We are, as Jesus said to Nicodemus, born again, regenerated, converted. Now Christian life can begin, a life of good ethics and morals not merely in outward deeds and demeanor but in our innermost thoughts and emotions.

God's moral law is still there for Christians, not as the source of Christian ethics and morals, but as the norm, as a guide or rule showing us what good works God wants us to do. Through the Gospel true love is instilled, and God's Ten Commandments are our guide (not our motive) for its exercise. The apostle Paul writes, "Love does no harm to its neighbor. Therefore love is the fulfillment of the Law" (Romans 13:10). Again, St. Paul: "The goal ... is love, which comes from a pure heart and a good conscience and a sincere faith" (1 Timothy 1:5).

It has been said, "Ethics teaches that man is a morally responsible being." Christian ethics go further. Through faith in the Gospel it *enables* a person to be morally responsible.

Prayer Suggestion

Ask the Holy Spirit to deepen your faith in Jesus and to make your life fruitful in every respect.

SPEAKING THE TRUTH

*Speaking the truth in love, we will in all things grow up
into Him who is the Head, that is, Christ. Ephesians 4:15*

Rumors, especially those involving prominent persons, can last a
long time. On July 9, 1850, President Zachary Taylor died suddenly.
Some believed he was poisoned and the rumor persisted. More than
150 years later the remains were exhumed, but no evidence of foul
play was found.

False rumors are lies, and they have fast feet. They are perpetuated because some people prefer them to the truth. The Bible speaks of
this. At the end of his gospel St. John corrected a rumor circulating in
his day because of what the risen Jesus had said to Peter: "The rumor
spread among the brothers that this disciple [John] would not die. But
Jesus did not say that he would not die; He only said, 'If I want him to
remain alive until I return, what is that to you?' " (John 21:23)

Some rumors are far worse. The Bible (Revelation 22:15) speaks of
malicious rumormongers as being in the same class with "those who
practice magic arts, the sexually immoral, the murderers, the idolaters
and everyone who loves and practices falsehood." Christ's enemies cir-
culated outright lies to account for the empty grave. They claimed the
disciples came by night and carried the body away.

Christians refrain from speaking and listening to rumors, especially false ones. St. Paul wants each reader to "put off falsehood and
speak truthfully to his neighbor" (Ephesians 4:25). Again: "Do not let
any unwholesome talk come out of your mouths, but only what is
helpful for building others up according to their needs, that it may
benefit those who listen" (Ephesians 4:29).

How can it be otherwise? Christians are like Christ, who speaks
the truth and is the Truth. He rose from the dead after completing our
redemption, establishing us in the truth that sets us free—and in truthfulness as a result.

Prayer Suggestion

Thank your Savior for being both your Exemplar and Enabler of
truth-telling.

SPEAKING OF WATER ...

He got up and was baptized, and after taking some food,
he regained his strength. Acts 9:18–19

"Throughout African-American culture, water symbolizes freedom, justice, and privilege," states Langston Hughes, an African-American poet, in *The Negro Speaks of Rivers*.

Rivers—and water as such—play a part in the Bible. A river, dividing into four headstreams, flowed out of Eden. The Jordan, flowing from beyond the Sea of Galilee to the Dead Sea, is mentioned often in the Bible; in it John baptized Jesus and many others. St. Paul and Silas met Lydia, the first convert in Europe, and other women gathered for prayer at a riverside near Philippi. In a heavenly vision St. John saw "the river of the water of life, as clear as crystal" (Revelation 22:1).

Water as such, whether it flows in rivers or is poured into a font when it is used for the sacrament of Holy Baptism, does more than symbolize "freedom, justice, and privilege." When connected with God's Word, as Jesus directs, it has the power to cleanse from sin, to grant freedom from the curse of the Law, to impart justice and other virtues of faith, to endow the baptized person, young or old, with the privilege of belonging to God's family with the right of inheritance guaranteed.

Water, with the Word, did all this for Saul the converted Pharisee, to whom Ananias of Damascus said, "What are you waiting for? Get up, be baptized and wash your sins away" (Acts 22:16).

Also your baptism and mine is a precious means of grace through which the Triune God grants a flood of blessings: "clothed ... with Christ" (Galatians 3:27), "forgiveness of your sins" (Acts 2:38), "washed ... sanctified ... justified in the name of the Lord Jesus Christ" (1 Corinthians 6:11), and a "good conscience toward God" (1 Peter 3:21). Let the rivers, or plain, simple, tap water, remind you of this.

Prayer Suggestion

Say thanks to the Triune God for the many blessings conveyed to you through your baptism.

BEYOND THE DEVIL'S "FAITH"

When He arrived at the other side ... two demon-possessed men coming from the tombs met Him. Matthew 8:28

The incarnation of the Son of God is confessed in the Nicene Creed. The only-begotten Son of God, it says, "was incarnate by the Holy Spirit of the virgin Mary and was made man." In ancient times the worshipers took special note of this solemn event by bowing when these words were spoken. The story is told that Satan, present at a worship service, was surprised to see a man not making this obeisance. He is supposed to have told the man that devils "would greatly rejoice and deem it an honor if the Son of God had become one of them."

Some people, from high-ranking theologians to common folk, have doubted that the Son of God truly became a human being and that Jesus is that one. But the devil has no problem with this. He knows better than to disbelieve the deity of Jesus. On many occasions the evil spirits, whom Jesus drove out of possessed people, openly proclaimed Him to be divine. The demons, expelled from the tomb-dwelling possessed men in the region of the Gadarenes, cried out, "What do You want with us, Son of God? ... Have You come here to torture us before the appointed time?" (Matthew 8:29) Similar demonic confessions were made on other occasions.

How do we confess our faith in Jesus as God's Son? St. James in his epistle (2:18–19) deplores a dead faith, a faith sometimes described as one of "the head and mouth," because it lacks good works as the outward evidence of the true and living faith in Jesus Christ as Lord and Savior. He says also that monotheism—the belief that there is but one God—is not enough. He writes, "Even the demons believe that—and shudder" (James 2:19).

The devil is at best a sullen "believer." While he must admit that Jesus is the true Son of God and the Savior of those who believe in Him, he himself, by his own choice, is excluded. We as human beings can be joyful believers, for it is our conviction that the Son of God became incarnate "for us and for our salvation."

Prayer Suggestion

Declare to Jesus that you believe in Him as God's true Son and as your Savior, thanking Him for salvation full and free.

On the Wings of an Eagle

I carried you on eagles' wings and brought you to Myself.
Exodus 19:4

On June 30, 1994, it was front-page news in the St. Louis *Post-Dispatch* that the bald eagle, on the verge of extinction in the early 1970s, was removed from the government's endangered species list. It has been America's national symbol since 1782.

The remarkable comeback of the bald eagle as a species coincides with the Bible's statement that the eagle rejuvenates itself. David (in Psalm 103), in praise of the goodness of God, states, "[He] forgives all your sins and heals all your diseases, [He] redeems your life from the pit and crowns you with love and compassion, [He] satisfies your desires with good things so that your youth is renewed like the eagle's" (3–5). This is a wonderful tribute to the grace of God, who does all this for believers because of the redeeming work of Jesus Christ, the crucified and risen One.

Eagles are mentioned often in the Bible. They have qualities that invite comparison with the love, power, and providence of God. These qualities include the tender care of the young, the strength of their wings, the swiftness of their flight, and their keenness of sight. Through Moses God reminds the Israelites how He carried them "on eagles' wings" (Exodus 19:4) as He brought the people out of Egypt to the Promised Land. In a special song of praise in Deuteronomy 32 Moses compares God's guardianship of Israel to the care of a parent eagle "that stirs up its nest and hovers over its young, that spreads its wings to catch them and carries them on its pinions" (v. 11).

In chapter 49 of his prophecy Jeremiah speaks of the Edomites "who occupy the heights of the hill … [and] build [their] nest as high as the eagle's" (v. 16). God is the believer's refuge and strength. He guards His people from evil by establishing them in safe places and surrounding them with His love. For this we praise Him.

Prayer Suggestion

Let your soul, heart, and mind magnify God in a prayer of thanks for His goodness to you in Jesus Christ.

CONSTANCY IN FAITH AND LOVE

After waiting patiently, Abraham received what was promised. Hebrews 6:15

People who visit Onondaga Cave in Missouri are told that its temperature is constant: Summer and winter, day and night, it is 57 degrees Fahrenheit. Elsewhere the world is given to ups and downs, as the hymn writer states, "Change and decay in all around I see."

People are given to inconstancy, even people who are Christians. Faith can weaken, and the fervency of love can subside. We are to expect this as the end of the world approaches. Jesus said, "At that time many will turn away from the faith. ... Because of the increase of wickedness, the love of most will grow cold" (Matthew 24:10, 12). This tendency prevailed from the beginning of Christianity. Through St. John, the Lord said He held this against the church in Ephesus: "You have forsaken your first love" (Revelation 2:4). The church in Laodicea had attained a constancy of sorts, but it, too, was displeasing to God: "You are lukewarm—neither hot nor cold" (Revelation 3:16).

In contrast to the fluctuations of human love and loyalty stands the permanence of the saving grace of God. The writer of the epistle to the Hebrews reminds his readers how God, faithful and true, had kept His promise to Abraham to give him a son and through him the greater Seed, the Messiah. As though the promise were not in itself sufficient, God confirmed it with an oath. At the fullness of time God fulfilled His promise by causing His Son to be born of a woman. Jesus Christ, born of the virgin Mary, is truly the woman's offspring of Genesis 3:15. He became our great High Priest when He entered the Holy of Holies to offer up Himself on the cross for our sins, then entering the Holy Place of heaven to intercede for us.

God's constant love in Christ, as attested in His steadfast, immovable Word, confirms us in our faith and love. We are both encouraged and enabled to do what St. Paul bids us: "My dear brothers, stand firm. Let nothing move you" (1 Corinthians 15:58). Our Christian response to God's love is: "Oh, may my love to Thee, Pure, warm, and changeless be, A living fire."

Prayer Suggestion

Declare your firm faith in, and love for, Jesus Christ, your Savior, asking the Holy Spirit to give you steadfastness.

BE WHAT YOU ARE

Do not think of yourself more highly than you ought, but rather think of yourself with sober judgment, in accordance with the measure of faith God has given you. Romans 12:3

The Bible in several places compares people to flowers, one reason being that they flourish for a while, then quickly fade away. Other parallels can be drawn. A writer in an outdoors magazine recently stated that "the dandelion is a weed that impersonates a flower." It may be asked: Do people of one kind at times pretend to be people of another sort?

We may know of people who don't want to be what they really are, going to considerable effort to disguise their identity. The problem of human dissemblance prevails also in Christendom. Some who are unbelievers at heart pretend to be Christians. They are called hypocrites. In ancient Greece, *hypokrites* were actors who impersonated other people.

Jesus said in the Sermon on the Mount, "When you pray, do not be like the hypocrites, for they love to pray standing in the synagogues and on the street corners to be seen by men" (Matthew 6:5). St. Matthew devotes the 23rd chapter of his gospel to Jesus' condemnation of the Pharisees, many of whom were hypocrites. The Lord said, "They devour widows' houses and for a show make lengthy prayers" (Mark 12:40).

If hypocrites are a spiritual nuisance, why are they not summarily excommunicated from the church? This cannot be done, for we cannot look into anyone's heart to see whether the true faith in Christ is present. Jesus made this clear in His parable of the tares among the wheat stalks. We are not to eradicate the hypocrites, for we would make too many mistakes. Jesus said we should let both grow together until the harvest. On Judgment Day our Lord will Himself make the separation.

Jesus' laissez faire does not imply that His church should condone sham Christianity. The church is to warn its members about the sin of hypocrisy. Holy Scripture, in the words of St. Paul, "is useful for teaching, rebuking, correcting and training in righteousness" (2 Timothy 3:16). It teaches us to be what we are. In the same chapter the apostle states also that God's Word, the Gospel, is "able to make you wise for salvation through faith in Christ Jesus." When we believe sincerely in Jesus as our Savior, we will try to keep His Word in good and honest hearts.

Prayer Suggestion

Pray that the Holy Spirit may keep you in the true faith and help you to confess it honestly before the world.

JESUS, THE TRUE CHRIST

Do not believe every spirit, but test the spirits to see whether they are from God, because many false prophets have gone out into the world. 1 John 4:1

There are diamonds and there are "diamonds." Among the latter are imitation gems made from hard-earth minerals in temperatures of 5,000 degrees Fahrenheit and above. They can be bought and sold, provided the buyer knows that they are not the real "mined diamonds." To sell them as such would be dishonest.

There is a true Christ and many false christs. Jesus said of the last times, "False Christs and false prophets will appear" (Matthew 24:24). Gamaliel, a respected teacher in Israel, mentioned two of them: Theudas and Judas (Acts 5:36–37).

In our time, the danger is not so much that religious leaders will claim to be Christ as that they will proclaim a false christ—they will misrepresent Jesus and His work. Those who say that He is not the Son of God are offering a fictitious christ, a make-believe "diamond" instead of the true gem that He is. Some leave Him out altogether. A modern false prophet was recently quoted as saying: "The only time you hear the name 'Jesus Christ' in our church is when the janitor falls down stairs."

In Galatia, false teachers claimed that Jesus did not fully redeem us and that therefore we are not saved by faith alone but by faith *and* good works. All who today proclaim a salvation by faith *and* something else—faith *and* good character, faith *and* a golden-rule morality, faith *and* human righteousness—preach only a partial Savior, and a partial Savior is none at all.

St. Peter is a true witness of Jesus. He confesses, "You are the Christ, the Son of the living God" (Matthew 16:16). He tells us that we were redeemed "with the precious blood of Christ, a lamb without blemish or defect" (1 Peter 1:19). This apostle is a spiritual jeweler offering us Christ as the genuine diamond.

Prayer

In your prayer renew your pledge of loyalty to Jesus Christ, true God and your one and only Savior.

LIVES THAT AGREE WITH LIPS

The Lord says: "These people come near to me with their mouth and honor me with their lips, but their hearts are far from me." Isaiah 29:13

When a branch of the St. Louis public library was to be closed for lack of use, some 2,000 persons of the neighborhood signed their names to a petition to keep it open. It was found, however, that only about 10 percent of the signers had library cards.

What people do very often lags far behind of what they say. Performances fall short of promises. Ideals considered good for others are not fulfilled by those who plead for them.

The mouths of many are far more "obedient" than their hearts, the Lord said through the prophet Isaiah. Lips say yes, but their lives say no. This inconsistency was noted by Jesus. That is why in Matthew 15 He quoted this text when the Pharisees insisted on observing the man-made ceremonial law of hand-washing but left the true Word and will of God undone.

During the days of Jesus' final suffering, the fickleness, if not the perversity, of human nature became most clear. Where was Peter on Good Friday after he had so strongly affirmed his loyalty to Christ? When Jesus announced His final journey to Jerusalem, Thomas said to the other disciples, "Let us also go, that we may die with Him" (John 11:16). Noble words, yes, but where was he after our Lord's arrest in Gethsemane? And where was he when on Easter evening the risen Savior appeared to the ten disciples?

Jesus said to Pontius Pilate that His servants "would fight to prevent My arrest" (John 18:36) if His were an earthly kingdom. Apparently many had promised to stand by Him. But where were they now—those thousands who after the miraculous feeding were ready to crown Him a king?

Our Lord, who gave His life for us, is certainly pleased when, in thankfulness, we come near to Him and honor Him with our lips, as we do in this devotion. It pleases Him above all if our declared loyalty passes from hearts to mouths, from lips to lives lived for Him. Then we are in harmony not only with ourselves but also with Him.

Prayer

Lord God, Father of our Lord Jesus Christ and our Father, help us to be true to You till death. Amen.

NOISE AND SILENCE

Sing joyfully to the LORD, you righteous; it is fitting for the upright to praise Him. Psalm 33:1

The superstition still prevails among some Chinese that noise drives away evil spirits. Hence on New Year's Day and on other occasions they set off firecrackers.

Does noise have significance for Christians in the practice of their religion? Several psalms as translated in the King James Version of the Bible call for making "noise." Later versions take the idea of "noise" away from cacophony and render the text as joyful praise supported by skillfully played instruments. Thus "play skillfully with a loud noise" in Psalm 33:3 of the King James Version becomes "play skillfully, and shout for joy" in the New International Version. The singing in many congregations is low-key, subdued, in fact, abominable. Much of our singing could be far more audible and joyful—not to drive away evil spirits but to let the Holy Spirit make His witness through us.

The exhortation to "make a joyful noise" (Psalm 100:1 KJV) seems to be in contradiction with this Word: "The LORD is in His holy temple; let all the earth be silent before Him" (Habakkuk 2:20). But there is no conflict. There are times in our worship, as in all of life, when we sing loudly for joy—on Easter morning, for example—and times when we quietly pray and silently meditate on God's wonderful Word and works.

In our world of noise and haste, we Christians need to recognize occasions for expressing the joy of our salvation in Jesus Christ. It is also good to find time to come humbly and silently before God to acknowledge His majesty, to confess our sins, and to listen to His consoling Word. Yes, sounds and silence have their places and appropriate times in the Christian's life.

Prayer Suggestion

Lift up your voice in prayer to express your Christian joy for salvation, and also quietly pledge your continuing loyalty to Jesus Christ.

LETTING GOD BE GOD

*Since the creation of the world God's invisible qualities—His
eternal power and divine nature—have been clearly seen.
Romans 1:20*

It is said that the Iroquois Indians were so impressed by the wonder of Niagara Falls that they worshiped it. French missionaries preached to them there, pointing out that the things in nature are the works of God, not God Himself. The ancient Greeks likewise blurred the distinction between Creator and creation, identifying the goddess Gaea with the earth. An echo of that error remains in the expression "Mother Earth," as though the earth, if not itself divine, at least has divine power. An even greater heresy, continuing to this day, is the belief that the human being is divine, either as part of God or as God Himself.

St. Paul, who penetrated the pagan world, ran across many religious beliefs. In Lystra, when he healed a crippled man, the people shouted, "The gods have come down to us in human form" (Acts 14:11). They tried to identify Paul and Barnabas with Hermes and Zeus, respectively. The apostle would have none of this. He said, "We too are only men, human like you" (v. 15). Then he proceeded to preach to them about "the living God, who made heaven and earth and the sea and everything in them" (v. 15). This living God sent His Son into the world to teach and to lay down His life for the redemption of sinners.

In his epistle to the Romans St. Paul points out that it is not only a sin but is already God's punishment when people, in their perversion of the truth, "worshiped and served created things rather than the Creator" (1:25). This is not letting God be God. This is the sin of rejecting the natural knowledge of God with which people are born and turning to creatures as idols.

Who is our God? What do we consider as our highest good? Is it gold or silver? Is it pleasure? Is it some human being? To fear, love, and trust in a created thing as though it were God is the master sin of idolatry. God wants us to keep the faith that He has revealed in Jesus Christ, His Son, through whose merit we have salvation.

Prayer Suggestion

Construct your own prayer, basing it on the theme of praising God from whom all blessings flow.

ADDING LOYALTY TO LOVE

The memory of the righteous will be a blessing.
Proverbs 10:7

Visitors at historic "Sunnyside" at Irvington, New York, home of Washington Irving, learn that he was not only a famous author but also a lawyer and foreign diplomat. "Sunnyside" never had a matron, for Martha Hoffman, to whom Irving was engaged, died before she was 18, and he remained a bachelor for the rest of his life. He did, however, carry her Bible with him wherever he traveled, at home or abroad. To love he added loyalty.

"The memory of the righteous will be a blessing" (Proverbs 10:7), states the holy writer. It is good to remember our benefactors, living or dead. St. Paul writes to Timothy, "I have been reminded of your sincere faith, which first lived in your grandmother Lois and in your mother Eunice and, I am persuaded, now lives in you also" (2 Timothy 1:5). Spouses, parents, pastors, and teachers are among those who have been a blessing to us. The author of the epistle to the Hebrews states, "Remember your leaders, who spoke the Word of God to you. Consider the outcome of their way of life and imitate their faith" (13:7).

Washington Irving did not have to live the 50 years alone after his fiance's death. He could have married someone else. He chose, however, to show his loyalty by remaining single. He honored the memory of his hoped-for bride by treasuring her Bible. Our departed ones have undoubtedly left us things, great thoughts, examples, and we are thankful for this. The greatest treasure, humanly speaking, we can leave behind are children who walk in the ways of the Lord. Timothy was a blessing who honored the memory of Lois and Eunice.

St. Paul goes on to tell Timothy, "Remember Jesus Christ, raised from the dead" (2 Timothy 2:8). Jesus is our dearest Friend, for He bore all our sins and griefs. We honor our Savior when, to our love for Him, we add loyalty to His Word and continue in it steadfastly.

Prayer Suggestion

Ask for the Holy Spirit's aid to bring to your remembrance the many blessings He brought you through those near and dear to you.

STRENGTH AND WEAKNESS

My grace is sufficient for you, for My power is made perfect in weakness. 2 Corinthians 12:9

It is not only the bite of a shark but also the sting of a jellyfish that can kill a person. People of physical strength can hurt others, but so can the physically weak when they tell lies, spread gossip, give wrong advice, write bad checks, steal.

But physical weakness can also have a constructive side. The apostle Paul at one time in his life had a debilitating "thorn in the flesh" (2 Corinthians 12:7), perhaps some kind of a physical ailment. But he nevertheless fulfilled his calling as Christ's witness. God gave him the promise: "My grace is sufficient for you, for My power is made perfect in weakness" (2 Corinthians 12:9).

Chapter 11 of the Hebrews epistle recalls the role of *Old Testament* saints who prevailed through their strong faith in the God of their salvation. It states their "weakness was turned to strength" (v. 34).

A similar chapter of *New Testament* saints could be written. In the temple of Jerusalem, presumably aged and physically frail, Simeon and Anna confessed strong faith in the Christ Child and told others of Him. In Joppa a woman named Tabitha (Dorcas in Greek) earned the gratitude of the poor for the great work she did, not with a sharp sword, not with a sledgehammer, but with the needle as a seamstress. We go next to Ephesus, where toward the end of the first century we find the apostle John, close to a hundred years old and so weak he had to be carried to worship assemblies. Yet he served faithfully and effectively, telling people about God's love in Christ. Back in Jerusalem, little children in the temple, so young and frail that they are referred to as "babes and sucklings," sing praises to Christ.

The physically weak in today's Christendom can and do render effective service to Jesus Christ, their Savior. Unable to do heavy physical work or to be world travelers as missionaries, they can and do, as the hymn lines suggest, "tell the love of Jesus" and can "say He died for all."

Prayer Suggestion

In Jesus' name ask God to show you the opportunities to serve Him amid your weakness … and handicaps.

WHEN PLANS CHANGE

During the night Paul had a vision of a man of
Macedonia standing and begging him, "Come over
to Macedonia and help us." Acts 16:9

On July 4, 1851, a railroad company began to lay track that was planned to run from St. Louis to the Pacific coast. It did not get any farther than the town of Pacific, 37 miles southwest of the starting point. Incompetence and corruption led to bankruptcy of the company and to a change in plans. It remained for another group to push on to Kansas City and beyond.

Quite often, changes in life's plans become necessary. The projected Tower of Babel was never finished. The Lord intervened because of the builders' pride. Jesus points out the folly of a man who laid the foundation for a tower which he could not complete because he had not first figured the cost. Similarly, Jesus points out, kings going forth to conquer must sometimes change their plans. Having underestimated the opponent's strength, they must ask for peace.

Changing one's plans is sometimes the better part of wisdom. God may intervene and put us on another road. During his second missionary journey St. Paul, accompanied by Silas, intended to revisit the young churches in the Asia Minor provinces and to start new ones, "but the Spirit of Jesus would not allow them to" (Acts 16:7). All doors were closed, for God had other plans. At Troas, not far from Homer's Troy, St. Paul had a night vision of a man asking him to "come over to Macedonia and help us" (Acts 16:9). In response, he and Silas left Asia Minor to be the first Christian missionaries in the continent of Europe.

Sometimes our best-laid plans go awry. We have to start over, asking God to help us to find the right path as we regroup. Amid all the changes in our world and in our lives, there is one constant: Our God is changeless. Jesus Christ is the same, today, yesterday, and forever. His Word abides forever. His saving love is today the same as it was when He walked the road to Mount Calvary to lay down His life for our salvation. This fact is the starting point when we must reroute our lives.

Prayer Suggestion

Pray for wisdom from God to guide you when changes occur in your life. Thank the Lord Jesus for being your traveling companion.

PROVIDING THINGS HONEST

Some people, eager for money, have wandered from the faith and pierced themselves with many griefs.
1 Timothy 6:10

We rightfully deplore house burglaries and street robberies by culprits carrying handguns. There are, however, also white-collar crimes committed in offices and boardrooms with different tools: pens, computers, falsified records, and outright lies. In a recent year three-fourths of the 500 largest companies reported major corporate fraud.

Since, as Jesus said, all sins, including theft, proceed out of corrupt hearts, it makes little difference what clothes the perpetrators wear, where they work, what education they have, and what methods they use. Thieves are thieves.

In a parable Jesus speaks of a rich man's manager who, through fraud, had wasted the owner's possessions. When he was discovered, he continued his dishonesty to secure a future for himself. This was white-collar fraud committed in a business office. Dishonesty was also practiced in political offices in the way the publicans collected taxes for the Roman government. For that matter, "white-collar" thievery was practiced in Jesus' closest group where a called and ordained apostle, Judas Iscariot, stole from the treasury.

It is a tribute to the transforming, heart-changing power of the Gospel when Christian men and women in business, government, and society as a whole "provide things honest in the sight of all men" (Romans 12:17 KJV). God calls on all of us to be faithful and honest stewards in whatever situations He has placed us. To that end He has given us new hearts and minds so "that we may lead a quiet and peaceable life in all godliness and honesty" (1 Timothy 2:2 KJV). It is also from the sin of greed, which is the basis for much dishonesty, that Jesus redeemed us. With our hearts set on the greater treasures of God's kingdom, we are enabled to fulfill our vocations honestly and thus glorify our Father in heaven.

Prayer Suggestion

Pray that the Holy Spirit, for Jesus' sake, may enable you to keep God's Word in a good and honest heart as you fulfill life's duties.

Our Use of Time

Teach us to number our days aright, that we may gain a heart of wisdom. Psalm 90:12

The people of this country have an average life span of 74.4 years. They spend 24 years in sleep and 13 years watching television.

Time is a precious gift of God. It is not given to us in the same measure or amount. Moses states, "The length of our days is seventy years—or eighty, if we have the strength" (Psalm 90:10). In His wisdom and love God determines a person's length of life. He graciously extended the life span of Moses to 120 years; he was needed during the critical times through which God's people passed. God, if He so desires, can extend a person's life even more. The risen Lord said to Peter concerning John: "If I want him to remain alive until I return, what is that to you?" (John 21:23)

Whether a person's life is long or short, the important thing is to use the time purposefully, that is, to the glory of God and to other people's good. The apostle Paul refers to this phase of Christian steward-ship as "redeeming the time" (Ephesians 5:16 KJV), or, as the New International Version has it, "making the most of every opportunity." He writes this because "the days are evil" (v. 16). Evil days offer so many opportunities to waste time in sinful, sex-saturated movies and those that feature slaughterhouse-type violence.

It is good for Christians to say with the psalmist, "My times are in Your hands" (Psalm 31:15) and to join in singing: "Take my moments and my days, Let them flow in ceaseless praise." When we use our time for honest work, we are praising God with our deeds. Why serve God with our time? The eternal Son of God entered our time and world to redeem us, so that "we might receive the full rights" (Galatians 4:5) as God's sons and daughters who joyfully serve Him. These rights include the inheritance of eternal life.

Prayer Suggestion

Take the time to thank God for His many blessings to you in your lifetime, asking Him also for His continued guidance as you serve Christ with your time.

GOD'S WORD AS WITNESS

Whether they listen or fail to listen ... they will know that a prophet has been among them. Ezekiel 2:5

God at times calls on persons to undertake heavy tasks. Consider this assignment of St. Paul: "This man is My chosen instrument to carry My name before the Gentiles and their kings and before the people of Israel. I will show him how much he must suffer for My name" (Acts 9:15–16). This is what God said of Saul to Ananias, who was to baptize him.

The prophet Ezekiel was called to a difficult and discouraging task. He was to preach repentance to Israel, a rebellious nation. Ezekiel was to know in advance that God's Word would be rejected. He might well have asked, "What's the use, Lord?" Ezekiel was to go and preach, the wall of unbelief notwithstanding. He was to do this for this reason: "They will know that a prophet has been among them" (Ezekiel 2:5).

The Lord, even today, sends His missionaries into the world, knowing full well, as these missionaries know, that many who hear God's Word will reject it. Then why go and peach? Jesus said, "This Gospel of the kingdom will be preached in the whole world as a testimony to all nations" (Matthew 24:14). This is the witness God bears to all mankind: "Christ Jesus came into the world to save sinners" (1 Timothy 1:15). Some will harden their hearts in sullen unbelief. Yet God wants them to hear this message. Having heard it, they will never be able to fault God for not giving them the opportunity to hear the truth of the Gospel.

You may not be in Ezekiel's position as a prophet. You are in a calling, perhaps as a parent, spouse, family member, housewife, wage earner, or worker in many fields. To you it may seem that your work and words as a Christian witness are in vain. Should you quit? Not at all. You continue to be Christ's witness by word and deed. You keep on saying that Christ Jesus is the Son of God who died for all sinners and then rose again. Why do this? So people will know that a Christian witness has been among them.

Prayer Suggestion

Say to the Lord Jesus in prayer that you are thankful for your redemption and that you will continue to be His witness.

THE TEST OF FAITH

"Woman, you have great faith! Your request is granted."
Matthew 15:28

Tests are quite common. Commercial products, especially medications, are tested before they are released to the public. People, too, are tested. They must pass driver's license tests, physical exams, Scholastic Aptitude Tests, and the like.

God, too, gives tests. He subjected Abraham's faith to a severe test when He told him to sacrifice Isaac, the son of promise. Jesus was tested three times in the wilderness, but by the devil. As a teacher, He gave an oral test to Philip when He asked, "Where shall we buy bread for these people to eat?" (John 6:5) We are expressly told, "He asked this only to test him, for He already had in mind what He was going to do" (v. 6). Jesus tested the faith of the Canaanite mother when for a while He seemingly ignored her pleas for her demon-possessed daughter. She passed the test with flying colors, for Jesus said, "Woman, you have great faith! Your request is granted" (Matthew 15:28).

We know that there are also tests of temptation for evil, and these originate with Satan, as did Jesus' temptations in the desert. Also the world—other people—can be the source. Job was tempted to commit suicide when his wife said to him, "Curse God and die" (Job 2:9). Judas Iscariot was tempted by his own inward sin, his greed, when he stole from the disciples' treasury and when, in the end, he betrayed Jesus for 30 pieces of silver. Satan was in on this, too.

What shall we do when tests of faith come to us? We do what Jesus did: adhere to the Word of God. We seek to grow stronger in our faith by frequent participation in the Lord's Supper. God gives us strength when we ask Him for it. We recall that Jesus overcame His agony in the Garden of Gethsemane and went forth to Calvary's cross to give His life for our salvation, being strengthened by God through an angel. We become more frequent in prayer, asking God to strengthen us. We apply ourselves to our work with diligence. Through these activities God will give us passing grades when He gives us His own SAT: Spiritual Aptitude Test.

Prayer Suggestion

Turn to your Savior and Lord in prayer for strength to meet every test of faith.

WHAT CHURCH BELLS SAY

*Come, let us bow down in worship, let us kneel before the
LORD our Maker. Psalm 95:6*

In this writer's boyhood in rural Nebraska it was customary to ring
the church bell when a member died. The number of strokes would
then give the person's age. On the day of the interment the bell was
solemnly tolled as the horse-drawn hearse approached the church. The
appropriate words of poet John Donne are often quoted, "Never send
to ask for whom the bell tolls; it tolls for thee."

At other times church bells announce glad tidings. Henry W.
Longfellow states this in the song *I Heard the Bells on Christmas
Day.* He said this about the belfries of Christendom as if to say to
unbelievers: "Then pealed the bells more loud and deep: God is not
dead, nor doth He sleep; The wrong shall fail, the right prevail, With
peace on earth; good will to men." The poet does not expressly say so,
but the hoped-for-peace—the peace with God—comes only to those
who believe that "God made Him [Christ] who had no sin to be sin for
us, so that in Him we might become the righteousness of God"
(2 Corinthians 5:21).

Church bells invite us to come to the house of God and to worship
Him there. They recite, as it were, the words of the Psalter: "Come, let
us bow down in worship, let us kneel before the LORD our Maker; for
He is our God and we are the people of His pasture, the flock under
His care" (Psalm 95:6–7). Again: "Enter His gates with thanksgiving
and His courts with praise" (Psalm 100:4). When we carry out what the
church bells invite us to do, we will receive the blessings of God in
rich measure. Then the hymn verse will come to us on our homeward
way: "From Your house when I return, May my heart within me burn,
And at evening let me say, 'I have walked with God today.' "

Prayer Suggestion

Finish this prayer: "Lord Jesus, I am glad I can attend Your house
because ..."

WE LIVE FOR CHRIST

For to me, to live is Christ and to die is gain.
Philippians 1:21

In *Don Quixote* the Spanish author Miguel de Cervantes (1547–1616) tells the story of a would-be knight who wants to do good things, in keeping with the ideals of knighthood. He wants to right every wrong and to dream the impossible dream. So he goes ahead and tilts at windmills, regarding them as evil giants.

Many people want to have a worthwhile mission in life. So they espouse causes and become crusaders. It is an axiom in physics that nature abhors a vacuum. This appears to be true also in a spiritual sense. Human nature, when it is no longer filled with religion, tends to make a "religion" out of secular causes.

We find many instances of this in the Bible. A spiritual vacancy, in many cases, was filled with something less than a worthwhile social cause—filled instead with pride, selfishness, and greed. Judas Iscariot was undoubtedly a believer when Jesus called him as an apostle. But as the ardor of faith and love left his heart, "Satan entered" (Luke 22:3); Judas became a mercenary, then a betrayer. Money became his "messiah," silver his "savior," and hoped-for gold his "god."

How important it is that we continually be filled with the Holy Spirit, leaving no room in our hearts for evil spirits to enter in! It is indeed proper for us as citizens to support necessary projects in the public domain. But we don't want secular causes in society and state to take away or compromise our commitment to Jesus Christ as our topmost priority. We want to keep saying with St. Paul, "To me, to live is Christ" (Philippians 1:21). And we have good reason. Christ loved us and gave Himself up for us. He is the object of our affection. To spread His saving Gospel in the world "on the wings of the wind" (Psalm 104:3) is our mission. This is far better than tilting at windmills to find meaning in life.

Prayer Suggestion

Give thanks to God for providing you with time and opportunity, talents and treasure, to live for Christ and His brethren.

GOD REMEMBERS

As high as the heavens are above the earth, so great is His love for those who fear Him. Psalm 103:11

If the St. Louis-born T. S. Eliot (1888-1965), who found fame in England as a poet and essayist, were to return to his boyhood home, he would find a large parking lot. Very likely, he would not be remembered by anyone.

The above is a very common experience of people who revisit the scenes of their childhood. In this respect, people are very much like flowers—perishable. The psalmist declares, "As for man, his days are like grass, he flourishes like a flower of the field; the wind blows over it and it is gone, and its place remembers it no more" (Psalm 103:15–16).

People are often forgetful. This is something Joseph experienced in Egypt. In prison he interpreted the dreams of Pharaoh's cupbearer. The baker was hanged, as Joseph said, but the cupbearer, who was spared, "did not remember Joseph; he forgot him" (Genesis 40:23). How human! But two years later, when Pharaoh had haunting dreams, the cupbearer came forward and said, "Today I am reminded of my shortcomings" (Genesis 41:9). He then suggested that Joseph be brought from prison to explain the king's dreams.

All the while there is Someone who remembers. The psalmist goes on to say, showing contrast: "But from everlasting to everlasting the LORD's love is with those who fear Him, and His righteousness with their children's children" (Psalm 103:17). God remembers us, however old we get and wherever we live. God's saving love in Jesus Christ attends us throughout life.

The God who remembers us is the same God we came to know in our parental home and whom we worshiped with simple childhood prayers. He is with us still. He recalls what we ourselves may have forgotten. But He does forget something—our sins, for which Christ died and of which we have repented. This is His promise: "I will be their God, and they will be My people. ... I will ... remember their sins no more" (Jeremiah 31:33–34). We thank God for His short memory in this regard.

Prayer Suggestion

Express your gratitude to God for continually keeping you in His grace and blessing you in Christ Jesus.

THE SLAIN LAMB

*On the tenth day of this month each man is to take a
lamb for his family. ... All the people of the community of
Israel must slaughter them at twilight. Exodus 12:3, 6*

When coal miners took canary birds with them into the deep
underground, the idea was not to hear them sing. The birds were to
give them warning. If they died, the miner knew that a deadly gas was
seeping into that area of the mine.

Animal-rights advocates do not approve of any misuse of God's
lesser creatures. But what about using *human beings* to one's advantage, even taking their lives to enhance one's own position? That is
exactly what King Herod did when he ordered the little boys of
Bethlehem killed. He hoped to dispose of the newborn King of the
Jews whom the Wise Men came to worship. To maintain his throne,
Herod believed, the toddlers had to die.

Some 33 years later the high priest Caiphas and his colleagues were
afraid of losing their position to the same Jesus. They said, "If we let
Him go on like this, everyone will believe in Him, and then the Romans
will come and take away both our place and our nation" (John 11:48).
So from their viewpoint, they sent Jesus to the cross for their own lives
and livelihood.

But God had the last word. By His overriding will, Jesus was the
Lamb of God sacrificed for the sins of the whole world. This truth was
anticipated throughout the Old Testament. Animals, including birds, were
brought as offerings. These sacrifices pointed the believers to the ultimate
offering—Jesus. Animal sacrifices, of course, did not have the power in
themselves to atone for sin, for the epistle to the Hebrews clearly states,
"It is impossible for the blood of bulls and goats to take away sins" (10:4).
It was always true, then as now, that the blood of Christ, the Lamb of
God, cleanses us from sin. The sacrifices that Old Testament believers
brought derived their forgiving power from what Christ was to do.

Canary birds in coal mines undoubtedly saved human lives. The virgin Mary at her purification had the choice of offering "a pair of doves or
two young pigeons" (Luke 2:24). In brief, animals, including birds, have
played parts in the overall unfolding of God's plan for our salvation.

Prayer Suggestion

Ask God to sharpen your consciousness with regard to the treatment of His lesser creatures.

GOD ANSWERS OUR PRAYERS

May my prayer be set before You like incense; may the lifting up of my hands be like the evening sacrifice. Psalm 141:2

Will our thoughts this morning be the same this evening? And when the day ends, what will be our longings? Edgar A. Guest expresses this wish: "I don't want to stand with the setting sun, And hate myself for things I've done." Edgar A. Poe, another poet, anticipates the solace of sleep: "For the heart whose woes are legion 'Tis a peaceful, soothing region." Thomas Ken penned those familiar lines from *Tallis' Canon*: "Forgive me, Lord, for Thy dear Son, The ill that I this day have done; That with the world, myself, and Thee, I, ere I sleep, at peace may be."

Believers mentioned in the Bible have looked ahead toward evening. The psalmist wants both his daytime and evening prayers to be acceptable to God: "May my prayer be set before You like incense; may the lifting up of my hands be like the evening sacrifice" (Psalm 141:2). Many times God reveals His love at eventide.

Consider that first Easter day when two disciples were walking to Emmaus and the as-yet-unidentified Jesus joined them. They wanted Him to be their guest. "Stay with us," they said, "for it is nearly evening; the day is almost over" (Luke 24:29). Christians throughout the world join Cleopas and his friend in wanting Jesus to spend the night with them. They know that His edifying words would open the Scriptures to them.

St. Paul's concern is similar to that of the poet Guest cited above. He doesn't want the emotions of the day, if evil, to be continued into the night and beyond. He writes, "Do not let the sun go down while you are still angry" (Ephesians 4:26). If the events of the day provoke anger, especially in situations involving a co-worker, it is best to make peace then and there.

As we look toward evening, we likewise ask Jesus to be our guest, our dear visitor, whose words will renew our faith in Him as our Savior from death and sin and as our Lord risen from the dead.

Prayer Suggestion

Look up Martin Luther's evening prayer in the catechism and use it as a model for your own prayer.

MAKING FRIENDS

I tell you, use worldly wealth to gain friends for yourselves.
Luke 16:9

An old saying in India has it: "If you're going to live by a river, make friends with the crocodiles."

Some places in the world are more dangerous than others. And some places, also some occupations and lifestyles, have special kinds of perils connected with them. Foresight is therefore important.

In a parable Jesus has an owner commend a dishonest manager for having acted with foresight when he made provision for his future. Jesus did not praise the manager for his dishonesty—he had the debtors falsify their account, thus currying favor with them as his future benefactors. Jesus praises him for his foresight, making the point that Christians likewise should look ahead to eternal life in heaven, there to be joined by those whom they have befriended. Many people will be in heaven because established Christians told them about Christ's salvation. Established Christians do this, not *in order* to be saved, but *because* they are saved. They do not merit heaven by good deeds; heaven is already theirs because of Christ's redeeming merit.

It is important to ask, What special hazards attend my life and my life's vocation? And if Christians know what they are, what provision are they making to protect themselves? If they handle the company's money, what are the "crocodiles" that are ready to devour them? What special temptations go with administering other people's funds? What are the moral pitfalls in school, in the home, in the community?

The important alternative is: How can we turn things around so that the temptations for evil will become opportunities for doing good? God is pleased when His people live circumspectly. He tells us through St. Paul: "Be very careful, then, how you live—not as unwise but as wise, making the most of every opportunity, because the days are evil" (Ephesians 5:15–16).

Prayer Suggestion

Ask your Savior to impart to you the gift of wisdom and foresight in your life.

FAITH FOUNDED ON FACTS

We were eyewitnesses of His majesty. 2 Peter 1:16

Fantasy, appeal to the imagination, fiction stories—these have a place in life, especially for children. Poets, authors, and composers provide the fictional wherewithal in and through the various media. Peter Ilich Tchaikovsky (1840–1893) uses the *Nutcracker Suite*, a ballet, to tell the story of a little girl and her magical Christmas gift, a nutcracker, that comes to life and takes her on an adventurous trip to the Land of Snow and the Kingdom of the Sugarplum Fairy.

Fantasy, while appropriate in the field of art and entertainment, is out of place in religion if the idea is to deny that the truths of the Christian faith are based on historical facts. Already in apostolic times some people claimed that the teachings of Christianity were myths and fables. Therefore St. Peter declares, "We did not follow cleverly invented stories when we told you about the power and coming of our Lord Jesus Christ" (2 Peter 1:16). He goes on to say that he and the other apostles were eyewitnesses of Jesus' ministry, especially eyewitnesses of His revealed glory as God's Son.

Jesus Christ is for real. He, the Son of the Highest, became incarnate and lived as a true human being among people. For this we have the back-up testimony of St. John, who writes that the disciples saw Him with their eyes and touched Him with their hands. God's Son truly became flesh, born of the virgin Mary. He truly suffered under the historic figure, Pontius Pilate, was crucified, died, was buried, and on the third day rose again.

Jesus Christ is not make-believe. The beautiful Christmas story of His birth is no myth. His deeds of love, many of them done with miraculous power, are not adventure stories. The angels who announced His resurrection are not sugarplum fairies. While we enjoy the music and narrative of the *Nutcracker Suite* and other masterpieces, we bear in mind that the story of Jesus and His love is the truth and that, believing in Him, we are saved.

Prayer Suggestion

Say your thank-You to God for the truth revealed to you in Christ Jesus, your Lord and Savior. Ask the Holy Spirit to keep you in the faith.

A LIFE OF OBEDIENCE TO GOD

How can a young man keep his way pure?
By living according to Your Word. Psalm 119:9

There are many ways of perverting and subverting the truth. One way was indicated by a university researcher who wrote, "Television emphasizes the deviant, so that it becomes normal." Abnormal behavior is represented as perfectly in order.

Another way of obscuring truth is the attempt to replace it with an outright lie. The devil tried it in beautiful paradise when he flatly contradicted God: "You will not surely die" (Genesis 3:4). At another time, in a most desolate region, he suggested to Jesus that He was not the Son of God. Satan perverts the truth also about himself. He, the prince of darkness, often poses "as an angel of light" (2 Corinthians 11:14). The devil teaches people to pervert the truth, as St. Paul writes in the opening chapter of Romans: "They exchanged the truth of God for a lie, and worshiped and served created things rather than the Creator" (v. 25).

We come back to the same theme: Deviant behavior is claimed to be normal. The same researcher writes, "Our culture used to give us boundaries. Today, there are no boundaries. Nothing is forbidden anymore." Because society no longer lays down moral and ethical guidelines for conduct and for making right choices, it becomes all the more important for us to study God's Word and follow it. The psalmist asks, "How can a young man keep his way pure?" He replies, "By living according to Your Word" (Psalm 119:9). This is sound advice for every Christian, regardless of age or gender. St. Paul writes to young Timothy that Holy Scripture "is useful for teaching, rebuking, correcting and training in righteousness" (2 Timothy 3:16).

Through the Gospel we are drawn closer to Jesus Christ. He declared His love for us by setting an example of obedience to God and then offering up His life to bring us into communion with God. Drawn by this saving love, we gladly walk in His commandments.

Prayer Suggestion

Give thanks to God for revealing to you the truth of salvation in Jesus Christ as taught in Holy Scripture.

THE WORD GETS THROUGH

Besides everything else, I face daily the pressure of my concern for all the churches. 2 Corinthians 11:28

There is a familiar saying concerning messengers of ancient times: "Neither snow, nor rain, nor gloom of night stays these couriers from the swift completion of their appointed rounds."

An even greater tribute must be given to the apostles whom Jesus appointed to go into all the world to deliver the good news of salvation. One could draw up a list of things that did not deter them. Neither the great distances involved, nor the indifference of many hearers, nor the hatred of the enemies of Christ's cross could keep them from completing their mission.

Such a list is contained in St. Paul's recital of the dangers to which he was exposed: five floggings, three beatings with rods, a stoning, three shipwrecks, dangers in cities and in the country. The list was not even complete when he wrote it, and he had many more hardships to endure, including a martyr's death in Rome. But despite every hindrance, the apostle delivered his message that "Christ Jesus came into the world to save sinners" (1 Timothy 1:15).

Through the centuries, neither snow, rain, nor gloom of night has kept Christ's messengers from proclaiming the Good News. They crossed "field and fountain, moor and mountain," using the available media of communication. At the time of the Reformation, Martin Luther's theses in defense of the Gospel spread over Germany in two weeks and in four weeks over all Christendom, thanks to the printing press. It seemed that the very angels themselves had been the messengers. As a matter of fact, the bearers of good tidings in all lands have been people, in most cases ordinary people.

Also in our day God speaks to our generation through His pastors and people. Through them He speaks the message of salvation in Jesus Christ, His Son.

Prayer Suggestion

Pray that God's Word may have free course in the world and be preached to the joy and edifying of Christ's holy people.

No Room for Assumptions

No one knows about that day or hour, not even the angels
in heaven, not the Son, but only the Father. Mark 13:32

"Occam's razor" is named after William of Occam, an English philosopher in the Middle Ages. A razor is for cutting. The expression means: When dealing with a proposition, we are not to introduce assumptions.

The faith we confess, for example, in the Apostles' Creed contains no assumptions. That Jesus was born of the virgin Mary, suffered, died, rose again, and ascended into heaven is duly attested by Holy Scripture. It is not assumptions we confess, but convictions founded on facts.

As if God's revelation of the way of salvation in Christ were not enough, people through the ages have introduced assumptions, doing this in an effort to answer questions not answered in the Bible. For example, it is asked: When will the Last Day come? The Bible doesn't say. But many have set dates only to be embarrassed when the time passed and Christ did not come.

There are other assumptions. A whole set of writings arose in the early church known as the New Testament apocrypha. These endeavor to answer questions about which the Bible is silent. They are filled with assumptions. The spurious Gospel of Thomas, for example, tries to fill gaps concerning the childhood of Jesus.

Whenever anyone in the church, even with the best of intentions, introduced assumptions—assumptions, for example, that we are saved by faith *and* good works, that the accounts of Jesus' miracles are myths, that our Lord did not bodily rise from the dead, that there will be no Judgment Day—it is time to use Occam's razor and cut away such unbiblical claims and traditions. What God has revealed in His written Word—in brief, that all people are sinners and that Jesus Christ, God's Son, died and rose again to save them—is what faith grasps for salvation.

We do well to study that Word that we may draw closer to Christ, the Perfect Truth.

Prayer Suggestion

Complete this prayer: "Lord Jesus, let my heart and mind be satisfied with the truths of Your Word. Let me not ..."

FELLOW CITIZENS

In Christ Jesus you who once were far away have been brought near through the blood of Christ. Ephesians 2:13

A man from an English-speaking country who was visiting Rome supposedly said that he enjoyed the sights, then added, "What I don't like is that there are so many foreigners here." He meant the regular inhabitants.

Every country, of course, has foreigners in its midst. Their presence is sometimes requested, unless they are tourists who bring business and then return home.

First-century Christians in the Roman Empire were regarded as disloyal and dangerous because they refused to offer incense to the deified Roman emperor. They were regarded as obnoxious foreigners. But it was all a mistake. Christ and the apostles taught their followers to be obedient, tax-paying citizens, rendering to Caesar what was his. They must, however, obey God rather than man when the government enacts laws contrary to God's Word.

While functioning as good citizens in the land, Christians are always citizens of a kingdom that supersedes all kingdoms: the kingdom of Jesus Christ. This latter is a kingdom of grace in which sins are forgiven to all who have faith in Christ, the Reconciler. It is a kingdom in which all believers, regardless of their station in the world, are equal. They are "fellow citizens with God's people and members of God's household, built on the foundation of the apostles and prophets, with Christ Jesus Himself as the chief cornerstone" (Ephesians 2:19–20). This kingdom of grace, also called the holy Christian church, the communion of saints, blends into the kingdom of glory, heaven. It is as the hymn writer states, "The saints on earth and those above But one communion make."

Christians are brothers and sisters in Christ. They are one. No one will claim, here in Christendom on earth nor in heaven above, as the visitor in Rome supposedly did, "There are too many foreigners here." All are fellow citizens in Christ's kingdom.

Prayer Suggestion

Pray for further enlightenment from the Holy Spirit on the privileges and obligations of your membership in Christ's kingdom.

FAITH AMID LIFE'S TROUBLED WATERS

Save me, O God, for the waters have come up to my neck.
Psalm 69:1

When Marco Polo, an early world traveler, returned to Venice, he had a hard time making people believe that the mighty, 3,000-mile-long Yangtze River in China was in places so wide that one could not see the opposite bank. Big rivers, in flood stage, grow even wider and seem like inland lakes.

So it is with the rivers of trouble. Their threatening waters sometimes seem so wide that the other side cannot be seen. Then comes more rain, making it utterly impossible to cross over in our frail boats.

Joseph in Egypt saw his problems multiply, making them seem like the flooding Nile. Sold into slavery in Egypt by his brothers, he was falsely accused of sexual harassment by Potiphar's wife and was committed to a foul dungeon. For pious Job, there was no end in sight as a whole series of afflictions befell him. He exclaimed, "Man is born to trouble as surely as sparks fly upward" (Job 5:7). For him the sparks led to a total conflagration of the life he had known.

Undoubtedly all of us have been in situations when we exclaim with the psalmist, "Save me, O God, for the waters have come up to my neck" (Psalm 69:1). Troubles beget troubles so that amid the inundation we cannot see the other side. But God did not forsake us. He assured us of His saving help. Our Lord does just that when we pray, "While the nearer waters roll, While the tempest still is high. Hide me, O my Savior, hide, Till the storm of life is past."

God will stand by us also in the future. He will stand by His promises. This fact remains, "If God is for us, who can be against us? He who did not spare His own Son, but gave Him up for us all—how will He not also, along with Him, graciously give us all things?" (Romans 8:31–32) So, when we, in the hymnist's words, "tread the verge of Jordan," we can bid "our anxious fears subside." In the end God will "land us safe on Canaan's side."

Prayer Suggestion

Pray to the Lord Jesus to give you stronger faith in Him when the waves of adversity threaten to roll over your soul.

GOOD JUDGMENT WITH FAITH

Hope does not disappoint us, because God has poured out His love into our hearts by the Holy Spirit, whom He has given us. Romans 5:5

"Build it, and they will come," says a young farmer to his wife in the movie *Field of Dreams*. So he prepares a baseball park in a cornfield. As the story unfolds, players from the past come to life, and spectators do arrive—all in fantasy, of course.

How extravagant can we become in our dreams, our plans for the future, our hopes for better days? Christian faith allows us—yes, bids us—to expect great things from God. But God has also given us reason, a mind. He wants us to exercise good judgment in all things.

In our prayers we may come with all boldness and confidence before our heavenly Father as, in Jesus' name, we make our needs and desires known. As we do this, we exercise our faith so that, whatever our suffering, we produce perseverance, and perseverance produces character, and character produces hope, as St. Paul teaches in the reading from Romans. That is how we Christians grow in godliness. That is how we maintain the upward look of faith as we keep our feet on the ground.

In harboring and expressing our hopes, desires, and dreams, we do well to remember what God has promised to grant us. He will not grant us things that are harmful, foolish, or fanciful—not a thriving ballpark in the midst of a cornfield. We may pray for temporal gifts: good health, a beautiful home, a well-paying job, and everything that comes under "daily bread" in the Lord's prayer, but we pray for these things with the condition that God should grant them if they are good for us and in accordance with His will. We let God choose the time and manner in answering our prayers.

For spiritual blessings, on the other hand, we pray unconditionally, knowing full well that He wants us to have them: forgiveness of sins, strength to serve Him, strong faith, and hope. Jesus Christ, our Savior and Lord, once for all suffered on the cross so that we might have them.

Prayer Suggestion

Let your prayer be for God, in Jesus' name, to grant you and the people around you the blessings needed.

FREE OF DEBT

Peter replied, "Repent and be baptized, every one of you,
in the name of Jesus Christ for the forgiveness of your sins."
Acts 2:38

Heavy indebtedness, to say the least, is a great hindrance. It keeps the debtors from getting ahead. Most citizens cannot comprehend the federal government's debt that runs into the trillions. But they can understand the handicap when nearly a fourth of the revenue collected goes to servicing the debt. The money used for this is taken away from needful items in the budget.

The effects of personal indebtedness are the same. Many persons cannot get ahead because of their debt burden. They need to cut corners, leading to all kinds of deprivation.

Even worse is spiritual indebtedness. Every person born into the world is a sinner, a debtor. Our *condition* of original sin leads to sinful *action*. The debt of sin, both as condition and as action, is huge—infinitely more burdensome than what any sinner-debtor could pay for. When Jesus in a parable describes a man as owing his master ten thousand talents, that is, several million dollars, He implies that everyone's life, spiritually speaking, is so deeply in the red that no significant restitution can be made. An accompanying evil is always that the burden of sinfulness keeps people from fulfilling the purpose for which they were created: to live to the glory of God.

All that we can do is to say, as the Latin has it, *Pater, peccavi,* "Father, I have sinned." When such a confession is made, together with the confession: "I believe that Jesus Christ, true God … and also true man … is my Lord, who has redeemed me," then our debt before God is totally canceled. Then, when we pray, "Forgive us our debts," God does just that. Then we are free of all spiritual debts, free to forgive our neighbor also, free to dedicate our lives to the service of Jesus Christ.

Prayer Suggestion

Express your gratefulness to God for forgiving all your sins for Jesus' sake and declare your willingness to serve Him gladly.

WE ARE PROTECTED

From within, out of men's hearts, come evil thoughts,
sexual immorality, theft, murder, adultery, greed, malice,
deceit, lewdness, envy, slander, arrogance and folly.
Mark 7:21–22

High above us and about the earth is the ozone layer that protects us against the ultraviolet rays of the sun. God, the Creator, planned a universe in which the forces of nature are balanced in such a way as to make life possible. Troubles ensue when people tamper with this balance. Floods, forest fires, droughts, the loss of living species, and other imbalances often result from our mismanagement of nature. Sending pollutants into the high levels of the atmosphere can lead to dire results.

Our natural world is often a mirror image of the spiritual sphere in which we as Christians live. The ozone situation is a case in point. The fall of the human race into sin resulted in total pollution. Think of what Jesus said, "Out of men's hearts come evil thoughts, sexual immorality, theft, murder, adultery, greed, malice, deceit, lewdness, envy, slander, arrogance and folly." As these sins proceed out of the heart, they create a wide-spread, high-rising contamination of human society.

To make it at all possible for Christians to survive in an immoral world, God in His wisdom and love made provision to shelter His people from the destructive "ultraviolet rays" of His Holy Law. This Law, so Holy Scripture testifies, demands, threatens, condemns, curses, and kills. It reflects the holiness of God. But God is not only holy and righteous, He is also merciful and gracious. He sent His Son, none other than our Savior Jesus Christ, to atone for all sin. For "God made Him who had no sin to be sin for us, so that in Him we might become the righteousness of God" (2 Corinthians 5:21).

The Gospel of Christ's reconciliation is our protective shield. It is our spiritual "ozone layer." As long as it is there and our faith in it continues, we are safe. Thank God for His saving Gospel!

Prayer Suggestion

Pray for the cleansing, purifying, protecting Gospel of Christ so that you may have continued spiritual life.

What Jesus Has Promised

Come to Me, all you who are weary and burdened, and
I will give you rest. Matthew 11:28

In his first speech as prime minister of England, Winston Churchill said, "I have nothing to offer but blood, toil, tears, and sweat." It was the time of World War II.

What does Jesus have to offer as our Leader and Lord? He speaks with frankness: "If anyone would come after Me, he must deny himself and take up his cross and follow Me" (Matthew 16:24). Again, this: "Do not suppose that I have come to bring peace on earth. I did not come to bring peace, but a sword" (Matthew 10:34). Our Lord did not say anything new. Ever since the fall of Adam and Eve into sin, words similar to those of the prime minister and of Jesus, our Savior, have been spoken to mankind in its state of spiritual warfare with God.

If this were all that could be said, no one would want to follow Jesus. But there is much more to say. If it were not for Jesus and His saving work, this is all there would be to life: blood, toil, tears, and sweat. Since God's own Son came into our world to take all the misery of sin on Himself, a great change has come about. Now those who follow Jesus are richly blessed. For them there is now no sword or warfare in their relation to God, but perfect peace and reconciliation.

It is a by-product of that peace that we can be at peace among ourselves. In our fellowship with God as His sons and daughters, and with ourselves as brothers and sisters, life's toils and tears turn to joyful service to Jesus. The sweat of the brow in which Adam and his descendants were to earn their bread is wiped away because in another garden Jesus agonized to the point that "His sweat was like drops of blood falling to the ground" (Luke 22:44). And what happens to our tears? To His people God declares in a promise as good as fulfilled: "[God] will wipe every tear from their eyes" (Revelation 21:4).

So we say, "Yes, Lord Jesus, we hear Your invitation and accept it gladly: 'Come to Me, all you who are weary and burdened, and I will give you rest' " (Matthew 11:28).

Prayer Suggestion

Give thanks to the Lord Jesus for His encouragement to bring all our burdens to Him.

JESUS, THE BREAD OF LIFE

"The days are coming," declares the Sovereign LORD,
"when I will send a famine through the land ... a famine
of hearing the words of the LORD." Amos 8:11

Overlooking Cobb Harbor on Ireland is a statue of a young mother and her two sons. It commemorates the many emigrants who had to leave their homeland because of potato famines, especially the one of 1847.

While physical famines are dreadful, they are superseded by the evil effects of the famine of the soul. The prophet Amos speaks of "a famine of hearing the words of the LORD" (Amos 8:11). It causes people to think more about God's Word as they seek help, for he writes, "Men will stagger from sea to sea and wander from north to east, searching for the Word of the LORD, but they will not find it" (Amos 8:12).

Moses conceives of spiritually hungry people trying to "ascend into heaven to get it [God's Word]" and look for it "beyond the sea." Spiritually hungry people go to out-of-the-way places for the Word when all the while, writes Moses, "the Word is very near you ... in your mouth and in your heart" (Deuteronomy 30:12–14). Today people also suffer spiritual starvation because they are ignorant of—or they out-right reject—the Word of God that is so near to them, so near as the power switch of their radio and TV set.

As for earthly food, it abounds when crops are good. Then droughts come, causing people to starve or to emigrate to other lands. So it is with the Word of God, our spiritual bread. When the prophet Samuel was still a lad and ministered under Eli, we are told that "in those days the Word of the LORD was rare; there were not many visions" (1 Samuel 3:1). Through the ministry of Samuel the situation was much improved. The Word then was plentiful. When God gives out His Word, whether in dew-drops or in deluges, it will accomplish what He desires.

To alleviate spiritual hunger, God did the ultimate. He not only gave us His Word in words but also to the fullest extent in the person of His Son. Jesus Christ is the living, life-giving Word. He is the Bread from heaven come to nourish our souls in this life and to prepare the road to heaven for us by giving His life on the cross. Now it is not necessary for us to cross oceans to find Him: He is near us in the Gospel.

Prayer Suggestion

Pray that Christ may more and more become the Bread of life to nourish your soul.

GOD FINDS LOST PEOPLE

Just as through the disobedience of the one man the many were made sinners, so also through the obedience of the one Man the many will be made righteous. Romans 5:19

In 1585, under the leadership of Sir Walter Raleigh, a colony was established on Roanoke Island off the North Carolina coast. When supply ships came from England in 1590, no trace of the colonists could be found.

The story of people missing is nothing new. In 722 B.C. the ten tribes forming the kingdom of Israel were carried into the Assyrian captivity, and nothing more was heard of them. Looking for lost people also brought the Lord God into the Garden of Eden after Adam and Eve had fallen into sin. They were not on hand, as usual, to welcome Him. Where were they? They were hiding among the trees of the garden because of guilty consciences.

The story of finding lost people is best told by Jesus Himself in the parable of the lost sheep. He tells how the shepherd looks for the sheep and, on finding it, carries it home on his shoulders with rejoicing. The recovery of the lost is even more poignantly told in the parable of the prodigal son.

Why is the experience on Roanoke Island repeated? Our world is full of changes that bring about population shifts. Time was when Christianity flourished in northern Africa and other regions later taken over by another religion. In our cities, internal changes have caused once-flourishing congregations to disappear. Also in rural areas economic, social, and perhaps also weather changes have brought about dislocations. The former all-purpose 160-acre family farms have been absorbed into larger organizations. One can go to many areas in North America and find abandoned mills, mines, and ranches. Empty villages and burned-out inner cities raise the same question: Where are the people?

Adam and Eve tried to get lost in Eden. But God found them and promised them a Savior: the woman's Seed, none other than Jesus Christ the Messiah. He wrestled in another garden—in Gethsemane—as the Second Adam to redeem the first Adam and all his children. Instead of hiding, Jesus boldly went forward to meet the enemy so that, in the end, He might give His life for all. Now the lost are found.

Prayer Suggestion

Thank God for His wondrous love in Christ in finding you and making you His own.

GOD'S WORD IS THE TRUTH

This is what we speak, not in words taught us by human wisdom but in words taught by the Spirit. 1 Corinthians 2:13

To err is human. We see this from big mistakes made in the secular world: the Edsel car, named for Henry Ford's son; the changed flavor of Coca Cola; the Susan B. Anthony dollar issued by the U.S. mint.

People make mistakes also in the church at large and in local congregations. Missions are opened in unpromising communities, churches are built in wrong locations, investments are not wisely made. Where and when human beings, imperfect despite their commitment to Jesus Christ, are at work, errors in judgment can be expected. The Bible tells us this through many examples. Elijah erred when he thought he was the only one in Israel still true to the Lord in an age of apostasy. John and James were off base in asking Jesus whether they should invoke fire from heaven to consume an inhospitable Samaritan village. St. Paul tells the Galatians (2:11) that St. Peter "was clearly in the wrong" when he refused to eat with Gentiles when Judaizers were around. St. Paul himself erred on occasion—in the choice of co-workers, in wanting to preach in a region when the Spirit said no, in being subject to conceit and vanity because of God's special revelations to him. Also in Christendom today people can err when they follow their own wisdom in things spiritual.

The apostles, while they did occasionally err in everyday affairs, were totally truthful and correct when the Holy Spirit moved them in their oral preaching and their writings of the New Testament Scripture. When speaking as the oracles of God, they were guarded from error. The Old Testament Scripture and the words of Jesus to them that the Spirit brought back to their remembrance were the source, norm, and standard of the apostles' doctrine.

It is by the written Word, also today, that all who preach and teach in the church are to be examined. If they are found to be in agreement with Scripture, then they should be honored and faithfully followed because they proclaim Christ Jesus as the only Savior from sin. The *sola Scriptura*—Scripture alone— emphasis of the Reformation keeps this truth before our eyes.

Prayer Suggestion

Ask the Head of the church, Jesus Christ, to keep all Christians steadfast in God's inerrant Word.

ON THE WINGS OF THE WIND

Salvation is found in no one else, for there is no other name under heaven given to men by which we must be saved. Acts 4:12

From time immemorial people have wished they could fly like the birds. Ancient legend has it that Daedalus, a Greek craftsman, and his son Icarus escaped from prison by attaching wings to themselves. In the Bible, the psalmist speaks of flying "on the wings of the dawn" and settling "on the far side of the sea" (Psalm 139:9), convinced of God's presence there, too. The prophet Isaiah says of those who hope in the Lord: "They will soar on wings like eagles" (Isaiah 40:31).

The time came when the dream began to come true. In 1908, at Kitty Hawk, North Carolina, Orville and Wilbur Wright ushered in the age of flight by flying their motored craft 45 miles in an hour and a quarter.

The airplane is a combination of wonderful inventions. It is being used in the service of the Gospel. In northern regions God's messengers use small planes to serve people spiritually in out-of-the-way places.

It is good and right to use the media of transportation and communication to bring God's saving Word to people wherever they are. In their day, the apostles used ships to preach Christ in faraway places. St. Paul was a world traveler by land and sea. From his many sea travels he learned much about ships and the forces that affect them: wind and water. During his last voyage to Rome to appeal his case to Caesar, he gave advice to the captain and crew before, during, and after a disastrous storm. He made use of whatever vehicles were then available to proclaim Christ and Him crucified.

Like the apostles, and like Christians through the centuries, we use the means that God puts at our disposal to bear witness to the same message that St. Peter proclaimed: "Salvation is found in no one else, for there is no other name under heaven given to men by which we must be saved" (Acts 4:12). That is the name of Jesus Christ, our blessed Lord and Savior.

Prayer Suggestion

Pray that the Christian church may continue to make full use of the available media for the preaching of the Gospel.

GOD, OUR PROVIDER

He [Messiah] has taken me to the banquet hall, and His banner over me is love. Song of Songs 2:4

Henry Shaw was a successful businessman in St. Louis. He set aside funds for beautiful Shaw's Garden. He also provided for a special service to be held annually in the church he attended. There was to be a sermon "on the wisdom and goodness of God as shown in the growth of flowers, fruits, and other products of the vegetable kingdom."

The same truth, on a smaller scale, is stressed in our houses of God. On special festivals and on ordinary Sundays flowers adorn our altars. On occasion, perhaps on Thanksgiving Day, food is brought to church for distribution to the hungry. These fruits of fields and gardens testify to the goodness of God as our Provider.

In the Old Testament the Israelites, by divine direction, were to observe festivals to the glory of God. During the Feast of Unleavened Bread a sheaf of the first harvested barley was presented to the Lord to consecrate the opening of the harvest season. Then came the Feast of Harvest, or Pentecost, marking the close of the wheat harvest. Loaves of bread baked from the first wheat flour were offered to God. These were basically religious festivals, not like secular county fairs. All male members over 12 years of age were to be present in Jerusalem for the celebrations. Jesus participated in these festivals.

New Testament Christians want every Sunday—every day, in fact—to be a time of thanksgiving to God for His goodness in providing for us through the products of the soil and through other gifts. They are especially thankful for the greatest gift of all—Jesus Christ, His Son and our Savior. Through Him comes our eternal salvation.

Indeed, "Fair are the meadows, Fair are the woodlands, Robed in flowers of blooming spring." But "Jesus is fairer and purer." In His great love for us He gave up His life that we might have eternal life.

Prayer Suggestion

Give thanks to God for all His gifts, notably for the gift of His Son as our Savior.

CHRIST, OUR TRUE TREASURE

Whoever loses his life for Me and for the Gospel will save it.
Mark 8:35

A ship, sailing from Panama to New York in 1857, was carrying gold prospectors from California. It was overtaken by a storm and began to sink. One man, with a fortune in his carpetbag, left it behind and saved his life. Another prospector found it impossible to abandon his gold, and he drowned.

Many important decisions have to be made in life. These involve not only material things, forcing a choice, perhaps, between investing in real estate or in a business. They also may involve lifestyles—whether to marry or to stay single, to live in a city or on a farm, studying to become a teacher or a nurse.

The ultimate choice has to do with life itself, whether to devote it to Christ or to mammon, to God or to gold. It is of utmost importance to devote oneself to the truths of God's Word, for a life thus lived is worth far more than all the wealth of the world. Our natural, or physical, life is a gift from the Creator and is to be valued as such. But besides our bodies we are endowed with immortal souls, inclusive of intelligence, speech, talents, and other mental and spiritual gifts from God. Human beings are thus set aside from other creatures of God. We are the special objects of His love.

Because of sin, however, whether greed, evil lust, pride, or desire for power, people are inclined to bargain away their lives in service to Satan and the sinful self. To prevent people from choosing the broad and easy way that leads to destruction, God prepared another way. He sent His Son into the world, not only to enlighten us as to life's values but to release us from bondage to sin. Through Christ's redemption He set us free to be His servants, yes, His redeemed children and heirs of eternal life. By faith in Jesus Christ we are enabled to choose what is good, to lead fruitful lives, and to glorify God on the road from earth to heaven.

No treasure—certainly not a carpetbag full of gold—is greater than life in Christ, for He redeemed us not with gold or silver but with His holy, precious blood.

Prayer Suggestion

Ask the Holy Spirit to keep you in faith in Christ and to guide you in making life's choices.

JESUS IS THE WAY

Jesus answered, "I am the way and the truth and the life." John 14:6

Big cities have their main streets: Michigan Avenue in Chicago, St. Catherine Street in Montreal, Kalakaus Avenue in Honolulu. In many places where the early Spaniards were we find a main road called *camino real*, or the King's Highway. Rome had its Via Appia on which St. Paul traveled on his last trip to Rome. Christians from the city came out to meet him and his group at the Forum of Appius and the Three Taverns.

On what important streets or highways have you traveled? In doing so, your destination may have been your parents' home, or a vacation site, or a place of doing business. You began with the prayer that God would grant you a safe journey. The plans you made allowed for changes. St. James writes, "Now listen, you who say, 'Today or tomorrow we will go to this or that city, spend a year there, carry on business, and make money.' Why, you do not even know what will happen tomorrow. ... Instead, you ought to say, 'If it is the Lord's will, we will live and do this or that' " (James 4:13–15).

Of all the important roads we may travel, none surpasses the way that leads to eternal life with God in heaven. It is the *camino real*, the heavenly King's Highway. It is the road on which Jesus traveled when He returned to the Father. When our Lord spoke of this, Thomas asked, "Lord, we don't know where You are going, so how can we know the way?" (John 14:5) Jesus had a ready reply. He Himself could directly approach the Father, but as far as we are concerned, He Himself is the Way to the Father. All of Holy Scripture is our spiritual road map showing that the only road to heaven is faith in the merit and mediation of Jesus Christ. It is for us to check our road map often, to make sure that we are on the right road.

Prayer Suggestion

Implore the Lord Jesus to walk with you as you travel the road leading to full communion with the Father in heaven.

LOVE SURPASSES KNOWLEDGE

My purpose is that they may be encouraged in heart and united in love, so that they may have the full riches of complete understanding. Colossians 2:2

People may have wondered why stations along the Kettle Valley Railroad in rugged British Columbia bore names like Juliet, Romeo, Iago, Portia, or King Lear. Andrew McCulloch, the chief engineer during the 1910–16 building era, was an ardent student of Shakespeare. With entertainment not available in these lonely places, McCulloch amused the workers in the evenings by reciting from the writings of the British bard.

It is good to be more than a one-dimensional person. One purpose of education is to broaden one's interest in things beyond one's immediate job.

St. Paul, in all humility and in due recognition of God's enabling grace, called himself an "expert builder" who laid a foundation on which others could build. As a spiritual "Andrew McCulloch" he entered the rugged regions of the pagan world and built a road for the Gospel of Jesus Christ. A man strong in the Christian faith, he was also strong in knowledge, laying all his talents at the foot of Christ's cross. He knew the Greek philosophers and poets, quoting them several times in his epistles.

The apostle wanted his young trainees to continue their education through reading. He writes to Timothy, "Do your best [the King James Version has "study"] to present yourself to God as one approved, a workman who does not need to be ashamed and who correctly handles the Word of truth" (2 Timothy 2:15). All the while St. Paul was telling the Ephesians—and is telling us today—"to grasp how wide and long and high and deep is the love of Christ, and to know this love that surpasses knowledge" (Ephesians 3:18–19).

Just to know Shakespeare gets no one to heaven, but to know the One in whom also Shakespeare professed faith—Jesus Christ as Savior—does.

Prayer Suggestion

Declare your loyalty to the Lord Jesus Christ, "in whom are hidden all the treasures of wisdom and knowledge" (Colossians 2:3).

GOOD WORKS SHOULD BE WELL DONE

Whatever you do, work at it with all your heart, as working for the Lord. Colossians 3:23

On an October day in 1989 the Communist regime of China executed 18 factory managers in a rice paddy while 500 plant workers watched. The charge: They had done "shabby work."

A church theologian stated years ago that Christians should not only do good works, but do them well. God is not pleased with careless, half-hearted efforts, especially when they result in the loss of customers or the disadvantage of employers. The Ecclesiastes writer declares, "Whatever your hand finds to do, do it with all your might" (9:10). Jesus applied Himself diligently to His assignments, saying, "My Father is always at His work to this very day, and I, too, am working" (John 5:17). Again, "As long as it is day, we must do the work of Him who sent Me. Night is coming, when no one can work" (John 9:4). The great work the Father had assigned to Jesus, His incarnate Son, was the making of restitution for the sin of the world. He endured death on the cross to do it.

The apostles, following the example of Jesus, worked faithfully as His ambassadors. They instructed their followers to do likewise and to avoid sloth. St. Paul wrote to the Ephesians, "Serve wholeheartedly, as if you were serving the Lord, not men" (Ephesians 6:7). He told the Colossians to work faithfully "not only when their [masters'] eye is on you and to win their favor, but with sincerity of heart and reverence for the Lord" (3:22).

"Shabby work," while it certainly does not call for a Chinese-style execution, is not for Christians. The latter strive for excellence because they are the followers of Jesus, of whom the people said, "He has done everything well" (Mark 7:37), and they are the children of the heavenly Father who, on surveying His creation, declared it to be "very good" (Genesis 1:31).

Prayer Suggestion

Seek the Lord's help to find pleasure and purpose in your daily work.

THE UPLIFTING POWER OF PRAYER

May my prayer be set before You like incense; may the
lifting up of my hands be like the evening sacrifice.
Psalm 141:2

"Lift up your hearts" is an invitation to worshipers in the Holy Communion service. The congregation responds, "We lift them to the Lord." Not only in formal church worship but also in our private devotions are we in need of lifting up our hearts in prayer.

In biblical times it was customary to lift up one's hands when praying. The psalmist prays, "May my prayer be set before You like incense; may the lifting up of my hands be like the evening sacrifice" (141:2). It was with uplifted hands that Moses on a hilltop prayed for the victory of Joshua and the Israelites over the Amalekites, and when he tired, Aaron and Hur upheld Moses' praying hands. Turning to the New Testament, we read these words of St. Paul to Timothy, "I want men everywhere to lift up holy hands in prayer, without anger or disputing" (1 Timothy 2:8).

God has both commanded and invited us to pray, but He has not prescribed what bodily posture we should assume when praying, whether to sit, stand, or kneel. The latter is most fitting, for it is "body language" expressing humility. The psalmist states, "Come, let us bow down in worship, let us kneel before the LORD our Maker" (95:6).

What about our hands when praying? A good Christian custom has been to fold them. We might also do what believers of old did when praying: lift them up. This would symbolize that we are lifting up our hearts to God. Faith in our Savior Jesus Christ dwells in our hearts. We ask Jesus to dwell in our hearts, cleansing them with His blood and keeping them clean and strong through the indwelling of His Spirit coming to us through Word and sacraments.

What is important when we pray is the *sursum corda*, the lifting up of our hearts. "It is with your heart that you believe and are justified, and it is with your mouth that you confess and are saved," writes St. Paul in Romans 10:10.

Prayer Suggestion

Close this devotion with a prayer in which you thank God with your heart, hands, and voice for His many blessings in Christ Jesus.

Speaking Clearly

If I want him [John] to remain alive until I return,
what is that to you? You must follow Me. John 21:22

"Reading from the same page" is an expression often used to point out the need for two (or more) persons to make sure that in the conversation they are talking about the same thing. No agreement can be reached when one is talking about apples and the other about oranges.

This is also true in religious discussions. The Bible records gross misunderstandings made by people who were not, so to speak, "reading from the same page." For example, Jesus was speaking about His forthcoming death and bodily resurrection when He said, "Destroy this temple, and I will raise it again in three days" (John 2:19). Some of His hearers, however, understood that as a reference to the temple building in Jerusalem. Again, when after His resurrection Jesus had a private talk with Peter, the subject of John's future came up. Our Lord had said that John would stay alive until His coming again "if I want him to remain" (John 21:23). The "if" is important. But Peter was not "reading from the same page." He thought that Jesus had said that John would never die, and this rumor prevailed for a while.

We do well to bear in mind that we can avoid unpleasant misunderstandings by always being clear in our words, especially when we talk about religion or matters of the Christian faith. The prophets of old, the psalmists, and then Jesus and the apostles set us examples in clarity of expression. They tell us the truths of salvation in clear language. Here is an example, both as to the statement of true doctrine and as to the exclusion of error: "It is by grace you have been saved, through faith—and this not from yourselves, it is the gift of God—not by works, so that no one can boast" (Ephesians 2:8–9).

When we all study the Holy Scriptures carefully, hearing, reading, marking, learning, and digesting them inwardly, we will understand ourselves much better when we speak to one another. We will be "reading from the same page."

Prayer Suggestion

Pray to the Spirit for a clear understanding of God's Word so that your faith may be strengthened and you can confess it more clearly before others.

CHRISTIAN VIRTUES

*The fruit of the Spirit is love, joy, peace, patience, kind-
ness, goodness, faithfulness, gentleness and self-control.
Galatians 5:22–23*

Seven is a holy number in the Bible. The prophet Isaiah (11:2-3) refers to the seven gifts of the Spirit. Wisdom is said to have seven pillars (Proverbs 9:1). The writer of Proverbs (6:16-19) lists seven sins that the Lord detests. These references may have been the basis for the medieval church's distinction between the seven vices and seven virtues.

From another religious source—from Maimonides, a Spanish rabbi of long ago—comes this: "A judge must have these seven qualifications: wisdom, humility, fear of God [reverence], disdain of gain, love of truth, love of his fellowmen, and a good reputation."

These are qualities everyone should have, whatever his or her station in life might be. *Wisdom:* "Be very careful, then, how you live— not as unwise but as wise" (Ephesians 5:15); *Humility:* "Clothe yourselves with humility toward one another" (1 Peter 5:5); *Reverence:* "Let us be thankful, and so worship God acceptably with reverence and awe" (Hebrews 12:28); *Avoidance of Covetousness:* "Keep your lives free from the love of money and be content with what you have" (Hebrews 13:5); *Love of truth:* "Whatever is true, ... whatever is right ... think about such things" (Philippians 4:8); *Love of fellowmen:* "Keep on loving each other as brothers" (Hebrews 13:1); *Good conduct and reputation:* "Conduct yourselves in a manor worthy of the Gospel of Christ" (Philippians 1:27).

These qualities are the fruit of faith, or the "fruit of the Spirit." This tells us how they are acquired. How different they are from the world's "morality." The latter have been compared to gilded nuts serving as Christmas tree decorations. Christian virtues are real; they result from Christ-centered faith and life. He who is our Savior from sin and the Enabler of the new life in Christ declares: "I am the Vine; you are the branches. If a man remains in Me and I in him, he will bear much fruit" (John 15:5).

Prayer Suggestion

Ask your Lord and Savior to live in you and make your life fruitful.

THE DEBTS ARE PAID

Christ redeemed us from the curse of the law by becoming a curse for us. Galatians 3:13

What shall a country do when prisons overflow with convicts? It is said that England, by the year 1789, had deported to Australia 160,000 people with prison records. Some had been imprisoned because they couldn't pay their debts. In the new world they could get another start.

Spiritually speaking, all persons since the time Adam and Eve fell into sin have been in need of forsaking the past and starting life with a clean slate. All had made many debts by their sins against God's moral law, the Ten Commandments. St. Paul states that "the handwriting of ordinances" or, as a newer version has it, "the written code, with its regulations" (Colossians 2:14), was against them. We were all head-over-heels in debt. And none of us could ever make restitution for our wrongdoing. Jesus made this clear in His parable of a man who owed his employer 10,000 talents. Even if his wife and children were sold into slavery, he could never repay. This is the situation of every sinner in relation to a holy God.

How does God deal with His debtors? He has a better plan than to export them to Australia. He doesn't want to banish them from His sight or to exile them to a planet where living conditions would be severe. Instead of sending them away to work out their own salvation, He sent His Son into the world and made Him the consummate Debtor in behalf of us all. With the price of His own blood, Jesus Christ paid for all our debts and set us free. No second payment, either by the Savior or by us, will ever be demanded. The written code is fulfilled, and the debts are canceled. This is what faith in the merit and mediation of Jesus Christ does.

The apostle states what the Christian's response to God's grace should be: "So then, just as you received Christ Jesus as Lord, continue to live in Him, rooted and built up in Him, strengthened in the faith as you were taught, and overflowing with thankfulness" (Colossians 2:6). Surely this is also how we react.

Prayer Suggestion

Say to the Lord Jesus that you want to live under Him in His kingdom and serve Him.

SERVING THE GOOD SHEPHERD AND HIS SHEEP

I am the Good Shepherd. John 10:11

In southern Missouri lives a woman whose main work is shepherding. Raising sheep, she said, "has full-time aspects." When lambs are due to be born, the owner must be there. Sometimes as many as ten lambs are born at Christmas time, cutting down on her holiday season.

In biblical times, women were involved in sheep care. We read that the daughters of a man named Reuel, in the land of Midian, led the flocks to water, with the shepherds sometimes bothering them. One day they were assisted by a refugee from Egypt, and this led to the marriage of Zipporah, one of the daughters, to the benefactor, Moses.

While shepherds were watching their sheep, as at the birth of Jesus, we can well imagine that their wives were giving loving, tender care to ailing sheep and lambs at home.

Jesus is the great Shepherd of the sheep. In John chapter 10 He stresses in what sense He is the ultimate care-taking Shepherd: "I am the good shepherd. The good shepherd lays down His life for the sheep" (John 10:11). He adds that He has the power to do this and to take up His life again with His resurrection. Before ascending into heaven, He appointed undershepherds, the apostles, who in turn trained successors to nourish Christ's flock with the Word of God. Through the centuries pious men were called and ordained by congregations to continue the work.

Faithful women have been active in the flock, serving their Lord by teaching and befriending especially the young in church, school, and home. They serve in many other capacities to advance the mission of the church. They walk in the footsteps of pious women who followed Jesus, ministered to His needs, and shared the Gospel with others. They were the last to leave the cross on Good Friday and the first at the empty tomb on Easter.

Christ's richest blessings rest on women today who serve as shepherdesses among His people.

Prayer Suggestion

Express your gratitude to God for the services of dedicated women in Christ's church today.

NOW IS THE TIME

Now is the time of God's favor, now is the day of salvation.
2 Corinthians 6:2

A man who writes a column in the St. Louis daily newspaper stated, after he had been baptized as an adult: "I wish I had received spiritual training when young. I believe it would have given me a better moral and ethical base from which to govern my life; I would have avoided many of the pitfalls of ego and arrogance."

The hymn writer, in addressing himself to Christ, stated his regrets in clear Christian terms: "Alas! that I so late have known Thee, Who art the Fairest and the Best ... Now bitter shame and grief I prove, O'er this my tardy love."

Regrets about being a latecomer are to be read between the lines written by St. Paul. He tells the Galatians, "The life I live in the body, I live by faith in the Son of God, who loved me and gave Himself for me" (Galatians 2:20). Great was the love the apostle had for his Savior, declaring it on many occasions and expressing great happiness in living his life in and for Christ. But think what he missed when, before his conversion, as Saul the Pharisee, he had not served Christ, instead "breathing out murderous threats against the Lord's disciples" (Acts 9:1). Surely it had to be the great regret in St. Paul's life that he had formerly "persecuted the church of God and tried to destroy it" (Galatians 1:13) when he could have devoted his time and effort to the upbuilding of the church.

Regrets do the individual no good when voiced after the time of grace has passed. The rich man of Jesus' parable was full of regrets when, at death, his soul landed in hell. It was then too late to change anything.

We take to heart the words of one who knew what he was talking about. St. Paul writes: "Now is the time of God's favor, now is the day of salvation" (2 Corinthians 6:2). The time for repentance is now. The time to believe in Jesus is today. What a joy it is to live for Him and to serve Him! Those who love the Lord and who, out of love to Him, serve others will never have regrets—only hearts full of gratitude for the work of the Holy Spirit in them.

Prayer Suggestion

Tell your Savior and Lord that you have repented of past sins and missed opportunities and that you are happy to turn your life over to Him.

GOD'S SUNSHINE

I have become its servant by the commission God gave me
to present to you the Word of God in its fullness.
Colossians 1:25

Government agencies and policy-making groups are asked to observe "sunshine laws" that are intended to make available their actions and resolutions to those who have the right to know.

God, too, is committed to "sunshine" principles. He has revealed to the world His plan of salvation. By themselves sinners could not know what God had in mind to bring the fallen human race back into fellowship with Him. God formed His saving counsel in eternity, before there ever was a sinful human race. With the coming of Christ and the proclamation of His Gospel, God's "sunshine" principle went into effect. St. Paul speaks of God's revealed grace in Christ as "the mystery that has been kept hidden for ages and generations, but is now disclosed to the saints" (Colossians 1:26).

God's saving grace was proclaimed in olden times by the prophets. This revelation, at first dim, was like light breaking through dark clouds. But at the fullness of time God spoke to us plainly through His Son. Jesus Christ, conceived by the Holy Spirit and born of the virgin Mary, is this divine Son. He is the Light of the world, the Sun of Righteousness with healing in its radiant light. Through Jesus Christ God emits His sunshine. He reveals to us His wondrous grace, the forgiveness of all our sins, and the perfect peace we have with Him in time and in eternity. We have this because Jesus Christ became the Second Adam to atone for all the sins of the first Adam and all his descendants.

When our Lord gave instruction to His followers to proclaim the good news of salvation to all the world, He put God's "sunshine" principle into effect. He wants the whole human race to know what Christianity teaches. He wants them to shed light on what Advent, Christmas, Easter, and Pentecost are all about. Away with secrecy, even with hesitancy! Let the sun of God's love in Christ shine so that a world sitting in darkness may know that the Savior is born!

Prayer Suggestion

Thank God for the revelation of His grace in Christ, asking Him also to help you spread the sunshine.

HOUSES OF DECISION

As for me and my household, we will serve the LORD.
Joshua 24:15

In Washington Crossing State Park, located in Buck County, Pennsylvania, stands a structure called "House of Decision." It got this name because in it George Washington and his staff decided to cross the Delaware River to attack the opposing forces at Trenton, New Jersey. They did so on Christmas night, 1776, and were successful.

Every home is in a sense a "house of decision." Important things have to be decided in the family circle about the daily work routines, about recreation, what to read, what to watch on TV, where the older children will go to college, and how to pay for it.

One matter exceeds all the family issues, namely, what is the family's relation to Jesus Christ? Joshua, the leader of the Israelites settled in the Promised Land, made a deep impression on the people when he announced at a mass meeting in Shechem: "As for me and my house, we will serve the LORD" (Joshua 24:15). In this house a right decision had been made.

In the New Testament we find many references to households where, through the Gospel, the Holy Spirit had led family members to declare Jesus Christ as Lord and Savior. St. Peter preached in the house of the centurion Cornelius. The Holy Spirit activated faith in those present and the whole household was baptized. The same events took place in the home of Lydia in Philippi and in that of the jailor in the same city. Another "house of decision" where the Holy Spirit probably did His work was the home of Philemon, to whom St. Paul wrote a letter.

If yours is a house where decisions comparable to crossing the Delaware have to be made, by all means make them. Say with Joshua that you and your house will serve the Lord Jesus. Trusting in the merit of Jesus Christ, you and your family will have peace with God and peace in the home.

Prayer Suggestion

Pray for the Holy Spirit's guidance when important decisions have to be made in your house.

SPIRITUAL WATCHFULNESS

Keep watch over yourselves and all the flock of which the
Holy Spirit has made you overseers. Acts 20:28

Several years ago a newspaper reported that a truck driver working for the highway system stopped to remove a warning sign that was deemed no longer needed. While he was doing this, he was struck by another truck and killed.

Caution in our spiritual lives is always in place. For one thing, we should not be too hasty to remove danger signs along the highway of the Christian faith. The evils may still prevail. In fact, some danger markers should never be removed. The writer of Proverbs states, "Do not move an ancient boundary stone set up by your forefathers" (22:28). What pertained to local geography then still applies to Christianity today. Warnings against sin, the temptations of the world, and the wiles of the devil are still needed.

While God's caretakers in the church look after the welfare of the people committed to their care, they are reminded by Holy Scripture also to be concerned about their own spiritual safety. This is stressed by the apostle Paul. In his meeting with the elders of Ephesus he said, "Keep watch over yourselves and all the flock of which the Holy Spirit has made you overseers. Be shepherds of the church of God, which He bought with His own blood" (Acts 20:28). And to Timothy he wrote, "Watch your life and doctrine closely" (1 Timothy 4:16).

In the home, fathers and mothers watch over their children, teaching them the meaning of God's love in Christ Jesus. They also need to look after their own safety as they travel the traffic-stricken highways of life. It would be a real tragedy if they were struck by the vehicles of sin and Satan and they lost their faith.

Years ago it was asked in a popular song, "Who takes care of the caretaker's daughter while the caretaker is out taking care?" Similarly, who takes care of the church's caretakers while they are taking care of their charges? The Lord does.

Prayer Suggestion

Pray for the continued guardianship of God over your faith and life.

FROM RAGS TO ROBES

Though He [Christ Jesus] was rich, yet for your sakes He became poor. 2 Corinthians 8:9

All people come into this world empty-handed, and that is also the way they will leave. Job writes, "Naked I came from my mother's womb, and naked I will depart" (1:21). St. Paul echoes the same truth: "We brought nothing into the world, and we can take nothing out of it" (1 Timothy 6:7). The rich man who had himself buried in his solid gold Cadillac, of course, left it behind.

How about the Son of God? Could He perhaps have come into this world with the symbols of incalculable wealth: gorgeous robes, diamond rings on His fingers, a solid gold crown on His head? Not if it was His purpose to take the place of all members of fallen mankind. But since He came as every sinner's substitute, He was born in deepest poverty. He came with nothing. His mother wrapped Him in scraps of cloth, in a "blanket" as one Bible version has it. In fact, in the Latin translation of Christ's nativity Mary has wrapped Him with *pannis*, that is, in tatters, remnants, rags.

When Jesus departed in death, He again had nothing, for the Roman soldiers appropriated His clothes.

How does Jesus' poverty benefit us? St. Paul tells the Corinthians, "You know the grace of our Lord Jesus Christ, that though He was rich, yet for your sakes He became poor" (2 Corinthians 8:9). Once for all our Lord enriched us with his poverty when, as our substitute, He exchanged the rags of our sinfulness with the robes of His perfect righteousness. Now we can stand faultless before God's throne. That robe, covering all our sins, is ours by faith in Jesus.

Without this robe, we are lost. But clothed in it, we are the best dressed people and welcome guests at the heavenly feast.

Prayer Suggestion

Make up your own prayer on the basis of the hymn lines: "Jesus, Your blood and righteousness, My beauty are, my glorious dress."

THE GRAVE WAS ROBBED

O grave, where is thy victory? 1 Corinthians 15:55 KJV

We cannot be sure where Christopher Columbus lies buried. Some say it is in the Dominican Republic, where his son is buried. Others say it is in the cathedral of Seville, Spain. Similarly, Daniel Boone has a gravesite in Frankfort, Kentucky, and another at Defiance, Missouri.

With Moses, the situation is different. The last chapter of Deuteronomy states that "to this day no one knows where his grave is" (34:6). While the apocryphal book, The Assumption of Moses, says that the archangel Michael carried Moses' body to heaven, the book of Jude (v. 9) tells us only that Michael disputed with Satan over Moses' body. Also the prophet Elijah has no grave, for also he was taken to heaven bodily.

Another who has no grave is Jesus. After His death on the cross His body was laid into Joseph's tomb. But on the third day He rose from the grave. The power of our Lord's resurrection was foretold by the prophet Hosea: "I will ransom them from the power of the grave; I will redeem them from death. Where, O death, are your plagues? Where, O grave, is your destruction?" (13:14) St. Paul repeated the substance of these words in his most comforting chapter in First Corinthians 15.

When we say the grave was robbed, we are not referring to the work of thieves who rob graves. We mean that death and the grave were stripped of their power over us when Christ, in proof of His conquest of sin and death, rose triumphantly from His tomb. Thanks to His victory, graves cannot hold back their occupants but must give them up when our Savior returns in glory on the Last Day.

The promise of the resurrection applies to all who died as believers in Christ, also to those whose graves have long disappeared and to those who never had a grave, like those who drowned in oceans. "The sea gave up the dead," writes St. John in the book of Revelation (20:13). In the end it makes very little difference where our graves are or whether they can be identified. The Lord Jesus knows where we are, and He will find us on that great Day.

Prayer Suggestion

Give thanks to the Lord Jesus for conquering death and the grave in your behalf.

SO CLOSE, YET SO FAR

*He [Jesus] said to him, "You are not far from the king-
dom of God." Mark 12:34*

In her autobiographical book, *Me*, the actress Katherine Hepburn,
although admitting her Christian roots, makes no profession of faith.
In fact, she denies having faith. Yet she has moments of truth. She
states, for example, "When you sin, you pay." (St. Paul explains: "The
wages of sin is death" [Romans 6:23].) Why did her marriage fail? She
confesses to selfishness: "It was Me, Me, Me."

Some non-Christians at times come close to confessing Christian
truth. In a dialog with Jesus, a scribe declared that loving God and the
neighbor "is more important than all burnt offerings and sacrifices."
He was obviously not a follower of Jesus, yet Jesus said to him, "You
are not far from the kingdom of God" (Mark 12:34). Again, after St.
Paul had stated his case to King Agrippa and appealed to him to
believe, Agrippa replied, according to the King James Version of the
Bible: "Almost thou persuadest me to be a Christian" (Acts 26:28).

We read in the Old Testament about Balaam, a pagan diviner, who
refused to prophesy against the Israelites as they moved through the
land of Moab toward the Promised Land. He said he would not do so
even if he received King Balak's "palace filled with silver and gold"
(Numbers 22:18). Instead he blessed the Israelites, uttering a messianic prophecy of the "Star that will come out of Jacob" (Numbers 24:17).
How far was he from the kingdom of God?

A person can be close to aspects of God's truth and yet be far
away from having faith in Jesus Christ as the Savior. Also in matters of
faith it is true: "A miss is as good as a mile." "Close," it is said in sport
circles, "counts only in horseshoes." Some can be said to be close to
Christianity because they know a great deal about the Bible or
because they are married to a Christian and sometimes attend church.
Yet, lacking faith, they are far from God's kingdom. The Bible is plain:
"Whoever believes and is baptized will be saved, but whoever does not
believe will be condemned" (Mark 16:16). God promises salvation to
all who put their trust in Christ crucified and Christ risen from the
dead.

Prayer Suggestion

Ask the Holy Spirit to keep your faith centered in Jesus Christ and
to give you the joy of living in Him and for Him.

FOUR KINDS OF LIFE

In Him was life, and that life was the light of men.
John 1:4

"Life" is a word occurring frequently in daily conversation. Sometimes it is not clear in what sense the word is used. It helps if we understand its usages. From a biblical perspective, we can distinguish four meanings of life.

First, as beings created by God, we have *physical* life. In Genesis we read, "The LORD God formed the man from the dust of the ground and breathed into his nostrils the breath of life, and the man became a living being" (2:7). Because we have bodily life, we breathe, eat, drink, work, and rest.

Second, as human beings, we have *mental-emotional* life. This sets us aside from animals. We can think, speak, and figure things out rationally. We can love. Jesus said, "Love the Lord your God with all your heart and with all your soul and with all your mind" (Matthew 22:37). In our time we notice a tendency to downsize the importance of the mind as having the power of reasoning and of making responsible decisions. Human behavior, it is claimed, is determined by one's physical genes.

Third, on the basis of Bible teaching we identify *spiritual* life, or faith active in love and in service to Christ. Unbelievers do not have it. St. John declares that Christ, the Son of God become man, is the source of this life: "In Him was life, and that life was the light of men" (John 1:4). It still is, for the Lord Jesus imparts and supports spiritual life through His Word and Spirit.

Fourth, Holy Scripture teaches that believers have the promise of *eternal* life. It is the extension of our present spiritual life. We have the foretaste of it in this present life in Christ but will realize the fullness of it in heaven.

The apostle John writes concerning Christ Jesus, "From the fullness of His grace we have all received one blessing after another" (John 1:16). These blessings certainly include life in its fourfold dimension. We have life in its fullness because Jesus gave His life for us.

Prayer Suggestion

Restate in your own words what the hymn writer states: "Take my Life, O Lord, renew, Consecrate my heart to You."

THE OVERRIDING WILL OF GOD

You intended to harm me, but God intended it for good.
Genesis 50:20

"God can use what He did not choose," declared a noted television evangelist. This is more than a play on words. It coincides with what the Bible teaches.

The fact that God can change the evil designs of people into good is heavily underscored in the life and work of Joseph as prime minister of Egypt. He told his brothers, "You intended to harm me, but God intended it for good to accomplish what is now being done, the saving of many lives" (Genesis 50:20). Earlier he had told them, "God sent me ahead of you to preserve for you a remnant on earth and to save your lives by a great deliverance" (Genesis 45:7). It was necessary, according to God's plan of salvation, to keep alive a remnant of Jacob's descendants, notably the tribe of Judah, for from the tribe of Judah the Messiah was to be born.

God did not choose—He did not so order or ordain—that a man named Saul the Pharisee should in his youth be educated in the wrong conceptions of the law of Moses and become self-righteous. But after Saul's conversion, God used the sharpened mind, the now properly directed zeal, and the power of speech of St. Paul to further the kingdom of Christ.

It was not God's choice that Christ's enemies should persecute the young church in Jerusalem and stone Stephen to death. But God used their evil plotting, directing it to a good outcome. The persecution had the good effect that it scattered the Christians to surrounding regions. Wherever those Christians went, they proclaimed and lived the saving Gospel of Christ.

In his sermon to the religious leaders in Jerusalem St. Peter cited the greatest instances of God turning to the eternal good of mankind the evil Christ's enemies chose to do: "You handed Him over to be killed, and you disowned Him before Pilate ... You killed the author of life, but God raised Him from the dead" (Acts 3:13, 14).

"Surely the arm of the LORD is not too short to save," writes the prophet Isaiah (59:1). This is still true today. What God did not choose He can use to bring about good outcomes in our time, in our world, in our lives.

Prayer Suggestion

Pray that God may, for Jesus' sake, turn the evil in your life to good outcomes.

SOMETIMES WE HAVE TO JUDGE

First take the plank out of your eye, and then you will see clearly to remove the speck from your brother's eye.
Luke 6:42

Some people stand for what is known as *laissez faire*, that is, let people do as they please. In support of this stance they quote the words of Jesus: "Do not judge, and you will not be judged. Do not condemn, and you will not be condemned" (Luke 6:37).

In words preceding the above, Jesus urges us to be merciful because our heavenly Father is that way. Further, He warns against self-righteousness, against having 20/20 vision with regard to someone else's faults but being blind to our own. Such people spot a "speck of dust" or a splinter in their brothers' and sisters' eyes when having a "plank" in their own. On the basis of this context, some say we ought never judge and condemn anyone, not even when moral wrongs are involved.

This cannot be what Jesus meant, for elsewhere He stated, "If your brother sins against you, go and show him his fault" (Matthew 18:15). Whenever Christians do this, they are not expressing arbitrary, personal judgments but are applying the prior judgments of God. The latter are the standard by which we live.

What kind of judging or condemning is Jesus forbidding? It is a judging that is loveless, without mercy, and is prompted by self-righteousness. Our Lord does not want us to presume to lay down moral principles, or a set of do's and don'ts, of our own making that exceed or fall short of what the Word of God says. The attempt to add to the Word of God was illustrated by the Pharisees, who added more than 600 laws of their own to the moral law of God. This is legalism.

Yes, there may come times when it is our Christian calling to point out to those near and dear to us that what they are saying and doing is wrong in the light of the Word of God. The intent is to be constructive and positive—as Jesus said—to "win" or "gain" the brother or sister, to be spiritually helpful to one for whom Christ died.

Prayer Suggestion

Ask God to give you the attitude toward, and the right concern for, brothers and sisters in the faith who err.

COPING WITH LIFE'S UPS AND DOWNS

"[N]o mind has conceived what God has prepared for those who love Him"—but God has revealed it to us by His Spirit. 1 Corinthians 2:9–10

Charles Mann, a defensive football end for the Washington Redskins, was asked how he could reconcile a rough sport with his professed Christianity. He remarked, "If Christ were on the football field, He would not be a wimp but would stand His ground." Then, applying his faith to the problems of the greater game of life, he said, "It is not by my strength or my talents, but it is God who gives me the power and wisdom to deal with life's ups and downs."

Jesus was not a moral or physical weakling. For His cleansing of the temple, He made a "whip out of cords" (John 2:15) and drove the sacrificial cattle and the money changers from the temple precincts. A wimp would not have done this.

It is worth pursuing what the athlete said about the greater contests of life taking place off the athletic field. Many are marked by ups and downs, victories and defeats, gains and losses. On fields more uneven than football gridirons, we are confronted by opponents far deadlier than the opposing players: sin within us, the world of iniquity, the designing devil. To hold our own against them until God gives us the victory, we need more than our own strength and talents. We need what St. Paul experienced: God's grace sufficient for us, with His power made perfect in our weakness.

What we also need to deal with life's up and downs is wisdom. Wisdom is more than knowledge or a mental accumulation of facts. It includes the ability to make right judgments on the basis of the facts at hand. Experience helps in this. Discretion, too, is a part of wisdom. These assets, said the football player, come from God. Especially the highest wisdom, faith resting in Christ's redemption, comes from God through His Word. The "Holy Scriptures," writes St. Paul, "are able to make you wise for salvation through faith in Christ Jesus" (2 Timothy 3:15). It is this wisdom that the Holy Spirit teaches and that He, through the Gospel, sustains in us. It is, in summary, the conviction that Christ Jesus gave His own life so that we might have forgiveness and the fullness of life.

Prayer Suggestion

Give thanks to Jesus, your Lord and Savior, for giving you the strength and wisdom to follow Him through life's thick and thin.

THE CROSS STANDS FOR STRENGTH

May I never boast except in the cross of our Lord Jesus Christ. Galatians 6:14

It is said that in Japanese culture the tree stands for strength.

Trees are mentioned in the Bible in various connections. The thought of strength and durability is suggested in Isaiah's reference to the believers as "oaks of righteousness, the planting of the LORD" (Isaiah 61:3). Fruit-bearing trees are symbols of spiritually productive Christians. In Psalm 1 a righteous person is compared to a tree that "yields its fruit in season" (v. 3). The individual cedars of Lebanon and other trees were used for Solomon's temple, symbolizing the individual believers who together constitute the holy Christian church, the communion of saints. In Jesus Christ, as St. Paul writes to the Ephesians, "the whole building is joined together and rises to become a holy temple in the Lord" (2:21).

Trees give wood for both constructive and destructive purposes. The Romans used wood to make crosses for the execution of their victims. Yes, a tree somewhere in the Holy Land became the cross on which Jesus was sacrificed for the sin of the world. St. Paul makes this clear: "Christ redeemed us from the curse of the Law by becoming a curse for us, for it is written: 'Cursed is everyone who is hung on a tree' " (Galatians 3:13).

The tree on Mount Calvary takes us back to the Garden of Eden where the devil used a tree to tempt Adam and Eve into sin. It was altogether fitting and right that the devil be himself overcome by a tree—by the accursed tree of the cross. This tree is now for us the symbol of our salvation in Christ. Now there is again a tree of life in the heavenly paradise. "To him who overcomes," writes St. John in Revelation, Christ "will give the right to eat from the tree of life, which is in the paradise of God" (2:7).

Yes, the tree of Christ's cross stands for strength in this life and for eternal life in the world to come.

Prayer Suggestion

Pray to God for the strength and joy always to glory in the cross of Christ.

CHRIST IS OUR PEACE

In Christ Jesus you who once were far away have been
brought near through the blood of Christ. Ephesians 2:13

During the Civil War, and probably in most land wars, many battles were fought near churches. At Shiloh in southwestern Tennessee, a bloody battle took place at Shiloh church. Another battle swirled around a Dunker church at Antietam, Maryland. A church seminary was involved in the battle of Gettysburg.

Tragic as it is for churches to suffer from warfare, it is far worse when battles are fought in the church itself. In the mother church in Jerusalem, founded on Pentecost Day, Grecian Jews "complained against the Hebraic Jews because their widows were being overlooked in the daily distribution of food" (Acts 6:1). But this was a minor skirmish in comparison with the much greater controversy over whether Old Testament ceremonial laws, like circumcision, must be part of New Testament Christianity. The conflict led to an apostolic convention in Jerusalem, where the principle of freedom from the mosaic law was once for all established.

The church in Ephesus was shaken by the same controversy. It needed spiritual guidance, and St. Paul provided it in his epistle. He wrote that Christ Himself "is our peace, who has made the two one and has destroyed the barrier, the dividing wall of hostility, by abolishing in His flesh the law with its commandments and regulations" (Ephesians 2:14–15). Because of Christ's obedience to the Law and His work of atonement (at-one-ment), we are fully and freely saved through faith in Him. This goes for both believing Jews and Gentiles, who are now one.

War continues in our world, and church edifices are still being destroyed. Disputes still arise in congregations and in entire church bodies. But the truth of salvation by grace—without the deeds of the Law, without a golden-rule morality, without human merit of any kind—stands firm. Standing on this foundation, Christ's church and its members are at peace.

Prayer Suggestion

Express your thankfulness to Jesus Christ for preserving and prospering His church on earth.

SPIRITUAL HEALING IN CHRIST

You have this in your favor: You hate the practices of the Nicolaitans, which I also hate. Revelation 2:6

Homeotherapy, a healing treatment, is said to date back to the ancient Greeks. "Homeo" in Greek means "like" or "similar." It says that the treatment is like the ailment. If patients had a fever, treat them with hot water.

This idea seemed to have spilled over into religious philosophy. Two churches addressed by St. John in Revelation, those at Ephesus and Pergamum, harbored the Nicolaitans, a sect very subversive to Christian morality. These people worked on the principle of overcoming the sinful flesh by exhausting it, that is, by accommodating its desires more and more until it was "satisfied." While Christianity taught that a person, empowered by the Holy Spirit, should oppose the flesh, the Nicolaitans used the "homeo" method—to act "like" or "similar" to what the flesh wanted.

Whatever the merits or demerits of homeotherapy may be, it is sure that the "treatment" of the Nicolaitans was downright satanic. It was bad spiritual "medicine." Little wonder that the Lord said through John that He "hated" what they were doing. The congregations addressed by John must put them out of their midst.

The idea of the Nicolaitans is not entirely dead. People in our culture are often encouraged to do what their sinful natures crave. They are told, "It is your right," or "If it feels good, it is right for you." This advice leads to sure self-destruction.

The right therapy is stated by St. Paul: "You were taught … to put off your old self, which is being corrupted by its deceitful desires; to be made new in the attitude of your minds; and to put on the new self, created to be like God in true righteousness and holiness" (Ephesians 4:22–24). Again, the same apostle: "Those who belong to Christ Jesus [those who believe in His atoning work] have crucified the sinful nature with its passions and desires" (Galatians 5:24). Only Christ is our spiritual Physician.

Prayer Suggestion

Pray that God, for Jesus' sake, may create in you a clean heart and renew a right spirit within you.

PEACE WITH GOD: BASIS FOR JOY

Come near to God and He will come near to you.
James 4:8

The Bible speaks of people enjoying themselves—at weddings, welcome-home occasions, parties, outings, trips. Families had a good time when they grouped together to travel up to Jerusalem for the festivals. The psalms of ascent reflect their joy, as David declares, "I rejoiced with those who said to me, 'Let us go up to the house of the LORD' " (Psalm 122:1). When in the Holy City, the people built booths or arbors to occupy for a week during the Feast of Tabernacles. We can imagine that the children especially enjoyed this "camping out" experience.

But some events were not enjoyable, like wars and the starvation sieges often preceding them. Under no circumstances are wars like picnics. When the first battle of Manassas was about to be fought at the outset of the Civil War, many people in Washington, D.C., including congressmen, thought it would be an interesting thing to watch. They came out in carriages, bringing basket lunches and wines. The "outing" ended in a rout, for both the Union troops and the spectators.

Wars, including the bloodless ones sometimes waged in the church, are no picnics. This is true especially when sin causes these controversies. St. James asks, "What causes fights and quarrels among you? Don't they come from your desires that battle within you? You want something but don't get it. You kill and covet, but you cannot have what you want. You quarrel and fight" (James 4:1–2). St. James knows of a much better way to receive what we want and need: Pray to God for it.

By contrast, how blest are congregations when Christ's peace prevails! The psalmist declares, "How good and pleasant it is when brothers live together in unity!" (133:1) This truly is Christ's peace, for He earned it for us on the cross. St. Paul writes, "Since we have been justified through faith, we have peace with God through our Lord Jesus Christ" (Romans 5:1). Peace with God is the basis for peace among ourselves.

Prayer Suggestion

Ask God for a full measure of the joy of salvation that is yours in Christ Jesus.

GOD AS HARVESTER

The soil produces grain—first the stalk, then the head,
then the full kernel in the head. Mark 4:28

A sidelight of the Civil War battle of Antietam pertains to the condition of the cornfield where the fighting began. General Joseph Hooker of the Union forces recorded this: "In the time I am writing, every stalk of corn in the northern and greater part of the field was cut as closely as could have been done with a knife."

War is somewhat of a harvester, but a destructive one. Something much better can be said of the grainfields Jesus used as an illustration of God's kingdom. In one of His parables He described how, unbeknown to the sower, the seed germinated, sprang up, and grew. He noted the stages of growth: "First the stalk, then the head, then the full kernel in the head" (Mark 4:28).

The Lord's point is: His followers sow the seed of God's Word and proclaim the Good News of the full and free salvation procured by Christ. As human beings, they can do the sowing only—they cannot do the converting and cannot accomplish spiritual growth—that is the work of God the Holy Spirit through the Gospel and the sacraments. He keeps people in the saving faith until God's own harvest time.

We see here from the stories of the two fields, first what human beings can do and not do. They can be very destructive, with the effects far more damaging than the ruin of a farmer's cornfield. Even when no formal battles are fought, people, with the devil always urging them on, can do untold harm to what God and God's people have built up. The second grainfield—the one in Jesus' parable—gives us comfort and courage. God is still in charge of His kingdom. His people do the sowing and watering, but He gives the increase. The Lord will, on that great Harvest Day, bring home the sheaves and gather the grain into His barn.

Believing this, Christ's sowers of the Word do not lose heart when they do not see immediate results of their testimony. Bringing people to the saving faith is God's department. He administers it well.

Prayer Suggestion

Let your prayer contain a special request for the good outcome of Gospel preaching through the world, to the glory of Christ.

DRINKING SPIRITUAL WATER

The water I give him will become in him a spring of water welling up to eternal life. John 4:14

In the brochure *Tips for Travelers* people are told to drink enough water to avoid dehydration. Further, they should remain aware of the hazards of water supplies in developing countries. They may be polluted.

The same two points can be made with regard to drinking spiritual water. First, we need the water of life to avoid the dehydration of the soul. Many people have an inner thirst, saying with the psalmist, "As the deer pants for streams of water, so my soul pants for You, O God" (42:1). The Word of God is living water, available in abundance. Jesus said to the Samaritan woman at Jacob's well, with regard to the one accepting His water: "The water I give him will become in him a spring of water welling up to eternal life" (John 4:14). This is another way of saying: Whoever believes in the Gospel of the forgiveness of sins, thanks to Christ's redeeming work, has the abundant life in Him, now and for eternity.

The invitation to quench the thirst of the soul is repeated throughout the Holy Scripture. The prophet Isaiah issues this invitation: "Come, all you who are thirsty, come to the waters" (Isaiah 55:1). In the closing words of Revelation St. John reissues the invitation, "Whoever is thirsty, let him come; and whoever wishes, let him take the free gift of the water of life" (22:17).

Besides avoiding spiritual dehydration, it is important to drink only the pure water of God's Word—the water kept free from pollution. From the beginning the devil has tried to deceive people and to induce them to imbibe the water from his poisoned wells. He has his human agents inviting passers-by not only to take a drink but also to fill their canteens for later drinks in life's journey.

Life is indeed like a trip. As we go through life we need to avoid spiritual dehydration and to make sure that the spiritual water we drink is pure.

Prayer Suggestion

Give thanks to the Lord Jesus for being the fountain flowing with grace and truth for your daily refreshment.

FIRM IN THE FAITH

My dear brothers, stand firm. Let nothing move you.
1 Corinthians 15:58

In recent years "stonewalling" has taken on a sinister meaning, as if a person wanted to hide the truth by surrounding it with a barrier. In the sport of cricket, it means playing a defensive game by keeping the other side from scoring. Perhaps a confederate general in the first Civil War battle of Manassas borrowed the term from cricket when, trying to rally his troops, he pointed to Gen. Thomas J. Jackson and his men and shouted, "There stands Jackson like a stone wall. Rally behind the Virginians."

The life of a Christian, so Holy Scripture teaches, is marked by spiritual battles. The enemies of the cross of Christ, led by Satan, try to route the believers and force them to surrender. This was attempted in Corinth. There St. Paul preached the Gospel, passing on what others had taught him, namely, "that Christ died for our sins according to the Scriptures, that He was buried, that He was raised on the third day according to the Scriptures" (1 Corinthians 15:3–4). These truths, said the apostle, were "of first importance."

But a kind of a "civil war" broke out in the Corinthian church, with some saying "there is no resurrection of the dead" (1 Corinthians 15:12). In reply, St. Paul started with the premise—and the promise—that Jesus was indeed raised from the dead. On this basic, duly attested truth he grounds the resurrection of all who had fallen asleep. Likewise Jesus said, "Because I live, you also will live" (John 14:19).

The key truth of Christ's resurrection as the basis of our own rising from the dead is still under attack. If it falls, the whole structure of Christianity falls with it. That is why we have to be like General "Stonewall" Jackson and the Virginians, as St. Paul bids us, "Stand firm. Let nothing move you" (1 Corinthians 15:58).

Prayer Suggestion

Ask the Holy Spirit to ground your faith firmly in Jesus Christ, who is the Resurrection, the Life, and the Rock of your salvation.

CHRIST'S UNITED NATIONS

I, when I am lifted up from the earth, will draw all men to Myself. John 12:32

After World War II, when displaced persons of many nationalities came to North America, it was said that a better comparison than the "melting pot" was the concept of a mosaic: Individuals were fitted into the total picture without giving up their personal identity. A line of poetry from Alexander Pope was recalled: "All are but parts of one stupendous whole."

The Christian church is a mosaic. It consists of people from "every tribe and language and people and nation," as St. John states in Revelation 5:9. All of them Jesus purchased with His blood, and to all of them He wants the Gospel of salvation preached.

While He was here on earth, Jesus ministered to the lost from the house of Israel, from whose midst He Himself had come. At the same time He came into contact with non-Israelites. During His journeys He addressed the Samaritans—the woman at Jacob's well and the thankful leper whom He had healed. He ministered to a Canaanite mother whose daughter was tormented by a demon, and He praised her persistent faith. The woman is described as a "Greek, born in Syrian Phoenicia." During our Lord's final Passover week in Jerusalem He greatly rejoiced when told that some Greeks wanted to see Him.

Jesus said, when He knew that His earthly ministry was soon to end: "I, when I am lifted up from the earth, will draw all men to Myself" (John 12:32). He was indeed lifted up from the earth when He was crucified. He declared in His night conversation with Nicodemus: "Just as Moses lifted up the snake in the desert, so the Son of Man must be lifted up, that everyone who believes in Him may have eternal life" (John 3:14).

Before being lifted up into heaven, the risen Christ made known His will that His disciples make other disciples from among all nations by baptizing them and teaching them that Gospel. The glorious mosaic of the Christian church is not yet complete. Many souls are to be added to fill out the picture. Epiphany is continuing.

Prayer Suggestion

Ask the Lord Jesus to bless the preaching of the Gospel so that many more persons may be added to His kingdom.

FAILURE NEED NOT BE FINAL

All the people in the synagogue ... got up, drove Him
out of the town, and took Him to the brow of the hill ...
to throw Him down the cliff. Luke 4:28–29

It is hard, if not impossible, for even the most capable persons to be successful in everything they undertake. For instance, Ferdinand de Lesseps of France did well in building the Suez Canal. But he failed in trying to construct the Panama Canal. The situation was different. The sand at Suez was easier to handle than the mountainous terrain of Panama. It remained for an American engineer, George W. Goethals, to complete the canal, which opened in August 1914.

Sometimes people fail through no fault of their own. They may meet circumstances beyond their control. Then, too, other people may interfere, causing setbacks. Think of young Joseph in Egypt. Appointed by Potiphar to supervise his household and entire estate, he was well on his way to success. But the owner's wife falsely accused him of sexual harassment and Joseph went to prison.

Consider the Lord Jesus Himself. In many Galilean cities His teaching and healing ministry was well received. But in His hometown of Nazareth He ran into a stone wall of resentment and unbelief.

St. Paul experienced something similar. Doors were opened to him and his companion in Iconium, Derbe, Lystra, and other communities. Then they reached a number of communities where the gates were shut. We are told that they were "kept by the Holy Spirit from preaching the word in the province of Asia" (Acts 16:6). God wanted the apostle to go somewhere else—to Macedonia, where he entered the continent of Europe with the Gospel and won many converts, including Lydia and her household in Philippi.

Has your life been like a seesaw ride? Have you experienced ups and downs? If so, take courage. We need always to go back to Jesus. He, the Son of God, became incarnate in our behalf. "He humbled Himself and became obedient to death—even death on a cross," writes St. Paul in Philippians 2:8. Rejected in His own town, He was with His resurrection "exalted ... to the highest place" (Philippians 2:9), to God's right hand where He reigns in glory over church and world.

Prayer Suggestion

Ask God for courage and strength to continue in your life's work despite setbacks you may have experienced.

Jesus, the Only Way to God

An angel of the Lord appeared to him in a dream and said, "Joseph ... you are to give Him the name Jesus, because He will save His people from their sins."
Matthew 1:20–21

More than 500 years before Christ's birth a philosopher in China, Lao-Tse, propounded the teachings of Taoism, which means the Way. He held that people should conform their lives to the quiet way of nature. "To withdraw into obscurity is the way of Heaven," he said.

Unlike this human philosophy, Christianity is a divinely revealed religion. It centers in Jesus Christ, who declared, "I am the Way" (John 14:6). While people today continue to say, as they have always in the past, that the many religious roads lead to the same heaven, our Lord made the exclusive statement: "No one comes to the Father except through Me" (John 14:6). In bearing testimony to Jesus, who had been crucified and was raised from the dead, St. Peter declared before the religious authorities in Jerusalem, "Salvation is found in no one else, for there is no other name under heaven given to men by which we must be saved" (Acts 4:12).

Jesus is the Way in a sense other than that He shows us how to love and gives us the Golden Rule. He is the one road to heaven. Only He has made restitution for all sin—in its many forms—that would keep people out of heaven. By His obedience and by His atoning death He reconciled the world of sinners to God, who, as our heavenly Father, has accepted us and made us His sons and daughters. God grants us His Holy Spirit to lead us to faith in the Savior and to implant Him into our hearts.

As persons redeemed, and through the Gospel and Holy Baptism made a new creation, we are able to walk on the way that leads to eternal life, all the while knowing that it is the way that surely brings us to our Father's house in heaven. In the first century, as the book of Acts tells us (16:17; 18:26; 19:9; 24:14), Christian believing and living was called the Way—something far different from Lao-Tse's Taoism. Much has happened since that time, but faith in Jesus Christ, God's Son and our only Savior, is still the one way to heaven.

Prayer Suggestion

Ask the Lord Jesus to strengthen your faith in Him as the only way leading to the heavenly Father.

THE KING OF HEARTS

Lift up your heads, O you gates ... that the King of glory may come in. Psalm 24:7

"Advent" and "adventure" are related words, not only because they come from the same Latin word (*advenire*, to come to) but also because both point to an exciting event and experience. What an adventure it is for us Christians to prepare ourselves for Jesus Christ, so that at His advent we may open the door of our hearts and let the King of glory come in!

The rule of this King is not political, external, or dramatic. Its power lies in the Gospel of the forgiveness of sins. People do not see it here, then there, for Christ's kingdom is within us. He is the King of hearts. He took us over when He redeemed us from sin and death with His own precious blood. Now we are His own, live under Him in His kingdom, and are comforted and blessed.

To "advent" and "adventure" we add a third related word: "venture." The Lord's Advent message invites us to come to Him in prayer, as the well-known hymn writer John Newton puts it:

> Thy promise is my only plea,
> With this I venture nigh;
> Thou callest burdened souls to Thee,
> And such, O Lord, am I.

We venture forth to the pleasant, delightful task to serve Him who first served us. Our Lord emphasizes that His yoke is easy and His burden light. Gladly and joyfully we assume our tasks as Christ's disciples: to venture forth to tell others the good news of His salvation, to visit the sick, to console the grief-stricken.

Advent is the time when we venture forth to meet the King of grace. He who comes to us wants us to come to Him also through the use of the Word and sacraments. His invitation is most appealing: "Come to Me, all you who are weary and burdened, and I will give you rest" (Matthew 11:28).

Who can refuse this invitation of the King of hearts?

Prayer Suggestion

Pray joyfully and thankfully to our Advent King, inviting Him to come into your heart and home with His blessings.

ADVENT REFRESHMENT

Jesus answered, "Everyone who drinks this water will be thirsty again, but whoever drinks the water I give him will never thirst." John 4:13–14

Christ's advent into our dry-as-dust world of sin is like a refreshing stream of water. "There is a river whose streams make glad the city of God," the psalmist declares (46:4). How true of Jesus Christ, the Source of living water!

Our Lord's entry into Jerusalem did "make glad the city of God." The Gospel account reads, "The whole crowd of disciples began joyfully to praise God in loud voices for all the miracles they had seen: 'Blessed is the king who comes in the name of the Lord!' 'Peace in heaven and glory in the highest!' " (Luke 19:37–38) In effect the people repeated the Gloria in Excelsis that the angels sang at Jesus' birth.

Jesus Christ refreshes and gladdens the souls of people because He removed the guilt and curse of sin. In St. Paul's words, "God made Him who had no sin to be sin for us, so that in Him we might become the righteousness of God" (2 Corinthians 5:21). This is the good news of the full and free salvation in Christ, and it is ours by faith in Him.

The Gospel of redemption is a power working effectively in our hearts. It is like a stream of water turning a desert into a garden spot. Thorns and thistles, spiritually speaking, no longer infest the heart. Instead it yields the fruit of the Holy Spirit. It brings health to wounded hearts.

In the Hall of Waters, a spa in Excelsior Springs, Missouri, four types of mineral water are available for drinking and for bathing. These waters are said to be good hydrotherapy—for good healing of various kinds of diseases.

Christ offers us His Word as healing water for the soul. Let Advent, the time of anticipation of Christ's coming, prompt us to quench our inner thirst by imbibing our Savior's living water.

Prayer Suggestion

Tell your Lord that you will gladly receive from Him the water of life and that you will share it with those around you.

THE HIGHWAY OF HOLINESS

A highway will be there; it will be called the Way of Holiness. Isaiah 35:8

When building modern roads, contractors shave down the hills and fill in the low places. They eliminate the curves to make the road run straight, thus cutting down on car accidents. They smooth out the rough places.

The above measures were taken when a state highway was built through the hills of northeastern Nebraska, where this writer grew up. Returning to his childhood home years later, he hardly recognized the area. The hills were flattened. Other once familiar landmarks—the rutted, high-center roads, the culverts in the low places, the barbed-wire fences—all were gone, even the buildings on the home places, since the space was needed to widen the highway.

The prophet Isaiah uses the language of road building when he writes, "In the desert prepare the way for the LORD. ... Every valley shall be raised up, every mountain and hill made low; the rough ground shall become level, the rugged places a plain" (40:3–4). Isaiah, of course, speaks of spiritual road building, of the changes that the coming Christ will effect in human hearts as He transforms sinners to receive Him.

Jesus Christ, whose advent in the flesh will soon be celebrated at this time of the church year, wants to enter all human hearts. But such access is prevented by sin. All people are sinners by nature and resist Him. They want no God, no Savior, to visit them. So they withdraw into rugged terrain: into selfishness, hatred, greed, pride, and liberty turned into license. Where they live there are no spiritual roads.

So God builds the highway, the "Way of Holiness." The Holy Spirit through the Word changes human hearts. He brings people to repentance and to faith in Jesus as the Savior. Now the way is open for Christ to come and for us to receive Him with joy. With Christ in our midst, we are on the highway to heaven.

Prayer Suggestion

Ask the Holy Spirit to open your heart fully to receive Jesus as the Savior who died for you and was raised.

CHRIST PAID THE PRICE

God presented Him as a sacrifice of atonement, through faith in His blood. Romans 3:25

When boarding city buses, we expect to pay the fare. In Amherst, Massachusetts, however, the buses carrying students from their residences to the three campuses in town have no fare boxes. The rides are free. Of course, the transportation isn't really free. The cost is defrayed in some other way.

All people in this world, whether old or young, rich or poor, are on a journey taking them from this world into the next. Jesus speaks in a parable about Lazarus, a beggar at a rich man's door, who died and "the angels carried him to Abraham's side" (Luke 16:22). The book of Jude declares that the archangel Michael was challenged by Satan over the body of Moses. An Old Testament figure, the prophet Elijah, ascended bodily to heaven in a fiery chariot.

If one were to picture conveyances carrying believers to heaven, would they have fare boxes? Does one have to pay? In the Bible God expresses Himself very clearly on this matter. Our money is not involved in anything pertaining to our salvation. Neither do good works and human merit count. St. Paul teaches, "By grace you have been saved—through faith" (Ephesians 2:8).

And yet, like in Amherst, the ride is not free. Somebody paid for it: our Lord and Savior Jesus Christ, God's own Son born of Mary. He came among us to give His life as a ransom for all. The price was tremendous for securing our free passage to heaven. It cost Him His holy, precious blood. "You are not your own; you were bought at a price" (1 Corinthians 6:19–20), declares St. Paul. Grace is not cheap. For us, careless sinning is out.

The Advent message calls us to repentance and to rejoicing because God's incarnate Son has done so much for us. Forgiveness and eternal life are ours, thanks to Christ's merit.

Prayer Suggestion

Express your heartfelt thanks to Christ, the Advent King, for His saving grace and the spiritual renewal He grants us.

Associates of the Prince of Peace

You are My friends if you do what I command.
John 15:14

Stories of the old West frequently refer to sheriffs taking groups of men with them to help preserve the peace against lawbreakers. Such a group, undoubtedly armed for the occasion, was called a posse or, in its longer form, *posse comitatus*. This is Latin, meaning men from the community empowered to act.

In a spiritual sense, Jesus surrounded Himself with a "posse" of 12 men whom He prepared to bring God's peace into the world and maintain it. Himself the Prince of Peace, He wanted the apostles to carry on His peace mission after His departure. They were closely associated with Him. He called them His friends. Given all authority in heaven and on earth, He empowered them to exercise the Office of the Keys, namely, the function of remitting and retaining sins. Pronouncing forgiveness to those who repented and believed in Christ as their Savior, the apostles, so to speak, used a key to open heaven. No earthly weapons, no power of the state, were to be used for this mission— only the Word of God, Law and Gospel. In Gethsemane He told Peter to put away his sword.

The apostles understood how their office was to be performed. St. Peter, for example, preaching in the home of the centurion Cornelius, said his mission was "telling the good news of peace through Jesus Christ, who is Lord of all" (Acts 10:36). What is more, the apostles knew they had to train others to eventually take their place. Thus, St. Paul, for example, surrounded himself with his own *posse comitatus*: Timothy, Titus, Silas, and many others. In local communities they had the assistance of dedicated women, like Lydia in Philippi and Priscilla (wife of Aquila) in several cities.

What about us, Christ's followers today? Will we, especially in this season of Advent and Christmas, volunteer to be Christ's peace corps, His *posse comitatus*, to repeat what the angel said: Peace on earth?

Prayer Suggestion

Say in your prayer how thankful you are that God's Son became incarnate to bring forgiveness and peace for you and for all people.

GOD'S VIRGIN-BORN SON

The virgin will be with child and will give birth to a son, and will call Him Immanuel. Isaiah 7:14

The Bible speaks of unusual conceptions and births. Some border on the miraculous. Isaac, a type of Christ, was born to Abraham and Sarah when they were long past ordinary parenting—he was 100 and she, 90. Similarly, John the Baptist, Christ's forerunner, was born of aged parents. There was something most unusual about Cain, the first son ever to be born for he was also the first murderer. It demonstrated early in the history of the human race that sin was a deadly reality and that the Second Adam was needed to undo what the first one had done.

As unusual as the birth of a firstborn son may have been, no one ever before, and no one born since, was ever born of a virgin. Jesus is the only one. Our Lord was truly the Son of God. He was conceived by the Holy Spirit and born of the virgin Mary, as we confess in the creeds of Christendom. This is in the creeds because Holy Scripture clearly teaches the virgin birth of the promised Messiah. Isaiah of old prophesied that the Savior would be born of a virgin. The evangelist Matthew tells us expressly that Isaiah's prophecy was fulfilled when Jesus was born of the virgin Mary. Further, the angel Gabriel told Mary that she would conceive and bear the Christ because "the power of the Most High will overshadow you" (Luke 1:35).

God has His reason for everything He does. He ordained that at the fullness of time His Son, who is our Lord and Savior Jesus Christ, would be "born of a woman," as St. Paul expresses it, so that as a true human being, in behalf of all human beings, he would be "born under law" (Galatians 4:4). He kept the law perfectly for us, and He bore the penalty for our disobedience. The outcome for us is this, and what an Advent-Christmas gift it is: We are God's beloved sons and daughters.

Prayer Suggestion

Praise God in your own words for the gift of His virgin-born Son, your Savior and Lord Jesus Christ.

We Rejoice with the Angels

Even angels long to look into these things. 1 Peter 1:12

Angels enter prominently into the account of our Lord's nativity. Christian art and music feature them during this season.

We know the sequence: First the angel Gabriel appeared to the priest Zechariah to announce the birth of John, the forerunner of Jesus. Then he visited Mary, a virgin in Nazareth, telling her that the Messiah would be born of her. On that most holy night at Bethlehem an angel announced His birth and then was joined by the heavenly host singing the Gloria in Excelsis. It was a repeat performance. At the creation heavenly music was heard when "the morning stars sang together and all the angels shouted for joy" (Job 38:7). The doxology at Bethlehem was proper, for in Christ a new creation in the spiritual realm came about.

The joy of the angels is most pure, most unselfish. It is vicarious, for they themselves were not directly involved in Christ's work of redemption. Yet they are most concerned about it. We can picture them standing tiptoed to catch a glimpse of God's eternal plan for mankind's salvation, as St. Peter writes, "Even angels long to look into these things" (1 Peter 1:12).

Angels teach us to rejoice because of the great things God has done in Christ for the salvation of the human race. They would find it hard to understand how some people, for whose eternal life the very Son of God gave up His life, can fail to thank and praise God. St. Paul describes the close relationship among Christians as members of Christ's body. Someone was very ill and got well. St. Paul writes, "If one part is honored, every part rejoices with it" (1 Corinthians 12:26). Not only the person who is the direct beneficiary will rejoice, but so also will those not directly involved. The angels teach us this. They themselves did not benefit from Christ's birth and from all that He was to do for us. Yet they rejoiced that Christ the Savior was born. Surely we will rejoice, too.

Prayer Suggestion

Thank the heavenly Father for sending His Son, who is the King of the angels, to be your Savior.

God's Son, Born in a Stable

But you, Bethlehem Ephrathah ... out of you will come for
Me One who will be ruler over Israel. Micah 5:2

Big, beautiful barns can be seen in America's rural heartland—in Iowa, Illinois, and Indiana. The best ones this writer has seen are located in the dairy country around Eau Claire, Wisconsin. They could easily give children the idea that Jesus was born in a stable of such dimensions. But such was not the case. The Church of the Nativity in Bethlehem stands over a cave believed to have been Jesus' birthplace. St. Luke's account says nothing about the place, only that Mary laid the baby into a manger. Apparently the place was a shelter with feeding facilities for cattle. What a humble place for the glorious Son of God to be born!

What is of importance, if not the structure, then is certainly the city where Jesus was born. The prophet Micah had foretold that the Messiah would come forth from Bethlehem in the land of Judah. Bible scholars in Jerusalem, when asked by King Herod where the Christ would be born, pointed correctly to the Micah passage. The Wise Men found the Christ Child there.

The birth of Jesus amid the most humble circumstances—in a primitive animal shelter and in a little town—emphasizes the great humiliation to which God's Son descended so that He might suffer and die for our sins. The Bethlehem birth experience cast its shadows ahead. Christ's entire life was one of self-denial, one of poverty and nonpossession. He, the heavenly Owner, was a borrower on earth. Unlike the foxes and birds with their holes and nests, He had no home of His own. And at the end He rode into Jerusalem on a borrowed donkey, ate the last Passover in another's home, and in death was laid into another man's tomb.

But with His resurrection Jesus was greatly exalted. Bethlehem's stable gave way to the heavenly palace. It all adds up to this: Jesus Christ is Lord, to the glory of God the Father.

Prayer Suggestion

Thank your Lord Jesus for becoming poor so that He might enrich you with all spiritual graces.

ADVENT ACCLAMATIONS

Hallelujah! Salvation and glory and power belong to our God. Revelation 19:1

The Scripture readings for Advent contain expressions of joy and anticipation that retain their appeal through the centuries.

The first of these acclamations is "Hail." The angel Gabriel addressed the virgin Mary with the words, "Hail, thou art highly favoured" (Luke 1:28 KJV). Or as a modern version has it, "Greetings!" (NIV). This was God's salutation conveyed through a prominent messenger. As far as we are concerned, God addresses us also, but He does it through an even greater ambassador of goodwill. "He has spoken to us by His Son," says the writer of Hebrews in 1:2. To each one of us God has sent Jesus Christ, who is not only the bearer of the Word— of the good news of salvation in Him—but is Himself the Word. This divine messenger from God stands at our door and knocks. His message is, "Hail, you are highly favored. You have forgiveness and peace."

A second Advent acclamation is "Hosanna." It was sung by the multitude that welcomed Jesus to Jerusalem. Basically, it is a petition derived from the psalms. It means, "O LORD, save us; O LORD, grant us success" (Psalm 118:25). The psalm closes with this call for a doxology: "Give thanks to the LORD, for He is good; His love endures forever" (118:29). This intent of "Hosanna" is also in our Advent hymns and prayers.

Our Advent acclamations reach a climax with "Hallelujah." Occurring frequently in the Psalter, it is the believer's exhortation to others to join him or her in giving praise to God. Hallelujahs are much in place as we prepare to celebrate the birth of Him who came to give up His life for the redemption of us all. The hallelujahs we now sing and speak are but weak lispings of the tongue in comparison with the great outbursts of praise that will make heaven's arches ring. A sampling is given in chapter 19 of the book of Revelation, where the great multitude in heaven gives expression to praise and thanksgiving. We are not yet present in that multitude, but we can even now join in singing the celestial hymn.

Hail, hosanna, and hallelujah are also our Advent acclamations.

Prayer Suggestion

Let your prayer now give expression to your joy and thanksgiving at the coming of Christ, your Savior.

Consistent Christianity

Woe to you, teachers of the law and Pharisees, you hyp-
ocrites! You give a tenth of your spices. ... But you have
neglected the more important matters of the law—justice,
mercy and faithfulness." Matthew 23:23

In Des Moines, Iowa, so the police said, a would-be bank robber handed the teller a long, poorly written note demanding a large sum of money. While the teller was trying to decipher the note, the would-be robber smoked a cigarette. But he stepped outside to do it to obey the bank's no-smoking sign.

Many people render uneven obedience. Jesus said to the Pharisees, who kept little man-made rules but transgressed God's great commandments, "You strain out a gnat but swallow a camel" (Matthew 23:24).

When Jesus comes again for judgment—the Advent message assures us that He will—He will find people doing much the same thing, ignoring God's great call to repentance but giving close attention to life's little dos and don'ts. They have no heart for the least of Christ's hungry and homeless brothers and sisters but have great sympathy for "animal rights." Christ will find growers and ranchers who, after good crops, plan to enlarge their facilities but give no thought to their spiritual welfare. If Christ were to come during the Advent season, He would find people shopping for trinkets but passing up the treasures God offers them in the Gospel.

As Christians we dedicate ourselves to the great truths of God's Word. We put first things first: Christ and our salvation in Him. St. Paul writes to the Corinthians, "What I received I passed on to you as of first importance: that Christ died for our sins according to the Scriptures, that He was buried, that He was raised on the third day according to the Scriptures" (1 Corinthians 15:3–4). The Son of God was born of the virgin Mary in Bethlehem so that He might redeem us from sin and death and then rise again from the dead.

The message of Advent prompts us to take the Gospel to heart, for it—not little man-made rules—is what Christianity is all about.

Prayer Suggestion

Request the continued guidance of Jesus, your Advent King, so that God's will may be done in all things.

IN PRAISE OF THE TRIUNE GOD

You received the Spirit of sonship. And by Him we cry, "Abba, Father." Romans 8:15

The three great festivals of the church year—Christmas, Easter, and Pentecost—give us the opportunity to meditate on the work of the Triune God in behalf of our salvation. All that pertains to Christmas involves not only the Son but also the Father and the Holy Spirit.

Christmas can be regarded as a festival that glorifies God the Father. True, it marks the birth of God's Son, but His Sender was the heavenly Father. Jesus stated repeatedly that He had not come on His own, but that the Father had sent Him. All that Jesus said and did conformed to the Father's will and redounds to His glory. A Christmas hymn dating back to an early century is entitled, "Of the Father's Love Begotten." Truly Jesus and the Father are one. They cannot be split apart. It was a misconception, and one that needed to be corrected, that a child expressed, "I like Jesus; He is nice. But I don't like that angry old God." God is holy and cannot abide sin. But in Christ He loves us, indeed to such an extent that He gave His Son and delivered Him up for us all.

At Easter time, as we celebrate the resurrection of Jesus, our thoughts are focused mostly on Jesus. But in doing so, we cannot exclude the Father, for He raised His Son from the dead, exalted Him highly, and set Him at His own right hand.

At Pentecost, we especially honor the Holy Spirit, the third Person of the Trinity. He is true God, equal with the Father and the Son. But in glorifying the Holy Spirit, we glorify also the Father and the Son, for it is from them that He came and still proceeds.

In the three great festivals of the church—the Nativity, the Resurrection, and the Spirit's Outpouring (Pentecost)—we celebrate the mercy and love of the Triune God for undeserving sinners. In the words of the Common Doxology, we "Praise Father, Son, and Holy Ghost."

Prayer Suggestion

Thank the Triune God for the revelation of His gracious will redounding to your salvation.

NOURISHED WITH SPIRITUAL BREAD

Then Jesus declared, "I am the bread of life." John 6:35

Bethlehem, like every other city, recorded its marriages, births, and deaths. Boaz and Ruth the Moabite woman, ancestors of Jesus, were married there. It was the birthplace of King David. Rachel died there when she gave birth to Benjamin, Jacob's youngest son. Above all, Jesus was born in Bethlehem, literally, "House of Bread."

Bethlehem was the proper birthplace for Jesus, the Messiah, for so Micah had prophesied. Further, Jesus, born in the House of Bread, declared, "I am the bread of life" (John 6:35). He said this during the lively discussion that followed His feeding of the multitude with five barley loaves and two small fish. In the give-and-take of this discussion Jesus sought to focus the minds of people on spiritual bread, on the Word of God, and on salvation in Him, the true Manna from heaven.

Human beings, no matter how full they are of earthly food, need inner nourishment. They need the truths that satisfy the hunger and thirst of the soul. They cannot be truly happy and satisfied unless they are at peace with God. This peace results from believing that Jesus died for their sins and that by faith in His merit and mediation they are declared just and righteous by God Himself. People need to be in the right relationship with God, for then they can relate properly to one another as human beings. Tempted by Satan in the wilderness to turn stones into bread, Jesus quoted these words of Moses, "Man does not live on bread alone, but on every word that comes from the mouth of God" (Matthew 4:4).

The celebrated "little town of Bethlehem," the House of Bread, yielded the Savior who is in every sense the Bread of Life. We honor the town in song and story, for, in the words of the song writer Phillips Brooks, "on thy dark streets shineth the everlasting Light," and that Light is Jesus Christ.

Prayer Suggestion

As you pray, "Give us this day our daily bread," include a petition for a steady diet of soul food through the Gospel of Christ.

AN UNHAPPY MORN FOR SATAN

The God of peace will soon crush Satan under your feet.
Romans 16:20

The English poet John Milton (1608–1674) begins his long poem *In the Morning of Christ's Nativity* with these lines: "This is the month and this the happy morn, Wherein the Son of Heaven's eternal King, Of wedded maid and virgin mother born, Our great redemption from above did bring." Toward the end he states that all the false gods—Baal, Moloch, Osiris, and all the rest—were most unhappy about Christ's birth. Why? They were losing their grip on the human race.

Sulking most of all, we can be sure, was the instigator of all idolatry: Satan. As the holy angels sang an anthem to the glory of God, the evil ones kept a sullen silence. Celebrate because the Savior is born? Never!

We learn from the Bible that the devil sought to hinder Jesus' ministry at every turn. He tempted Him to the sin of disobedience in the wilderness. He sought to penetrate the inner circle of the disciples by taking over the heart of Judas Iscariot. He prompted Peter to try to talk Jesus out of going to Jerusalem to suffer and die, and our Lord had to rebuke Him with these hard words, "Get behind Me, Satan!" (Mark 8:33) Jesus knew that the devil tried to prevent Him from atoning for the sins of humankind. He said to the arresting band at Gethsemane, "This is your hour—when darkness reigns" (Luke 22:53). Surely Satan rejoiced when Christ's lifeless body was laid into Joseph's tomb. Paul Gerhardt declares in an Easter hymn: "They in the grave did sink Him; the foe held jubilee."

If the above was Satan's consistent agenda—and it was—we can be sure Christ's birth as the Savior of sinners was no happy event for him. But not giving up, and we can also be sure of this, he prompted King Herod to slay all the young male children at Bethlehem, hoping to include the Christ Child in this slaughter.

But Satan did not prevail. Christ did, and for that reason we rejoice in all of our Lord's triumphs, from Bethlehem's crib to Calvary's cross.

Prayer Suggestion

Give thanks because Jesus, the woman's offspring, crushed Satan's power.

A MODEL FOSTER FATHER

[Mary said:] "Your father and I have been anxiously searching for You." Luke 2:48

Do stepfathers and foster fathers in modern homes have a biblical model? They do. He is Joseph, the provider, protector, guardian, and guide for Jesus, the virgin-born lad in his house.

Joseph was an honorable man in relation to Mary, his betrothed. He believed what God told him about the child Mary was going to have and promptly married her.

Joseph was a superb foster father to Jesus. You say: "That was easy, for Jesus was sinless and always behaved perfectly." Sinless, yes, but having become a true human being, God's Son went through all the phases of childhood and youth. He needed to learn, to be helped, to know how to get along with people, to study the Scriptures, to practice prayer. We are told this about Jesus' development: "Jesus grew in wisdom and stature, and in favor with God and men" (Luke 2:52). Joseph played an important role in the life of the youthful Jesus. The relationship was so close, so natural, that Mary said on finding Him in the temple, "Your father and I have been anxiously searching for You" (Luke 2:48).

By trade, Joseph was a carpenter, teaching the building skills to his foster son, for Jesus likewise was called a carpenter (Mark 6:3). A story, probably a made-up one, relates that Joseph and Jesus carved out yokes for oxen, making them so well that they would not chafe the animals' necks. We cannot imagine Jesus doing sloppy work, and He did say later in life that His yoke on people was easy.

Did Joseph have biological children? We don't really know. People at the time did refer to Jesus' four "brothers" and His "sisters." But in biblical times such terms for family members sometimes referred to relatives in a wider sense. For example, Abraham in the Old Testament referred to himself and Lot as "brothers" when they were really uncle and nephew, respectively. Also, if Jesus did have actual brothers and sisters, would He on the cross have committed the care of His mother to the apostle John?

As close to Jesus as he was, Joseph found his salvation in none other than his familiar foster son. Also we are saved by the one who came to save His people from sins—Jesus.

Prayer Suggestion

Ask for God's help to become a dedicated and devoted role model for those in your family.

ISAIAH FORESAW CHRISTMAS

Speak tenderly to Jerusalem, and proclaim to her ... that her sin has been paid for. Isaiah 40:2

Recently it was announced that the debt of the United States government had risen to 4.6 trillion dollars. A trillion is a number reached by multiplying a billion dollars a thousand times—a figure beyond the average person's comprehension.

The Bible speaks of sins as incomprehensible in number. The 10,000 talents a man owed according to Jesus' parable is such a figure. No one can repay that debt. The hymn writer states: "Could my zeal no respite know, Could my tears forever flow, All for sin could not atone." Because this is so, God created Christmas. He ordained that His Son should be born of a virgin mother because only that Son could pay the debt. And He did. That, in the final analysis, is what Christmas is all about.

Isaiah was one of God's foremost spokesmen proclaiming God's forgiveness. He lived and labored around 750 B.C., midway between Moses and Christ. Isaiah was a man of many talents and titles: prophet, inspired writer, chaplain to King Hezekiah, and "the evangelist of the Old Testament," as someone has said. He proclaimed the Gospel in these words, "Comfort, comfort My people, says your God. Speak tenderly to Jerusalem, and proclaim to her that her hard service has been completed, that her sin has been paid for, that she has received from the LORD's hand double for all her sins" (Isaiah 40:1–2).

This sounds very much like a "double dip" of divine forgiveness, and that is what it is. The New Testament evangelist John puts it like this: "From the fullness of His grace we have all received one blessing after another," or as the King James Version states: "grace for grace" (John 1:16). St. Paul says the same: "Where sin increased, grace increased all the more" (Romans 5:20).

Isaiah very plainly states the basis for God's forgiveness. He testifies how the Messiah, born of a virgin (7:14), would in due time be "stricken by God, smitten, and afflicted" (53:4). This Sufferer would take up our infirmities, sorrows, and sins. He is none other than Jesus Christ. Yes, Isaiah foresaw the first Christmas we still celebrate in our times.

Prayer Suggestion

Give thanks to God for the rich measure of His forgiving grace in Christ Jesus.

DAVID AND JESUS: TWO KINGS

He [God] promised beforehand ... regarding His Son,
who as to His human nature was a descendant of David.
Romans 1:2–3

If Christ's birthday were celebrated in heaven, David would certainly be one of those present. He was deeply involved in the historical events of our Lord's nativity.

Joseph, accompanied by Mary, went to Bethlehem for the census because "he belonged to the house and line of David" (Luke 2:4). Bethlehem was David's town in the land of Judah, and there Jesus was born.

We read in the gospels that Jesus was often hailed as "the Son of David," which was a messianic title. Our Lord's kingship was thus declared, but it differed from that of David. It did not consist in resurrecting the throne of David in Jerusalem. Jesus' kingdom, a spiritual one, far transcended that of David. In it He ruled as the Son of God and the world's Savior. On the basis of Psalm 110 Jesus established that He was not only David's son but also his Lord. David also looked to the Messiah for salvation. In Psalm 22 the psalmist David, the "sweet singer of Israel," foretold the Messiah's crucifixion in minutest detail. St. Peter, in his moving Pentecost sermon, made plain that David believed in the coming Messiah and foretold His resurrection. Jesus is this Messiah.

The life of King David is intertwined with that of Jesus in that both were shepherds, David as the keeper of his father's flocks at Bethlehem, and Jesus as the Good Shepherd. It was on David's Psalm 23 ("The LORD is my Shepherd") that Jesus based His designation as the Good Shepherd in John 10. How fitting that the news of the Good Shepherd's birth was first announced to shepherds at Bethlehem!

Would King David attend Jesus' birthday were it celebrated in heaven? Undoubtedly so. But a much more important question is: Will you and I observe His birthday here on earth? Will we celebrate it because "life and salvation He does bring"?

Prayer Suggestion

Ask the Holy Spirit to prepare your heart for a worthy celebration of the birthday of Jesus, your Savior.

PILGRIMS ON EARTH

In My Father's house are many rooms. ... I am going there to prepare a place for you. John 14:2

When James J. Hill built the Great Northern Railroad, he did much to open up the great Northwest to people wanting to take up land and build homes. For himself, in St. Paul, Minnesota, he built a mansion of 32 rooms, where at one time he entertained more than 2,000 guests. Despite his heaven-on-earth home, Hill was a pilgrim on earth. He died in his mansion on May 29, 1916.

St. Luke's account of our Lord's nativity speaks of travelers on earth. The itinerants were not only Joseph and Mary but also the people who crowded the inn at Bethlehem. While Jesus' birthplace, a stable of sorts, was most primitive, the guests in the inn didn't have it so good, either. The inn was by no means a modern motel. It was merely an enclosure where feed and water was available for the animals and where the travelers could rest for the night. Elsewhere in the resting place for caravans where the Good Samaritan took the man beaten up by thieves, there was at least an innkeeper who would look after the victim.

The crowded inn at Bethlehem, as well as the stable where the Holy Family stayed, helps to illustrate why Jesus, the Son of God, left His Father's mansion of many rooms in heaven and became a pilgrim on earth. He came, fulfilled His atoning work, rose from the dead, and ascended into heaven, thereby preparing a place for us in heaven as our permanent home.

Even if we all had homes as large and as comfortable as Mr. Hill's, we would not consider ourselves permanent residents on earth. All believers are pilgrims. Abraham, the father of them all, considered himself to be a stranger and sojourner in Canaan, living in tents. "He was looking forward to the city with foundations, whose architect and builder is God," states the writer of Hebrews (11:10). He adds that all the believers, all those heroes of faith he describes in chapter 11, "admitted that they were aliens and strangers on earth" (v. 13).

We are thankful for our homes which we can decorate for the holidays and where our families can gather. All the while we remain mindful of St. Paul's words, "Our citizenship is in heaven" (Philippians 3:20). And we eagerly await a Savior from there, the Lord Jesus Christ.

Prayer Suggestion

Thank the Lord Jesus for preparing a home for you in heaven.

The Lord's Advent Advance Man

*In those days John the Baptist came, preaching in the
Desert of Judea and saying, "Repent, for the kingdom
of heaven is near." Matthew 3:1–2*

Evangelists, today as in the past, have preached in strange and
seemingly unproductive places. In a New York subway, a man recently
tried to preach to morning commuters as they came and went. He lifted
up his voice above the train noises as he preached on these words of
Isaiah, "Seek the Lord while He may be found" (55:6). What a place
and time for a sermon!

One could wonder whether John the Baptist could get people to
listen while setting up his pulpit in a desert where nobody lived.
Should he not have preached to the multitudes in Jerusalem? But John
chose the right place. Surprisingly, great crowds came to him there
"from Jerusalem and all Judea and the whole region of the Jordan,"
Matthew reports (3:5). The people confessed their sins and were baptized by John in the river Jordan.

John had a definite calling. He was the forerunner of Jesus, the
herald who announced the presence of the Messiah in the person of
Jesus of Nazareth. He was, as Isaiah (40:3) had foretold, "the voice of
one calling ... in the wilderness." The prophet Malachi likewise had
referred to the forerunner as the messenger who would prepare the
way for the Messiah.

John the Baptist and Jesus were distant relatives but may not have
been personally acquainted with one another in previous years. They had
a good relationship. Not for a minute would John presume to be the
Messiah himself, as some had suggested. Instead he testified to his disciples as he pointed to Jesus, "Look, the Lamb of God, who takes away the
sin of the world" (John 1:29). And Jesus recognized the faithfulness of
John in which his greatness lay. He said, "Among those born of women
there has not risen anyone greater than John the Baptist" (Matthew 11:11).
Jesus added a good word, too, about John's humility: "yet he who is least
in the kingdom of heaven is greater than he" (Matthew 11:11).

John was Christ's Advent advance man. We do well to take his
words to heart and look to Jesus as the Author and Finisher of our faith.

Prayer Suggestion

Give thanks to God for the faithful testimony of John concerning
Jesus, the Lamb of God.

PROMISES, PROMISES

Christ has become a servant of the Jews on behalf of God's
truth, to confirm the promises made to the patriarchs
so that the Gentiles may glorify God for His mercy.
Romans 15:8–9

A song sometimes heard at church weddings although it contains no Christian sentiments is *Oh, Promise Me.* It mentions growing love, comparing it to flowers, to "violets of early spring, which come in whispers ... and sing of love unspeakable that is to be." Through the words of the soloist, bridegroom and bride promise such developing love. It is a sad fact, however, that the promised love sometimes turns to weeds rather than flowers, with the marriage pledge becoming an unfulfilled performance.

Human beings, even Christians, sometimes falter in their promises. But God never does. He stands behind His Word. Through the Old Testament centuries He promised to send a Savior from the sin Adam and Eve and all their descendants had committed. The first promise, known as the protevangel (first Gospel) was given to our first parents in Genesis 3:15. It was the promise of the woman's Seed, or Offspring, crushing the serpent's head. The promise of redemption was renewed to Abraham and the other patriarchs. With increasing clarity the prophets, such as Moses and the psalmists, comfort the believers with the promise of the coming Messiah, who would atone for their sins. Clearest of all was the testimony of Isaiah in his 53rd chapter, where he spoke of the Messiah as God's Servant bearing the sins of all.

Undoubtedly there were times when the faithful anxiously asked, "When will the Savior come?" Perhaps some doubted whether God had remembered His people. But God kept His Word. In due time Christ was born. God fulfilled His promise, as the hymn verse states, "What the fathers most desired, What the prophets' heart inspired, What they longed for many a year, Stands fulfilled in glory here." With eyes of faith we, too, see God's promise fulfilled in Christ.

Prayer Suggestion

Give thanks to God for fulfilling His promise to send us the Savior in the person of His Son, born of Mary.

KEEPING CHRISTMAS CHRIST-CENTERED

Salvation is found in no one else, for there is no other name under heaven given to men by which we must be saved. Acts 4:12

Some years ago Christmas was often written as X-mas. The letter X in algebra stands for the unknown. But Christ, who revealed the Father and Himself to us, is not unknown. So it was necessary at the time to stress: Keep Christ in Christmas!

In our times, secularists want to declare ours a post-Christian age and to suppress all Christian awareness in schools and community life. Objection is raised to manger scenes in the public square. Then the temptation is great to fill the vacuum with old pagan rites, such as the observance of the winter solstice, falling on December 21 or 22, when the sun is farthest south of the equator.

As Christians we want to keep Christmas what it truly is: the birthday of Jesus, who, as the Lord told Joseph, "will save His people from their sins" (Matthew 1:21). St. Peter struck the same keynote when he told the enemies of Jesus, "Salvation is found in no one else" (Acts 4:12).

It would be a strange birthday celebration indeed if we left Christ out of it. Then there would be nothing to celebrate—no basis for joyful festivities, no theme to dwell on in sermon and song, no incentive for giving gifts in appreciation of God's great gift to us, His own Son.

Moved by the Holy Spirit, let us keep Christmas Christ-centered and receive all the blessings God intended for us to have: full salvation, "to the praise of His glorious grace, which He has freely given us in the One He loves" (Ephesians 1:6). We can rejoice over the angel's announcement that Christ the Savior is born. We can join the shepherds and bow down and worship Him. We can sing the Christmas hymns and carols with great delight. We can, along with the first witnesses of our Lord's nativity, "spread the word concerning what had been told them about this Child" (Luke 2:17).

Prayer Suggestion

Pray for a renewal of Christmas as the festival that celebrates the birth of Jesus Christ, the world's Lord and Savior.

CHRIST, OUR REPRESENTATIVE

The Word became flesh and made His dwelling among us.
John 1:14

It can be said that John Quincy Adams, the son of United States President John Adams and himself a later president (1825–29), stepped down in the latter part of his life. For 17 years after his presidency he rendered distinguished service as a member of the House of Representatives.

A much greater "demotion" can be ascribed to the Son of God. He really stepped down. From eternity Jesus Christ was the Son of the Highest, very God of very God. He was, as St. Paul exclaims, "God over all, forever praised! Amen" (Romans 9:5). But He "made Himself nothing, taking the very nature of a servant" (Philippians 2:7). The Advent season with its message of Christ's incarnation prepares our hearts and minds for the celebration of His nativity.

We are not left in doubt as to why God's Son became incarnate. He, as Jesus Christ, became one of us so that He might take our place in rendering obedience to God's Law, which we have transgressed and to bear the penalty for our transgressions. He, so to speak, entered the assembly of sinners to become our representative, as John Quincy Adams did in behalf of his political constituents. None of us could come before the judgment throne of God, plead innocent, and receive a sentence of forgiveness. Only Jesus, the Son of God, could do this, and He did.

It was for our redemption that God's own Son was born of Mary, serving as our substitute from the cradle to the cross. He came not in royal splendor but as a servant, as He Himself declares, "The Son of Man did not come to be served, but to serve, and to give His life as a ransom for many" (Mark 10:45).

Now at the right hand of God, Jesus still represents us as He pleads for us before our heavenly Father.

Prayer Suggestion

Ask God's blessings on the Advent season as you and those with you meditate on the coming of Jesus for our salvation.

A NIGHT OF LIGHT

God is light; in Him there is no darkness at all. 1 John 1:5

In all of the church's liturgy and literature there is hardly a passage surpassing the sublime words of the Collect for Christmas Eve: "O God, because You once caused this holy night to shine with the brightness of the true Light, grant that we who have known the mystery of that Light here on earth may come to the full measure of its joys in heaven." As we pray these words, we stand on the borderline of two worlds—the temporal and the eternal, the comprehensible and the incomprehensible. The truth we can grasp is linked up with transcending reality.

Physically, the night (or early morn) of Jesus' birth was as dark as any night preceding or following it. Yet it was a night that shed its light abroad in all the world. Its celestial radiance verified the birth of the Son of God, the Light of the world. This Light comes from the Father "who lives in unapproachable light, whom no one has seen or can see" (1 Timothy 6:16). Again: "God is light; in Him there is no darkness at all" (1 John 1:5). But the same God became visible in His incarnate Son. The same God who made the light shine at the creation and sent His Son, the Light of the world, gave illumination once again when He "made His light shine in our hearts to give us the light of the knowledge of the glory of God in the face of Christ" (2 Corinthians 4:6). In the birth of His Son, and in all that this Son said and did, God made known His saving, life-giving love for us.

Because our salvation lies in the Christ Child, Christmas Eve shines most brightly. It casts its radiance abroad everywhere—over Bethlehem, over Jerusalem, over modern cities boasting their own "great white way," over fog-blanketed London, over the City of Lights (Paris), and over the peaceful suburb or hamlet where you live. Everywhere God has turned on the light of the Gospel, even over the Land of the Midnight Sun. Rejoice over this Light as you worship in church tonight, with the sanctuary all lit up and the lights of the Christmas tree shining.

Prayer Suggestion

As you give thanks to God for Christ, pray that you may come to the fullness of joy in heaven.

CHRIST, THE SAVIOR, IS BORN

The Word became flesh and made His dwelling among us.
John 1:14

The most beloved of all Christmas carols undoubtedly is "Silent Night, Holy Night." The words were written by Joseph Mohr and the melody by Franz Gruber, both of Salzburg, Austria. Originally written in German as "Stille Nacht, Heilige Nacht," it has lost nothing in the translation. Stanza three hails the birth of Jesus Christ as that of the Son of God, from whose holy face radiantly beams the light of love divine. Truly, God so loved the world that He gave His only Son to be its Redeemer.

The Son of God is the second Person of the Holy Trinity. He is "God of God, Light of Light, very God of very God," (true God from true God), as we confess in the Nicene Creed. He is equal with the Father and the Holy Spirit in every way.

It was for our salvation that this Son of God "came down from heaven and was incarnate by the Holy Spirit of the virgin Mary." He assumed His true human nature into His Person. He who is true God is also true man. On the human side, Jesus Christ was involved in another trinity. Artists portray Him as a member of a human family consisting of Joseph, Mary, and the infant Jesus. He became a part of mankind, the worldwide family that embraces all families. He did so, that in Him, as God had promised to Abraham, all the families of the earth might be blessed.

The Christmas account proclaims in words and in the Word, who is Jesus Christ, that God "wants all men to be saved and to come to a knowledge of the truth" (1 Timothy 2:4). For this purpose He sent His Son to be the "one mediator between God and men, the man Christ Jesus, who gave Himself as a ransom for all men" (1 Timothy 2:5–6).

Today we come with joyful hearts to worship this divine Mediator lying in a manger. Together with the shepherds we thank God for "the One and Only [Son], who came from the Father, full of grace and truth" (John 1:14).

Prayer Suggestion

Thank the heavenly Father for sending Jesus into the world for the salvation of sinners and for their adoption as God's sons and daughters.

THE ADORNMENTS OF FAITH

If anything is excellent or praiseworthy—think about such things. Philippians 4:8

In many churches and homes Christmas trees are decorated with ornaments that symbolize the Christian faith: the Epiphany star, alpha and omega, lamb with a banner, or the letters IHS. These add meaningful beauty to the tree.

Christians themselves are like trees adorned with the fruits of faith, like the tree of life "yielding its fruit every month" (Revelation 22:2). As spiritual trees, what adornments or evidences of faith do we desire and pray for? In Galatians 5:22–23 St. Paul writes, "The fruit of the Spirit is love, joy, peace, patience, kindness, goodness, faithfulness, gentleness and self-control." It is through the Gospel and the sacraments that the Holy Spirit creates and preserves faith in the saving merit of Jesus Christ. This fruit is genuine, unlike gilded nuts hanging on Christmas trees.

Another enumeration of Christian virtues is found in 2 Peter 1:5–7, where the apostle presents this golden chain of Christian qualities: "Add to your faith goodness; and to goodness, knowledge; and to knowledge, self-control; and to self-control, perseverance; and to perseverance, godliness; and to godliness, brotherly kindness; and to brotherly kindness, love."

In the Philippians passage indicated above, which is intoned with "Rejoice in the Lord always," St. Paul opens up another treasure chest of the jewels of Christian life. He urges godliness, because "the Lord is near," and at Christmas time we can say, "the Lord is here." He would have us replace anxiety with prayers containing petitions and thanksgivings. Then, having assured us of the peace God gives us in Christ, he bids us to give thought to this string of pearls: whatever is true, noble, right, pure, lovely, admirable, excellent, and praiseworthy.

How different are lives adorned with these virtues compared with the tinsel and gaudy glitter and litter with which people of this world decorate themselves! Now is a good time for us to sparkle with the likeness of Christ.

Prayer Suggestion

Pray to the Holy Spirit to work all good within you.

ONLY GOD IS GOOD

To the King eternal, immortal, invisible, the only God, be honor and glory for ever and ever. 1 Timothy 1:17

The Christmas carol "Good King Wenceslas" tells how the king with his servant trod through the snow to bring food and fuel to a poor man. It makes a good story. Another thing the not-so-good King Wenceslas (or Wenzel) did was to torture a churchman of Bohemia, John of Nepomuk, and throw him into the Moldau River to drown because he refused to tell him the secrets the queen had confessed to him.

It is easy to refer to people as "good." When someone becomes the victim of a tragedy, the neighbors usually say what a good person he or she was, even when it is not so. Jesus was not in favor of dealing loosely with "good," especially when the element of flattery is involved. One time a rich, but self-righteous, young man rushed up to Jesus, bowed before Him, and asked, "Good teacher, what must I do to inherit eternal life?" The Lord said, "Why do you call me good? ... No one is good—except God alone" (Luke 18:18–19). Jesus knew that this youth wanted to be praised for all his good deeds.

"Good" or similar adjectives can be applied to some persons. Joseph, Jesus' foster father, is described as "a righteous man" (Matthew 1:19), and another Joseph, in whose tomb Jesus rested, is called "a good and upright man" (Luke 23:50). At Joppa, a Christian woman named Dorcas "was always doing good and helping the poor" (Acts 9:36). Despite their natural, inborn sinfulness and the sins they commit, Christians by their faith are declared to be good in God's sight because of the righteousness that Christ earned for them. Thanks to their baptismal grace, they are growing in goodness. Christians are never perfect, but they are always striving for the goal of what is good and right.

In a true sense, as Jesus said, only God is good, so good, in fact, that He loved us all while we were yet sinners, sending His one and only Son, our Lord Jesus Christ, to give His life for our salvation. God, the Father of Jesus and our heavenly Father, is truly a good King. Fully sharing His saving love is His Son, who is the King of kings and Lord of lords. To Him be glory forever!

Prayer Suggestion

Thank the heavenly Father for sending His Son, Jesus Christ, into the world for your salvation.

SIMEON'S THANKSGIVING

Lord, as You have promised, You now dismiss Your servant in peace. Luke 2:29

Simeon, a righteous and devout man in Jerusalem at the time when the Savior was born, lives on in the song Nunc Dimittis, or "Now You Are Dismissing." It is a song of joyful thanksgiving to God for the salvation He has revealed and bestowed in Jesus Christ, His Son. Along with other songs from Luke's gospel—the Benedictus of Zechariah, the Magnificat of Mary, the angels' Gloria in Excelsis—Simeon's song was among biblical hymns sung by early Christians.

The reading from Luke indicated above explains how Simeon came to speak these words. When Mary and Joseph brought the infant Jesus to the temple for "their purification according to the law of Moses" (Luke 2:22), Simeon was there to greet them. The Holy Spirit, having previously revealed to him that he would not die until he had seen the promised Savior, had prompted him to come to the temple at this time and to speak his blessing on the infant Jesus.

Simeon had waited for the redemption of Israel. Now all was fulfilled. Now he could depart in peace, for with his own eyes he had seen the Savior sent for the redemption of Israelites and Gentiles alike. We can sing with him, "Let us, O Lord, be faithful, Like Simeon to the end, So that his prayer exultant May from our hearts ascend: O Lord, now let Thy servant Depart in peace, I pray, Since I have seen my Savior And here beheld His day."

Are we as ready to go as Simeon was? The Russian writer Ivan Turgenev, in his novel *A Living Relic* has death visit a sick and aging peasant and say to him, "I am sorry that I can't take you now." It happens often that younger people who would like to live must go, while old ones would just as soon die because they think there is nothing more for which to live. With Simeon in the temple it was different. He was ready to meet his God, not out of boredom or a sense of frustration, but because he had seen the promised Savior. Now everything else would be anticlimactic. In due time God called him home with peace of mind.

Prayer Suggestion

Express thanks to God for having brought you to faith in Jesus Christ, the promised Redeemer.

GROWING UP WITH JESUS

Jesus grew in wisdom and stature, and in favor with God and men. Luke 2:52

It has been said that people change every seven years. There may be something to that. When born, we are cradle-fast infants. Seven years later we are boys and girls of considerable mobility. Add seven more years, and we are young teenagers. At age 21 we are young adults, and seven years later, mature adults, and so forth.

Jesus, the Son of God become a true human being, grew naturally, going from one phase to another as He grew mentally, physically, spiritually, and socially. We meet Him first as an infant lying in Bethlehem's manger. In due time He was circumcised and then presented in the temple. Then came the flight into Egypt. Next we read that as a 12-year-old lad He stayed behind in the temple in Jerusalem. He followed Joseph and Mary back to Nazareth and was obedient to them in home and workshop.

Then follows a quiet period of 18 years. St. Luke breaks the silence by saying, "Jesus Himself was about thirty years old when He began His ministry" (3:23). After this the four gospels have much to tell us about Jesus' ministry of preaching and healing. The gospel accounts are long introductions to the main events: our Lord's suffering and dying to redeem us, and His rising again to put the seal of certainty on His messianic work as the sole Savior of sinners. After 40 days He ascended into heaven.

From what we know of Jesus' life, we cannot discern changes every seven years. We know, however, that all events in His life and ministry proceeded according to God's plan, and Jesus became aware of that plan. Already as a lad of a dozen years He knew He must be about His Father's business. He knew also that His mission could not begin before John the Baptist had announced His Messiahship. Until that time Jesus was a carpenter.

We need to ask: Are we maturing in a well-balanced manner, which includes spiritual growth? Are we daily growing in the grace and knowledge of our Lord Jesus Christ, and in that respect following His pattern of growth? The writer of Hebrews (5:11–14) wants us to advance beyond the ABCs of Christian faith and understanding. He tells his readers to proceed from the milk of the Word to solid foods as they become adults. So let us ever grow with Jesus!

Prayer Suggestion

Ask the Holy Spirit to give you not a *childish* but a *childlike* faith in Jesus.

GOD'S SAVING LOVE TO EACH ONE

God so loved the world that He gave His one and only Son.
John 3:16

It is said that a little boy of Chinese ancestry, who was named Lo, came home from Sunday school and told his mother that he was mentioned in the Bible. When she asked where, he replied, "Lo, I am with you alway, even unto the end of the world" (Matthew 28:20 KJV). In a way Lo was correct—not that his name was mentioned in the Bible but that he was meant and included in every promise of God.

When we read that God so loved the *world*, all mankind, to the extent that He gave His own Son, some might think of a faceless crowd, of people en masse. But when in His words to Nicodemus Jesus spoke of the *world*, He stated emphatically that each person is included—none is left out. And when our Lord goes on to say, *"whoever* believes in Him shall not perish but have eternal life" (John 3:16), He again stresses that no penitent, believing sinner is disqualified, for God's saving grace embraces each one.

The two great truths stand side by side: Christ died for all and His concern is for each individual person. As the Good Shepherd He guides and guards the flock, and when one sheep or lamb is lost, He goes after it, for He gave His life also for that one person. St. Paul tells the Corinthians not to cause a weak brother to sin against his conscience, for it was also for this person that Christ died.

The message of the Christmas-Epiphany season is that Jesus Christ came into the world to be the Savior of each one. He wants to be received by each one, as we sing: "Joy to the world, the Lord is come! Let earth receive her King; Let every heart prepare Him room."

So we can agree: While our names are not specifically mentioned in the Bible, we are one and all included in every promise of salvation. More important than having one's name in the Bible—some unbelievers like Pontius Pilate are named but are not saved on that account—is to have one's name in the Book of Life. Into that sacred volume our names were entered when we came to faith through Holy Baptism. Our standing with God is secure. God hears this prayer in a baptismal hymn in behalf of a person baptized: "Write the name we now have given, Write it in the book of heaven."

Prayer Suggestion

Thank the heavenly Father for His saving love in Christ, His Son, and for including you in the promise of salvation.

THE RIGHT TIME IS NOW

Many will say to Me on that day, "Lord, Lord, did we not prophesy in Your name, and in Your name drive out demons and perform many miracles?" Matthew 7:22

The medical world speaks of a brain problem called dyslexia. A person so afflicted reads words backwards. The word "was" is seen as "saw."

One may speak of spiritual dyslexia. One form of it is the backward look on one's life, with people wishing at life's end that they had done what they should have done from the beginning. It is like a motorist looking in the rearview mirror to see where he has been, instead of looking ahead to see where he is going.

The end of the year brings to mind the end of time when Jesus will return in glory to wind things up for the church and the world. In the text He repeats what many will say to Him on that day. They will recite their pretended good works as the basis of their plea for acceptance into heaven. However the plea cannot be accepted, for the people in question look back on things they themselves chose to do instead of doing the will of the heavenly Father. Now is the time to do the works of God.

The heavenly Father wants us to do the works of mercy that give outward evidence of the saving faith in Jesus Christ, the Savior from sin and death. Our Lord makes plain what these works are in His discourse on the separation of the righteous from the unrighteous, as a shepherd separates the sheep from the goats.

Surely the rich man in Christ's parable, who neglected poor Lazarus at his doorstep, in the afterlife—seeing Lazarus in heaven and finding himself in hell—wished he had done God's will. He attempted to live his life backward: from the afterlife to the present one, from the world beyond to the world here and now. Can it be done? Jesus would say, "No way!" Instead He tells us through biblical spokesmen, "Now is the time of God's favor, now is the day of salvation" (2 Corinthians 6:2).

At year's end, we express regret at not having done God's will as He desires. But in His grace He gives another year, with many opportunities to serve Him.

Prayer Suggestion

Ask the Lord Jesus to keep you from hindsight and to open the eyes of faith to what lies ahead that you may serve Him as He desires.

Devotions for Special Festivals and Occasions

GOD SET THINGS STRAIGHT AGAIN

God ... made His light shine in our hearts to give us the light of the knowledge of the glory of God in the face of Christ. 2 Corinthians 4:6

A woman in the entertainment field who has never been married recently declared, "I say I'm divorced so people won't think there's something wrong with me."

In a society where sin prevails, the abnormal is often represented as normal, especially when majority behavior rather than God's Word sets the tone. Thus truth is replaced with lies, fact gives way to fiction, and light yields to darkness.

The great sin is that unbelief strips God of His glory. Consider how plainly and poignantly St. Paul describes the evil trade-off: "They [people of the pagan world] exchanged the truth of God for a lie, and worshiped and served created things rather than the Creator—who is forever praised. Amen" (Romans 1:25). Again, "Although they claimed to be wise, they became fools and exchanged the glory of the immortal God for images made to look like mortal man and birds and animals and reptiles" (Romans 1:22–23).

But God was not willing to let mankind live in the darkness of sin and in the distortions of Satan. He set the record straight when He, the Creator who in the beginning created the light in our physical world, once more made the light of truth to shine in our hearts. This He did when He sent His Son, Jesus Christ, to be the Light of the world. In Him and through Him God revealed the glory of His grace, that is, His down-to-earth love that brings erring sinners back to the truth.

And to what truth? This, that the way of salvation is found in Christ, who went from the cradle to the cross to give His life so that we may have eternal life. This fact is set straight again, for which reason we celebrate Christmas: "To the praise of His [God's] glorious grace, which He has freely given us in the One he loves. In Him we have redemption through His blood, the forgiveness of sins, in accordance with the riches of God's grace" (Ephesians 1:6–7).

Now that we know the truth of God's grace, we can walk in the true light, not in man's flashlights that lead away from the truth and turn the abnormal into the normal.

Prayer Suggestion

Glorify your Lord God for revealing His amazing grace through the gift of His beloved Son, Jesus Christ.

MOUNTAIN CLIMBING IN LENT

Many peoples will come and say, "Come, let us go up to the mountain of the LORD." Isaiah 2:3

Mountain climbing is a strenuous undertaking. It requires planning and preparation. One must establish a base camp, have the necessary equipment, beware of the hazards: glacial ice, avalanches, falling rocks. The climbers must be dressed properly to withstand the cold winds. They must carry tents and food supplies. But they will put up with all hardships in anticipation of arriving at the top.

Consider how much more difficult spiritual mountain climbing would be if it all depended on us. The invitation we extend to one another, "Come, let us go up to the mountain of the LORD, to the house of the God of Jacob" (Isaiah 2:3), would be a call to an impossible journey if we hoped to come to God by our own efforts. No one would be equal to the task of doing all that God commanded. We are by nature not equipped to scale the heights of holiness. The dangers are too many, the tasks required too great, the effort far too demanding. The long and short of it is that we cannot be saved by doing the works of the Law.

Yet we have reached the mountaintop of salvation, thanks to Jesus Christ. He is the pioneer of our faith. He proceeded step by step to climb Mount Calvary with the burden of all our sins on His back. He is truly the Lamb of God who takes away the sin of the world. He went ahead to prepare for us the way to heaven, clearing away the obstacles and providing rest stations so that we can follow Him all the way to heaven. This is our consolation as today, Ash Wednesday, we begin to climb "Calvary's mournful mountain."

We know, of course, that living the Christian life is not a carefree pleasure trip, for Jesus tells us, "Small is the gate and narrow the road that leads to life" (Matthew 7:14). Here our Lord is referring to life as Christians must lead it in a world of sin. The daily struggle is not put forth to gain forgiveness, peace with God, and eternal salvation. Rather, it describes the grateful effort of those who have already received all the blessings of divine grace and who, out of a deep sense of thankfulness, gladly and willingly follow in the footsteps of Jesus.

Yes, the invitation to mountain climbing stands: "Come, let us go up to the mountain of the LORD" (Isaiah 2:3).

Prayer Suggestion

Ask the Lord Jesus to give you the willingness and strength to begin the Lenten journey with Him.

CHRIST'S TRAVAIL OF BODY AND SOUL

He shall see of the travail of His soul, and shall be satisfied.
Isaiah 53:11 KJV

It is said that the picture "The Praying Hands" represents the toiling hands of a friend who gave up art and took a job to enable Albrecht Duerer to become an artist. What we see are really "The Toiling Hands."

The hands of Jesus were both praying and toiling hands—first for carpentry work and then to heal the sick and otherwise to help troubled people. It took great effort to do what Jesus did to fulfill His preaching and healing ministry: traveling about, enduring the heat of the day, putting up with insufficient rest at night. Jesus Himself spoke of the need to do the Father's work during the short time available to Him.

It is especially proper to refer to Jesus' redemptive activity as work—as labor, toil, travail. It required great effort to endure all that our Lord suffered as He carried His own cross and was later nailed to it. The prophet Isaiah, known as "the evangelist of the Old Testament," clearly foretold the Passion of the Messiah in his 53rd chapter. God in heaven was mindful of what His Son on earth was suffering as the sinners' Substitute, for the prophet writes: "He shall see of the travail of His soul, and shall be satisfied" (53:11 KJV).

"Travail"—the word is closely related to "travel," which required great exertion in early days. The word for "travail" in the original Hebrew text is *amal*, which stands for labor, toil, trouble, misery, distress, suffering. This is how Martin Luther translated the term in the German Bible: "*Darum dass seine Seele gearbeitet hat*"—"Therefore, because His soul worked," that is, toiled to the utmost, the heavenly Father accepted His sacrifice as sufficient for the salvation of all who believe in Jesus. The prophet adds: "By His knowledge My righteous Servant will justify many, and He will bear their iniquities" (Isaiah 53:11).

To the praying and toiling hands of Jesus—and to His feet that amid travail walked throughout Palestine and beyond—we add His toiling soul. With His whole being our Lord gave Himself to the work of our redemption.

Prayer Suggestion

Say to the Lord Jesus that thousand, thousand thanks shall be given to Him for His travail in your behalf.

CHRIST, OUR HEALER

Whenever you eat this bread and drink this cup,
you proclaim the Lord's death until He comes.
1 Corinthians 11:26

Because people continued to suffer from the wounds of sin, Jeremiah asked: "Is there no balm in Gilead? Is there no physician there?" (8:22) Balm, a vegetable oil, was used as an ointment for wounds.

Is there no spiritual balm for wounded souls, and is there no physician to administer it? There is, and the Good Physician is Jesus Christ. St. Luke, himself a physician, quotes Jesus as saying, "It is not the healthy who need a doctor, but the sick. I have not come to call the righteous, but sinners to repentance" (Luke 5:31–32). This was our Lord's reply to those who objected to His eating with publicans and sinners.

As our Good Physician Jesus has the means for spiritual healing—healing that is, generally speaking, good for the whole person, even on the mental side. His remedies are the Word and the sacraments. The words Jesus spoke "are spirit and they are life" (John 6:63). Holy Baptism, which He instituted, is "the washing of rebirth and renewal of the Holy Spirit" (Titus 3:5). Holy Communion, which our Lord likewise established, conveys to us His true body and true blood given and shed for the strengthening of our faith in the forgiveness of our sins.

Do we need this spiritual balm, this healing sacrament? Yes, because we are all suffering from the sickness of sin and are therefore in need of the healing Jesus imparts. It is needed now as much as it was when Jesus instituted it on Maundy Thursday. The treatment is still the same. Christ's means of grace give spiritual life and relieve the pain of the soul. They are the balm of Gilead we should receive often.

Prayer Suggestion

Do what your Lord did the night He was betrayed: Give thanks to God for His saving grace as you commune today.

SORROW MINGLED WITH JOY

Sorrowful, yet always rejoicing. 2 Corinthians 6:10

A man who has been active in many radio and television programs has described Christians as "people who celebrate Good Friday all year long." What he said is partly true, partly untrue. It indicates how hard it is for people outside of Christendom to see the complete picture of Christian faith and life. Quite often they see only one side of what personal Christianity is all about. What to them is an either/or may well be a both/and. Both is true of Christians: They are "sorrowful, yet always rejoicing" (2 Corinthians 6:10).

On Good Friday we are indeed sorrowful—sorrowful that the innocent Lamb of God was put to death on a cross, sorrowful that members of the human race could sink so low as to crucify the Lord of glory, sorrowful that also our sins contributed to His death. This sorrow is genuine, showing true repentance. The mood of Good Friday is clearly expressed in hymns sung on this day. We solemnly sing Bernard of Clairvaux's "O Sacred Head, Now Wounded." Again: "O darkest woe! Tears, overflow! What heavy grief we carry! God the Father's only Son In a grave lies buried." And such sorrow is in various forms expressed not only on Good Friday but on other days as well.

But there is more to Good Friday than the tokens of sorrow: tears, black paraments on the altar, a silence of respect. There is also hope and joy. There is rejoicing, indeed not yet the full joy of Easter, but "always rejoicing" because Christ's death spells life for us. Because He made atonement for our sins, we are assured of forgiveness and peace with God. Such rejoicing springing from hope is likewise not a one-day affair, for we are "always rejoicing" amid life's sorrows and disappointments.

Are we Good Friday Christians all year long? Yes, but as people who know that gloom must yield to gladness.

Prayer Suggestion

Say to Jesus that you confess your part in causing His death but that you rejoice in the salvation He brought you.

His Presence in Joseph's Garden

Mary Magdalene went to the disciples with the news:
"I have seen the Lord!" John 20:18

In the Meditation Garden at Graceland in Memphis, Tennessee, where Elvis A. Presley lies buried with his mother and a grandmother, one sees a life-size stone statue of Jesus. It is a reminder to the multitudes of annual visitors that Jesus, risen from the dead, is the Lord of life.

All who have ever believed in Jesus Christ through the centuries as the Resurrection and the Life and have passed away are as yet resting in their graves. Jesus' grave, however, is empty. Our crucified Savior, having completely finished His redeeming work, rose from the dead, thus lending full validity to His promise that on the Last Day He will—in spirit and in truth—be present in all cemeteries or wherever the bodily remains of the believers rest. He will be there to summon them to everlasting life with Him in heaven.

Mary of Magdala, that Easter morning, saw Jesus alive in Joseph's garden. It was a special favor—a reward of grace—to her for lingering at the empty tomb after the others, as St. John reports, had gone "back to their homes" (20:10). Mary heard His voice as He called her by name. She was able to testify, "I have seen the Lord!" (John 20:18) While she was not to hold on to Him physically (for He had not yet returned to the Father), we can be sure that she held on to Him spiritually for the rest of her life. Although Jesus ascended into heaven, that contact would remain. And she will see Him again and will hear His voice when He, the Good Shepherd, returns to summon all His sheep, living and dead.

It matters not where our graves will be, the risen Savior will be there, not as a stone statue but as the living Lord.

Prayer Suggestion

Complete this prayer: "Lord Jesus, because You have risen from the dead, it is now my firm conviction that You …"

OUR GUIDE INTO ALL TRUTH

*All of them were filled with the Holy Spirit and began
to speak in other tongues as the Spirit enabled them.
Acts 2:4*

People visiting historic places need tour guides. A guide does not go behind the group and drive them with a whip; he does not force or compel. He goes before the people and leads them.

The Holy Spirit, so Jesus promised, would come after the Ascension and lead the disciples into all truth—into the right understanding of all the words and acts of Jesus for the salvation of the world.

As our Guide into all the truth, whether Law or Gospel, the Holy Spirit leads, enlightens, remonstrates, seeks to persuade, and pleads. He does not make walking robot Christians of us or pound the truth into us with a sledgehammer. He invites all to accept Christ as their Savior. Yet some people still say no to the Gospel.

This is not to say that the Spirit offers divine grace on a casual, take-it-or-leave-it basis. Nor does He expect man to convert himself, partially or totally, by his own reason or strength. It is always and altogether by the power of the Spirit that anyone comes to faith, for "no one can say 'Jesus is Lord,' except by the Holy Spirit" (1 Corinthians 12:3).

When the Holy Spirit guides us into all the truth, He asserts His power through the Gospel, so that "the Word ... [will be] mixed with faith in them that heard it" (Hebrews 4:2 KJV).

Our heavenly Guide engages human guides to lead us into all truth. He once sent Philip the Evangelist to the desert road from Jerusalem to Gaza to explain the Scriptures to the Ethiopian official who was reading in his chariot. Such guides, on a regular basis, are the called pastors and teachers. At times the Spirit sends special envoys to clarify a point for us—perhaps a next-door neighbor, a seat partner on a plane, a family camping next to ours during vacation. He has many spokespeople, including you and me.

Prayer Suggestion

Enlarge on this prayer, "Holy Spirit, let me speak—and let me listen—when truth needs to be told so that ..."

GOD'S REVELATION IN WORLD AND WORD

Oh, the depth of the riches of the wisdom and knowledge of God! How unsearchable His judgments, and His paths beyond tracing out! Romans 11:33

Theodore Steele, a painter, had these words written over the fireplace of his mansion in scenic Brown County, Indiana: "Every morning I take off my hat to the beauty of the world."

The writer of Ecclesiastes in the Bible gives credit to whom it is due when he declares: "[God] has made everything beautiful in its time" (3:11). Even after the fall of mankind into sin and the effects it has on nature, there is beauty in the world. Katherine Lee Bates paints a colorful word picture in her song "America, the Beautiful," speaking of "spacious skies," "amber waves of grain," "purple mountain majesties," "fruited plains," and all this extending from "sea to shining sea." How wonderful the world must have been when God first made it! What we now see in many places: urban slums, eroded soil, rivers and lakes filled with filth—this is man's doing.

"Splendor and majesty are before Him [God]; strength and glory are in His sanctuary," writes the psalmist (96:6). The Bible speaks of worshiping God in "the beauty of holiness" (Psalm 29:2 KJV). Solomon's temple was a thing of beauty. God's house, also today, should reflect the beauty He Himself created in the greater sanctuary that is His world.

In His world God has revealed not only beauty but also wisdom, might, and justice. While these qualities of the Creator are so evident that also the heathen are aware of them, there are other truths that God revealed only in His Word. In the Holy Scriptures God made Himself known as triune—as Father, Son, and Holy Spirit. Running through this revelation like a golden thread is the love of God. This love is especially seen in His desire to bring all people into a saving relationship with Him through His Son. Jesus came into the world to reconcile sinners by dying for their sins. The whole Scripture bears witness to Jesus Christ.

Through God's Son all things were made: the universe with its awesome dimensions and its beauty observable in our world. To Him, as the Indiana artist said of the world, we take off our hats.

Prayer Suggestion

Pray that the Triune God may open your eyes to the beauty of His world and your heart to the glory of His grace in Jesus Christ.

Giving Thanks for Daily Bread

Jesus then took the loaves, gave thanks, and distributed to those who were seated. ... He did the same with the fish.
John 6:11

"In comparison with the Great Depression of the 1930s," said Norman Vincent Peale, "the recent recessions are like Sunday school picnics." Many people went hungry then, joining long lines to soup kitchens. Someone with a light touch said, "We occasionally see signs: 'Keep off the grass.' In the Depression they read, 'Don't eat the grass.' "

The multitudes that came to Jesus in an uninhabited area were told to sit down, for "there was plenty of grass in that place" (John 6:10). But the hungry people didn't have to eat the grass; Jesus had real food in mind for them. He satisfied the hunger of all by miraculously multiplying five small barley loaves and two small fish—a boy's lunch—into food for all.

During the Thanksgiving season we are especially mindful of, and thankful for, the daily bread God provides for us. And by "daily bread" we mean more than bread baked in ovens; we mean also clothing, housing, jobs, medical care, education, good government. God does not, as a rule, provide for us with gifts directly from heaven, like the manna of old. Nor are we fed in such a wonderful manner as Jesus used. Still, it is a miracle in a way that seeds grow into plants and trees yield food to eat. God is at work in nature for our benefit.

In a much larger sense God has provided for us spiritually. By the miracle of undeserved, divine grace He gave us His Son, Jesus Christ, as the bread of life. We live not by bread alone but also—and especially—by the Word of God which nourishes our souls and, in fact, our whole being. Jesus Christ is the personal Word. He is God's Son, very God of very God, who for us and for our salvation gave His life. In Him we live, move, and have our being. What grounds for thanks!

Prayer Suggestion

Give thanks to God for His many blessings, especially for the gift of His Son, our Savior Jesus Christ.